NEPTUNE'S TRIDENT

Spices and Slaves: 1500-1807

'The Trident of Neptune is the Sceptre of the World.'

Antoine-Marin Lemierre

A HISTORY OF THE BRITISH MERCHANT NAVY
VOLUME ONE

NEPTUNE'S TRIDENT

Spices and Slaves: 1500-1807

RICHARD WOODMAN

WITH A FOREWORD BY HRH THE PRINCESS ROYAL

For Chris, to whom I owe everything

Frontispiece: Mercantile Sloops, not to be confused with the naval sloop-of-war (which was a larger, brig or ship-rigged, vessel), or the faster cutter (the rig of which was almost identical, but which was rarely used for commercial cargo). Despite their small tonnage such modest merchantmen trafficked across the Atlantic, as well as ran in the coastal and short-sea trades. The drawing is by Baugean. (Author's Collection)

First published 2008

The History Press
The Mill, Brimscombe Port
Stroud, Gloucestershire, GL5 2QG
www.thehistorypress.co.uk

© Richard Woodman, 2008

The right of Richard Woodman to be identified as the Author
of this work has been asserted in accordance with the
Copyrights, Designs and Patents Act 1988.

British Library Cataloguing in Publication Data.
A catalogue record for this book is available from the British Library.

ISBN 978 0 7524 4814 5

Typesetting and origination by The History Press
Printed in Great Britain

CONTENTS

PART THREE
'The Grandest Society of Merchants in the Universe'
British Shipping in the Indian and Pacific Oceans, 1707–1793

BUCKINGHAM PALACE

I am delighted to write a Foreword for the first of this five-volume history of the British merchant marine. This ambitious project places what became a national Merchant Navy squarely within its historical context, alongside but not over-shadowed by the exploits of the Royal Navy. Indeed, the roots of both sea-services are indistinguishable and the British mercantile marine was, like the Industrial Revolution, one of the great empowering dynamics of the 19th Century.

The beginning of international hydrography and meteorology, the development of the steam-vessel, the opening of new trades, mass emigration to Canada, the United States, South Africa, Australia and New Zealand, the carriage of affordable foodstuffs, including tea, grain and frozen meat, were all pioneered by British merchant ships. On the eve of the First World War the British merchant marine was the largest in the world and accounted for about 40% of global tonnage, and twice in the 20th Century what had been recognised as a national Merchant Navy gallantly served the nation in its struggle with Germany.

Today we are apt to forget these facts, although 95% of our imports by volume still arrive by sea. Ships have become larger, ports are no longer visible within our cities and our national merchant fleet has declined. But we remain an Island, dependent on trade, and Richard Woodman reminds us of the importance of merchant ships and our debt to the seafarers – men and women – who manned them.

Anne

INTRODUCTION

'Others may use the ocean as their road;
Only the English make it their abode.'
Edmund Waller (1606–87)

No history of Britain can ignore the Industrial Revolution, nor the fact that Britain
was the world's workshop for almost a century; no history of Britain can gloss over
the imperial expansion that resulted in one sixth of the earth's landmass being ruled
from London; indeed, no contemplation of our present state can be properly understood without a rudimentary knowledge of the foregoing. By common and universal
consent Great Britain was the modern world's first super-power, acquiring sufficient
geo-political strength, influence and economic muscle to influence its present-day
state. In the eighteenth century her interest in the slave-trade had a profound impact
upon the economic and social development of the West Indies, the echoes of which
resonate yet. In the nineteenth century, after exporting criminals and indentured
labour, British and Irish emigration enabled a diaspora to North America and the
Antipodes of both the desperately poor and the better-off. Another, less well known,
shift of population was effected as a direct consequence of Britain's *volte face* in her
abolition and active suppression of the slave-trade: a new mass movement of Indian
and Chinese 'coolies', indentured to take the place of liberated slaves.

Thus, as if obeying some respiratory and reflexive law, Britain has of late produced a new increasingly non-indigenously inhabited country which is painfully
breaking new ground in terms of a population composed of mixed races and cul-
tures, all attempting to resolve ancient and irreducible questions of varied religious
faiths set amid strongly entrenched secular values. This extraordinarily eclectic and
volatile *demos* has yet to embrace commonly agreed societal *mores*, though it lives
under the continuing ambivalent and traditionally expedient compromise of 'the
Crown in Parliament' which seems – at least in the short-term – to be adaptable
and durable.

To what do we owe this situation, unique to the Britain of the twenty-first century?
The short answer is to our imperial past, to our early social engineering and reform,
and the general enabling wealth which was produced from all these factors. This in
turn, we are led to believe, was itself due to the Agrarian and Industrial Revolutions
combined with a post-Napoleonic pre-eminence and stability, the *Pax Britannica*, and
a slow progress in social reform. Latterly the slave-trade has been included, if only to
exemplify and represent the exploitative talents of our forebears.

British initiative, inventiveness and engineering led the world and, although other nations were to adopt, modify and exceed these accomplishments, the British achievement from the middle of the eighteenth century was in the very vanguard of change and at the dynamic heart of it.

A closer examination of the culmination of British hegemony following the defeat of Napoleonic France reveals as its power-base a vast maritime empire. To this must be added those places – such as South America and China – which, though outside the imperial Pale, were nevertheless commercially linked with Britain and British investment and which, in turn, contributed to the wealth of Great Britain. To what, one might therefore reasonably ask, did the British owe this disparate territorial spread with its closed markets, sources of abundant raw-materials and influential agrandisements? The glib answer is to its navy, its Royal Navy. 'Trade', it was confidently asserted by the imperialists – and widely believed by all who were told – 'followed the flag'. Trade was good for all participants, whether they were within the imperial family or outside beneficiaries of its benign intercourse; the fact that it *followed* the flag – with which came a neat package of good-governance, justice and territorial integrity – meant that the flag itself was a manifestation of essential goodness. Setting aside the imperial balance sheet of profit-and-loss, this fundamental assertion is not merely inaccurate, it is a perversion: trade did *not* inevitably follow the flag, it was almost always the other way round. In fact the British Royal Navy has usurped the credit of a second, but not secondary, maritime asset possessed and nurtured by the British: that is to say its once vast mercantile marine.[1]

Although late on the maritime scene – following the Portuguese, Spanish and Dutch – the British soon came to dominate the oceans of the world not simply by the naval power-projection available to them after the end of the Napoleonic War in 1815, but by the often aggressive, sometimes amoral – and always opportunist – ambitions of her merchants and their ability to facilitate trade by means of shipping. Almost nowhere in conventional mainstream history will you discover an analysis of British merchant shipping as an historical instrument of empowerment and imperial expansion, let alone of social advancement and the betterment of mankind. Yet it was unequivocally a fundamental engine of history (and the benefits that it was then axiomatic to assume were part-and-parcel of progress), so-much-so that in 1921 the United States' ambassador to the Court of St James was moved to eulogy.

'I deem it no exaggeration to say,' Mr J. W. Davis claimed, 'that whether in war or peace, the British Mercantile Marine has rendered more service to more men or more nations than any other human agency.'

This is a powerful and unambiguous encomium and not one lightly dismissed as unimportant; the more so since it was uttered by the representative of our most aggressive maritime competitor. It is, of course, subjective and of its time, and it refers to outcome not method. But it also highlights the *fact* of cause producing profound effect. Moreover, if not true in the absolute sense, how is it that such a claim, if so important, has been ignored? Even in a country to which it has contributed so much, merchant shipping has never been properly appreciated, either socially or historically, because in the first place it was never in the shipowners' interest to expose it to public

acclaim. From humble beginnings, shipowners became patrician in outlook, secretive
in their dealings and often astute enough to work outside the formal constraints of
national regulation. Indeed, national regulation often compels them to adopt such
apparently shady practices in pursuit of profit. Furthermore, despite the social cachet
of a few individual ship-masters and their ships, the generality of a remote, largely
disconnected and shifting seafaring population enjoyed little claim to social inclusion
in a society which – perversely enough – fostered exclusivity as a self-perpetuating
dynamic. Secondly, by being out of sight, seafarers were out of the public mind and
when they did impinge upon it, usually did so in unfortunate circumstances. Disaster
and shipwreck were their chief professional advertisements, drink and disorder their
personal and social manifestations. To these unfortunate characteristics the generic
lumping of all ranks, from ship-masters to galley-boys, as 'merchant seamen' without
any distinction of hierarchical responsibility, fixed in both the political and the popular mind a status for this floating population which lay near the nadir of imperial and
national social pretension. This was reinforced at one end of the social spectrum by
the employment of numerous ethnic minorities such as Goanese stewards, Sudanese
firemen, Chinese, Indian and West Indian sailors; and at the other a combination of
vested-interests which acted against the attainment of professional standing by the
large, articulate and able – but fatally dispersed – officer-corps. Thirdly, by its very
nature merchant shipping is historiologically associated in the most pejorative way
with the perceived evils of both imperialism and the period immediately preceding
England's – and specifically England's – rise to power. This most especially attaches to
its involvement with Tudor privateering, the ambiguous exploits of Drake and his ilk,
and the Atlantic slave-trade, along with the revolting circumstances and conditions in
which it was prosecuted. Whatever moral equivocations these amoral practices raise,
they took place and were, for many, the only means of earning a living. Fourthly, the
lack of glamour of merchant shipping, its rather disparaged existence for the benefit
of private 'trade' – with all the pejorative connotations that this has in the British
psyche – along with its supporting, subordinate and secondary role in time of war, has
left it outside the ambit of formal history and guaranteed that it was always going to
be outshone by the naval service that sprang so directly from it.

Such have been the singular glories of the Royal Navy that, uniquely, the brilliance
of the naval aura eclipses all else in the way of British maritime endeavour. These
complex and often subtle and insidious influences have entirely diverted the fleeting
attention of the British populace from its other, more demotic, valuable and great
maritime activity: merchant shipping.

It would be an exaggeration to say that this disinterest extends to ships themselves.
Merchant ships have been subjected to specialised focus as fascinating artefacts and
a considerable amount of technical data about them is available to those minded to
seek it. A few studies of merchant shipping have been made, usually in connection
with the First or, more likely, the Second World Wars and these are often soporifi-
cally academic; some recent historians have carried out major reviews of Britain's
maritime empire and her command of the world's oceans, but these have been drawn

from a core of naval-centric considerations, occasionally usurping the achievements of merchantmen as having been *naval* exploits, and often blurring the historical truth expressed by Archibald Hurd in the preface to his war history of the mercantile sea-service in the First World War. Hurd wrote that upon the outbreak of war in 1914: 'It was forgotten by the British people that the British Merchant Navy had a war history dating back to a period anterior to the founding of the Royal Navy.'

Other histories of the British merchant marine have concentrated in technical achievement, almost entirely excluding the people – largely, it has to be said, men – whose lives affected these momentous events. What has never been attempted, I submit, is an intimate history of the British mercantile marine as an engine of imperial expansion and maintenance, and as an important and influential factor on the making of the modern world. It is neither an unequivocal record of beneficent goodness, nor entirely a catalogue of exploitation, despite its under-pinning motive of profit and its occasional unequivocal forays into the thoroughly reprehensible, even the downright wicked, at least in terms of modern *mores*. The exploits of the mercantile marine did however *happen*, and for that reason alone need airing. That it all happened and in doing so earned – and continues to earn despite its now polyglot composition and compromised flag-status – considerable sums in 'invisibles', is more than a minor footnote to the national balance sheet. Even today, with a barely perceptible merchant fleet, the earnings of British shipping are greater than that of British agriculture or aerospace.

Howsoever we view the modern world with its global markets, the close inter-relationships of competing economies within the so-called global-village, its brilliant technologies set off against its petroleum-based and gargantuan appetites, its grim determination to expand and develop at variance with the preservation of a small planet, its human greed set against the logic of human-need, its racial, cultural, religious and intellectual differences, we can remain assured of one constant: shipping remains vital. No less than 97 per cent of all the goods we carry home from the supermarket arrive on our coast by way of merchant ships. So too do the oil products we guzzle on a daily basis.

Although for complex reasons these goods are now rarely borne in British ships, the historical actions of the British merchant fleet in the seventeenth, eighteenth, nineteenth and twentieth centuries were fundamental to the creation of our world today.

In this book I have attempted to draw together a number of threads which all contribute to this vehicle of world trade. I touch hardly at all upon the building and technical development of ships to satisfy the demands of the trades in which they earned their livings;[2] more influential in the context of this work were the factors and motives which drove their owners to recognise or create and then exploit opportunities. Having sketched the scientific advances that enabled trade to be conducted with increasing reliability, I also touch upon the recruiting and regulation of a seafaring population of variable quality along with the wider, supportive infrastructure that existed across the globe to service shipping and seafarers. This important element provided, loaded and discharged cargoes; dry-docked, provisioned and repaired its battered carriers – or bottoms – and equipped and serviced those who went to sea in a variety of capacities. I have also tried to illuminate the men, and a handful of women, who owned, commanded and manned the thousands of merchant ships that flew the mercantile red ensign of Great Britain in its heyday. Unlike Arkwright, Watt, Newcomen, Telford, Macadam and other luminaries of the Industrial Revolution, few have heard of owners like Bowrey, Bibby, Brocklebank, Holt, Thomson; or Willis, Wigram, Currie, Anderson, Leyland, Booth, Mackay; let alone Macrae, James, Hutchinson, Crow, Wright, Hamilton, Beecroft, Dance, the Scoresbys (father and son), Forbes, Kemball, Woodget, Evans, Golding and thousands of other ship-masters who drove their ships across every ocean on the planet. Among these ship-masters were some amazing characters whose contribution to human progress might have been greater had they enjoyed better social status. As early as 1572 a British merchant ship-master had identified the connection between mosquito bites and malaria. 'But', as Dr Ann-Mary Hills points out, 'typically this accurate observation was ignored by the medical profession for some 250 years'. Thirty years later James Lancaster was administering anti-scorbutics to his men while a number of merchant masters were among the first British hydrographic surveyors; none are remembered today. Only a handful of these men in command of transatlantic liners in the first half of the twentieth century briefly became household names; most fulfilled their tasks in what Joseph Conrad, himself a naturalised British master-mariner, considered 'a useful calling', but several achieved great things, some endured tribulations of epic proportions while others fomented or suppressed mutinies, fought fires, brought disabled ships into port or simply underwent the awesome rigours of the ocean to bring butter to the British breakfast-table. Others went to war.

To some extent these achievements have been demeaned by the ease and speed with which highly tuned racing yachts may be driven round the globe. The advances of technology make navigation today a thing of almost kindergarten simplicity but also provide back up, rescue and routing to a degree unimaginable to those lonely men who often fought the elements for weeks at a time to conduct their ships from one place to another. These were not self-indulgent voyages made to smash a record just for the sake of it, though there was no lack of competition. Although by the 1850s 'races' were frequently and unofficially entered, no passage was undertaken other than to make a profit or, if in ballast, to pick up a cargo and keep a vessel gainfully employed. If this was not romantic – a concept to which few seafarers subscribe – it was a reality in which the hardship of everyday experience called forth standards of seamanship and navigational skill lost to us today, even in the highly regulated and protective world of the modern sail-training ship.

It also formed character among those who lived their working lives in such an environment; not always admirable, often appalling and tyrannical, but occasionally heroic. Here, in the microcosm of ships over many generations, can the best and the worst among us be found.

Most of these mariners were modest men – for the landsmen understands so little of the sea-life that the seafarer desists from anecdote, preferring the company of his own kind – and much of this vast endeavour was essentially mundane, to be taken in the stride. Most voyages were successful and profitably accomplished, and therefore unremarkable, at least to the superficial analysis of both seaman and land-lubber. But the extent of this collective effort was enormous, perhaps the more so when seen as something now gone, past, supplanted by new exponents of an ancient art to which the British were initially late in coming, but who dominated at its climax, before the technological revolution of our own age.

As an account of the life it attempts to record, history is inevitably complicated and, in the telling, is equally inevitably simplified. It is in this process of simplification that commercial shipping has been lost: it was private and profitable, had little to do with crowned-heads and embroiled governments usually only when the latter demanded to interfere or required its services. That is not quite so. Certainly at the end of the eighteenth century Britain began an industrial revolution which, by the middle of the 1800s, had made her the world's workshop. But the former would never have led to the latter had not a British mercantile marine existed, enabling cause to achieve effect. It is in this essential role of facilitator that what began as the 'merchants' service', became synonymously the merchant service or the mercantile marine, to find a final flowering as the 'Merchant Navy'. In this incarnation, and composed not merely of British nationals in the narrow sense, it twice saved this country in the first half of the turbulent twentieth century. Elsewhere I have argued that between 1939 and 1943 it did no less than save the civilised world.[3] This was no mean achievement and it arose from a history as full of daring, opportunism, amorality, skulduggery and courage as any other field of human endeavour. So, in short, this is essentially a book about men and ships.

Although on the face of it this is the narrow story of *British* achievement, unlike that of the Royal Navy the history of the British mercantile sea-service has a far wider international context, as that American ambassador of 1921 was polite enough to acknowledge. It was my privilege to be trained and to serve in the last years of the post-war British Merchant Navy. Since then I have watched a slow decline in British shipping, followed by an uncertain renaissance as a small mercantile marine belonging to a quondam global maritime power only as long as shipowners retain their vessels under its flag. Notwithstanding this, in 1971 the government decided to dispose of much of the carefully preserved crew records of the British Mercantile Marine, believing they were of no historical value, though the University of Newfoundland had the good sense to plead the case for a proportion. Sad though these facts are, at the very least, they give those of my generation of British seafarer – and in particular of its loyal but disregarded officer-corps – a unique perspective of the workings of history, of decline and fall, and the transient nature of all things.

NOTES

1. As J.B. Condliffe points out in *The Commerce of Nations*: 'From the early 17th Century onward colonisation and trade are inseparable, and shipping is closely tied to both'; to which may be added J.R. McCulloch's assertion that: 'Navigation and naval power are the children, not the parents – the effect, not the cause – of commerce'.
2. See Woodman, R., *The History of the Ship*, Conway Maritime, 1997 and 2005.
3. See Woodman, R., *The Real Cruel Sea, The Merchant Navy in the Battle of the Atlantic, 1939–1945*, John Murray, 2004.

ACKNOWLEDGEMENTS

I wish to thank the following people for their kindness and generosity in helping with the preparation of this volume. Some have assisted with information or advice, giving of their expertise and time; others have furnished documentary material from their family archives while yet more have given permission to use illustrations from their collections free of charge. I am most grateful to them all: Dr David Cordingly; Captain Aris Finiefs; Rob Gardiner; Captain Joshua Garner; The Lord Greenway; Michael Grey; Mr R.G. Hart; John Keay; M. Philippe Petout of St Malo; and to Captain Ian Smith of The Marine Society. My thanks also go to Rear Admiral Jeremy de Halpert and Mr Peter Galloway, respectively the Deputy Master and Secretary of the Corporation of Trinity House, for permission to use paintings in the Corporation's possession, and to the Master and Wardens of the Honourable Company of Master Mariners for the use of material in the Honourable Company's archives.

Special thanks must go to Richard Joslin of the N.R. Omell Gallery, and Richard Green and Susan Morris of the Richard Green Gallery for their wonderful help and generosity in sourcing some of the illustrations; and to Paul Ridgway and John Robinson for their helpful advice in drafting the text. My thanks for their professional help to Chris Rawlings at the British Library, Nathaniel Pendlebury at National Museums on Merseyside, Melissa Atkinson at the National Portrait Gallery and Doug McCarthy at the National Maritime Museum. I am, as always, indebted to my agent, Barbara Levy, whose long-suffering support has been invaluable. Finally, to the dedicatee, my firmest friend and partner without whom I should long since have abandoned this particular ship goes my warmest and liveliest appreciation. The rest, she knows.

Richard Woodman
Harwich, 2008

NOTE ON METHOD

To tackle such a vast subject presents the writer with certain difficulties, the resolution of which it is perhaps best to explain to the reader. This is the first of five volumes and so to produce a coherent narrative I have in general followed a chronological sequence, beginning around 1500, but touching lightly on the first Elizabethan Age, and taking the first part of the story to the Act of Union of 1707, which created 'Great Britain'. This conveniently marks a point from which the naval and mercantile sea-services part company. The next historical milestone is the Treaty of Paris in 1763 which conferred upon British shipping the freedom of the seas, saw the foundations of undisputed British power in India and secured her dominance of North America, but the general disregard of trade for the formalities of treaties and other such political and martial culminations, reduces the value of such conventional break-points. Insofar as the British mercantile marine is concerned the themes of historical exposition broadly consist of commercial aggression, political turmoil, war and social opportunity, along with the creation of markets for shipping and a continuous development in shipbuilding. The various dynamics which drive this narrative required their enablers. These consisted – besides merchants seeking cargo-capacity – of shipowners, ship-managers, shipping agents, ship-masters and seafarers generally. The huge variety of endeavour created by the interplay of these elements, however, flies off in all directions, making the discipline of rigidly following a time-line dull, disconnected and – in truth – impossible. It has therefore proved expedient, both for the author's wits and the reader's interest, to divert from an absolute conformity with chronology in order to draw to a conclusion a particular train of events.

This first volume follows British shipping globally until the Treaty of Paris in 1763. It then extends the time-line until 1807 in the case of the slave-trade, when the traffic was abolished in British ships. Similarly, the developmental aspects of the all-important trade of the East India Company are related in some detail until well beyond 1763, penetrating the years of the First World War with France in order to introduce the contentious matter of impressment, to sketch-in the manner in which the trade with India was managed, and to record the early stirrings of British hydrography. The story of merchant shipping in the wars between 1763 and 1815 is, therefore, reserved for the second volume, *Britannia's Realm*.

This book is not about the morality of trades or the practices of the shipping that supported it. Though rarely the case, trade may occasionally be equitable; to a greater or lesser extent, it is more likely to be exploitative. Shipowning and ship-management were – and remain – unequivocally so. Such was the grandeur of its most successful exponents, and such the indigent state of their meanest employees, that to argue anything else is as pointless as it is manifestly untrue. Such inequities – obvious to us through the lens of hindsight – were neither as obvious nor as troublesome to those either enjoying the benefits of shipowning or suffering from its worst excesses at the time in question. One exception to this is the impressment system which the reader may find much made of – particularly in *Britannia's Realm* – largely because it was a more dominant feature of the maritime fabric than one might at first imagine, and I make no apology for this. Such inequities, dreadful as they were, were in part cause and in part consequence of their own era and need to be set in contemporary context. We should not lose sight of the fact that, while generations of seafarers endured appalling conditions and only a few major and disturbing movements were initiated to end them, service at sea in merchant ships was for many young men a way out of grinding poverty ashore, a highway to material success and social advancement. Its reverse: drunkenness, arrogance, brutality and exploitation alas inevitably accompany such a large and dynamic movement in history. Even piracy, of which for a time the English were masters, was a golden road for some.

I have therefore made no attempt to either bowdlerise, or render politically correct, contentious terminology within the text. Both would seem to be dishonest. If an activity, object, or group of people was known in its time by a certain name, then that is the term I have used. I apologise if this causes offence; it is not intended to. Likewise I have stuck to the seaman's tradition of using the feminine gender for ships, even when they possess male names. It is an old prejudice and not one I wish to give up.

Although I make use of quotations, to save space and preserve the reader's patience these are not invariably referenced; all come from books listed in the bibliography. In general I have used traditional place names but, where it seemed helpful, I have parenthetically added the modern equivalent, for example: Bombay (Mumbai). On account of a long British seafaring tradition in which native names were rendered into seafaring *patois* and frequently enshrined in log-books – the best known of which is Ushant for the French island of D'Ouessant, off the Breton coast – I have usually retained the familiar English form.

I have not greatly troubled the reader with ships' dimensions, such data being available elsewhere. However, where appropriate I have occasionally referred to a vessel's burthen tonnage, a measure of capacity based on an ancient wine-cask, or 'tun', containing 252 imperial gallons. It was the method by which medieval ships were taxed and is evidence that one of our earliest trades was the import of wines from the French dominions of English kings. Tonnage by burthen serves to the end of our period, shortly after which tonnage measurement was reformed.

On the other hand, to give a fuller appreciation of what merchant ships routinely undertook, amid the events of note I have included a number of detailed voyage accounts in a particular trade. I have also applied a similar focus upon particular shipping ventures where these exemplified a trade and its complex workings and I am aware that I have ignored others, which cannot be helped.

The final three volumes of this series, *Masters Under God*, *More Days – More Dollars* and *Fiddler's Green*, bring the surprising history of the British merchant marine up to date.

MAPS

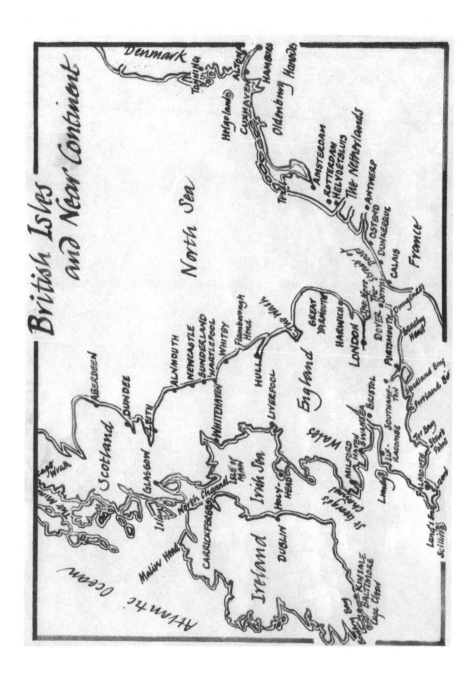

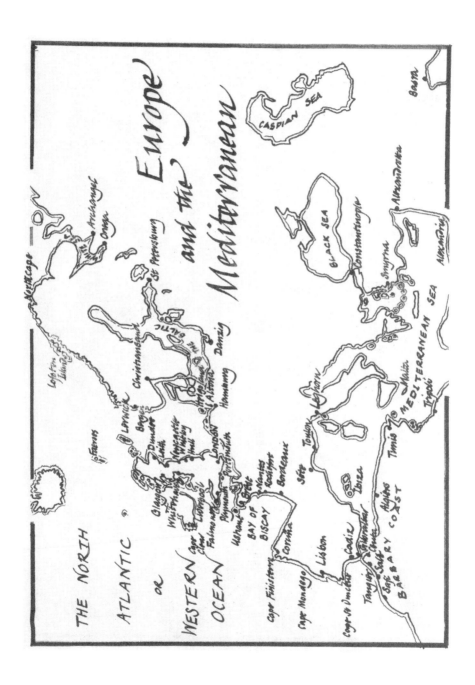

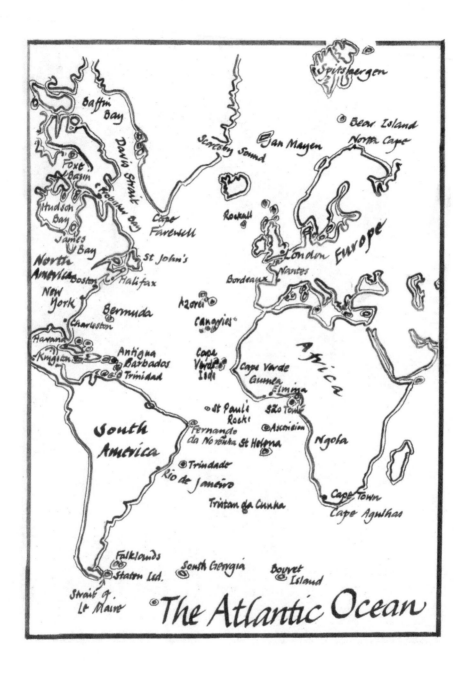

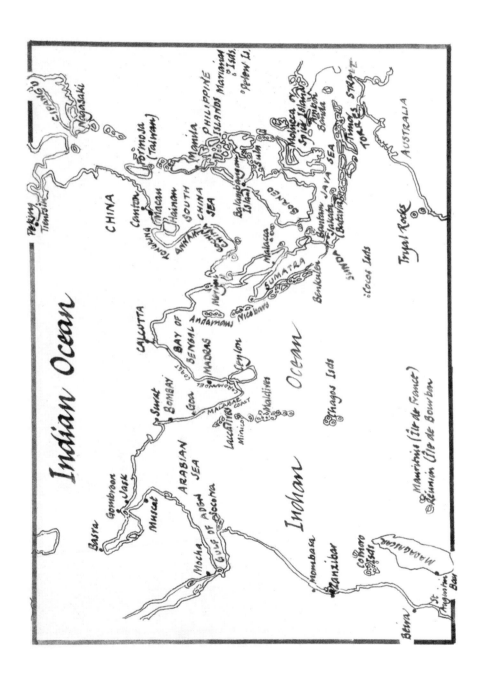

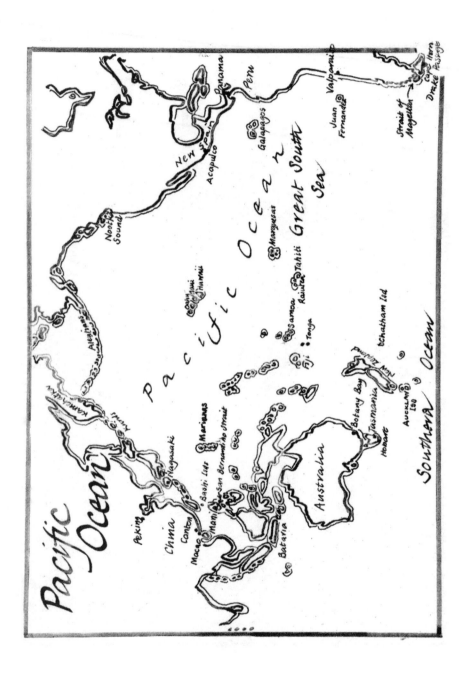

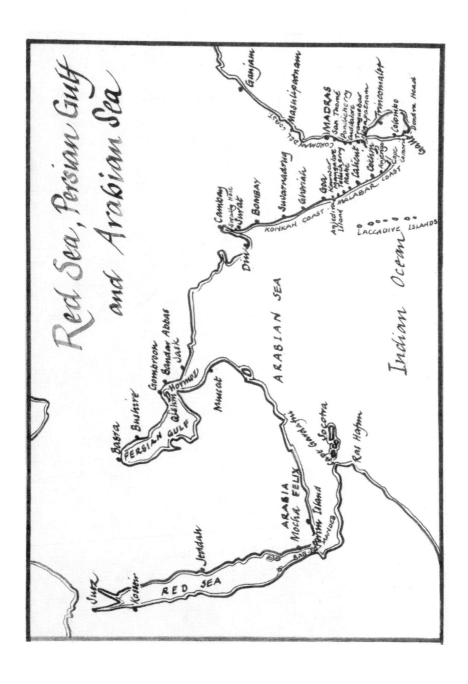

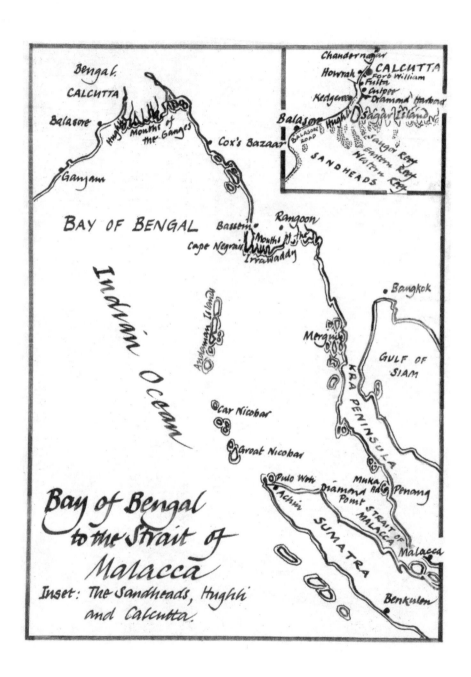

Bengal.
CALCUTTA
Balasore
Ganjam
Mouths of the Ganges
Hugli
Cox's Bazaar

BAY OF BENGAL
Bassein
Rangoon
Cape Negrais
Mouths of the Irrawaddy

Indian Ocean

Andaman Islands

Bangkok
Mergui
GULF OF SIAM

KRA PENINSULA

Car Nicobar

Great Nicobar

Pulo Weh
Muka Rd.
Diamond Point
Penang
Achin
STRAIT OF MALACCA
SUMATRA
Malacca
Benkulen

Chandernagar
CALCUTTA
Howrah
Fort William
Fulta
Chipee
Kedgeree
Diamond Harbour
Balasore
Hugli
Sagar Island
BALASORE ROAD
Saugor Reef
Eastern Reef
Western Reef
SANDHEADS

Bay of Bengal
to the Strait of
Malacca
Inset: The Sandheads, Hughli
and Calcutta.

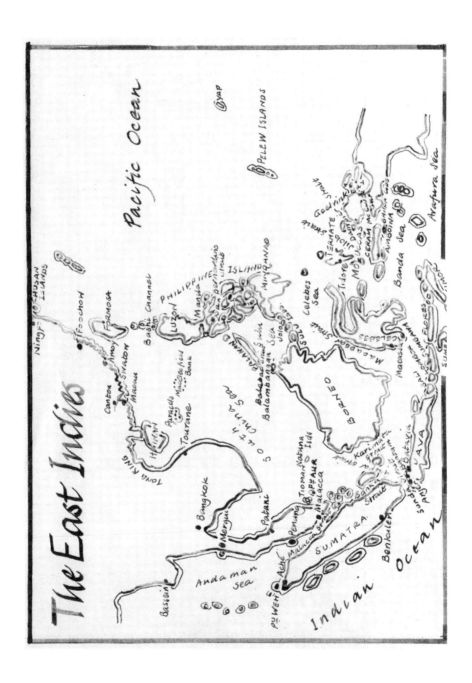

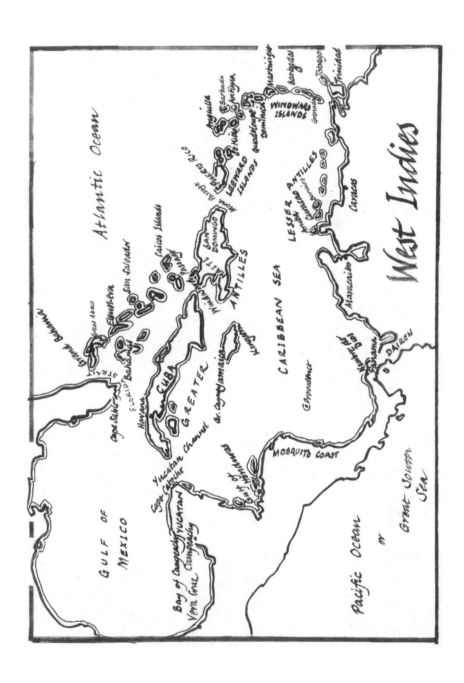

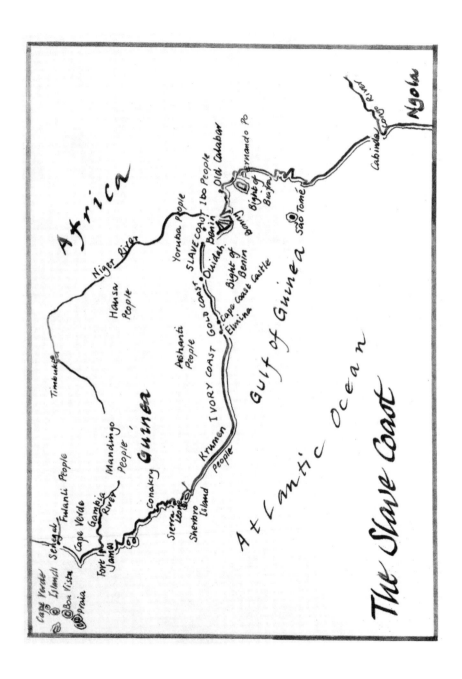

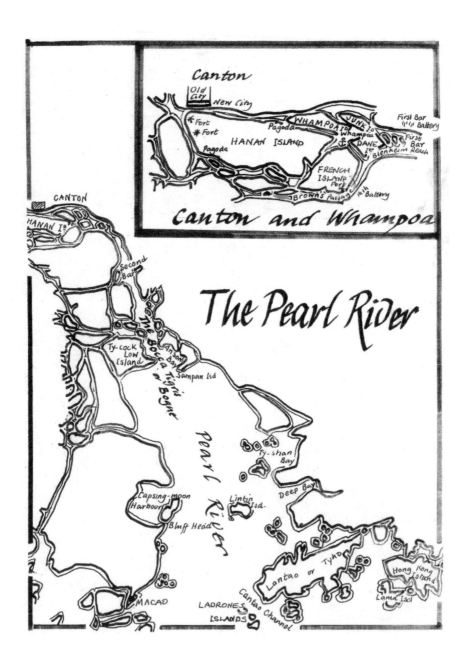

PART ONE

'The Trade of the World'

English Shipping 1500–1707

'He that is the Lord of the trade of the world is Lord of the wealth of the world.'

Sir Walter Ralegh

ONE

'AT THE DEVOTION OF THE WIND AND SEAS'

The Lure of Distant Lands, 1500–1707

The European discovery of land on the far side of 'The Western Ocean' may well have occurred long before Columbus, but it was only after 1492 that the presence of a new world began a powerful working upon the collective consciousness of the European mind. From the viewpoint of her sea-power, both naval and mercantile, which was at its zenith sometime about the middle of the nineteenth century, it is odd that among the nations of Europe Great Britain was a relative latecomer to maritime ambition. That the mantle begun with Portugal and Spain looking seawards and cultivating the dream of exploitable riches and eventually – after their temporary union in the late seventeenth century – a single sea-borne empire, later fell upon the British, is one of the extraordinary surprises of history.

Europeans were not the only adventurers. The Chinese Empire dispatched a number of exploratory expeditions but abandoned these around 1421 after the return of the imperial eunuch Zheng He on the grounds that little would profit the Middle Kingdom from such enterprises. At about the same time that the Chinese are thought by some to have been systematically quartering the globe, the Portuguese were astir, tentatively moving down the African coast and out into the Atlantic. Soon they had doubled the Cape of Good Hope and reached India and then the Spice Islands of the Moluccas; not long afterwards they colonised 'the Brazils'. The Spanish, meanwhile, having headed west to annex the West Indies and destroy the ancient civilisations of Central and South America, crossed the Isthmus of Panama. Such was the hold these two Iberian states appeared to have upon the globe that the Pope was resorted to in order to pacify competing national ambition between the two rival Catholic countries by the Treaty of Tordesillas of 1494 and its subsequent modifications. It followed that both retained power in their vast maritime empires for centuries, in the case of Spain drawing a wealth that kept her a dominant force in Europe until the Napoleonic era. Shortly after the conquest of the Philippines by Legaspí in 1565 (almost fifty years after the adventurer Ferdinand Magellan met his death there) Urdaneta discovered the westerly winds of the North Pacific provided a practical eastwards passage back to Mexico, enabling the establishment of the annual voyages of the great treasure, or 'Register', ships that were soon necessary to the Spanish economy. These, alternatively known as Manila or Acapulco galleons, maintained a continuous trans-Pacific service until 1815, by which time Spain's American colonies were in open revolt and seeking independence. This shipping route was the oldest and longest continuously maintained cargo-service in history.

Although several of these fabulously laden ships either foundered or were wrecked, only four were lost to an enemy, that enemy being first England, and later Great Britain. Under threat of Catholic conquest and enflamed by both commercial greed and frustration at exclusion from western waters under the Papal writ enshrined at Tordesillas, English seamen began their first major incursions onto the high seas.

From earliest times English kings had used merchant ships as military transports and, from time to time, as warships. The mustering of fleets of armed merchant bottoms was the standard medieval method of 'raising' a navy. Indeed some monarchs actually had an interest in merchantmen; Edward IV, for example, invested in profitable ship-owning. Nor were the succeeding Tudors indifferent to exploitable exploration: in 1497 Henry VII encouraged the Venetian adventurer Giovanni Cabot to venture west to Newfoundland from which arose English participation in the cod-fishery of the Grand Banks. Later, at Bristol in 1551, Giovanni Cabot's son Sebastian founded the 'Company of Merchant Adventurers'.

In 1514 Henry VIII incorporated the guild of shipmen and mariners of the Trinity House both to regulate pilotage on the river Thames and to provide charitable benefits to 'decayed mariners'. Henry VIII also had the first naval graving-dock built at Portsmouth, establishing both the naval dockyard and what would become the Royal Navy distinct and separate from the nation's merchant shipping, but not yet strong enough to operate without mercantile reinforcement.

Nor were his subjects idle. In 1542 an English trading fort was built on the coast of Brazil and in 1551 one Thomas Wyndham set out in the 150-ton *Lion* to begin the first of a series of annual voyages to West Africa, returning with gold, iron bars, sugar and fruit. The consequence of this was to involve England in the notorious slave-trade. Two years later, in 1553 and under the aegis of the Company of Merchant Adventurers, Sir Hugh Willoughby and his chief pilot, Richard Chancellor, in the *Bona Esperanza*, the *Bona Confidentia* and the *Edward Bonaventure* attempted to reach Cathay, as China was then known, by way of a north-east passage. The expedition was a disaster, for they failed in their objective, being separated in a gale. Willoughby discovered only the frozen wastelands bordering the Arctic Ocean where he and many of his men perished. Richard Chancellor in the *Edward Bonaventure* pressed on, to land in the northern territories of the Tsar of Muscovy, thereafter travelling to

Moscow to be received by Ivan the Terrible. Chancellor was drowned returning from his third voyage to Russia in 1556, but from this encounter grew a most important trade route to the ice-free northern ports of Russia supported by the joint-stock 'Muscovy Company' which was founded in London in 1555. Following this northern enterprise, in 1561, ambitions turned south: following Wyndham, John Hawkins made three voyages to Africa founding another joint-stock company entitled 'The Merchant Adventurers for Guinea' to exploit the transfer of black Africans across the mid-Atlantic as slaves.

A second attempt to reach China was made by Martin Frobisher in 1576 by way of the north-west passage. It met with no success, but confirmed English colonial ambitions in North America, for in 1583 Humphrey Gilbert led an expedition to found a colony at St John's, Newfoundland, to promote the important cod-fishery.[1]

The roots of English, and ultimately British, sea-power lay in conflict. In the mid-sixteenth century the hatred between England and Spain arising from religious difference was excited by the exclusion of English adventurers from the riches of the West Indies and Spanish claims on the mainland of South America. The aggressive, legally equivocal operations of men like Francis Drake, self-seeking men whose personal ambition chimed in with Elizabethan foreign policy, served the English state well. While they were fundamental in the establishment of an English Royal Navy, they were equally influential upon the development of a versatile, heavily built, armed merchant-ship which became a man-of-war when required.

Most famously it did so in 1588 when Drake was appointed vice admiral to Lord Howard of Effingham, the Lord Admiral of England, and with his private ships joined the main fleet in defeating the Duke of Medina-Sidonia's *Armada*. This, combining with the various expeditions conducted by English and English-sponsored navigators among which has to be counted that of Thomas Cavendish, whose return from his two-year circumnavigation occurred just as the Armada was falling apart, conveyed an impression of considerable English maritime power. This was an illusion.

In the years before the reign of Elizabeth I, when compared with other European powers – including the nation-states of Venice and Genoa, and the Hanseatic ports of Hamburg and Lübeck – English merchant shipping was small in terms of tonnage and numbers. Its most prominent and durable feature was to be its east coast coal trade, supplying 'sea-cole' from the mines of north-east England to London. According to Ralph Davis, English shipping as a whole consisted of: 'A meagre coastal traffic, a fishery of moderate scale, [and] a trickle of carrying traffic with the Low Countries, Spain, Portugal, France and the Baltic...' Some of this commerce might have been intrinsically valuable, but it was not high in volume and it is the volume of trade that creates a demand for shipping tonnage.

In 1598 the Hanseatic League's London headquarters, the Steelyard, was closed as a result of internal schism, Dutch competition and political turmoil, rather than any overt act on the part of the English Government. Nevertheless, the revolt in the Netherlands against Spain initiated the beginnings of the decline of Spanish power on the European continent and a shift in export strategy by English merchants, marked a quickening of English trade. Gone was the reliance upon the single-market for English wool and broadcloth following a crisis in 1550. Moreover, the defeat of the Ottoman Turks at Lepanto in October 1571, though failing to extirpate the Barbary corsairs, nevertheless enabled English trade with the Levant to flourish as the 'precursor of all English long-distance enterprise'. Elizabethan England was courted by the Sultan in distant Constantinople, who required a supply of tin, lead and 'bell-metals', the last released onto the open market from the dissolution of the monasteries and all wanted for the casting of cannon and the manufacture of shot. Even expertise in seamanship became an exportable skill. In exchange came wine, raisins, olive oil, expensive spices and silk brought overland from far and fabled Cathay. This trade, carried in what was popularly known as 'the Smyrna fleet' was, like that to Muscovy and West Africa, in the hands of a joint-stock enterprise, the 'Levant Company'.

The Joint Stock Company, set up by investors buying stock in a company established for a specific purpose, was the mechanism by which early English voyages were financed. It was to be the model for all such overseas expeditions and enterprises, attracting enormous amounts of capital while, at the same time, minimising risk by diversifying investments among several discrete ventures. Drake's notorious but single-purposed circumnavigation, in which Queen Elizabeth I secretly invested, gave enormous returns and is an example of the first, limited-objective joint-stock company. A less inhibited remit was adopted by the original East India Company, established at the end of 1600, by spreading the risks among the several ships making the initial voyages to India. In a joint-stock company shareholders elected a managing Board of Directors and had some initial say in the company's establishment. Thereafter they profited in proportion to their private investment and usually did very well. Dividends were paid out in money, but when capital returns were low and payment might weaken the company's position, the dividends were either postponed or, if remaining homeward cargo was available, could be liquidated from its sale on the open market by the shareholders.

Nevertheless, the joint-stock company proved both flexible and viable for English mercantilism and was, moreover, a great advance upon the anachronistic guilds or Government-sponsored enterprises that had preceded it. Not only did it open up the exotic trade with the orient, initially that of pepper and nutmeg, but it made possible the colonisation of North America – Jamestown being a product of the Virginia Company. The durability of the system, though much modified over time, is best exemplified by the East India Company which, by the time of its dissolution in 1858, had become the *de facto* ruling body of 'British' India.

The establishment of a joint-stock company was by a private Act of Parliament or Royal Charter, and winding them up required revocation of such instruments. Unfortunately they were not always successful, for the disadvantage of such an arrangement was that just as they enjoyed the profits, shareholders stood to lose all: in underwriting a company's debts there was no limit to their liability. While shareholders of the Royal African Company, established in 1672, enjoyed the amoral fruits of the slave trade, the backers of the South Seas Company had a different experience, as we shall see.

The Levant Company had been formed in 1585 and Elizabeth I had backed it with half the required capital of £80,000. It established trading houses in the Levant to trade with the subjects of the Ottoman Turk and its ships ran the gauntlet of interception by the piratical navies of the semi-autonomous Ottoman Pashaliks along the Barbary coast of north Africa, who were not only active in the Mediterranean but raided north as far as Iceland and south-west England in quest of plunder and slaves. Consequently vessels built for the service of these joint-stock companies had to be capable of self-defence and were well able to serve as men-of-war: both the Muscovy Company's *Edward Bonaventure* and the Levant Company's *Merchant Royal* fought against the Spanish Armada. Equally, in time of war, the seasonal sailings of these companies' ships made them vulnerable to attack. In 1590 ten homeward-bound vessels belonging to the Levant Company – the so-called 'Smyrna fleet' was attacked off Gibraltar by Spanish galleys. In a six-hour running fight the Spanish were beaten off with little apparent loss to the English.

The richness of this trade, which commanded freight rates of up to £7 per ton, was enormous. It was said to 'set 100,000 people to work' as England exported woollen cloth, lead, tin, hides and fustian – a coarse cloth made from cotton and flax – in exchange for imports of raw silk, cotton, mohair, currants, malmsey, tannin and oakgalls for ink. The company's ships called at Marseilles, Genoa, Leghorn (Livorno), Zante, Cephalonia, Crete, Smyrna (Izmir) Constantinople (Istanbul), Alexandretta (Iskanderum, the port for Aleppo), Cyprus, Tripoli, Alexandria and Algiers. Trading in many of the Levantine ports was conducted through established 'factories' where English agents were resident and such posts were maintained in Alexandretta, Constantinople and Smyrna until the Levant Company's monopoly was revoked in 1753 and the trade thrown open.

Indeed its very wealth attracted the attention of enemies and the Smyrna convoy became directly embroiled in the War of the English Succession (1689–97, sometimes known as King William's war, following the accession to the English throne of the Prince of Orange as King William III). As a consequence of the political situation the homeward Smyrna convoy of 1693 was enormous and comprised both English and Dutch bottoms. In expectation of its approach, a powerful Anglo-Dutch fleet was sent south to meet it and bring it safely home. Unfortunately the main allied fleet ran short of victuals and most of the men-of-war put about, with only Sir George Rooke's ships supported by a small Dutch squadron continuing south. Better prepared, the French combined their squadrons from Brest and Toulon, intercepting the convoy off Cape St Vincent on 17 June. Fortunately Tourville, the French admiral, took some persuading that what approached was a fleet of merchantmen not a battle-squadron, but the presence of the Dutch men-of-war caused Tourville to divert part of his fleet which the Dutch gallantly engaged, two of their men-of-war immolating themselves in a furious fight which allowed the convoy to scatter. Rooke observed that this was 'one of the best judged things I ever saw' but although three-quarters of the convoy escaped, no less than ninety-two laden merchantmen were captured or sunk. Although the majority of these were in fact Dutch, the losses in London alone were of equal value to the damage caused by the Great Fire of London in 1666. For their part, the French liquidated their prizes for 30 million *livres* which equated to their entire naval budget for the previous year. King William, whose interests lay in both London and Amsterdam, was devastated, while the verdict of the House of Commons fell upon the naval commanders-in-chief who were guilty of 'notorious and treacherous mismanagement'. The political consequences of this débâcle were considerable, but this was not to be the last catastrophe to befall a mercantile convoy failed by the navy to which it looked to for protection in time of war. The next, as we shall shortly observe, was to follow in a little over two years.

The Hanseatic decline, caused by conflict elsewhere in Europe, created a vacuum in the Baltic, drawing English shipping into that enclosed northern sea, while Italian commercial influence in London waned, being replaced by home-grown expertise. The English, with a sense of opportunism, embraced the notion that they could exploit the recession of Spain's maritime power but this expansion was not unopposed, for in their new freedom from Spain the Dutch were driven by the closure of European markets to search for new sources of wealth, looking eastwards for alternatives. England and the United Provinces, both otherwise insignificant countries, both Protestant and fired with a new ethic, were to emerge as bitter rivals who would fight each other within the coming century. At first all the advantages lay with the Dutch: independence combined with stolid, consensual Protestantism to establish the rule of law without the wild excesses of other revolutions. Banking rapidly made Amsterdam the pre-eminent European financial centre, its merchants lent their entrepreneurial skills, its shipyards provided the means and its seamen the daring, to work an economic miracle. Detail helped; the entire Dutch nation lived in intimate contact with the sea; it was sensible to the vagaries of the weather and tides, and had learned the virtues of organisation. Moreover, in the *fluyt*, with its adaptability for trading to both the Baltic and the Mediterranean, they produced an able cargo-carrier and efficient sailer capable of being built cheaply and worked by a minimal – and economically optimal – crew. The republican spirit of the Seven United Provinces combined with the strictures of a raw capitalism to create an important feature of Dutch shipping which spread elsewhere but was never adopted until too late by its English rival. This was a flat shipboard hierarchy which minimised social difference and enabled small crews to function well, uninhibited by stifling considerations of relative status.

However, there was one thing the Dutch could do nothing about, and that was the shallowness of their home waters. Despite the employment of hollow 'camels' to lift and carry deep-laden merchantmen across the Zuyder Zee, neither their merchantmen nor – more significantly – their men-of-war could be built deep and large enough to combat the rising naval power of what in due course would no longer be merely England, but Great Britain. Such transitions were slow, though speeded by the final outcome of three Anglo-Dutch wars and aided by successive mounting discomfiture of the French, who followed the Spanish as a major naval nation. But the English, along with their fellow Scots, were never able to run ships on minimal manning levels and herein lies one small part of their ultimate decline as a maritime power: they were – *par excellence* – a victim of their own success. The British never produced anything as efficient as the *fluyt* – though they acquired numbers of them as prizes – nor anything quite as intuitively adept as the Dutch sailor. Again, this excellence was a proclivity, never to be equalled in Britain where it nevertheless became an article of national faith to assume Britannia's maritime expertise was supreme.[2] The British affinity for the sea-life was partial, not general, accruing only to sections of the public which were geographically isolated. In the event the British proved better at producing officers than ratings and, of course, in contrast to every other European country including what eventually became the Netherlands, it would have a larger maritime population. This latter circumstance guaranteed success for a modest inferiority in quality – a comparison that might be made with equal cogency if of less impact or importance with such as the Norwegians – until profitable shipowning so resided in the margins of ship-management that manning levels and the pay-scales of seafarers became crucial to the existence of a national merchant fleet. This was another element that guaranteed eventual decline. Other factors bore fruit when the repeal of the Navigation Acts in the mid-nineteenth century was finally played out over a hundred years later.

But all of this lay in the future; in the early seventeenth century, as the twin crises of Civil War in England and collision with the Dutch loomed, the foundations of British maritime supremacy were laid by the English. New markets were opened up, new import and export trades were established: peace with Spain reopened trade with that country and Portugal; uneasy dominance of Ireland improved the commerce across the Irish Sea; the combination of colonial expansion in North America and the cod-fishery on the Grand Banks off Newfoundland, which provided a market for African slaves and portable protein for British armies, saw the rise first of Bristol, and later that of Liverpool. A further combination of an expanding Royal Navy requiring so-called 'naval-stores' – consisting of turpentine, resin, flax, ship and spar-timber, iron and hemp – added to the already thriving general trade with the Baltic to make this route of paramount importance to the British economy and the ports of her east coast. To this might be added the vigorous coastal trade which, in the absence of good roads, and the presence of a coal trade, a passenger trade and a rising industrial base, made the movement of commodities by sea a viable enterprise and a national necessity. Such successes bred success, encouraging investment, shipbuilding, port expansion and even personal ambition. Men rose socially and while the incomparable Cook may be singular, there were many, many more such as he in the preceding two centuries.

In 1582 an inventory of 1,600 merchant ships revealed that only about 250 were in excess of 80 tons burthen but, as Ralph Davies makes clear, this number rapidly grew and by the end of the century:

the east coast coal trade had trebled in volume in thirty years. The Iceland fishery seemed flourishing; across the Atlantic went over two hundred ships for the

Newfoundland fishery, which had employed only thirty in 1574. Nearly every branch of the shipping industry … was advancing rapidly; and a few days before Christmas, 1606 the *Susan Constant*, *Godspeed* and *Discovery* sailed from London to begin the American colonisation which was ultimately to be the greatest expansive force of all.

Then, of course, there was India, and beyond the subcontinent lay fabulous Cathay and the spice islands of modern Indonesia. Trade in eastern seas meant confrontation with the decaying power of Portugal and the newly invigorated Dutch, but in 1583 an English adventurer named Ralph Fitch had made an overland journey to India. Returning in 1591 he aroused interest in London and, in due course, on 31 December 1600 the first English East India Company was founded with an initial capital of £72,000 and a royal charter granted by Elizabeth I. This event marked the uncertain and almost unnoticed conception of 'British' India. Although it was not yet India upon which what would become popularly called 'John Company' fixed his rapacious eyes, the terms of this incorporation granted the company exclusive and monopolistic rights of trade in eastern seas beyond the Cape of Good Hope. Under the wealthy Sir Thomas Smythe, the 125 merchants who constituted 'The Governor and Merchants of London trading into the East Indies', each invested as much capital as they wished to venture, and profited in proportion.

Smythe had been born in 1558. As a mature man he had been appointed 'Farmer of the Customs' and private banker to Elizabeth I. Following the failure of the Jamestown Colony in North America, Walter Ralegh and his associates transferred the proprietorship to him, Smythe having been one of the original 'London Council for the Plantation of Virginia'. Related to a Lord Mayor of London and himself a graduate of Oxford University, Smythe was, at twenty-three, an incorporator of the Levant Company and, by thirty, a principal in the Muscovy Company. He then became attracted to the Virginia project, at the same time backing James Lancaster in his first voyage into the Indian Ocean in 1591. Knighted in 1603, Smythe was, according to Keble Chatterton:

> Far-sighted … financially adventurous yet full of cool prudence … one of the very few rich men in England… Without his insight, his steadying and driving force, his powers of organisation, the future history … and the growth of [England's] Merchant Navy, might have been a very different story.

Smythe's stewardship of the East India Company increased its capital value from an initial investment to some £1.5 million in his twenty-one gubernatorial years, for it was part of Tudor foreign policy to marry the state's ambitions with those of its wealthiest citizens who:

> at their own adventures, costs and charges as well for the honour of this Our Realme of England, as for the increase of our Navigation [meaning shipping], and advancement of Trade.

Between 1601 and 1607 several East India 'fleets' were sent out. The Company even attempted to find another route by way of the Davis Strait, sending Captain George Waymouth in quest of a north-west passage in 1602, but the main effort was by the Cape of Good Hope towards Java, Sumatra (Sumatera) and the Moluccas in quest of spices. Pepper was the most sought after of the spices, being a more agreeable food preservative than salt, but coriander, nutmeg, ginger, mace, cinnamon, cloves, turmeric and cardamom were also in demand.

The first of these voyages was led by the experienced and Portuguese-speaking James Lancaster, and consisted of five vessels which left in April 1601. Lancaster had ventured into Arctic waters and served against the Spanish Armada; his voyage under the aegis of the new company may have been inspired by the arrival of the *Richard of Arundel* off Limehouse in 1591. Her master, James Welsh, landed a cargo of thirty-two barrels of palm oil, 150 elephant tusks and, significantly, 587 bags of pepper. Lancaster had already made a pioneering voyage into the Indian Ocean. Scurvy had struck early, two men dying 'before wee passed the line and divers sicke, which took their sickness in those hote climates.' In fact Lancaster had encountered and recognised with remarkable acuity all those evils which were to beset long voyages in the succeeding centuries and which were to vex the authorities responsible for them. The weather, Lancaster found, was:

> unwholesome from 8 degrees of Northerly latitude unto the line, at that time of the yeere, for we had nothing but Ternados, with such thunder, lightning and raine, that we could not keep our men drie 3 hours together, which was an occasion of the infection among them, and their eating of salt victuals, with lack of clothes to shift them.

The three remaining vessels, *Penelope*, *Edward Bonaventure* and *Marchant Royall*, continued to the Cape where the last named was sent home with the sick. The *Penelope* soon afterwards foundered, and Lancaster in the *Edward Bonaventure* finally reached Indian waters after many vicissitudes; he was seriously ill off Sri Lanka when he was 'more like to die then [sic] to live' and he lost his ship on the homeward passage, arriving in London with only a handful of men.[3]

On this his second voyage Lancaster bore letters of commendation from Elizabeth along with gifts to sundry 'Indian Princes'. Lancaster hoisted his flag in the *Red Dragon*, a 600-ton privateer built in the Royal dockyard at Chatham in 1595 as the *Mare Scourge* for the Duke of Cumberland, one of Smythe's fellow-founders of the East India Company. The remainder of the small fleet consisted of the 300-ton *Hector*, commanded by John Middleton; the 260-ton *Ascension*, commanded by William Brand, a 'grave and discreet merchant' who spoke Arabic, Spanish and Portuguese; the 240-ton *Susan* under John Heywood, and the small storeship *Guest* (or *Gift*). All except the last were armed, the *Hector*, *Ascension* and *Susan* having been purchased by the East India Company from the Levant Company. Lancaster was appointed 'Generall of the Fleet', a term then standing in place of admiral, with Middleton as his vice admiral, and the entire company numbered some 480 men. As their chief pilot, or navigator, they had John Davis the Arctic explorer who had just returned from a voyage to the Spice Islands in a Dutch Indiaman, the *Leeuw*. The fleet was well appointed and besides seamen, included factors and pursers in anticipation of trading opportunities. To this end thirteen different English cloths, tin, iron, lead and luxuries such as pistols, toilet implements, cutlery, plate, plumes, spectacles and drinking glasses were loaded as trade-goods, and a trading-imprest of £11,267 in silver was carried. The ships left Woolwich in February, but it was April before they finally departed from Dartmouth.

A degree of confusion arises from the contemporary use of the generic noun 'fleet' for such enterprises (a practice that lasted into the nineteenth century), and the necessary appointment of a hierarchy of 'general, admiral, vice admiral' and so forth which conveys to the modern reader the sense of these being naval expeditions. They were not. Lancaster's 'fleet' was commercially speculative in concept, backing and constitution, its vaguely diplomatic veneer being entirely subordinate to its mercantile purpose and its hierarchical 'ranks' merely reflect the convention of the day.

On their way south in June they captured the richly laden Portuguese Indiaman, *São Thomé*, and transferred her looted cargo of wine, oil, olives and spices into two of their number. A few weeks later they took out of the *Guest* all usable spars and stores, broke down her upper-works for firewood 'and so left her floating in the sea' a derelict. By the time they reached the Cape of Good Hope scurvy had a hold on the men in most of the ships, though Lancaster had learned from his previous experience and:

> brought to sea with him certaine Bottles of the Juice of Limons, which hee gave to each one, as long as it would last, three spoonfuls every morning... This Juice worketh much better, if the partie keepe a short Dyet, and wholly refrains salt meat, which ... and long being at sea is the only cause of the breeding of this Disease.

Lancaster's ships sailed again on 29 October and soon ran into heavy weather, thereafter finding it necessary to recruit at Antongil Bay on the coast of Madagascar from mid-December until early March, 1602. Here, amid a degree of discontent and near-mutiny, during which the *Ascension*'s surgeon, Christopher Newchurch, attempted suicide by poison, Lancaster augmented his stock of citrus fruit, rice, peas, beans, oxen and chickens by bartering with the indigent population; sadly not all his sick recovered, several men dying of dysentery. At the burial the ceremonial discharge of a gun killed Brand of the *Ascension*:

> and the boatswaine's mate of the same ship. Many others were hurt and besprinkled with the bloud of these massacred men, who, going to the burial of another, were themselves carried to their owne graves.

They had built a small pinnace as tender to the squadron before Lancaster sailed on 6 March, after which the fleet headed north-east across the Indian Ocean and made a brief landfall on the Nicobar Islands before anchoring off Aceh or Achin (Aché) on the north-west extremity of Sumatra on 5 June. Here contact was made with Dutch traders who, despite orders to repulse English shipping, were sufficiently intimidated to make no objection to Lancaster's ships loading with spices and what pepper there was. Lancaster himself was borne upon the back of an elephant following a larger pachyderm bearing Queen Elizabeth's letters in its *howdah*, to an audience with the local ruler. The elderly obese Ala-udinn Riayat Shah received Lancaster cordially, but the pepper harvest had been poor and the prospect of trade was uncertain. Accordingly Lancaster sent the *Susan* further south to Priaman and, while his factors tried to drum up more cargo – a matter taking some months – Lancaster took the *Red Dragon*, *Hector* and *Ascension* into the Strait of Malacca in quest of plunder. On the afternoon of 3 October they encountered a Portuguese carrack, the *São Antonio* which they attacked after dark and boarded next morning, taking out of her quantities of calico on its way to China from Madras. Lancaster then returned to Aceh where the *Ascension* was loaded with the accumulated pepper and sent home. On 9 November Lancaster in the *Hector*, made for Priaman to pick up the half-loaded *Susan*. Leaving Heywood with orders to sail homewards as soon as he was full, Lancaster then headed for Bantam to the east of Anjer at the eastern end of the Sunda Strait, arriving on the 16th. Here, with 'a very greate peale of ordnance, such an one as had never been rung there before…' and after securing permission from the local rajah – a ten-year-old boy – Lancaster established a trading station and sent William Starkey in the Madagascan-built pinnace to replicate this in the Moluccas.

On 20 February 1603 Lancaster weighed the *Red Dragon*'s anchor and headed for home with another 'greate peale of ordnance'. John Middleton had died and the *Hector* was now commanded by her master, Sander Cole. On their way the two ships ran into a cyclone which:

> continued a day and a night, with an exceeding great and raging sea, so that in the reason of man no shippe was able to live in them; but God, in his mercie, ceased the violence thereof and gave us time to breath and to repair all the distresses and harmes we had received, but all our ships were so shaken, that they were leakie all the voyage after'. Further bad weather was encountered in May when 'the seas did so beate upon the ships quarter, that it shook all the iron-work of her rother [rudder]; and the next day in the morning, our rother broke cleane from the stern of our shippe … [which] drave up and downe in the sea like a wracke.

After monumental labours, entailing one member of the crew going overboard, a jury-rudder was fashioned from the mizzen-mast, but this failed within hours. With the *Hector* standing-by and his men anxious to abandon ship Lancaster, anxious not to lose his valuable cargo, coolly sat down and wrote to Smythe:

> Right Worshipful Sir,
>   What hath passed in this voyage, and what trades I have settled for this companie, and what other events have befallen us you shall understand by the bearers hereof

… I will strive with diligence to save my ship, and her goods, as you may perceive by the course I take in venturing mine own life, and those that are with mee. I cannot tell where you should look for mee, if you send out any pinnace to seek mee because I live at the devotion of the wind and seas. And thus fare you well, desiring God to send us a merrie meeting in this world, if it be his good will and pleasure…
Your very loving friend,
James Lancaster

He succeeded in putting this remarkable epistle aboard the *Hector*, along with orders for her to proceed homewards, but Cole steadfastly remained with his 'Generall' until the sea moderated whereupon, with his best swimmers, he lowered a boat and came to Lancaster's aid. The incident says much for the loyalty Lancaster inspired, for the reinforcement assisted the *Red Dragon*'s company in rigging a second jury rudder and, thanks to improvisation, skill and dogged persistence, brought the ship under command again. Doubling the Cape they headed north, a man being killed when the slings of the main-yard gave way and flung him overboard. The two ships took on fresh water and hogs at St Helena, recruiting the sick with greens and fresh fruit until leaving on 5 July. At last, on 7 September 1603:

We tooke sounding, judging the Land end of England to be fortie leagues from us. The eleventh day [of September] we came to the Downes, well and safe to an anchor; for the which, thanked be Almighty God, who hath delivered us from the infinite perils and dangers, in this long and tedious Navigation.

The voyage had cost some 180 seamen their lives, including Middleton's, largely due to scurvy, but spirits ran high as the *Hector* and the *Red Dragon* worked their way up 'the River of Thames' to find moorings off Woolwich. Loaded with over 1 million pounds avoirdupois of pepper at 8s the pound in their holds, the profits to the East India Company ought to have been immense. This was not the case for the market was glutted by the Dutch who had shortly before this amalgamated their separate eastern commercial enterprises into a single entity, the *Vereenigde Oostindische Compagnie* (VOC, or the United East India Company) with an immense capital of £540,000. In London pepper stood at 1s 2d to the pound and there were few buyers for it.

Despite the knighthood conferred upon the remarkably stoic James Lancaster, the year of 1603 was unpropitious. Good Queen Bess had died in March and King James VI of Scotland had ascended England's throne as James I. He had brought with him, it was rumoured, several noisome infections, most obviously that of the plague, which made one of its periodic and devastating appearances in London, wiping out about a fifth of the population and depressing trade. Nevertheless, by accepting a quantity of pepper in return for their stakes, the Company's directors were induced to support further voyages and, on the completion of a second, dividends rose to a spectacular 95 per cent. Further 'fleets' followed; the next under Henry Middleton, a relation of the first fleet's vice admiral, and including the *Hector* and *Susan*. The latter foundered when homeward bound, but the remainder reached home in May 1606. For the third venture Captain William Keeling, who had formerly sailed in both the *Hector* and *Susan*, was appointed General of an expedition for which £53,000 capital had been subscribed, but of which only £7,280 had been expended in trade-goods. This expedition had a wider purpose, combining the efforts of both the East India Company and the ailing Levant Company.

The Levant Company had been disbanded in 1603, hit by the losses to the Barbary corsairs and rendered unable to meet its obligations under its original charter. However, in December 1605 the new King James I had reconstituted it 'in perpetuity' and it benefited from eastern trade, buying spices in London and re-exporting them to Constantinople.[4] This general reinvigoration coincided with a changing situation in the east. Earlier that same year a trade-war had resulted in the Dutch wresting the fabulous spice trade from the Portuguese with the capture of the Moluccas; then they in turn were dispossessed in the following year by Spanish forces from the Philippines. The fluidity of this state of affairs attracted the notice of ambitious merchants in London, hence the dispatch of William Hawkins aboard the *Hector*. The 105-ton *Consent* appears to have sailed first, on 12 March 1607, Keeling heading for the Moluccas. The other two ships, *Hector* and the *Red Dragon*, left on 1 April and, upon reaching Socotra, the *Red Dragon* headed for the Indies and the Hector steered north for Surat. It was hoped that Hawkins, a Turkic-speaking member of the Levant Company, who left London charged with an embassy from James I to the Mughal emperor Shah Jahangir, would secure a 'Grant in Trade'. Hawkins's landing at Surat was contested by the Portuguese but he succeeded in reaching Agra, where his ability to converse with the emperor ensured imperial interest and some degree of personal favour, though he failed to persuade Jehangir to throw up his agreement with the Portuguese. Further similar embassies were sent out by the Levant Company and King James I, but with no better success, nevertheless the expedition made a good return on investment and Hawkins remained behind attempting to persuade 'the Great Mogul' to change his mind in favour of the English.

For his part, Keeling had arrived in the Moluccas only to find he was unable to trade. Instead, he cunningly showered silver to the tune of £2,949 on the owner of Javanese *praus* carrying cargoes of cloves and encouraged the factors sweltering in the tropic heat at the 'English factory' at Bantam, on the western extremity of Java. In this wise a cargo was accumulated and, after the accounts had been reckoned following Keeling's return home on 9 May 1610, the expedition had yielded a profit of 234 per cent, the cargo of cloves acquired for under £3,000 selling at £36,287.

By this time the East India Company's Directors, now recognised as serious rivals by both the Dutch and the Portuguese, had petitioned James for a revision of their charter enabling them to acquire more and larger ships. While other eastern voyages were in train the company built the *Trades Increase*, an immense ship of 1,293 tons burthen, launched by the king himself on 13 December 1609 from the Company's own recently acquired shipyard at Deptford. It was a splendid occasion; a fine dinner was given to the king and his courtiers, served on Chinese porcelain. The acquisition of the Deptford shipyard was a significant marker of the Company's confidence, despite its enemies in its trading area, for it was acquiring a fleet of significant size, employing some 2,500 officers and seamen in addition to the clerks, ship-wrights, blacksmiths, caulkers and other tradesmen now toiling in its new premises. Most important, despite Hawkins's failure at Agra, over one hundred factors were scattered in what the Company increasingly regarded as its 'possessions', its factories or trading-stations along the Indian coast and across the Bay of Bengal. An audit in 1621 estimated that English woollens, iron, tin, lead and other goods to the value of £319,211 had been exported in return for imports valued at purchase at £375,288, but sold at market prices of £2,044,600.

Against this enormous profit must be offset the considerable costs of the ships and crews, the fact that voyages took many months, so that although the first twelve voyages yielded profits of never less than 138 per cent (at a time when interest rates were about 8 per cent per annum) there was always anxiety and risk attached to them. Moreover, as the numbers of ships engaged in the trade increased, losses began to be experienced, exceptionally that of both ships in 1608. It was all very well for Lancaster to break up the *Guest* to his fleet's advantage, but the loss of the *Susan* was costly and most of these early East Indiamen came to unhappy ends. By this means the expendable nature of ships in pursuit of wealth became a subconscious consequence of trade in the English psyche. While continuing to penetrate the Mughal Empire the *Ascension* was wrecked on shoals at the mouth of the Amlicka River, some 54 miles from Cambay (Khambat) on the Gujarat coast in 1609, and the redoubtable *Hector* capsized and sank while being careened off the coast of Java in 1617. The *Red Dragon's* fate, as befitted her origins, was closely linked with the establishment of English power in India, and occurs later.

Soon the Company's ships were venturing beyond the Indian seas. Sir Henry Middleton, sailed from England in the *Trade's Increase* in 1610 with the 90-ton *Darling* and *Peppercorn*, Captain Nicholas Downton in company. Leaving the latter ship at Aden, in November Middleton passed through the Strait of Bab-el-Mandeb intending to anchor off Mocha and trade for the *Arabica* coffee bean. Unfortunately:

About five a clocke, in luffing [and] in being much wind, we split our mayne toppe sayle, and putting abroad our mizzen, it split likewise; our Pilots brought our shippe a ground upon a bank of sand, the wind blowing hard, and the sea somewhat high, which made us all doubt her coming off … we did what we could to lighten our ship, sending some good a-land and some aboard the *Darling* … we land[ed] as well our Wheat-meale, Vinegar, Sea-coles, Pitch and Tarre … and other provisions … as well as Tinne, Lead, Iron, and other merchandise to be sould, and staved neare all our [fresh] water.

These were desperate measures and although the ship was refloated Middleton had been captured by Arabs and both he and his ships were obliged to languish until his release was secured and it was late September 1611 before he arrived at Surat. The delay and news of the travails of the English in the Red Sea had reached Portuguese ears and seven armed Portuguese vessels awaited Middleton's arrival. So too did William Hawkins, eager to be repatriated after his fruitless sojourn at Jehangir's court. All Middleton achieved was the embarkation of Hawkins and a retreat to the island of Socotra off the Horn of Africa, where he left letters of warning to others who followed him before making for Perim Island in the Strait of Bab-el-Mandeb to trade directly with Arab and Indian vessels. Here he wished to barter for calico – cotton goods from the Indian port city of Calicut – to exchange in the East Indies for spices.

Meanwhile the next ships to attempt to trade with the remote Arabian provinces of the Ottoman Porte were on their way under Captain John Saris. Saris had sailed as a factor on the Company's second voyage and served at Bantam until October 1609, when he had returned home in the *Hector*. He was made general of the eighth voyage and with the *Hector, Clove* and *Thomas* was sent out under a *firman* from the Sultan at Constantinople to trade at Aden and Mocha. Alarmed at Middleton's news of hostility in Arabia Felix (modern Yemen) which he picked up at Socotra, he nevertheless continued, encountering Middleton trading at Perim. The two men concluded a plan to make the best of things before Middleton, having secured a cargo of trade-goods, sailed for the Spice Islands in the *Trade's Increase* with the *Peppercorn* in company.

Middleton's great ship had, however, begun to suffer a common curse of wooden ships: the heavy fouling of her bottom by weed and marine growth. They were also eaten into by the mollusc *teredo navalis*, or 'ship-worm', a voracious lover of oak found in vast numbers in tropical seas. To combat these ills various concoctions of greasy, usually tar- or tallow-based formulations were smeared, or 'payed', on the bottom, but they were an imperfect anti-dote. It had therefore become the practice while in a safe haven in the Spice Islands to 'heave a ship down' or careen her. This entailed lightening her as much as possible, of taking out of her all her upper spars, anchors, stores and cargo and then, at a location where she could lie in sheltered water sufficient to float her but close enough to run ropes and tackles ashore, to heave her over on her side. Then began the laborious task of hand-scraping her bottom, re-caulking as necessary for the homeward voyage, and 're-paying' the exposed planking or, as seems possible, doubling the planking with expendable, locally obtained hardwood, probably *seraya* or *ramin*. Careening had to be done twice, once for each side, and might take many days.

A suitable 'careenage' had been found at Bantam on the Java coast and was one reason why the place had recommended itself as a site for a factory. Here the *Trade's Increase* was accordingly hove-down. It is inferred that the crank, or unstable nature of this great ship, contributed to her downfall, for the details of her end are uncertain. Other hints suggest that numbers of her crew died, probably of malaria for which the area became notorious for a rapid infection: 'all her men died in the careening of her,' quotes Chatterton, and this is lent substance by a further anecdote that numerous hired Javanese also died 'in the work before they could sheath one side'. As a consequence of this terrible drain on resources 'they could hire no more men, and therefore were forced to leave her imperfect, where she was sunke in the Sea, and after[wards] set on fire by the Javans'. The sequence of events is unclear, though the date of her burning is said to have been 19 November 1611 and one consequence was that the loss persuaded the Company's Directors not to build so large a vessel in the future. It is possible that the *Trade's Increase* had had to be abandoned six months before her firing, for Middleton himself died at Bantam on 24 May, it is said of a broken heart.

But not before the *Peppercorn* had sailed for home, Downton saluting Middleton with 'five shot' and embarking on a passage fraught with difficulties, not least of which was a fire. This, usually catastrophic to a wooden ship, was started by the cook, Richard Hancock, who was 'o'erguzzled with drink', but the flames were extinguished before it got too firm a hold. More mundanely she leaked badly, her worn sails split at the slightest sign of a squall and carried away some of her standing rigging. Wear-and-tear was to trouble these ships for some years yet, without the added complications of imperfect navigation and a lack of charts. Downton lost his reckoning as he sought the Chops of the Channel, missing the Scillies and stretching too far north to make his landfall off Ireland, putting into Waterford. In addition to the parlous state of his ship, Downton had lost many men to disease, chiefly scurvy, but his arrival marked the end of this, the 'sixth voyage'. Notwithstanding the loss of the *Trade's Increase* and its dubious trade practices, the sixth voyage returned 121 per cent on investment.

For his part, Saris had done even better. From Perim he had stretched across to the Spice Islands and then, in the *Clove*, he had gone on to the almost fabled land of Cipangu, or Japan. The Japanese were resistant to outsiders but the Portuguese had a small foothold at Nagasaki. Although Japan was later to close its doors to all but the Dutch, Saris was favourably received by the Shogunate officials, largely owing to the good offices of the Englishman William Adams, then resident in Japan.[5] Saris's trade prospered and, on his eventual return to London, his voyage realised 218 per cent.

Such ventures relied heavily upon chance. The Court of Directors wanted regular trading rights. Unable to take no for an answer, the Company successfully persisted in breaking down the barriers raised against trade with the Mughals. In 1611 Anthony Hippon, who had served as master in both the *Red Dragon* and the *Hector* in 1606 and 1607, took command of the *Globe* – the first East Indiaman to be built at Blackwall – in 1610 and on reaching India he established a trading post at Pettapoli in the Bay of Bengal. This was the first formal English 'post' in India and far distant from Agra. It lasted until abandoned in 1687 owing to pestilential fevers carrying off the factors, but a more permanent factory had by then been established at Surat. Hippon himself died on the east coast of the Malay peninsula on 9 July 1612 before the end of the *Globe's* voyage.

The tenth fleet 'sent out' in early 1612 under the command of Captain Thomas Best consisted of the *Red Dragon* and the *Hosiander*. These made for Surat and anchored in Swally Hole on the Tapti River, adjacent to the city. Learning of yet another attempt on their monopoly the Portuguese governor at Goa despatched Admiral Nuño de Cunha with four men-of-war and some two dozen local *grabs* to root out the English. The Portuguese squadron arrived off Swally Roads on the afternoon of 29 November full of seamen, soldiers and lascars. Best immediately weighed and stood out to sea where he could use his guns and avoid being boarded by overwhelming numbers.

A few ranging shots were tried before night fell and it was next morning before the action was joined. Best was contemptuous of his opponents:

> Yf mine eyes had not seene, I could not belevd ther basenes and couardlynes. That these 4 galleons they have no better in all thesse countries. In burthen … from 700 to 900 and 1,000 tons; good ordnance (better than we have any), but so small use they make of them, with so little skill, that a man would never desire a better enymy.

Playing his broadsides on his 'enymy', Best fell back into the Tapti estuary on an ebb tide, drawing his deeper-draughted foe after him. Three of Da Cunha's ships ran aground, to be pounded by the *Red Dragon* and *Hosiander*, and when the flood refloated them the action continued until dark, whereupon both forces anchored. English casualties were two killed and one man wounded while the Portuguese lost in excess of 150 dead and many incapacited. Despite attempting to renew the action by putting to sea next day and manoeuvring in the offing until 3 December, Da Cunha remained at anchor and Best withdrew across the Gulf of Cambay to reprovision at Mahuva. There, on 23 December, Da Cunha renewed the action. It rumbled on for two days, Robert Standish, surgeon of the *Hosiander* remarking that they:

> gave them such banges as maid ther verie sides crack; for we neyther of us never shott butt were so neere we could not misse. We steered after the [*Red*] *Dragon*, and when she was with [engaging] one we were with another. And the truth is that some of them were glad to cutt [their anchor] cables and be gone.

Finally a fire was started aboard Da Cunha's flagship. 'This day we tore them most cruellie,' Standish wrote:

> We see swimming by our ship peeces of tymber, boords and ould hatts and clothes. Ther sailles were almost torne from [the] yards, some of them, and their tackeling (running rigging) cutt in peecces.

This humiliation meted out to the Portuguese was welcomed by the Mughul Emperor, greatly reducing Shah Jehangir's hostility to the new-comers. Soon afterwards he relented and permitted the Company's ships to trade at Surat, Gogha (Gogo) and Cambay, this last giving access to the vast caravanserai of Ahmedabad some miles inland, while Surat was established as a permanent factory and remained the pre-eminent English trading-post until displaced by Bombay (Mumbai) in 1661. Best loaded a cargo of Indian cotton 'piece-goods' and on 17 January headed for Sumatra to exchange this for spices, particularly pepper. Here, 'out of sight of the Hollenders' and offering the local growers better rates for their produce than the Dutch, Best broke into the Dutch monopoly and traded at four anchorages along the Sumatran coast.

English factors were at Ceram (Seram) by March 1613 where a confrontation occurred between a young Dutch factor named Coen and the commander of the

Indiaman *Darling*, John Jourdain, but within a few years, in addition to Aceh and Bantam, English trading-posts had been set up near Jakatra (Jakata) contiguous to the main Dutch station on Java; Pattani on the east coast of the Malay peninsula; and at Macassar on Celebes (Sulawesi).

Meanwhile in India clumsy Portuguese efforts to oust the English toe-hold in India by capturing a Mughal ship as a bargaining chip misfired and resulted in war between Jehangir and the Portuguese. The English 'eleventh fleet' arrived at Surat in October 1612 and consisted of four Indiamen, one of which was the *Enterprise* commanded by Christopher Newport. Having made five voyages to Virginia, losing one ship, the *Sea Venture*, on Bermuda, before sailing for the east, Newport's career is typical of his era (he was to die at Bantam in 1617). On the eleventh fleet's arrival its general, Nicholas Downton, was invited by Jehangir to join his war on the Portuguese as an ally of the Mughals, but Downton had orders not to compromise diplomatic overtures between London and Madrid and his refusal resulted in a ban on trade by Jehangir. Downton was now caught between two fires, for the Portuguese Viceroy at Goa, Dom Hieronymo de Azevedo, took personal command of his forces and descended upon the anchorage at Swally Road with six galleons, two armed carracks and sixty *grabs*.

Seeing the enemy approach on 18 January 1615 Downton decided to remain anchored in shallow water, forcing Azevedo to anchor and consider his position. Two days later the smaller, lighter-draughted Portuguese ships weighed and moved up on the flood tide, eager to cut-out the nearer Indiaman, the *Hope*. From the 650-ton *New Year's Gift* Downton saw the *Hope* boarded. Ordering his other two ships to cut their cables and set sail, the *New Year's Gift* moved towards the beleaguered *Hope* where a fierce hand-to-hand conflict raged on her deck. Firing incendiary shot the English ships set fire to the *Hope*'s assailants and the *Hope* herself. Azevado, watching from his huge flagship, saw his three vessels drift onto adjacent shoals and burn to the water. As for the *Hope*, though damaged, she was saved despite his men having fought 'with greater resolution' than one English participant had 'never see[n] menn fight'. English dead amounted to five; Portuguese losses were far greater.

Humiliated, Azevedo resumed his attack in early February, but the fireships he sent in on the tide drifted harmlessly past the anchored Indiamen and on 3 March Downton's now fully laden ships sailed out past the remaining Portuguese and headed to sea. Azevedo weighed in pursuit, but declined battle when Downton's ships rounded-to and ran out their guns. Azevedo gave up the pursuit and left Downton to make for Bantam. Downton's defence had effectively ended the war with the Mughals and, having discomfited Azevedo, placed the English in the ascendancy. In 1618 the arrival of Sir Thomas Roe in the *Charles* as ambassador to the Mughal court resulted in a treaty in which, in exchange for trading-rights, the Company would guarantee Mughal shipping protection against Portuguese attack and the depredations of pirates. This was an important provision, for in these years piracy proliferated, practised by all manner of men from all manner of backgrounds: Arabs, Englishmen, Portuguese, the French, and it was largely for this reason that Indiamen were so heavily armed. In

1611 the Second Act of Piracy was passed through the English Parliament – the first had been in 1536 – empowering the Courts of Admiralty throughout King James's possessions to try, condemn and execute free-booters. Since these operated only in North America and the West Indies, the consequence was that the displaced pirates set up bases on the coast of Madagascar from where they could plunder all European Indiamen as they made their laden way home. This was more than a mere flourish, for not only did the East India Company's armed ships increasingly intervene in local conflicts on the Mughal side to enforce their guaranteed protection, but local vessels flew flags indicating they were under the English Company's wing. In 1679 Captain Keigwin reported sighting a *shibar* 'having English colours' and 'showing by her ensign she belonged to the English or [was] under their protection'.[6] Similarly a report from the factory at Surat alluded to local vessels chartered on freight by its factors as 'wareing our colours', and thereby obtaining 'creditt', and of Indian merchants preferring the Company's ensign to 'a ship under the [Mughal] King's collour'.

Prestigious and creditworthy though this protection might have been, its practical value is less certain for this was – as we shall see – an era of unromantic piratical lawlessness. Roe, writing in connection with his agreement with the Mughal emperor, justified the increased responsibility assumed by the Company in Indian waters on the grounds that 'iff measures bee nott tayken to prevent such [piratical] expeditions, wee shall have the seas full of them and all trayde ruyned'. Despite any misgivings entertained by the Court of Directors in London, this accession of power, particularly as a license to make war on the enemies of the Mughals, greatly enhanced English prestige and puissance in Indian waters. It was from this point that the East India Company began its expanding hegemony over the subcontinent, an encroachment that culminated in the occupation of the entire Indian subcontinent.

Piracy and the Portuguese remained problematical. So too did the Dutch, not least because, despite the rivalry between the two trading nations, they were Protestant, and English mariners did not hold the same antipathy towards them as towards the Catholic Iberians. In March 1616 four English Indiamen and a pinnace trading at Pulo Wai in the Banda islands were confronted with nine Dutch Indiamen intent on driving the trespassers out. All those who sought to outwit a monopolistic company were known as 'Interlopers' and one, Samuel Castleton, had been employed by John Company to attempt to break into the Dutch domain. Now in the Company's *Defence*, Castleton sought to negotiate but was driven off and could find no island willing to trade for fear of savage Dutch reprisals. Castleton died before his ships retired to Bantam, to be replaced by Nathaniel Courthorpe who, in the *Defence* and with the 569-ton *Swan* in company, returned to the Banda Islands with orders to hoist English colours on Pulo Run and establish an English presence.

By Christmas 1616 Courthorpe, after reaching an accommodation with the local chief, landed guns and fortified his anchorage. The Dutch under Cornelis Dedel arrived in three Indiamen from Banda Neira on 3 January 1617 only to find Courthorpe, besides his own men and guns, had mustered a large force of armed islanders. Dedel retired for reinforcements and a few days later a small vessel taking soundings offshore was fired upon by the English batteries. This seemed to have deterred the Dutch and the *Swan* departed to load pepper at Ceram. On her return, however, she was attacked, overwhelmed and seized, her captors 'much glorying in their victorie and showing the Bandanese that the King of England might not compare with their great King of Holland'. Worse was to follow for the crew of the *Defence*, tired of languishing at anchor off Pulo Run, mutinied and, taking their ship to Banda Neira, surrendered to the Dutch. Abandoned ashore Coulthorpe with his loyal officers, seamen and factors, was blockaded; he dug in for a siege.

The news of Coulthorpe's isolation reached Bantam along with a demand from the Dutch governor at Jakatra for Pulo Run to be given up. In response two Indiamen, the *Attendant* and *Solomon*, were sent to relieve Courthorpe but were taken by the superior Dutch blockading squadron and rumours quickly spread that their men were harshly treated by their captors. The hitherto amicable relations between the two nations broke down, particularly in Bantam where the seamen of both countries fought running street-battles. Matters might have quietened down during a long stalemate but in March 1618 Laurens Real, the Dutch governor, was replaced by the young, zealous and ruthless Jan Pieterszoon Coen.

A few months later, in November, a new English Resident, Captain John Jourdain, arrived at Bantam. The two men had clashed at Ceram five years earlier where the older Jourdain had claimed a right to trade since 'the countrie was as free for us as for them'. Jourdain now arrived with a fleet of five Indiamen with which, reinforced by the six already in the archipelago, he intended to force the issue to a conclusion, holding a council at Bantam on 28 November when they 'with one consent resolved to lay hold upon all occasions to redeem the disgraces and losses done to our Kinge and Countrie'. When a Dutch ship, the *Zwarte Leeuw*, anchored unwittingly off Bantam she was seized as a prize. Coen heard of this while assembling his ships in the Moluccas with the intention of intercepting Jourdain as he attempted to relieve Courthorpe. He immediately moved on Jakatra and burned the English factory to the ground. Meanwhile the *Zwarte Leeuw* was also set on fire, thanks to the carelessness of drunken English seamen looting her.

The two fleets met off Jakatra a few days before Christmas. Eleven English Indiamen under Captain Sir Thomas Dale, and including Hawkeridge in the *Thomas* (see Chapter Two), fought 'a cruel bloody fight' and 'soundly banged' the seven Dutch vessels. Coen withdrew towards the Moluccas, whereupon the war embroiled the local rajahs. The Rajah of Jakatra laid siege to the Dutch fort there which, he claimed, had been erected close to his own capital without his permission. Dale, unable to reach Pulo Run, made common cause with the Javanese prince and joined the siege. By February the garrison was close to capitulation but at this juncture a rival Javanese noble, the Pangaran of Bantam, claimed the Dutch fort himself. Arguing that neither it nor the English factory at Bantam had any rights, he demanded the Dutch fort was turned over to him otherwise he would burn the English post.

Dale, a servant of the Company, had little alternative but to withdraw his support from the Rajah of Jakatra and retire to Bantam to preserve the Company's investment.

With their situation eased, the besieged Dutch took heart and were soon rewarded when Coen entered the road with his fleet and raised the siege. While the Dutch thereby strengthened their hand, the English fell apart. Dale and Jourdain quarrelled over what should be done next and their final decision was disastrous. While Jourdain left with two ships, the *Hound* and *Sampson*, to pick up cargoes from the factory at Pattani, miles away on the Malay isthmus at the southern extremity of peninsular Thailand, Dale proceeded to Masulipatam (also known as Bandar and modern Machilipatnam) on the Coromandel coast to refit his ships.

Coen fell upon an undefended Bantam and carried out the threat of the Pangaran. Leaving the English factory in ashes, Coen sent his three best-armed Indiamen in pursuit of Jourdain. Caught unawares miles away from Java quietly at anchor off Pattani, Jourdain discounted the advice of his officers as the Dutch squadron stood into the bay. Urged to cut his cables and meet them under weigh, Jourdan claimed this would seem like flight. Carrying the last of the land-breeze into the road the Dutch anchored close to the English ships and in the windless dawn of 17 July 1619 they opened fire. Two of their Indiamen, one ahead and one astern of the *Sampson*, clapping springs on their cables, brought their broadsides to bear to rake Jourdain's ship from both ends. The third Dutchman veered alongside the *Hound*. The outcome was a foregone conclusion, despite the resistance of the East India Company's men, for only five small guns aboard the *Sampson* could be brought to bear and after two hours of murderous fusillade Jourdain ordered a white flag hoisted and clambered onto the rail to hail his opponent. He was met with a storm of musketry and fell back upon his own deck, his chest shattered, one of a dozen dead. The *Hound* resisted for a further half hour and then she too succumbed.

Dale, meanwhile, was also dead; having contracted malaria he expired on 9 August, soon after reaching Masulipatam. He had been succeeded by Captain Martin Pring of the *James Royal*, but Pring proved indecisive and remained off the Indian coast.[7] In the absence of the English force, the active Coen captured an English Indiaman in the Sunda Strait and, two months later in October, seized four more off Tiku, Sumatra, bringing his total to eleven prizes. The ruthless Coen, who ran rough-shod over the inhabitants of the archipelago and galled 'the natives with a sharp spur' was deprived of absolute victory. Even as Pring, prodded into action with the arrival of three ships as reinforcement from Surat, was in the Sunda Strait approaching Bantam Bay on the 8 April 1620, he met an outward-bound Indiaman bearing dispatches from London. These informed Pring and all the Company's servants that the rival East India Companies had reached an agreement under which the English were to reoccupy Bantam and enjoy half the Javanese pepper trade and one third of the Moluccan spice exports, largely nutmeg. In return the English company would contribute to the maintenance of Dutch forts and, should the occasion arise, the two would combine forces against incursions from the Portuguese or the Spaniards. This agreement had been signed ten days before Jourdain's death and the news did not reach Pulo Run until November. By then the wretched Nathaniel Courthorpe had been a month in his grave. It had been an unnecessary conflict but its outcome – at least in the short-term and irrespective of its cost – enabled the English to further consolidate their position against the Portuguese.

Among the principal objectives of the English was silk, then chiefly obtained from Persia (Iran) where the Shah was engaged in intermittent war with the Ottoman Turks to the west. The silk-trade had been entirely in the hands of Arab, Mughal and other Indian traders who regularly crossed the Arabian Sea under the influence of the favourable monsoon, but soon after their arrival in the Indian seas the Portuguese had sought to arrogate to themselves as much of this as possible.[8] To this end they had established a fortress on the island of Hormuz at the narrow entrance to the Persian Gulf, determined to secure as much silk as possible and thereby dominate the European market for this beautiful material.

In 1616 the 600-ton Indiaman *James* landed her eager supercargo, the factor Edward Cannock, at the port of Jask, standing on a peninsula to the east of the entrance to the Strait of Hormuz. Cannock proceeded overland to wait upon Shah Abbas and plead the case for trade with the English. He was received with reciprocal enthusiasm, the Shah being eager to open trade with a European power other than the Portuguese and thereby outflank the Ottomans, who controlled the European terminus of the silk-road to China. He allowed Cannock 3,000 bales of silk on credit, claiming King James I as his brother.

Now, however, the Portuguese went onto the offensive and they possessed greater resources having for some time been conjoined with Spain. In 1618 Philip III sent out an ambassador to persuade Abbas to evict the English. Don Garcia de Silva y Figueroa failed, even receiving hints that the Shah 'had a resolution to tayke Hormuz from the King of Spane's hold and deliver it unto the English nation'. So enraged with the tone of Philip's letters was the Shah that he tore them up and flung them in the hapless Figueroa's face, immediately granting the gleeful English sole rights in the silk trade.

Having received news of this rebuff, Philip next despatched a small squadron of five well-appointed men-of-war under an admiral known popularly as the 'Pride of Portugal' from his successes against the Mughals. Ruy Freire de Andrade arrived off Hormuz in June 1620. The annual English fleet of four Indiamen had left the Thames in February under Captain Andrew Shilling in the large 800-ton *London*. Shilling's fleet divided off Socotra, the *London* and the *Roebuck* making for Surat, with a native *grab* purchased for local use, while the *Hart* and the *Eagle* headed for Jask to load silk. On anchoring in Swally Road, Shilling was informed by Thomas Kerridge, the British 'President' – the English factories in England having acquired the grandiloquent title of 'presidencies' – of the presence of the Hispano-Portuguese men-of-war. Shilling took council and it was decided to discharge sufficient trade-goods for Kerridge to accumulate homeward cargoes for them while they proceeded towards Jask. They encountered the *Hart* and *Eagle* to the east of Jask, on their way back to Surat after learning of Andrade's fleet at Hormuz. Undaunted, Shilling ordered the two ships to put about and join him, proceeding towards Jask to prosecute the silk-trade in defiance of an enemy and ready to fight if necessary.

On approaching the anchorage they descried Andrade's ships at anchor under the promontory of Jask, but it fell calm and it was next day, 17 December, before a light westerly zephyr enabled Andrade's ships to move. They carried the breeze down upon their quarry and until mid-afternoon the two squadrons manoeuvred, exchanging occasional shots. By this time Shilling, with a red flag at the main-masthead of the *London*, had gained the weather gage and, setting fire to the *grab*, ran her down towards the Portuguese. Unfortunately the forlorn-hope aboard the *grab* abandoned her too soon and the opportunity was lost, the action ceasing at sunset with both fleets anchoring about ten miles apart.

Next day Andrade was to windward but made no attempt to renew the fight. Shilling took advantage of the breeze and made for Jask where his ships broke-bulk and landed English woollen broadcloth, iron, tin and lead, along with chests of silver with which to purchase silk. Meanwhile Andrade moved up the coast, receiving reinforcements from Hormuz and by Christmas both captains-general were ready to resume the contest. Shilling, however, was pinned in the anchorage by a wet onshore wind. Superstition began to stir among the English seamen who 'were perswaded that the Portingales had brought with them … a witch to bring them continuallie a faire wind'. But on 28 December 'the Lord gave us a prettie Easterlie gale,' wrote Richard Swan, a mate of the *Roebuck*, and Shilling moved upon his enemy.

> The grete ordnance from our whole fleete plaied so faste upon them, that doubtlesse not one of these galliounes, unless their sides had become impenetrable, had escaped us. About three of the clocke in the afternoon, unwilling after so hot a dinner to receive the like supper, they cutt their cables, and drove with the tyde until they were without range of our gunnes. And then theyre frigates [colloquially native craft, probably grabs, employed as auxiliaries] came and towed them awaie wonderfully mangled and torne.

Having driven the Pride of Portugal back towards Hormuz, Shilling re-anchored off Jask, loaded silk and left for home on 14 January, but it was far from the end of Iberian influence in the region, for Andrade turned his ire upon the Persians, raiding the Mekran coast. Abbas, meanwhile, had besieged a Portuguese fort on the large island of Qeshm to the west of Hormuz, but he was unable to prevent his enemy being reinforced from the sea without any ships to enforce a blockade. On the arrival of four Indiamen and a pinnace at Jask in mid-December 1621 Abbas threatened denying the Company's factors any trade unless he first received help. Their leader, Edward Monnox, boarded the *Jonas* and confronted Captain John Weddell with the problem. In short, Monnox argued, notwithstanding the difficulties renewed hostilities would cause at home, if English trade were to prosper, Hispano-Portuguese power had first to be broken. With Company losses set against compromising a distant Government's policy, greed prevailed and Weddell gave his support, providing he shared the plunder and the tolls levied on the Strait of Hormuz.

On 22 January the English ships closed the batteries of Qeshm and began a bombardment which lasted some days after which Andrade, who had commanded the defence, surrendered on 1 February. The Pride of Portugal was humbled and sent to Surat with hundreds of prisoners in one of the ships and two pinnaces. Weddell then embarked about 3,000 Persian troops and headed east for Hormuz, landing the Shah's forces. The city was over-run and the Portuguese driven into their citadel under the walls of which were drawn the five remaining ships of Andrade's fleet.

Closing, the *Jonas* and her consorts repeated their bombardment, almost knocking to pieces two of the Portuguese ships and persuading the defenders to withdraw their guns into the fortress. As this was in train, a small craft was sent in with a single gun which was fired at point-blank range into the hull of Andrade's quondam flagship, the 1,500-ton *Todos los Santos*. Penetrating her waterline, the great ship filled and sank at her moorings, heeling as the tide ebbed and left her aground. Meanwhile Abbas's troops were sapping towards the walls of the citadel and, placing mines, blew a breach through which they launched a ferocious attack on 17 March. With immense courage the Portuguese garrison threw their assailants back, but their will was broken and they beat a parley and sent a flag of truce to negotiate with Weddell rather than Abbas. Consequently an agreement to capitulate in honourable terms was reached and on 23 April 1622, St George's Day for the English victors, the saint's flag was raised above the fortress in place of Portuguese colours.

The successful taking of Hormuz by the Anglo-Persians marked the end of Portuguese and Spanish ambitions in the region. An attempt to retake Hormuz was made in 1625, but was defeated by an Anglo-Dutch fleet, as will be seen, but the tide of history had turned against the Lusitanians. Though still entrenched at Goa and, on the coast of China at Macao where, as we shall presently see, they were to be of use to the East India Company, the Portuguese were in decline: English mercantile fortunes, on the other hand, were on the rise, though there were obstacles yet to be overcome.

It could not be expected that a man of Jan Pieterszoon Coen's stamp would rest content sharing the exploitable wealth of the archipelago with the English. A man of fearsome reputation who reputedly killed 15,000 Indonesian Bandanese during his tenure of office, he was fiercely loyal to the VOC. 'The English,' he fulminated in an assessment of the accord between the two rival companies he sent to Amsterdam in May 1620, 'owe Your Excellencies a great debt of gratitude for they had assisted themselves straight out of the Indies, and you have put them right back in the middle again'. Distant from his principals he acted with more autonomy than Weddell, for his contempt of the accord was marked by his orders to his factors and garrison commanders that it was Dutch writ that actually ran throughout the islands. Indeed, harking back to a mythical, classical Dutch age, Coen had the chief post at Jakatra renamed Batavia and, despite its location on low land surrounded by malarial mangrove swamps, it was in his lifetime to become the capital of Dutch rule.

As for the English presence, Coen allowed only a miserable warehouse and residence at Amboina alongside the grand Dutch post. The English found Dutch officials difficult and the burden of supporting the islands' defences heavy; the land allocated to them for their factory at Batavia was in a marsh 'from which arose miasmas conducive to the quotidian-ague', or malaria; one factor at Batavia who refused a Dutch order was flogged; and the natives were intimidated from enjoying open intercourse with the English merchants. This maintained low prices to the local producers of spices, despite the willingness of the English to pay more. Complaints reached the Directors in London and, faced with Dutch intransigence and over-stretched in their resources, they decided to withdraw the Company's factories in the Moluccas and at Banda Neira. The Royal Navy would take the islands in 1810, but for now the East India Company was content to consolidate its position elsewhere. In view of what now happened in the Spice Island, this was an irony of tragic proportions.

While these matters were being debated in London, the ambitious Coen now decided to move against the English, arguing that once faced with a beneficial *fait accompli*, his own Directors in distant Amsterdam would condone his actions. He chose as his objective the little factory at Amboina. Here one Gabriel Towerson was the East India Company's factor. Described as easy-going, Towerson ruled a mixed English enclave of two dozen writers, tally-clerks, storemen, errand boys and a brace of Company soldiers armed with two muskets, half a pound of powder, three hangers and a touching trust in their neighbours. Towerson occasionally dined with his Dutch counterpart, the governor Herman van Speult, and in February 1623 requested some casks of beer be sent up from the English post at Batavia as a gift to Van Speult.

Amboina (Ambon) commands a sheltered bay on the western end of Ceram and its chief defence rested with the 200-strong Dutch garrison under Van Speult. Aware of Coen's Anglophobia and in receipt of secret orders, Van Speult assured Coen:

> that our sovereignty shall not be diminished or injured in any way by English encroachments, and if we may hear of any conspiracies of theirs … we shall, with your sanction, do justice to them suitably, unhesitatingly and immediately.

Thus did Van Speult condemn his behaviour ante the event for, even as Towerson requested 'some beer or a case of strong waters' to please his colleague, van Speult was concocting a case and stratagem against the Englishman. A Japanese soldier-of-fortune serving the Dutch as a guard was arrested after asking a fellow soldier some questions touching the fort's defences. Suspicious, but also seeking a pretext, Van Speult had the mercenary put on the rack and hot irons applied to his feet, from which a confession was extorted implying an insurrection was imminent. Some other itinerant Japanese were rounded up and also tortured, confirming the story, but it was not until a drunken Englishman, following a row with one of the Dutch trading staff, threatened to set the man's house on fire, that Van Speult had the pretext he wanted. The Englishman, charged with intended incendiarism, was racked and readily agreed to whatever Van Speult suggested. In this way a full-blown conspiracy implicating Towerson was 'uncovered', just as Van Speult had hinted to his master that it would be.

On the morning of 15 February 1623 Van Speult summoned an unsuspecting Towerson and accused him of plotting to take over the fort and murder the garrison. An incredulous Towerson was led away in irons, his people soon afterwards following. Next day, a Sunday, the Dutch put their brother Protestants to the torture. Spread-eagled, their faces bound with water-sodden cloths, the English were slowly suffocated until, upon the point of death, they were released, then made to vomit before this treatment was repeated. If this failed to elicit a confession – and there were six boys among Towerson's people – further horrors were added. Candles were applied to the soles of the feet and, of course, the genitals. All thus tortured broke and confessed, though one, John Clarke, resisted so that his body swelled enormously. The broken men were allowed a little time to recover from their ordeal. On the flyleaf of his account-book one clerk wrote:

> Through Torment we were constrained to speak that which we meant not, nor ever once imagined. They tortured us with Extream Torment of Fire and Water that Flesh and Blood could not endure it … they have put us to Death Guiltless of our Accusations.' Another wrote in his prayer-book: 'I was obliged to confess what I never knew, or else go to the Torments which rather I would suffer I did Confess that which as I shall be saved before the Almightie is Not True.

Towerson found an old bill and scribbled upon it in a shaking hand, 'Gabriel Towerson now appointed to die Guiltless of anything that can be laid to my charge. God forgive them this Sin, and Receive me into His Mercy.' This relief afforded his prisoners, Van Speult, had Towerson and eight of his colleagues, nine Japanese and one Portuguese over-seer brought forth and beheaded.

News of this atrocity reached England in May 1624, helping to stoke up a popular hostility against the Dutch which combined with commercial rivalry to provoke three wars later in the century, but for now the Directors continued with their withdrawal, closing the factory at Batavia and holding on, for the moment at least, to the post at Bantam from where a diminished trade was continued with the Moluccas and Sumatra.

The loss was not much felt in the counting-houses in London. Nor was there great disappointment when Weddell failed to open trade with China. In 1637 he entered the Pearl River in the *Dragon*, a navigation forbidden to foreigners and, although he landed near Canton, he was turned away empty-handed. It was then of little moment. Expansion in India was adding more and more commodities to the lading of the East Indiamen at Surat and elsewhere on the Malabar and Coromandel coasts. Ships could load both trade goods for the archipelago or, better still, homeward cargoes. In addition to silks and carpets from Persia and coffee from the Yemeni coast of Arabia Felix there came from the subcontinent itself cotton and calico, varieties of dyes and more, richly woven carpets. The lands south of Goa yielded pepper, cardamom and a coarse form of cinnamon, and here too cloves and nutmegs from the Moluccas might be picked up, having been brought thither by Arab and Indian traders. By tapping into the traditional trade, Company factors, succeeded in largely circumventing the pro-scriptions of the Dutch, to the ultimate disadvantage of the latter. From the Malabar forests came ebony and teak – later to be extensively used for shipbuilding – while the rich southern interior produced wheat and millet.

The vast extent of India began to dawn upon these early traders for, along with exports from the post at Pettapoli, there came from Bengal salt, sugar, more silk and – essential for artillery as an ingredient of gun-powder – saltpetre (potassium nitrate). From the post at Masulipatnam on the Coromandel coast near the mouths of the Krishna River established in 1611, English expansion moved north and east. Masulipatnam itself was close to the cotton-producing Golconda, a region which also contained diamonds, rubies and other precious and semi-precious gemstones. However, the anchorage was poor and the city lost influence after the founding of Fort St George at Madras in 1639, finally falling to the Dutch in 1686 to be held by them for four years.

Although there was no harbour at Madras either and the Indiamen rode at anchor in an open and exposed roadstead – making landing both cargo and passengers a hazardous operation for many years – Fort St George and the adjacent city of Madras became in time one of the East India Company's three major Presidencies. Fort St George soon afterwards superseded Bantam in administrative importance until it gradually gave way to a more important Company settlement. But what – with Bombay and Madras – would ultimately become the pre-eminent of the Company's three greatest Presidencies, was then of minor significance as the Company's ships penetrated the many mouths of the Ganges. Ascending the Hughli in 1651 they landed and set up a factory. In time this would become Calcutta.

Although in this expansion lay the foundations of an immense commercial – and later political – empire, the fortunes of the East India Company remained uncertain, constantly compromised by the wars of native Indian princes, and in competition with other European nations. The most immediate problem remained the Dutch, with whom Commonwealth England went to war in 1652. The Dutch took and colonised the hinterland of Saldanha Bay at the southern tip of Africa, establishing Cape Province as a vital staging post on the long voyage to India and the orient. The Swedes and Danes also established East India Companies, neither of which threatened the English position. However, in 1664, fostered by Colbert, a French Company, the *Compagnie des Indes Orientales*, was formed and in 1674 secured a post at Pondicherry, south of Madras near Cuddalore.[9]

Ironically it was at home that the Company struggled most, having excited the hostility of James I's successor, Charles I, in its opposition to his taxes. The East India Company's financial base was far less sophisticated than that of its Dutch counter-part. The individual stock investment in the annual 'fleet' had been superseded in 1612 by the merging of all investment in common capital to the tune of £740,000. Factors, in bidding for different fleets, found themselves in artificial and unnecessary competition. This combined arrangement ran for four years until 1617, during which twenty-nine Indiamen had loaded for the east. Four were either lost or so worm-eaten that they had to be broken up, two had fallen into the hands of the Dutch and, by the end of that year, while fifteen were still seeking full cargoes in the east only eight had actually returned home. In the next twelve years fifty-seven ships were sent out to load the cargoes collected by the smaller pinnaces the Company had caused to be built for service 'on the coast', picking up small quantities of produce and bringing them in to the factories for storage until an ocean-going Indiaman arrived.

So far, so good, but the increasing wealth of the Company's Directors and its influence on European politics ran ill in Government. The sexually ambivalent James I had appointed his favourite George Villiers, Duke of Buckingham, as Lord Admiral, an appointment he retained in 1625 when James was succeeded by Buckingham's near contemporary and friend, James's son Charles I. Buckingham was a rapacious, arrogant young man who, if not the old king's catamite, loved intrigue on a grand scale and enjoyed a voluptuous indulgence in life's luxuries. Although his turbulent life was to be ended in his thirty-sixth year by assassination, Buckingham's cupidity was attracted to the wealth reputedly aboard Weddell's ships returning from Hormuz. As a consequence he persuaded Parliament to lay an embargo on the seven Indiamen preparing to sail for India from the Thames in 1624, ostensibly in order to mulct his share of the plunder of Hormuz in his capacity as Lord Admiral. Such was the influence of the King's favourite, that the ships lay off Tilbury until the Directors had surrendered over £10,000.

King Charles I also disliked the autonomy of the Court of Directors and found a pretext for interfering over the contentious matter of the private trade allowed the Company's employees. As this was almost impossible to prevent, it had seemed expedient to regulate it so that it did not interfere with the Company's own trade and take up capacity aboard the ships illicitly. However, by the 1620s it was getting out of hand, not least in the specifics of crown revenue. Charles issued a proclamation following the:

> many abuses … laytely crept intoe the East India trayde by reason of the practice of officers and others ymployed by the sayde Companie and their confederates in gaining att theyre own profit by driving a secret und underhand trayde wherebye his Majestie is defrauded of his Customs and Subsidies and the sayde Companie of its Freyte and Goodes. [An allowance of] 'Suche onlie as may be packed in a chest of Fower Foote long, one foote and haulf a foote broade, and one foote and one hauf deepe. Duble this quantities being permitted to Commaunders, Factors, Pursers … and Master's Mates'.

This might have been reasonable for the ship's company, but scarcely pleased the factors and inferior Company clerks and writers who went east to endure privations, disease, and isolation to make their fortune as well as serve the Company. The consequence was that many adopted the accepted oriental trading practices of *back-sheesh*, breeding a culture at odds with the supposed regularity and probity of English manners at home, and relying upon the confidential services of India Company sea-officers to handle their letters of credit on commission. This was a dichotomy of circumstances more than a matter of double-standards; it was to permeate all levels of trade and ensured a degree of 'doing-favours' that knitted the commercial-fraternity together, particularly within John Company itself which, in due course, became dynastic in its structure, both afloat and ashore.

Such involvement affected the building, owning and management of the Indiamen themselves, various measures being taken to detach complex issues of personal interest, as will be seen presently. Such occurrences were invariably cast in an unfavourable light, particularly when envy – both of money and power – sought exposure. The growing moralism inherent in Parliamentary politics and the Puritan faith was augmented by the sudden access of power available to the House of Commons in its dispute and triumph over the king. Parliament also conceived a strong animus against the Company and its wealthy merchants, charging it with 'exporting the treasure of the kingdom, it being alleged that £80,000 had been sent out yearly in money'. To this were added two more charges: destroying the country's timber stocks by recklessly building large and extravagant ships which used wood required by the Royal Navy, and finally complaining that its demand for crews reduced the numbers of seaman available to the Royal Navy. This was a multiple irony for a number of reasons: the Company took up large numbers of landsmen and trained them; it paid its seamen and mariners regularly and – significantly – it had better managed its seafarers than the Caroline navy, particularly in the matter of scurvy.[10] In 1649, amid civil turmoil and internecine strife, the Commissioners of the Navy forced a loan from the Company of £4,000, but in 1654 Oliver Cromwell, the Lord Protector, having formalised a peace-treaty with Lisbon, obtained the concessionary right for English ships to trade with any Portuguese possession. In the long-term this had an important consequence in the Company's dealings with the Chinese Empire through Macao; in the short-term it enhanced profits to the extent that in 1655 Cromwell drew a loan of £50,000 from the Directors and later that year, desperate to pay the seamen in Robert Blake's naval squadrons after their service against the Dutch, ordered the Company to advance £10,000 for the purpose. In return for rescuing Parliamentary Government, Cromwell conferred a new charter, establishing a permanent joint-stock company.

The protracted upheaval of the English Civil War had to some extent affected the Company's business, despite its attempts to remain aloof. Its roots in a city with strong Parliamentary sympathies ensured it was on the winning side. Nevertheless the divisions it caused had repercussions within the Company, none more so than the strange case of the 400-ton *John* and the barratry of her master, Captain John Mucknell. A Royalist and a frequent drunk, Mucknell sailed for Surat in February 1642 carrying no less than £30,000 in specie to fund the Company's trade. This was more than the customary imprest for a single voyage and the Directors sent as surety the merchant Edward Knipe. He was Mucknell's antithesis, a sober, sanctimonious Puritan, with a contempt for seamen and a belief that as a merchant his was the superior position on board. The consequences were predictable; Knipe began his criticisms against a fellow factor, acquainting 'him that his manner and carriage did rather become a fiddler than a merchant'. In a revealing admission, Knipe:

> spake nothing in prejudice of his birth. I will say nothing in defence of itt because the partie thatt tolde mee he was born in Venice of an Irish father and a Venetian mother, did nott acquaint mee that they were lawfully married.

Such piety was entirely discomfited by the captain's drinking, especially since Mucknell seemed to enjoy the company of some of his juniors. In his cabin, Knipe observed, Mucknell entertained 'the most debausht, and ungodly people in the shippe' roaring that he was 'a prince at sea, the proudest man upon the face of the earth, an Englishman and if I was to be born again, I would again be born an Englishman!' He was then wont to add – at least according to Knipe: 'I am a Cockney and that's my glory!' Helplessly Knipe tolerated these jolly scenes, intending to remove Mucknell from his command when they arrived at Surat, but in August they anchored off Mozambique and Knipe went ashore. Here he encountered a Portuguese merchant who requested passage to Goa for his household, which included a number of black slaves. Since passage-money was involved to the benefit of the Company, Knipe assigned the merchant and his wife the master's cabin. Mucknell, when he heard of this, demurred violently and Knipe, in consultation with the ship's chaplain, bethought himself as having gone too far. He sent the chaplain to placate Mucknell with a bribe of 200 gold *reals*, an offer that appeared to have caught Mucknell in the throes of alcoholic remorse, for the deal was concluded with a heartfelt promise of 'reformacion of his life and conversacion'.

Delighted with the outcome and the captain's apparent contrition, Knipe next accepted an invitation to go ashore on the Comoros Islands, lying in the Mozambique Channel between the mainland and Madagascar. Here, while the hands ostensibly sought wood and water, the reformed Mucknell enjoyed a picnic with Knipe, his fellow merchants, and their Portuguese passengers. At some point a message came stating that two of the seamen were fighting aboard the *John*; Mucknell went to assert authority. It was the last the picnickers saw of him.

Once aboard the *John*, Mucknell called the hands aft and announced that he was dispossessing the Company in favour of the King and added the inducement that such loyalty would be recompensed with a share of the specie on board: 'You thatt are for the Kinge and will agree to this motion hold up your hands'. All but eighteen agreed and the objectors were clapped in irons. Mucknell then weighed anchor and sailed south. An encounter with another English ship resulted in a drunken orgy at the end of which three visitors to the *John* remained with her, being 'Too druncke toe be put into their boate'. Mucknell then returned home, to berth at Bristol, which had declared for the King and where the grateful monarch received Mucknell's contribution of the *John*'s specie to his war-chest. Mucknell was rewarded with a knighthood and the 'loyal' crew was paid a bounty in *reals*, being promised more, each 'according to his deserte' after the king's restoration. As for the *John*, she was armed and commissioned into Charles's extemporised new navy – the country's 'Royal' Navy having largely declared for Parliament. Meanwhile, far away, the marooned Knipe and his fellow castaways were obliged to beg humble-pie from the Comorans until an outward bound Indiaman conveyed them all to Surat.

At the Restoration of the Monarchy in 1660, the bankrupt Charles II was keen to raise funds and saw, as Cromwell had done, that the East India Company, by its close relationship with the state, had to assist the centre of power. In his self-serving way Charles II conferred enormous advantages upon the Company, first by the acquisition of Bombay. It had long been clear that ship-repair facilities had to be made available in the east and that new sails, spare rope, spars and anchors must either be carried or stocked at the distant factories, but the problems of ship-worm and bottom-fouling argued for more permanent dockyard facilities than mere storage depots. It was considerations of this nature that persuaded the Company's Court of Directors to seek property of their own and, ironically it was obtained from the old enemy, the Portuguese. As part of her dowry, Catherine of Braganza brought to her marriage to Charles II in 1661 a brace of foreign possessions – Tangier (which was to become a hideous drain on resources) and the Portuguese port of Bombay (which was not). In 1668 this was ceded by the Crown on a lease at £10 per annum to the Company which, although it complained about a 'great burden and expense', found it a far superior location to Surat. In the neighbouring hinterland teak was available for shipbuilding and it was not long before the port contained the slipways of ship-yards. Bombay prospered, rapidly acquiring a mixed population of 60,000 souls and in 1687 it became a Presidency.

To consolidate his, and the Company's, positions Charles also further enforced the monopoly and thus improved the position of the English in the wake of the end of the Third Dutch War (1672–1674). As a partial offset to the Dutch acquisition of the Cape, in 1673 the Company occupied the island of St Helena as a valuable staging post and these measures revived the Company's fortunes which were under serious pressure from the war and the inroads of English Interlopers. These independent-minded merchants disputed the legality of the Company's monopoly and traded directly with the indifferent locals. Large fortunes were to be made upon the hazard of a single voyage, so it was impossible to prevent this trespassing which was further encouraged by the enormous and expanding volume of trade. Even with Charles's intervention on its behalf, the East India Company suffered from legal process when it moved against what it considered illegal shipping, risking claims of restitution in the Admiralty Court. Such compensation could be costly: the *Andalusia* realised £30,000, the *Bristol* as much again. It was also claimed in Parliament that, irrespective of the monopoly enshrined in the Company's charter, it was a principle of English liberty that a man might trade – at his own hazard – wheresoever he pleased.

Another more reprehensible opportunity open to adventurers and fortune-hunters was that of young men joining the Company's service and, once on the Indian coast, resigning to sell their services to local potentates, even to distant monarchs of considerable powers. One, Samuel White, left the Company's service to join that of the King of Siam after first becoming one of a number of mercantile adventurers who commanded ships trading across the Bay of Bengal. One of their chief freights was in live elephants. This was a lucrative, dangerous and specialised trade, each ship carrying 'from fourteen to twenty-six of these vast creatures' which were highly valued in India as engines of war. Each pachyderm had to be provided for with 'at least seventy banana trees ... for the sixteen or twenty days crossing' and they had to be kept tranquil throughout the passage, for fear of them becoming over-wrought and damaging the ship with their tusks. White commanded one of these vessels, the *Derrea Dowlat*, for two years until he secured an appointment as Shahbandar – or harbour-master, customs-officer and tax farmer – at the then Siamese port of Mergui. Here, White shamelessly lined his own pockets with the most blatant rake-offs and unscrupulous fiddles, seemingly fearless of the consequences and even commissioning notional 'Siamese men-of-war' which he sent out under his own orders on piratical cruises. Such men, individual and colourful but often wholly amoral, engaging in local wars as well as trade, built ships to fulfil their ambitious projects. These vessels formed what in effect became a second, Indian-based, British merchant fleet of so-called 'Country-wallahs'.

Often possessed of considerable physical courage, as well as a complete lack of scruples, these independent ship-masters often imbibed eastern culture and maintained considerable state. One William Hedges recorded in his diary that on:

> Sept. 26, 1683. Capt. Alley came up to Hughly in his Barge, rowed with English Marines in coats with Badges, and 4 Musicians. He put himself into a great Equipage, like an Agent, and took about 70 or 80 Pens to wait upon him. [Calling upon the Mughal governor, Alley was] habitted in scarlet richly laced. Ten Englishmen in Blue Caps and Coats edged with Red, all armed with Blunderbusses, went before his pallankeen, 8 Peons before them, and 4 Musicians playing ... with 2 Flags before him.

Dining with Captain Lake of the Company's ship *Prudent Mary* on 13 November, Alley and 'divers Interlopers' made 'great mirth and jollity by firing guns all afternoon'. So seductive was the convivial company that Lake was moved in his cups to proclaim that 'if he did not like the Company's employment that voyage, he would turn interloper the next'. While they might be tolerated on the Indian coast – though they undercut Company freight-rates – these men and their ships were not to be countenanced on the main carrying-route home to England. Nevertheless their commercial aggression was such that they were soon taken into partnership by local investors, usually but not exclusively Parsees, owing to their expertise. This led in due course to the ousting of the traditional – usually 'Moorish' or Muslim – traders from their traditional trade-routes which in turn led to the increased commerce of Bengal, and the final supremacy of Calcutta as the seat of the Company's power and influence. We shall hear more of them later.

The ships employed in the 'Country-trade' were locally built of highly durable teak to conventional European design. They operated in Indian and China seas alongside the legitimate East Indiamen which they resembled and often exceeded in size. In addition to exotic elephants they carried all the variety of commodities trafficked across the region, and often bore the illegal Malwa opium that was finding its way into China, often by way of Mergui and then across the Siamese isthmus to the banks of the Maenam River from where it was picked up for onward shipment by Chinese junks.

The Company's own armed coastal vessels kept clear of this trade, being employed to bring cargoes into the main ports for trans-shipment into the ocean-going Indiamen. By degrees, according to the circumstances, some of these armed coasters were used for policing duties against interlopers, and against both Arab and Indian pirates; such ships were commanded by Company officers who in due course matured into the Bombay and Bengal Marines, private navies which were the counter-part of the Sepoy levies that came to form the Company's private army. The gradual assumption of territorial aggrandisement beyond the confines of trading factories began to permeate the thinking of the Directors in London, led by their 'despotic chairman' Sir Josiah Child who was reputed to retain his position by bribery.

By the Restoration in 1660 the joint-stock system was giving way to the practice of share-holding, a practice that had become common among shipowners and is discussed later. By the time that William of Orange had become William III and displaced Charles II's unrepentantly Catholic brother James II in 1688, the East India Company's principals owned about three dozen vessels ranging in size from 100-ton pinnaces, to 800-ton ships. Its fleet annually carried out from England about £70,000 worth of lead, tin, English broadcloth and high-value manufactured luxuries, in return for oriental produce. Of this the most significant was the appearance of the first China tea in 1667, a tiny consignment of a mere 100lb arriving not by English Indiaman, but by way of the continent, courtesy of the Dutch. However, its fashionable and expensively exotic benefits were to establish a lucrative and influential trade. All this immense flow of material wealth can scarcely be quantified: it annually yielded the English Exchequer £60,000 in Customs duties, and the Company's shares sold for five times their face value. By the end of the seventeenth century East Indiamen of 1,300 tons were being launched into the Thames, mounting up to seventy guns and the Company had extended its trading posts still further. Benkulen on the west coast of Sumatra was established in 1685 when, following the loss of Bantam to the Dutch in 1683, pepper plantations were planted over a 300-mile stretch of the fertile coast. For the first time the Company grew a commodity for which it had a ready market, thereby securing and consolidating supply and reducing costs.

In that same year, 1685, the first cargo of China tea carried by an English East Indiaman, the *China Merchant*, was loaded at Amoy, cutting out the Dutch as suppliers to the English market. The Chinese, however, soon restricted trade to Canton, the ships of the 'foreign devils' – *fan kwai* – being allowed no further than an anchorage at Whampoa, 13 miles from Canton itself. In permitting this, the Emperor K'ang-Hsi established a set of eight rules which were to cause the Honourable East India Company and its Committee of Selectmen no end of tribulation in the ensuing 150 years. The situation remained virtually unchanged until the issue was forced by an overweening Great Britain in the Opium Wars of the mid-nineteenth century.

The imperial Chinese rules forbade the entry of foreign men-of-war into the Pearl River, or other Chinese waters. The foreign factors were allowed access only to their prescribed national factories at Canton where they might reside as bachelors between September and March; this was the North-East Monsoon season in the South China Sea and hence the time for trade. Their families were to be confined to the Portuguese enclave at Macao and the numbers of servants they took with them to Canton was strictly limited. Visits to Canton, pleasure trips and the use of sedan-chairs were denied to foreigners, although walking-out in the Honan Island public-gardens was permitted three times a month in groups not exceeding ten persons. All Chinese pilots, agents, merchants, lightermen and junkmen in contact with the foreign-devils had to be licensed, providing a rich source of private and imperial revenue to the Mandarins, while all actual contractual commerce could only be carried out through the approved traders of the *Co-Hong*, or *Hong* for short. However, both parties were beholden to the emperor's personal merchant at Canton and Customs Gatherer – the *hai kwan pu*, or 'Hoppo' as the British inevitably styled him. No credit could be advanced, and smuggling was illegal. Provided that the foreigners kept within these strictures they were not subject to Chinese law, except in the case of a homicide involving a Chinese person, in which case the suspect was to be handed over to the imperial magistracy.

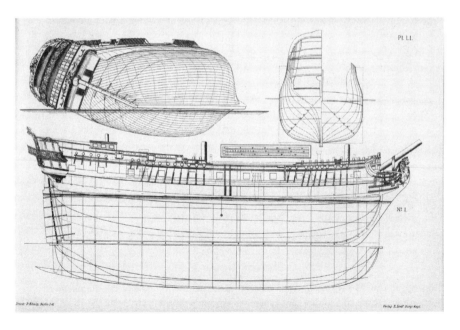

An English East Indiaman of about 600 tons burthen from Frederik Hendrik Af Chapman's *Architectura Navalis Mercantoria* of 1768. (Author's Collection)

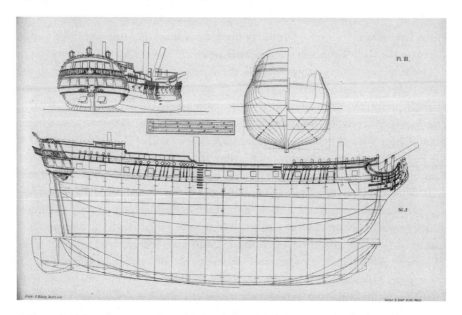

A frigate-built merchantman of 761 tons burthen measuring 136ft on deck, with a beam of 36ft and a maximum draught of 19ft. Such a vessel would be ship-rigged. From Frederik Hendrik Af Chapman's *Architectura Navalis Mercantoria* of 1768. (Author's Collection)

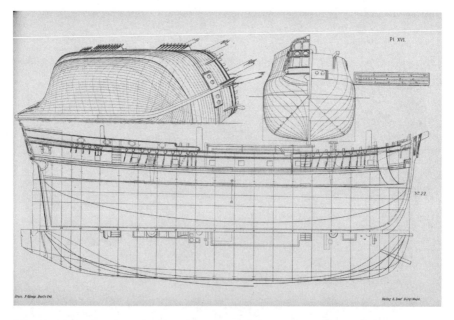

Ship-rigged Cat. At 833 tons burthen this cat represents a workhorse of the merchant fleet, strong, capacious and slow, but capable of voyaging world-wide. Note the large hatch amidships, the plain head and lack of decoration. From Frederik Hendrik Af Chapman's *Architectura Navalis Mercantoria* of 1768. (Author's Collection)

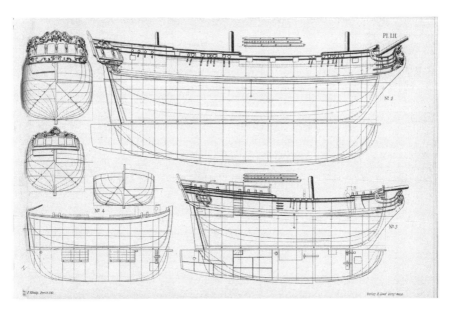

A West Indiaman of about 270 tons burthen from Frederik Hendrik Af Chapman's *Architectura Navalis Mercantoria* of 1768. (Author's Collection)

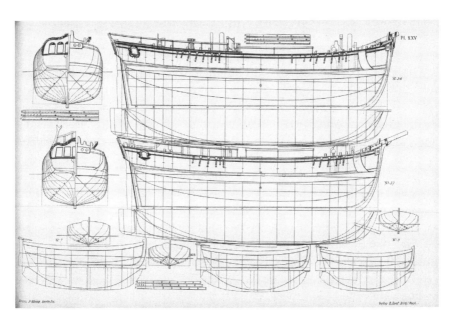

Smaller, two-masted Cats and ships' boats. Top: a snow-rigged cat of 316 tons burthen and 84ft in length. Note the 'horse' or lighter spar rising abaft the main-mast to which the luff of the mizzen was secured and which chiefly distinguishes a snow from a brig. Middle: a similarly plain, but brigantine-rigged cat of 80ft length and 227 tons burthen. Bottom: three yawls of various sizes. From Frederik Hendrik Af Chapman's *Architectura Navalis Mercantoria* of 1768. (Author's Collection)

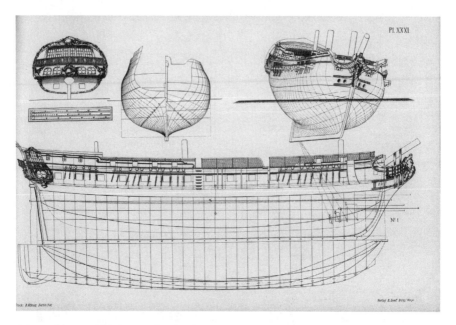

PL XXXI

A large, ship-rigged Privateer-frigate of 40-guns comprising twenty-eight 18-pounders and a dozen 6-pounders. Such a vessel represented a substantial investment, being of about 900 tons burthen and having a crew of 400. These ships were also used as slavers. From Frederik Hendrik Af Chapman's *Architectura Navalis Mercantoria* of 1768. (Author's Collection)

Commanders of Indiamen did not enjoy the same privileges in China as they were to in India, though they could occasionally visit Canton and partake of the limited liberties of the Company's factors with whom they had dealings. For the crews, access for a run ashore was limited to the islands around Whampoa where, surrounding the *bankshall*, or office, of the harbour authorities – minor functionaries in the imperial hierarchy – there grew up stews and grog-shops to pander to the seamen. Brothels were thoughtfully provided by the enterprising Chinese aboard sampans elaborately decorated with flowers – hence the euphemism 'flower-girl' for a common whore. Despite these restrictions, the wily factors and Selectmen soon came to complex accommodations with the Hong merchants and the Hoppo. Bribery, or *cumshaw*, was seen as an added 'duty' to be paid by the one side and levied by the other to oil the machinery of trade. The advantages of this flowed both ways and reflected the energetic writ that increasingly ran through all the dealings of the Company with their trading partners in the east.

Much of this aggressive policy was under the chief direction of Sir Josiah Child, whose brother John was President at Surat, and it led in India to a less happy outcome. Harassment of the tiny station on the Hughli – which by edict from Agra was unfortified – led to the sending of an expedition against the Mughal forces there. The subsequent war damaged the hitherto good relations between the new Mughal emperor, Aurengzeb, and the English. However, the Mughal state still relied upon the

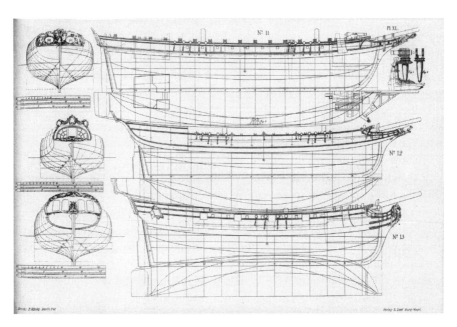

Three Privateers. Top: a schooner-rigged vessel of 94ft in length and two main guns, one a chaser and the other fitted amidships (see inset). Manned by about 100 men she also mounted small swivel guns along her rail and could be pulled by ten pairs of 'sweeps' or large oars. Middle: a smaller, 70ft long schooner-rigged privateer of 2-guns and 50 men, pulling eight pairs of sweeps. Bottom: although only 62ft in length this single-masted sloop-rigged privateer was pierced for and mounted ten carriage guns, could be pulled by seven pairs of sweeps and had a crew of 50 men. From Frederik Hendrik Af Chapman's *Architectura Navalis Mercantoria* of 1768. (Author's Collection)

agreement with the Company to act as a protective force to its own merchant shipping and a peace was patched up. During the conflict the chief factor at Hughli, Job Charnock, had discovered a deep-water anchorage further upstream. With fortifications proscribed, what Charnock wanted was a place where the Company's ships' guns could cover the otherwise defenceless factory. The location was as low-lying and fever-ridden as Batavia, but by dint of effort Charnock and his men toiled through the wet season of the south-west monsoon, to raise bunds and build warehouses – known as 'godowns' in the east – on the drier ground. The work went on for some years and even excited local suspicion which resulted in hostile attacks. To protect the settlement and in defiance of Aurengzeb's edict, Charnock raised a small fort in 1696, and in building Fort William laid, as it were, the foundation stones of Calcutta. There was little the Mughals could do to oust the opportunist new-comers and by 1700 the success of the new port raised it to the status of a Presidency.

This increase of the political power of the Company was augmented elsewhere. By 1686 it had established high-courts at Madras and Bombay and was granted powers by parliament to try seamen captured practising piracy. Hitherto such felons had to be sent home for trial in London, but the new rights enabled a swifter and more effec-

tive justice to be done and the first case to come before the new court was that of
the crew of the *Royal James*. After mutinying, these men had turned pirates. The three
ring-leaders were hanged, while another three had 'P' branded upon their foreheads
and were deported in chains. In another case of twenty pirates captured off Malacca,
the court was inclined to me merciful. 'In consideration of the small damage done', all
were to be branded and deported, excepting two, chosen by 'the fortune of the dice'
who were hanged 'for Terror's sake'.

By now the Company's ships no longer engaged in speculative ventures, or expeditions, but plied regular routes. This stability saw a career structure emerging for
the senior officers, though these were far from the aspiring gentry of the following
century. It was part of Child's policy to encourage a fierce loyalty by allowing commanders and their officers the 'indulgence' of a regulated amount of private trade.
Such an incentive was of benefit to all, not least in encouraging a degree of private
exploration for new sources of produce. This, however, often entailed great risk and
was far from being one-sided. Late in 1660 Robert Knox, on his way to the Malabar
coast in the Indiamen *Anne*, ran into bad weather and was blown far out of his way,
putting into the immense land-locked natural harbour of Trincomalee on the north-
east coast of Sri Lanka to refit and repair. Knox had been an Interloper, or 'free-trader'
as he would have preferred to have been called, but had joined the Company's service
and had his son, also named Robert, with him as a mate. Whilst lying in Trincomalee
the *Anne*'s people were attacked by the Rajah of Kandy's men who made prisoners of
the younger Knox and fourteen others. The ship escaped, reaching Surat on 15 March
1661 (where she was bought for local trading and renamed *Hope*), but all efforts by
Captain Knox to secure the release of his son failed. Although three of his shipmates managed to escape and the others settled in the country taking local wives, the
younger Knox and another officer, Stephen Rutland, were confined by their captors
for twenty years. On their eventual release and interview by the Court of Directors
back in London, the two men were compensated with £20 and £10 respectively.

Thinking Robert Knox a resourceful fellow, Sir Josiah Child – an unpleasant man
whose 'Influence and Interest' was, Knox afterwards said, 'so great by pleasing and
displeasing whom he pleased' and who involved Knox in a court-case before he
sailed – appointed Knox to command a new ship. This was the small 165-ton *Tonquin
Merchant* which had been built largely to Child's account by Sir Henry Johnson at
Blackwall. In order to fit himself for command, Robert Knox attended one of the
growing number of 'mathematical schools' teaching the rudiments of navigation. His
subsequent adventures are complex, but he endured much. His first voyage in command was without incident, but the second made up for this. Departing in May 1684
with orders to assess the prospects of settling at Tristan da Cunha he was then to
land on Madagascar and 'procure Negrosse' as Company labourers at St Helena. Then
he was authorised to load trade goods from any Indiaman lying at anchor and load
£2,000 the Company would have awaiting him there before proceeding on a 'new
discovery or projecting voyage' which was to 'passe through the Straits of Bally (Bali)
and so into the South Seas; and there to serch for a trade amounge those Islands, and

Robert Knox, 1641–1720, the East India mariner who sailed with his father in the *Anne* and was captured when she put in to Trincomalee for repairs. Knox senior omitted paying his respects to the Rajah of Kandy, Rajasinha II, who distrusted all Europeans having been cheated by the Dutch, and thus Knox junior and a ship-mate spent twenty years as prisoners in Ceylon. Knox later became a protégé of Sir Josiah Child and commanded the *Tonquin Merchant*. (Whereabouts of original unknown. © Courtesy of the Bodleian Library)

thence to Timore … to buy any sort of Comodities that … would turne to Benefett of the Company'.

The *Tonquin Merchant* ran into a cyclone off Madagascar and when she finally rode at anchor and Knox went ashore to barter for slaves, he so angered the local chief that he was lucky to escape with his life. He had to endure another incarceration, this time mercifully brief, but sailed for St Helena empty-handed. By now the *Tonquin Merchant* was short of supplies and scurvy appeared. Anchoring off St Helena, Knox went ashore and watched as his now mutinous crew cut the anchor-cable and headed for home. With only the clothes on his back Knox secured a passage on a home-ward-bound Indiaman and had the galling experience of seeing his ship anchored in Plymouth Sound. She soon afterwards sailed to Cowes from where her men were summoned to appear before the Court of Directors in London and explain their con-duct. According to his own account Knox was accused 'with all the scandalous crimes they could invent, but the highest … was short allowance [of rations]'. Knox's crew had, however, brought their ship home, a fact weighing in their favour.

Relations between the Company and the denizens of its lower-decks were not good at the time. Not for the last time in the history of British shipping did easy profits detach the profiteers from those who earned them. Nor were many of those responsible for crew-welfare much better.[11] Nevertheless, such expressions of discon-tent concerned the Directors, many of whom were opposed to, but intimidated by,

Child and they worried about whether 'they should have no seamen to serve them hereafter'. As a consequence of all this, the unfortunate Knox was regarded as a Jonah, but while several Directors wished to placate the seamen at Knox's expense, the wily Child assisted Knox in taking out a civil suit against their bonds for good behaviour. Having recovered some of his outlay, Child now compelled Knox to contribute to the refitting of his ship.

Having endured all this Knox sailed again in 1686 with a royal commission to engage in the war then being fought against the Mughals under Aurengzeb. In this he failed, his sole capture being a Persian vessel whose owners protested, compelling Knox to relinquish his prize at Jask. He arrived home amid another row in the Company court-room over the finances of his voyages. His third trip to Madagascar, Benkulen, Madras, the Hughli and, on the way home, Barbados, was more successful, but he declined a new command built to Sir Josiah's eccentric design on the grounds that 'it would be hazardous in bad weather to be at sea in her' and fell out with Child over the matter of private trade. His indignation was further incensed when the counting-house clerks presented him with a bill of commission for £45 on a quantity of cotton brought home on his first voyage, and charged £11 for the loss of a dozen pieces of fabric from a cargo worth £90,000. To Child's fury Knox now refused to serve as factor at Isfahan, St Helena or Benkulen, such was his disillusion with his 'ungrateful masters'. Instead Knox embarked upon an interloping voyage in the *Mary*. It was not a success and he afterwards retired, aged 60.

An equally contentious contemporary of Knox was Edward Barlow. Running away from his poor home in Lancashire, Barlow worked for an uncle in a tavern on the Thames, soon afterwards joining the Commonwealth man-of-war *Naseby*.[12] He was in this ship during the Restoration, saw action in the Dutch wars and it was after ten years of naval and merchant sea-service that he joined the East Indiaman *Experiment* as a seaman. After an Indian voyage the *Experiment* went to China, loading from junks sent down from Canton to Macao, the Portuguese factory at the entrance to the Pearl River. On her way home, off the Sumatran coast in December 1672 and ignorant of the outbreak of hostilities, the *Experiment* was captured by the Dutch and it was almost two years before Barlow arrived home. His survival raised a serious matter common to all merchant seamen: that of their right to be paid wages after a ship was lost, either by Act of God or war. Since it was held that 'freight is the mother of wages' and the loss of a ship deprived the ship's owner from generating the money from which he paid his seamen, Barlow received nothing beyond a compassionate gratuity, and in this he was fortunate, since it was granted out of the cynical assumption that 'it may conduce to the Company's service, and to the encouragement of those in their employ'.

Despite this Barlow shipped out again in the *Kent* as a petty officer. He was rising in the service and wholesale sickness among his officers combined with his own abilities saw him promoted to chief mate by the time she arrived home. It was in this capacity that he next sailed in the *Delight* in 1683 but in July, when they lay off Aceh, Barlow became embroiled in a dispute with Captain John Smith. An incensed Smith 'took up a carpenter's adze, offering to cut me over the head' the upshot of which was that Barlow was turned out of the ship.

Left to fend for himself, Barlow begged a passage aboard a free-trader, making his way to the Hughli where the factors befriended him. A chief mate's vacancy having occurred in his old ship, the *Kent*, Barlow arrived home but was unable to seek redress against Smith and shipped out again, serving successively as mate of the *Rainbow*, *Sampson*, *Sceptre* and the *Wentworth*. This ship was one of the first vessels which, following the *Experiment*'s tentative but successful prospecting voyage to Macao, opened in 1699 a regular trade with China. This was to pander to, and profit from, the growing English craze for tea-drinking, and as chief mate Barlow must have gained some influence in handling this new, but delicate, taintable and perishable cargo. He next joined the *Fleet*, a frigate-built Indiaman of 280-tons owned by Samuel Ongley and also bound for China. The ship's captain was young and inexperienced, a protégé of the Court of Directors, and he leaned heavily on the truculent, tarpaulin Barlow, fomenting another row before the ship had reached the Chinese coast. Only on the return voyage, when coming under the convoy of HMS *Kingfisher*, did the *Fleet*'s commander feel strong enough to dismiss Barlow, persuading the *Kingfisher*'s captain to embark Barlow as a passenger. Barlow confesses to his own 'plain-speaking' and admits a measure of guilt for these contentions, but he paid with further loss of pay and privileges and the politics and progress of Barlow's later years are confused. He may, or may not have acted as captain of the *Sceptre* in 1698 while that ship was on the Indian coast and at the instigation of the Governor of Bombay, Sir John Gayer. Certainly it appears that he had sufficient funds to buy the 160-ton *Liampo* in 1705, and charter her to the Company with himself as master.

There were others who have left less of a mark, but whose voyaging was no less enterprising. In about 1685, a certain Captain Goodlad visited Mindanao and, finding a cargo, left a letter with the local Sultan 'directed to any Englishmen who should happen to come hither' informing them that he had established a tariff of rates for trade in the Philippines.

Under the stability brought by the Restoration of the monarchy, the Company – if not its seafaring servants – prospered mightily. Social order and an inflow of wealth found the country swept by 'the India craze'. Silks, muslins, painted cloth called chintzes, were all in demand, despite the cries of distress from the traditional silk-weavers in London's Spitalfields. While the court of the Merry Monarch reflected this luxury, residual Puritan carping and the widening gulf between rich and poor focussed green eyes upon the Court of Directors, that mercantile clique 'of men with long heads and deep purses' which had 'set up an incontrollable Power in themselves'.

This, they had certainly done, much in the manner of their ownerships and management of their ships. The acquisition of their own shipbuilding yard at Deptford in 1609, adjacent to the Royal Dockyard and close to the maritime centre of Trinity House's first premises, had placed East India ship-construction in the forefront of the industry. William Burrell, a shipbuilder of Ratcliffe and a committee member, had been appointed Surveyor General, overseeing this complex site with its riverside wharf, wet and dry-docks, storehouses and smithies; its carpenters', coopers' and shipwrights' workshops, rope-walk, sail- and draught-lofts; its slaughter- and salt-houses and its vict-ualling-yard. The whole site was expanded in 1619 and there was even a gun-powder mill which, besides charcoal and sulphur, used the salt-petre brought back from India.

Burrell himself undertook a multiplicity of tasks, combining his work for the Company with the duties of a Commissioner of the Navy and master-shipwright in the neighbouring Royal Dockyard. He supervised the laying down of a vessel's lines in the draught-loft and travelled extensively in search of timber. He resisted any attempts to wrest from his central control cheaper ships, countering suggestions that tonnage could be more economically obtained by building in Ireland because he could not over-see the work 'whereby many faults would be to their great prejudice and danger of the shipping'. He did, however, seek economies by acquiring land downstream on the north-bank at Blackwall, reducing the rent burden at Deptford and enabling some land to be given up in 1631. Much of the Blackwall property was the marshland which insulated the Isle of Dogs and made the digging of deep enclosed docks easier. Extensive piling and in-filling was necessary but the Company already had moorings laid off the creek surrounding the debouchement of the tribu-tary Lee into the Thames, and there was a causeway providing access both to the City and the lime-kilns of Limehouse. From Blackwall moorings lighters had long been provided by Thomas Watson & Co. to enable the incoming Indiamen to send their cargoes upstream to Custom House Quay and Wool Quay, so the site, once developed, would prove advantageous. Ten years after the founding of Deptford, the Company had another extensive shipbuilding yard at Blackwall, the first vessel using it having been the *Red Dragon*.

Such was the success of the Blackwall with its hundreds of labouring craftsmen that in 1648 the Court of Directors relinquished the Deptford yard, retaining only some wharfage and stores which were turned over to warehouses and became known as The Stowage. The savings to the Company were immense and, sensing further economies, in 1650 they sold Blackwall to Henry Johnson who also began construct-ing men-of-war for the new Commonwealth Navy. After the Restoration in 1660 Johnson switched increasingly to building East Indiamen. In January 1661 Pepys vis-ited the yard by barge, to see 'a brave new merchant man which is to be launched shortly, and they say is to be called *Royal Oake*'. Johnson became the principal builder for the Company until his death in 1683, being succeeded by his son. Both were committee-men of the Company and after Johnson junior's death the yard was leased on to Johnson's manager, Philip Perry. Perry's son John took it over in 1776 and pur-chased the entire Blackwall estate in 1779. All these men had close associations with the Company and its Indiamen. By 1742 this vast, open facility consisted of 'a wet dock, three dry docks, one double and two single, as well as building slips for many ships of war'. Other building yards flourished in the vicinity, the frames of great ships rising above the flat-banks of the river, their launching days gay with silk and bunting flags, ornate swags, bands playing and guns firing. Such occasions were attended by the Company's big-wigs and their ladies, the waters of the Thames filled with the wherries of the watermen who conveyed them thither, while other observers, such as the Elder Brethren of Trinity House enjoyed a day out in their buoy-yacht.

Thus developed a practice of East Indiamen being built privately, but in yards owned by members of the Court; moreover they were built not to the Company's own account, but for private owners who were themselves Directors. Thus the Company itself avoided the risks and administrative burden of shipowning, chartering-in ships owned by its principals. Most such Indiamen were majority-owned by one Director with others holding minority-shares. Often the masters were among these minority share-owners, a system that acted as an incentive to a captain's efficiency and vigilance, but it was a system that attracted criticism: such benefits were obfusc and invisible to the denizens of London, whereas the opulence of the Company was not.

Nevertheless, with a new charter granted in 1693 the Company's finances and position seemed secure enough; yet this was an illusion. Politically the Company enjoyed few favours at court, its former attachments to James II leaving a bad odour. Moreover, as mentioned earlier, war with France was raging. On 16 July 1695 the homeward-bound East India convoy was engaged south of Ireland by a French squadron of six line-of-battleships and two fireships commanded by Amiral Le Comte de Nesmond. The losses were considerable, consisting of the *Princess Anne of Denmark*, 670-tons, the 750-ton *Defence*, the 650-ton *Resolution*, the 500-ton *Seymour* and the 400-ton *Success*.[13] Following the interception and havoc wrought to the Smyrna convoy twenty-five months earlier, this was another disastrous blow to both the country and the Company. French men-of-war and, perhaps more pertinently, French corsairs are considered to have seized approximately 4,000 English merchant ships as prizes during the War of English Succession (1689–1697). This begged the question not so much of whether the Royal Navy was incompetent at defending the nation's sea-borne commerce, as to whether the provision of adequate trade-protection was a proper function of the Royal Navy.

For the East India Company this was a woeful time, for besides these war-losses there was an alarming rise in the interloping of independent traders encouraged by the decisions of the Court of Admiralty mentioned above, to award compensation against the Company. In 1694, as will be seen presently, an attempt was made to set up a Scottish company and some India commanders sought to defect to it. Knox was one, for the Directors ruled in 1696 that the untrammelled private trading indulgence was to be withdrawn from its sea-officers, those wishing to trade would, in future, pay a premium of 18 per cent. It was, complained Knox, 'like the Pope who cannot Dispose of his pardons to eate flesh in Lent, etc, without Money'. Though, as we have seen, the problem of private trade had excited envy previously, its worth outweighed its defects and niggardly controls only created resentment in the Company's sea-officers – a particularly sore point in Knox's case after his long captivity and consequent miserly 'compensation', though he had 'gotten an estate' by his subsequent travails.

In the Indian seas the Company suffered further from piracy, mutiny and a straining of its relationship with the Mughal emperor, Aurangzeb, which is enlarged upon later, but matters nearer home were more pressing. By the mid-1690s, a crisis arose when, with the Government needing a loan of £2 millions sterling, a group of merchants in opposition to the Company and all involved in backing interloping ships, offered the sum at 8 per cent and a request for its own charter. The offer, which entailed a political bias in favour of the Whigs, was accepted and the charter granted, the *arrivistes* entitling themselves the New East India Company. They established a factory at the town of Hughli, after which the arm of the Ganges was named and which lay far above the Old Company's post at Fort William, beyond the new French factory at Chandarnagar and the Dutch one at Chinsura. Meanwhile an act opening the commerce to free-traders was passed in 1699, a further destabilising influence.

The consequences were near-catastrophic for both parties. While the New Company was jealous of the Old, the general public hated both while lapping up all the commodities the companies could provide and they could afford. Such vast riches accruing to a few men then, as now, excited envious indignation and that English desire for humiliation. It seemed for a while that both enterprises would sink, alarming a Government dependent upon the revenues this fabulous trade raised. To avoid this disaster the two boards were persuaded to agree to amalgamate. In 1707 the 'The United Company of Merchants of England Trading to the East Indies' was formed with capital of £3.2 millions; the *quid pro quo* was an interest-free loan of £1.2 million to the Government. Although a new charter was granted, to last until 1726 and later extended to 1766, the timing of the amalgamation was augmented by other simultaneous events, resulting in a near miraculous change in the new united company's opportunities. The first was the Act of Union between England and Scotland, harnessing Scottish commercial ambition to the enlarged state of Great Britain; the second was the distant death of Aurengzeb at his camp in the Deccan on 20 February 1707. The first was to augment the new United Company's power-base and native resources; the second marked the beginning of the end of the Mughal Empire. Soon dignified as the 'Honourable East India Company', the United Company was to be sucked inexorably into the power vacuum of an India falling into fragments.

NOTES

1. The importance of the cod-fishery to several European nations, especially Portugal, France and England arose from the fact that dried cod was, apart from salted meat and cheese, one of the few methods of storing protein for consumption in winter. It was therefore a highly desirable and portable commodity, becoming even more so during the European wars of the seventeenth and eighteenth centuries when entire armies were sustained in the field by dried-cod.

2. I intend no contention in this claim, for it seems to me that, as will be seen, class and perceptions of class distinction lay – and still lie – at the heart of the British social order, to the detriment of that other essentially English notion, the Common-weal. I make a claim for the *inherent* (note the emphasis as generic and not specific) superiority of the Dutch as sea-farers based upon the simple fact that, at the time of writing, 2007, they

remain a formidable force at sea while the British presence, seemingly unassailable in, say, 1950, has almost entirely vanished.

3. Several such expeditions ended in disaster, the best known being Henry Hudson's in search of the north-west passage (see Chapter Two). A lesser known one was that under Benjamin Wood, an experienced West Indian navigator. In 1596, under the aegis of Sir Robert Dudley, son of Elizabeth's favourite, the Earl of Leicester, a voyage was proposed west through the Strait of Magellan to Cathay. Armed with diplomatic letters to the Great Khan of China, Wood's fleet consisted of the *Bear*, the *Bear's Whelp* and the *Benjamin*. They sailed, never to be heard of again, a disappointment that might have put period to English enterprise had not rivalry with the Dutch re-ignited the London merchant speculators.

4. 'Perpetuity' meant, in fact, some 220 years. The Levant Company was not wound up until 1825.

5. Having served at sea in the 1590s and learning of opportunities in India, Adams had joined a Dutch expedition sent westwards through the Strait of Magellan. The little fleet of five ships was battered by bad weather and Adams was the sole survivor of the last of them, the *Charity*, being washed ashore on the island of Kyushu. Refused permission to leave, Adams made himself useful to the authorities by way of his expertise in shipbuilding and navigation, skills that earned him the gift of an estate near Yokosuka and a Japanese wife. Learning of the English factory at Bantam he sent thither a message, prompting Saris's visit. Afterwards Adams received permission to leave Japan and became a servant of the East India Company, making several voyages to Cochin-China and Thailand, but he returned to Japan several times and died there in 1620.

6. Keigwin's letters of 19 and 21 November (quoted by Sir Evan Cotton) makes both these points for he was, at the time, acting as commodore of a small squadron blockading the island of Karanja, near Bombay, after its seizure by the Mahratta king, Shivaji. A *shibar* was a large vessel, similar to a *pattamar*, of 200–300 tons burthen.

7. Pring was, nevertheless, a competent seaman. In 1617 he had had trouble with the *Royal James* leaking, reporting to the Company on 12 November that approaching Surat the ship suddenly started making water: six feet in four hours, followed at a rate of thirteen inches the hour with the pumps going. Help was obtained from the other ships to man the pumps and after several attempts to stop it 'we basted our spritsail with oakum and let it down before the stem of the ship and so brought it aft by degrees; in which action it pleased God so to direct us that we brought the sail right under the place where the oakum was presently sucked into the leak; which stopped it in such sort that the ship made less water the day following than she had any day before from the time of our departure out of England'. Mindful of the fate of the *Trade's Increase*, attempts to careen were not very successful, but the leak was stopped so that 'since we came afloat her bends are much righted and she hath remained very tight'.

8. Influenced by the temperature of the thrusting landmass of the Indian subcontinent, the dry north-east monsoon blows across these seas from November to April. The fiercer south-west monsoon from May to October carries moisture across India, producing the rainy season. A similar phenomenon occurs as far east as the South China Sea influencing the carriage of tea by both Indiamen and their elegant nineteenth-century successors, the tea clippers.

9. Colbert had the first French East Indiamen built in The Netherlands where the necessary expertise resided, ordering that they were especially grandly decorated into order to impress the Indian merchants and rajahs and thereby steal a march upon his English rivals.

10. Charles I's attempts to build up the Royal Navy, particularly through raising Ship-Money from a tax on inland towns was not only one of the causes of his violent rupture with Parliament and the consequent English Civil War, but demonstrates the disconnection felt

by Middle-England from the sea and sea-power. Despite the grandeur of his warships, epitomised by Phineas Pett's magnificent *Sovereign of the Seas*, the morale of the Caroline Royal Navy's seamen was constantly near-mutinous. Mismanagement and corruption ensured the Royal Navy declared in large measure for the Parliament in the ensuing Civil War.

11. A laxity had infected the Company's surgeons who dispensed with daily inspections and became 'very careless of a poor man in his sickness'. Medical examination consisted of taking a sick man 'by the hand when they hear that he hath been sick two or three days, thinking that is soon enough, and feeling his pulses when he is half-dead, asking when he was at stool, and how he feels himself, and how he has slept, and then giving him … medicines on the point of a knife, which doeth as much good to him as a blow upon the pate with a stick'.

12. This was following the First Dutch War (1652–1654), in which the Royal Navy fought mostly in the North Sea and English Channel, though two actions were off Italy. The Second Dutch War was after the Restoration of King Charles II in 1660 between 1665 and 1667.

13. The *Seymour* had been sent out as an interloper and was purchased during her voyage by the Company who had a cargo for her. The *Defence*, *Success* and *Resolution* were, after their capture, refitted and sent out under English colours as decoy corsairs. The last named was built for Sir Josiah Child. Indian Ocean piracy is dealt with in a subsequent chapter.

TWO

'IN THE BELLY OF ALL COMMERCE'

The English in the Western Ocean, 1500–1707

The Treaty of Tordesillas of 1494 attempted to resolve the competitive differences between Spain and Portugal, the two Christian states which were then the pre-eminent European maritime powers. By papal condescension, each was granted the free hand of exploitation throughout an entire hemisphere of the globe. While a nominal meridian was agreed in the Atlantic, no corresponding longitude was resolved on the far side of the planet where, as we have seen, the Portuguese claimed the Moluccas and the Spaniards the neighbouring Philippines. Such an arbitrary decision took no account of any possibility of a change in the *status quo*. Roughly a century later Spain's largely Protestant vassal state of the modern Netherlands revolted, while Elizabeth I's nominally Protestant realm of England challenged Spanish – and Catholic – hegemony at sea. Both were at war with Spain and found in the Caribbean flaws in the structure of the vast and immensely rich empire directed from a distant Madrid.

Ironically, these weaknesses were exploited because of internal divisions within England, herself disintegrating into civil war, fed in part by the peace secured by Elizabeth's successor, James I of England and VI of Scotland, and exacerbated by his son's extortionate demands in building up a naval fleet. This was a double irony, for Charles I's necessity for a powerful navy was a result of his peace-loving father's neglect if it, a poor decision on James's part given the wandering and lawless tendencies of his independently minded subjects who named their first colony in his honour. But James was keen to profit from their endeavours, and in 1604 – while inveighing against the noxious weed – the king declared a duty payable on imports of tobacco, introduced by Ralegh some time before the establishment and tragic failure of the Jamestown colony.

While religious differences among English land-lubbers provided the engine for a nascent colonisation, English merchant navigators were also looking west to the New World. Ambition prompted them to pursue a disastrous search for a northern route into the Pacific. Following the tentative thrusts of Davis and Frobisher touched upon in Chapter One, Henry Hudson was to seek the North-West Passage. His early two voyages of 1607 and 1608 had been made on behalf of the Muscovy Company and had been in search of that older grail, the North-East Passage, following the wake of the Dutchman Willem Barentz into Arctic waters. In 1609 Hudson was engaged by the Dutch East India Company. Leaving the Texel in the *Half Moon* he was compelled to abandon another attempt to force the ice off Spitsbergen. Quashing an incipient mutiny among his crew he persuaded them not to give up the enterprise, offering an alternative. Doubling Greenland, Hudson sought a passage to the westwards to the Pacific, which he then believed existed around the fortieth parallel. Reaching Virginia on 28 August, he headed north and found instead the river that bears his name, claiming the adjacent island as New Amsterdam in the name of the United Provinces.

On her way home the *Half Moon* put into Dartmouth, where Hudson found himself in trouble, forbidden to further serve the Dutch. Making a virtue of necessity he raised interest in his new quest among London merchant investors, chief among them Sir Dudley Digges. In April 1611 Hudson set out again, in the *Discovery* of 55 tons, on a doomed voyage. By August he had penetrated the great bight that is named after him, but became embayed in what is now James Bay, an inlet of the greater Hudson's Bay. Here the *Discovery* was beset by ice and forced to over-winter, her people at first subsisting upon the small willow ptarmigan until the spring migration left them desperate. They ate anything 'how vile soever,' wrote Abacuck Prickett, not eschewing 'The mosse of the ground … and the frogge (in his ingendering time as loathsome as a toade) …' Later, with the spring melt, they obtained fish; by June the *Discovery* was free of the ice and things might have turned out well, for Hudson had demoted his troublesome mate Robert Juett and replaced him by the able Robert Bylot. Soon afterwards, however, Hudson inexplicably hid the charts and navigational instruments, and down-graded Bylot.

The *Discovery's* company had by now consumed the last of their ship's biscuit and cheese. Scurvy appeared, a catalyst for disloyalty and fear, fomenting internal hatreds, and provoking a mutiny led by Henry Greene. On 23 June Hudson, his son John and a handful of loyalists, were cast adrift and abandoned, never to be seen again. Thanks almost entirely to Bylot the *Discovery* was extricated from the great bay and began to make her way home. A vicious encounter with the Inuit resulted in the death of several of the mutineers, including Greene who had originally been Hudson's protégé.[1]

Although the nine survivors had acquired a stock of sea-birds, these soon ran out as they sailed for home. Privation continued to take its toll: Juet died from 'mere want', the rest despaired. Thanks to the outstanding efforts of Bylot, however, the *Discovery* reached England in September 1611, the absence of Hudson provoking a series of laboured enquiries that dragged on and on. Prickett's account of the voyage was suspect, but he was Digges' representative on the expedition and it was seven years before anyone was arraigned for the murder of Hudson. After prolonged judicial indecision four men were accused, Prickett, but not Bylot, among them. However, any conviction failed for lack of evidence, the survivors blaming Greene and others among the dead.

By now other considerations supervened: Bylot had been assisted in extricating the *Discovery* by a strong favourable current from the west, inducing the conviction that despite the disaster, Hudson's Bay was indeed the entrance to a strait leading westward to the Pacific. This notion penetrated the highest circles, reaching Prince Henry of Wales who, with 160 merchant-adventurers, now backed a second expedition. This was to be commanded by the Welshman Thomas Button, who had seen naval service in Irish and West Indian waters. He would command the *Resolution* with the *Discovery* as consort, and Robert Bylot would accompany Button as pilot. Button's orders were to return to Hudson's Bay and observe the current.[2] 'If it come in Southwest, then you maie be sure the passage is that waie; if from the North or Northwest, your course must be to stand upp into it.' Despite the presence of both Bylot and Prickett, there was no mention of searching for Hudson.

Button's expedition of 1612 reached its apogee on 13 August when the two ships could proceed no further; they had reached the western side of Hudson's Bay and could find no passage in that direction. The *Resolution* and *Discovery* wintered in a river where several men died, but Button occupied his crew in activities that would not have disgraced a later age. After their release from the ice, the ships coasted north in another attempt to find the elusive strait to the west but, having surveyed over 500 miles of coastline, Button gave up, returning to the Thames in September 1613, still convinced that the passage existed.

Meanwhile, in Button's absence, in July 1612, no less than 300 merchants, many of them his backers, had formed the optimistically named Company of Merchants of London, Discoverers of the Northwest Passage. Undaunted by Button's failure the *Discovery* set out again in March 1614 under a relative of Button, William Gibbons, but he failed to justify Button's confidence and was beset by ice off the coast of Labrador, from whence he soon came home. Once again the little *Discovery* was made ready. It was now Bylot's turn to command, and with him as navigator went the exceptionally able William Baffin. The two men made a formidable team; Baffin was an experienced Arctic hand who had been in the service of the Muscovy Company and had made several voyages to the Spitsbergen whaling grounds. Most importantly he understood the determination of longitude by lunar observations and, despite the crudity of his instruments and the complexity of the calculations, was among the first navigators to determine longitude at sea, long before the invention of the chronometer. Baffin was also outstanding as a surveyor.

Avoiding the trap of Hudson's Bay, the *Discovery* remained in higher latitudes and penetrated further west, but in July 1615 she too was baffled by ice. Bylot and Baffin had discovered the strong tides and had spent days observing them, Baffin concluding that these were tidal streams generated not in the distant Pacific, but in the adjacent Atlantic. Such was his standing and the confidence reposed in him by the expedition's backers that this explanation was accepted, but the ardour of the Northwest Passage

Company remained undiminished and in February 1616, Bylot and Baffin were again on their way in the faithful *Discovery*. Rounding Cape Farewell they headed into the Davis Strait, passing farther north than their eponymous predecessor, and discovering the great bight that bears Baffin's name. 'On Midsummer Day,' Baffin recorded, 'our shrowds, roapes and sailes were so frozen that we could scarce handle them; yet the cold is not so extreame, but it may well be endured'. By July the *Discovery* had passed the 78th Parallel but could penetrate no further and Bylot turned south and 'ranne along by the shore'. Exploring the numerous indentations that they named after the expedition's backers, they came upon Lancaster Sound on 12 July 1616. Despite the width of the entry, from the aspect of the distant backcountry Baffin concluded that this was one more deadend, and the *Discovery* continued south.

> Here our hope of passage began to be lesse every day, for from this Sound to the southward wee had a ledge of ice betweene the shoare and us … [and] made an end of our discovery, and the year being too farre spent … wee determined to goe for the coast of Groineland to see if wee could get some refreshing for our men.

This decision was prompted by the onset of scurvy, the remedy for which was known to these remarkable men, even in 1616.

> We found great abundance of the herbs called scurvie grass, which we boiled in beere, and so drank thereof, using it also in sallets (salads), with sorrel and orpen, which here groweth in abundance. All our men within eight or nine dayes space were in perfect health and so continued till our arrival in England.

In writing to Sir John Wolstenholme, a prominent and influential figure in the Northwest Company and an 'incorporator' of the East India Company, Baffin concluded: 'There is no passage, nor hope of passage, in the north of Davis Straights [sic]. We having coasted all, or neare all the circumference thereof, and find it no other than a great bay.' In passing Lancaster Sound they had unknowingly crossed what would prove two centuries later to be the entrance to the sought-after route to the west. Robert Baffin was a distinguished mercantile sea-officer, but he now passed into the service of the East India Company and obscurity. He made several surveying voyages in the Persian Gulf, producing splendid charts and adding to the growing hydrography of the east, but joined the attack on Hormuz where he was killed in the assault on the fortress of Qeshm in 1622 mentioned in Chapter One.

Conclusive though the submissions of Bylot and Baffin might seem, imagination is an emotion not subject to reason. Other nations were demonstrating an interest in the Arctic. In 1605 English ships had been employed by the Danish king to establish trade with the Inuit and in 1619 a Danish expedition under Jens Munk set off. It was a catastrophe, only Munk and two companions returning to Copenhagen, a circumstance that laid the matter to rest for a few years, but in London the desire to find what formed itself into a certainty in the minds of men like Wolstenholme promoted further attempts. In January 1617 the East India Company's 'Court of Committees' assembled and were informed by Wolstenholme of:

> …an intende tryall to be made once again in discouringe the Norwest passage … [because] a greate tyde of floode runnes, and riseth sometimes 17 or 18 foote in height, wch is supposed cannot bee butt by some current from the sea in some other place, wch in probabilitie may proue the desired passage…

It was intended to be led by a Captain Bullocke but the arrangements and appointment of its leader are of more than passing interest, demonstrating the width of adventurous experience and the vicissitudes of existence as they figured in the life of one long-obscured ship-master of the period.

William Hawkeridge was a Devon man, a cousin of the great Stuart naval architect Phineas Pett. He first sailed with Captain (later Sir) Richard Whitbourne of Exmouth in 1610, when Whitbourne commanded a ship in the Newfoundland fishery trade in which Hawkeridge sailed as his 'servant'. This, often a term for an apprentice, seems to have been the case, for by 1612 Hawkeridge was a member of Button's expedition to Hudson's Bay.[3] It is possible that in accompanying Button, Hawkeridge was serving as a mate, if not the master of an accompanying pinnace, and in 1618 Hawkeridge, as we have seen in the previous chapter, served as 'a Captaine in a ship to the east Indies…', commanding the *Thomas* in a voyage to the Moluccas, during which he fought alongside Dale in his action with Coen. Thereafter Hawkeridge's movements are obscure, but the *Thomas* probably foundered off Java, leaving Hawkeridge to continue in the East India Company's service, possibly in command of a local 'Country' ship or as agent for the Company. In August 1622 Mr Fursland, a Company factor writing to the Directors from Batavia, mentions that Hawkeridge was returning home as a passenger aboard the *Lesser James* because:

> hee deserues better imployment then att present wee are able to give hime, hauing sufficiently and carefully p'fourmed the chardges imposed vppon hime, which we referre vnto your Wor'ps consideracones, to reward him…

However, on the homeward passage the ship's master, Captain Roberts, fell ill and, as had been arranged, Hawkeridge succeeded him. It appears that during his tenure of command, the *Lesser James* encountered a Chinese junk which was attacked – perhaps after it attacked the *Lesser James*, for the point, though inferred, is not explicit – and pillaged her of 1,500 *reals*. Hawkeridge is alleged to have profited from this loot, but the details are obscure, as is the length of his period in command, for he was not master at the conclusion of the voyage when, against Company regulations, the *Lesser James* touched the Irish coast before making the Thames.

Back in London by the summer of 1623 Hawkeridge was pursuing the Company for wages and expenses that may have been withheld against his perceived misconduct. On the other hand Hawkeridge was vociferous in his public protestations against the calumny of the Directors, bringing a legal action against them. Claim and counter-claim were laid before the Admiralty Court and although the matter of the junk and the landing in Ireland were aired, the tone of the proceedings does not conduce to Hawkeridge's outright guilt. Whatever it was he had done, it was more irregularity than offence. However, the Court of Committees resolved that it was:

> thought fitt to cast vpp the value of his goodes and moneys in the Companies handes, and, having deducted for his disseruice … such a proportion as may in some reasonable sorte punish his errors and deterre otheres, to order him the rest.

Accordingly Hawkeridge was admonished for not having dissuaded the stop at Ireland, from which he had himself profited by private trade. Hawkeridge countered this with the explanation that the *Lesser James* had favoured a northerly course to make a landfall on the Irish coast in order to avoid the hostile Dutch, who laid a course for Ushant and the coast of France. By this he implied that their indulgence in private trade in Ireland – which the Directors could not stop – was purely fortuitous. However, Hawkeridge wished to:

> wype away these staynes and sett him[self] upright againe in their favours. He also endeaured to bring to their remembrance that, at his going forth, it pleased the then Courte of Committees to promise him that they would winke at any reason-able matter he should bring home; but none of the Committees remembered any such thing…

He submitted to the Directors's decisions, but remained aggrieved, afterwards speaking 'bigg wordes against the Company'. The dispute was finally resolved by a reduction of the mulct imposed upon Hawkeridge, but the connection between him and the East India Company was to be severed. 'The Court [of Committees] ordred that Captayne Hawkeridge's bond shall bee delivered vppe vpon sealing of a genrall release'.

While this convoluted story was unravelling, elsewhere in the City the indus-trious Wolstenholme had been busy meditating another voyage to search for the North West Passage. To this end he had, 'amongst my friends, raised a reasonable good stock' and had, moreover, negotiated to take-over a naval pinnace, the *Lyon's Whelpe*.[4] This was to be released by King James I to his Lord Admiral, the Duke of Buckingham, who would 'make [her] over to us in consideration of his adventure'. Thus Buckingham would buy into a private expedition, His Majesty having 'con-tented to bestow in free gift vppon his Grace' the *Lyon's Whelpe*. This arrangement was arrested when, on 27 March 1625, James died, whereupon it was swiftly resolved by the new monarch. Within days of his accession Charles I approved of 'an action of great importance to trade and nauigation' which he thought 'fitt to cherish and advance'. Thus the *Lyon's Whelpe* was released from naval service to the 'Duke and his assigns … to use & imploy the said Pyñace as his owne proper ship'. A month later, on 30 April 1625 a Royal Warrant authorised the Commissioners of Customs to release to Captain William Hawkeridge £200 worth of Spanish *reals*, revealing that this imprest was intended to provide the new expedition's leader with trading capital once he reached the Indies 'because it is vncertaine what English commodities will vende in those parts'.

In his preparations Wolstenholme went further, drawing Hawkeridge's name back to the attention of his fellow Directors, and soliciting the East India Company's assistance. Wolstenholme requested that when the expedition's two ships – for there are references to a second vessel – reached the East Indies, the East India Company's factors should:

> use them kindly, but also suffer them to lade their shipps from thence for England, with peppr. One of the Committees disliked the mocon, being of the opinion it were better the adventure were lost than that the said passage should be discovered; for that it will greatly p[re]judice the Companies benefit and trade…

In the end the Company compromised: the ships would be succoured, but pepper would only be loaded if no Company ships were available, and even then the cargo was to be to the Company's account at a freight of £20 'the Tunne'.

Hawkeridge, whatever his standing among the Directors of the East India Company, was probably uniquely qualified to command 'soe weightie an Enterprise', possessing as he did experience of both the Arctic and the East Indies. There are hints that he was released in order to undertake the expedition on the influential Wolstenholme's recommendation. Certainly his very public dispute with the Company seems to have counted in the estimation of Wolstenholme and possibly his personal faction among his fellow 'Committees,' or Directors. Many of these men were not opposed to the discovery of a new passage to the Pacific, having invested heavily in earlier expeditions. Indeed the Company's current Governor, Sir Thomas Smith, was, like Wolstenholme, an 'adventurer' in the new enterprise, a mark in its commander's favour. The precise dates of Hawkeridge's voyage are obscure and, from Foxe's second-hand and self-confessed 'Confused Accompt' (account), its details are lost. What remains is sketchy and muddled, but the voyage was a failure; Hawkeridge was, in the words of Miller Christy, 'either very incompetent or very unfortunate'. He broke no new ground nor made any achievement of note, unless it was squirreled away by Foxe for his own purposes, one possible reason for Hawkeridge's voyage having been expunged from history.

Hawkeridge cannot have been entirely incompetent, nor without resource, for afterwards he resumed trading, commanding and freighting a vessel of his own. But he was certainly very unfortunate, for he lost her, her cargo and his liberty when she was overwhelmed and seized by twelve Algerine corsairs in 1631. Mewed up in Algiers, the destitute ship-master petitioned Trinity House for relief. 'His ransom of £250 cannot be paid without charitable help. He lost £2,000 when the ship, of which he was sole owner, and her goods were captured', the Brethren noted. Christian 'hartes' were moved 'to commiserate his case and minister to his libertye' which was accomplished so that on 15 June 1633 the great shipbuilder Phineas Pett recorded that he travelled from Chatham to Portsmouth 'accompanied with ... Captain William Hawkeridge, newly returned from captivity.'

Of Hawkeridge's exploratory voyage one thing is clear, particularly from the engagement of King Charles and Buckingham, both of whose exploits were attracting hostile scrutiny in Parliament. This was the need to bury its failure, otherwise it killed any inclination of mercantile speculators to reconsider the hazard, and simultaneously dashed the hopes of other ambitious seamen. Curiously, the dice was to enjoy one last throw when, in 1631, Luke Foxe, an ageing ship-master possessed of an 'itch' to resume the search for a strait into the Pacific, resuscitated the interest of the City's investors, notably the Arctic patrons Sir John Wolstenholme and Sir Thomas Roe.

Foxe, a 'facetious, but energetic and capable, Yorkshire seaman' was a rough and hardy mariner of forty-five whose contempt for the emerging class of scientific 'mathematicall seamen' was outspoken. These men, Foxe seems to have believed, 'looke forth and tremble at the rising of every wave', a perjoration that might for personal reasons have been aimed at Hawkeridge rather than Baffin, but was certainly meant for Captain Thomas James. Fired by rivalry the Merchant Adventurers of Bristol determined to send their own expedition under James, a gentlemanly and able navigator, who was to command the *Henrietta Maria*. Rivalry stamps these twin expeditions, which left England within days of each other in May, for while James's vessel was named after the queen, Foxe's pinnace was named *Charles*, after the king.[5] Despite this, both had received royal approval and, in anticipation, both commanders bore letters from the Court of St James to the 'Mikado of Cipangu', as the Emperor of Japan was then known. After his previous experience, this seems to have been as much as King Charles was prepared to venture on the new expedition's behalf.

There, however, the similarity ended: Foxe had recruited old Arctic-hands; James turned several away, apparently disdaining their services. Both vessels penetrated Hudson's Bay and, on 29 August, met near James Bay whereupon the courteous James entertained Foxe to a dinner of game. The suspicious and gleefully contemptuous Foxe wrote after the encounter, during which they were beset by a squall that 'threw in so much water as we could not have wanted sause if we had had roast mutton,' that he perceived James 'to bee a practitioner of the mathematicks' who was 'no seaman'. Notwithstanding his dismissal of 'the mathematicks' Foxe carried out a running survey of the as yet unexplored coast of Hudson's Bay before leaving the area. He sailed north into the basin that today bears his name and is, in fact, an entry into the passage to the west. With scurvy now rife, the *Charles* headed for home, entering the Thames in October to the surprise of Foxe's backers.

Despite his education, James fared less well. The *Henrietta Maria* had been aground on several occasions and struck a rock in James Bay, thus giving James's name to the scene of Hudson's earlier tragedy. In order to lighten his ship, James now jettisoned his coal and then lingered in the bay. This delay forced him to over-winter as the ice formed round the *Henrietta Maria* and trapped her. However, a gale blowing onshore caused the ship to drift to leeward in the ice, causing damage and forcing James to a second decision. Having built some huts on the surrounding ice, he decided to sink his ship to prevent her further movement. In so doing, he hoped to be able to raise her again the following summer, but the action demoralised his men who were 'almost dead with cold and sorrowes'.

In case his plan failed they built a boat, but the winter drew on and scurvy struck. By May four men had died, a fifth of James's crew, but the weak survivors began breaking the ice up in the *Henrietta Maria*'s flooded hold and manhandling it out of the ship. By July she had been refloated and, skirting the ice, James retraced his outward passage, though he too turned north once clear of Hudson's Bay. Thereafter he headed for home, arriving in October 1632, establishing a curious British tradition that was to stick to Polar exploration until the very end of the so-called 'Heroic Age'. Lauded for his initiative and his extreme privations, all of which were revealed in a published account of his ordeal, the gentlemanly James became the hero of the hour. Having covered a greater distance than any of his predecessors Foxe, for all that he had not lost a man and had withal produced surveys superior to those of his rival, was ridiculed. Foxe's real achievements were lost in the public assumption that his early return was somehow inferior to James's gritty endurance.

Notwithstanding these inequities, whether or not there was a geographical passage to the Pacific ceased to matter to many merchants in both Bristol and London. Ice rendered any such straits impassable and they refused to throw good money after bad. Besides, they had a nutmeg of consolation. Timber and whales were obvious natural resources available from land and sea, but there was another rich source of wealth in the icy wastes of the far north of America: furs. In the face of this, further speculative exploration was pointless; enthusiasm for Arctic exploration was to dwindle some-what, though not to die. Upon its full revival, it was no longer a commercial venture for merchant seamen, but a national, even a supranational matter, fit for the ener-gies of the Royal Navy, the ambitions of its officers, and a part of the greater global hydrography of a new era.

The pragmatic merchants of London knew when to cut their losses and when opportunity beckoned. In an environment that teemed with otter, mink, ermine and, most importantly, beaver, there lay profit enough; besides, they had losses to recoup. But England was to be overtaken by civil war and, moreover, there were other more pressing matters; trading opportunities opening up with the new colonies of North America and – setting aside trade with the Far East, the Baltic and the Arctic whale-fishery – the growing slave trade. There was also the very real threat to valuably laden shipping passing to and from the Mediterranean posed by the pirates of Barbary.

English attempts to establish both overseas settlements and overseas trade – as opposed to home and European trade – resulted in 'a series of disparate and chaotic colonial adventures' for which the crown showed little enthusiasm. Worried about offending either France or Spain, James I's lack of support beyond the minimal had results fatal for his subjects and their backers' purses. Although James granted monopolies to vari-ous joint-stock companies, he did little else. The Guinea Company (the Company of Adventurers of London Trading to the Parts of Africa) of 1618 had abandoned both its factory and trade as unviable as early as 1621; the Amazon Company, gaining its monopoly in 1619, foundered soon afterwards. The tragic failure of Ralegh's adventure in Guiana – which disobeyed James's injunction not to attack the Spaniards – resulted in Ralegh losing his head. Nor did James's unwisely granted monopolies meet with approval throughout his kingdoms. In enforcing their rights over the northern right-whale fishery, the London-based Russia Company found itself in dispute with the whaling companies of Kingston-upon-Hull, an argument that allowed the Dutch to exploit the differences between the two and to dominate the settlement of West Spitsbergen along with the fishing of its wondrously eutrophic waters.

However, in an age of religious ferment, there were other dynamics abroad which over-rode the pragmatism of mere merchant trading. Although the Roanoke colony of 1597 had failed, Sir John Smith's founding of Virginia in 1607 was, under Smith's dynamic leadership, more successful, notwithstanding the loss of the *Sea Venture* on Bermuda in July 1609 and the subsequent disagreements between her crew and Captain Christopher Newport and his colleagues of the Virginia Company. In 1620, the *Mayflower*, commanded by Captain Christopher Jones of Harwich, made her trans-Atlantic voyage with religious dissidents, landing them beyond Cape Cod upon Plymouth Rock in Massachusetts. The success of the fragile colony was due in no small measure to that of the Massachusetts Bay Company – another joint-stock enterprise – along with increasing migrations, of which the most significant was that of 1630 led by John Winthrop. Connecticut and Rhode Island were the first offshoots of Massachusetts, but extending settlement gradually created what later became New Hampshire and Maine. Transatlantic voyages with emigrants became an increasing commonplace and Bristol a port-city of imperial importance. Further north, meanwhile, the French were penetrating modern Canada, establishing the fortress of Louisbourg on Cape Breton Island and up the St Lawrence corridor where Quebec and Montreal would rise. In addition, four years after the Pilgrim Fathers stepped ashore by way of Plymouth Rock, the Dutch followed suit, landing on Manhattan Island to found the city of New Amsterdam on the claim made in 1609 by Hudson.

In due course these settlements would become great ports, but in the early years of North American colonisation it was in home waters that English maritime commerce was in trouble for this was the misnamed 'golden-age' of piracy, an era of great anarchy at sea. James's political pursuit of peace, at variance with his predecessor's long quarrel with Spain that so answered the rapacious ambitions of her seafaring subjects, now disinherited them. Widespread unemployment caused numbers of seamen to carry on seafaring by virtue of what they considered a birthright upon which they conferred a sort of justification by a notional floating fraternity.

Nor, alas, was James in a position to suppress this dangerous maritime rebellion of his own subjects. Indeed such was his neglect of the Royal Navy that a Captain Richard Gifford bemoaned its post-Elizabethan decline: 'we have no such shipping nor such affection to sea affairs; neither have we such seamen to put in execution, and few that know the right way to perform any royal service.' Condemnation seems universal; comments by others in 1626 run likewise: 'More ignorant captains and officers can hardly be found, and men more careless of his Majesty's honour and profit…' There were further animadversions on the following year when: 'Such a rotten miserable fleet, set out to sea, no man ever saw. Our enemies seeing it may scoff at our nation.'

It was this state of affairs that prompted the new king, Charles I, to embark on his disastrous and troubled efforts to make amends, but although the kingdom might be deficient in naval officers and an efficient navy, it was not entirely devoid of competent sea-officers. Not for the last time it was left to mercantile interest and initiative to protect its own shipping.

Throughout the seventeenth century the nominally Ottoman Turkish possessions along the North African coast had maintained a quasi-*jihad* upon the trade of Christian Europe. From Tripoli, Tunis, Bona (Bône), Algiers and Morocco, swift oared-galleys capable of short, high-speed chases, seized the under-manned merchant ships of all nations. The luxurious and despotic courts, under whose banners this particularly durable form of piracy flourished, provided not only a ready market for all goods seized, but enjoyed an insatiable appetite for white 'Christian' slaves. Many of these were sent to the galleys, employed on massive building-works, or sold as menials to those who could afford them. Such was the success of these denizens of 'High Barbary' – the name derives from the Berber tribes of North Africa – that many captives, unable to escape and resigning themselves to making the best of it, 'turned Moor' and fought alongside their captors as renegades. These individuals, maintaining what was by now an internationally condemned English appetite for piracy, often rose to high positions of influence, assuming Berber titles and privileges and using their seamanship and knowledge of their home-coasts to profit by raiding them. Most who turned their coats enjoyed a lifestyle of comparative ease, far more attractive than the drudgery of merchant seafaring.

By the early seventeenth century a Flemish renegade named Simon Danser had encouraged the Barbary pirates to turn to sail and their fast lateen-rigged vessels vastly extended their raids. In due course they 'learnt for themselves to handle European rigs and heavy guns, and needed Englishmen or Dutchmen purely as subordinates'. These Muslim pirates, with their admixture of quondam Christian adventurers, wrought havoc among the isolated coastal fishing communities of all littoral states. Among these characters was an Englishman named Verney,[6] and another Dutchman, Jan Janszoon of Harlem, who assumed the title of Murad Rais and raided Iceland, taking 400 men, women and children into captivity. A few years later, in 1631, he fell upon the Irish town of Baltimore, enslaving at least 109 men, women and children – some say more. These were sold in Algiers, where a French monk witnessed the pitiful sight: 'Women were separated from their husbands and the children from their fathers'. As Sir Francis Cottingham, one of James I's clerks, mentioned in noting the insolent audacity of the Barbary pirates, 'I have never known anything to have wrought a greater sadness and distraction in this court than the daily advice thereof'.

Alongside Arabic pirates of 'Turkish' origin and Muslim faith, the host of renegade Christians is noteworthy. If not exactly typical, the career of the Englishman John

Ward demonstrated how far an ambitiously amoral man might rise. The apostate Ward, who had sworn to 'become a foe to all Christians, bee a persecuter to their trafficke, and an impoverisher of their wealth' took a Venetian vessel, the *Reneira e Soderina*, valued at £100,000 in a sensational capture in 1607. He became so powerful that he employed a 'vice admiral', Richard Bishop, who in 1609 was active in the Irish Sea with a dozen sail and whom we shall meet again presently. Ward himself had, for obscure reasons, turned pirate to prey on shipping for the trade-goods they could resell, but soon realised that Christian seamen proved 'white gold' of an easier conversion. According to one of his captives, an English seaman named Andrew Barker, Ward's success at supplying the Bey of Tunis with slaves so ingratiated him with the Bey that he was given 'a very stately house, farre more fit for a prince than a pirate'. Here Ward lived 'in a most princely and magnificent state'.

The persecutor of Iceland and Baltimore, Murad Rais, also reaped honours, the Moroccan sultan making him governor of the port of Safi where he held court 'seated in great pomp on a carpet, with silk cushions, the servants all around him', acting 'in the manner of royalty' and providing a port of replenishment for his purely English confederates. But Baltimore itself did not escape the stain of piratical reputation. Despite the fact that it had suffered from the renegade Dutchman's attack in 1631, the same port, along with Crookhaven to the west, was said to produce pirates of its own and 'the women of Baltimore were reported to be all the wives or mistresses of pirates'.[7]

But it was the indiscriminate ransacking of coastal villages that troubled an impotent Government in London for the impudent 'Moors' landed on Lundy Island, fortifying the high-ground commanding the anchorage, the ruins of which are still known as Morisco Castle. In establishing their lighthouse at St Agnes in the Isles of Scilly, the Elder Brethren of Trinity House were obliged to pierce the tower for defensive musketry, while in late July 1625 'Sallee Rovers' ravaged the English west country, abducting an entire congregation from Mount's Bay one Sunday as the parish attended matins. The following year they raided Looe, from which they kidnapped eighty fishermen. They 'seized divers people about Padstow' and even entered Plymouth Sound. In all twenty-seven ships and 200 people were carried off. 'Lovinge and kind father and mother,' wrote Robert Adams, one of their victims, 'I am here in Salley, in the most miserable capivitie, under the hands of most cruell tyrants…' He was made to work at a mill like a horse from morning until night, 'with chains upon my legges of 36 pounds waights a peece'. His letter reached its destination, for Adams sought ransom: 'I humbly desire you, on my bended knees, and with sighs from the bottom of my hart, to commisserat my poor distressed estate, and seek some meanes for my delivery out of this miserable slavery'.

More common than such wholesale and pitiful abduction was the taking of merchantmen at sea. Deeply laden and rarely well manned, they were easily overtaken and often easily overwhelmed, though a determined resistance usually paid off. Most vessels trading under the aegis of the Levant Company and bound for the eastern Mediterranean were armed, their owners obtaining first a certificate of necessity from

Trinity House and then a warrant from the Lord Admiral to licence their carrying of ordnance.[8] Another expedient was to obtain a Letter-of-Marque as a license to arm a merchant ship even if no predatory plans were mooted by her owners or master. Both procedures were adopted during the lifetime of the *Sampson*, a large 500-ton vessel built at Limehouse in 1625. Part-owned and commanded by William Rainsborough, the *Sampson* was employed in the Levant trade and in 1627 was engaged to convey the chattels of Sir Thomas Phillips, appointed ambassador to the Porte at Constantinople.

Rainsborough was the son of a London shipowner and ship-master who, by 1625, had become an Elder Brother of Trinity House. He was 'regarded as one of the most experienced and capable seamen of his time and was frequently consulted by the Lords of the Admiralty on maritime matters', sitting on a Commission to examine methods of manning the King's ships. Rainsborough was prominent in an age when men of his ilk – particularly those in London – still provided their ships and even their persons for naval service. In 1635, 'when a fleet under Admiral the Earl of Lindsay with Sir William Monson as Vice-Admiral was equipped for service against the French and Dutch, it included five ships provided and maintained by the City of London'. These included the *Sampson* and the *Royal Exchange*, both part-owned by Rainsborough, while he himself was appointed to the command of *Merhonour*, forty-four guns, Lindsay's flagship, taking with him William Cooke as sailing master.[9]

Lindsay's task was to maintain the traditionally claimed 'Sovereignty of the English Channel' against a Franco-Dutch fleet then off Portland 'in a bragging pretence of questioning His Majesty's prerogative of the Narrow Seas'. In addition to warding off Dutch raids on the coast, Lindsay was charged with clearing English waters of pirates, including 'Turks', to protect trade and 'to guard against any infringement of the Customs'. Success, though claimed, was at best only partial and was certainly temporary. During the winter Rainsborough joined Sir John Wolstenholme as one of several commissioners appointed to enquire into the management of the Chatham Chest (see Chapter Three), and the following year was again appointed flag-captain, this time to the Earl of Northumberland in HMS *Triumph*.[10]

In common with other members of his fraternity, Rainsborough, had been intimately involved with other measures to combat the 'grievous scourge' of the Barbary raiders. In 1619 a large sum had been raised to ransom captives and Trinity House was charged with finding a further £2,000 for each of the two succeeding years. The City merchants then determined to send a dozen armed ships against the Barbary pirates, putting up £40,000 for the task. They also requested help from the Levant Company and all merchants and companies trading to Iberia. Trinity House advised that a levy on all London ships would spread the cost among those who stood to benefit and avoid evasion, but the outcome was a raging controversy; whingeing merchants demanded Trinity House made up the money and the Elder Brethren, devoid of funds for such a thing, in turn petitioned the King. It was not a good time for the monarchy and nothing was done beyond the brethren recommending that merchantmen proceeding into the Mediterranean should do so in 'fleets', or convoys, for mutual self-protection.

In 1633, however, alarming rumours that an enormous pirate fleet was preparing at Algiers prompted Trinity House to urge the wholesale issuing of Letters-of-Marque which the brethren rather naively claimed would end piracy in a year. If this was an appeal for aggression on the part of the nation's merchant masters it fell on deaf ears, but during this period Trinity House received a steady stream of pleas for help from some of the families of the hundreds of mariners who had fallen into the clutches of the Barbary corsairs. Hawkeridge was but one of many whose pathetic representations reached London.

The widow Mary Temple deposed in 1614 that her husband John had been 'captured by pirates' on several occasions 'during the last three years'. Finally, the previous May when master of the *Peter* of London he was captured of the coast of Barbary by three ships of war manned by Turks and Moors, and four Christians. He was taken to Sallee in Barbary and so misused that he died within eight days. One of the crew was murdered, the rest tortured, and the boy forced to be circumcised and 'turn Turk'.

Temple had lost £120 in the *Peter and Mary* and his four small children were thereby impoverished. On 6 June 1623 when the *Hope for Grace*, laden with salt and oil from Aviero in Portugal, was taken by 'Turks', it was not only Captain Thomas Short and his crew who were seized. The London merchant Robert Mathew, taking passage in the ship, was taken with the loss of 'his whole estate'.

> The captain of the Turkish ship sold him for 350 Barbary ducats which at 8 s[hillings per ducat] *amounts* to £140. He lives in misery in iron chains, is forced to grind in the mill like a horse all day long, is fed on bread and water, and insufficient of that, and is tortured to make him turn Turk [i.e. abjure Christ and embrace Islam]. A great ransom has been set on him which, because of his losses, he cannot procure without charitable aid.

Another widow, Elizabeth Ensome, petitioned in January 1626 on behalf of her husband Robert who had been taken when homeward bound from the Canary Islands the previous April. At the time of her capture, the *Unicorne* of London had been 'within 10 or 12 leagues of Scilly'. Again Ensome lost 'the whole of his estate' indicating his wealth was tied up in his ship and her cargo and was sold at Salé. Sold as a slave he was under coercion to turn apostate, subjected to cruel usage and with a ransom set at £250 – the amount of his lost investments – his wife and their three children were destitute.

William Kempster, master of the 140-ton *Paule* of London was taken by corsairs in December 1631 and he and his crew 'of 15 were carried to Algiers where they live in miserable slavery'. This was the last straw for Kempster and the vicissitudes of a mariner's life are exemplified by his plight. He had lost £100 invested in the *Rose* when she foundered in 1627, £240 when a corsair from Dunkirk 'took and sank his bark' and the following year:

> a French man-of-war pillaged him when he was homeward bound ... whereby he lost £100 in cloth, victuals and money. His total losses amount to about £640. He and his crew are unable to pay their ransom...

John Croft, master of the *Flying Drake* of Lyme, was 'honest and maintained his wife and family by his industry'. In 1632 the *Flying Drake* had made a voyage to Viana do Castelo in Portugal and on her homewards passage she was seized by pirates.

> He and his crew lost all that they had on the voyage and were sold as slaves at Algiers. They have been cruelly misused to make them forsake Christ and serve Mahomet. They cannot be released without the payment of ransoms which they and their poor wives cannot procure. Together with their wives and children, they will perish without charitable relief.

Occasionally a ship might escape the Barbary corsairs: Captain George Hatch, master of the *Barbara* of London reporting that nine Christians had 'brought a small ship into Portland Road'. They had been captured by an Algerine vessel 'but had overcome 29 Turks who had held them captive…' But such a turning-of-tables was rare and the experience of John Browne, 'mariner of Wapping' who was captured twice, first in about 1618 when 'master's mate of the *God Keepe* of London, Richard Boyer master' and again in March 1623 when a master's mate in the *Mathew and Judeth*, Henry Tatton master, were more common. Both ships were returning home laden from Faro.

Nevertheless, the most notorious of all the Barbary pirates remained the 'Sallee Rovers' who issued from the port of New Salé on the Atlantic coast of the sultanate of Morocco. However, in 1626, these men threw off any pretence at loyalty to the Sultan, and began to operate independently. The hostility of the individuals who made up the mixed crews hitherto operating under the Sultan's protection and flag – and to which they would in time return – was deeply rooted. In addition to the traditional antipathy existing between Muslims and Christians, the population in Morocco had been swelled by the wholesale eviction of Muslims from Spain that had begun after the triumphant *Reconquista* of Ferdinand and Isabella in 1492. Imperfect at first, this had been given impetus by King Philip III who, in 1610, had expelled the final million remaining 'Moors', many of whom were actually of mixed blood. Most fearsome of these were a group who had resettled in the mountains of Andalucía and became known as *Los Hornacheros*. Some 4,000 of these desperate, ferociously independent and lawless people headed south for the shores of Morocco.

Motivated by this imposed migration, a general revenge upon Christians combined with the Prophet's injunction to convert the infidel, to provide a moral imperative on the one hand. On the other, the perceived immorality of this course of action was compromised by those Christians who turned apostate. Seamen who took their Christianity lightly and owed no personal allegiance to anyone – and they must have been legion – saw attractions in turning their coats, notwithstanding their apostasy. Indeed many may have found Islam attractive for several reasons, and seamen who deserted either before or after capture, often forsook very little. One William Appleby, a seaman in the *Elisabeth Consort* of London, deserted when the ship was on a legitimate and protected trading voyage to Algiers. Appleby was known to have been 'to sea with Turkish pirates against Christians' but later turned up in London suing for his wages. In June 1619 the Elder Brethren of Trinity House gave as their opinion that in forsaking his ship he who 'wilfully runneth from a ship in the time of his voyage runneth also from his wages'.

Appleby was small beer, a man who could not stick at his defection but wanted his bread buttered on both sides. But there were others astir, men who also turned to piracy who were neither 'Moors' nor 'Turks' but home-grown Englishmen, several of whom not only had their bread buttered, but more than adequately honeyed. Among these was a certain Peter Easton. Easton commanded a 'powerful squadron with nothing to fear from the English navy' and had 'at least twenty ships'. He disdained the rule of law, remarking, 'I am, in a way, a king myself'. 'Going on account,' the euphemism most used by self-justifying pirates was, as Captain John Smith explained, entirely attributable to that lack of 'imployment for those men of warre. So that those that were rich rested with what they had; those that were poore and had nothing but from hand to mouth, turned Pirats...' In the years between 1580 and 1603 the English seafaring population had grown three fold, to about 50,000 men, a situation which provoked the Earl of Salisbury, within days of King James's accession and the abolition of state-licensed privateering on the grand scale that year, to complain that: 'All sailors of late are fallen into such vile order that they shame not to say that they go to sea to rob all nations, and unless the captain consent thereto, he is not fit...'

This election of commanders had promoted the notion of 'a pirate confederation' operating in the Atlantic under an 'admiral', Ward's protégé Richard Bishop. Elaborate measures were taken to get rid of loot by means of 'purse-bearers' – from which the title 'purser' derives – and corrupt agents ashore. The confraternity of pirates was fragile; each man was out for himself and alliances lasted only as long as mutuality was necessary. In 1607 Sir Richard Hawkins's brother-in-law, Captain Owen, had faced a mutiny of his eighty-man crew who promptly elected another to command them. Peter Easton initiated his rise by breaking from Richard Robinson and he in turn was deserted by hundreds of his men during his cruise off Newfoundland and North America in 1612. Whatever their morals, the three principal 'admirals' of the confederation, Bishop, Easton and Mainwaring, were remarkable seamen. Of Bishop it was said when that worthy was seeking a royal pardon in 1610:

> he is by farr the most sufficient man amongst them all; both for Cowncell and Commaund, as he was always well accompted of, by Sir John Norris, under whom he served in the warres of those tymes; I heare withal that he is a man of good temper and moderation, (for one of that Corse of liefe), and a keeper of his word.

In the summer of 1609 Bishop was reported to have mustered eleven well-armed ships and some one thousand men off the Irish coast, Peter Easton being his vice admiral and Thomas Francke his rear admiral. While a naval presence was maintained in Irish waters to suppress piracy, it was wholly inadequate. In 1608 the duty fell to Captain Williamson in the king's ship *Tremontane*. Williamson managed to corner Captain Tibalt Saxbridge in Baltimore but:

> Captaine Jeninges and Captaine Bishoppe with theire shippes came downe to the saied Williamson, and anchored the one on his bow and the other on his quarter within pistol shott, and the said Williamson beeinge then as it seemed not fitt to fighte with them put for them a flagg of Truce.

Williamson was then bought off and Bishop in due course received his pardon, settling in Ireland and building a house near Schull – though he could not quite renounce his former occupation, for it appears he often harboured old comrades there. No did his pardon lead to an end of piracy, for he was succeeded by Easton who increased the size of the fleet so that: 'These men, thus furnished, threaten the world'.

For the hapless ship-master encountering such a pirate, the practice was to remove him as a hostage against the good behaviour of his crew while his ship was looted. Such was the usage meted out to Captain William Oakes of the *Primrose* of London who met Captain Thomas Francke off Cape Finisterre in 1609. The master of the *Gift of God*, having been plundered by Easton, was charged with a declaration:

> to tell the merchants on the exchange that he [Easton] would be a scourge to Englishemen, sayeing he had no Englishe blood in his belly and therefore esteemed Englishe men no other than as Turckes and Jews.

Notwithstanding this denial of nationality, Easton appears to have come from Dartmouth but adopted the colours of Savoy, from whose Duke he had received a pardon in 1613, presumably thereby transferring his allegiance. He is described as having a 'rude and savadge' countenance while 'his speech and carriage is slow, subtile and guilty'. Lying off Cape Finsterre in the 160 ton, twenty-two-gun *Fortune* in March 1611, he took the Dutch vessel *White Swan* from Tenerife laden with Canary wine, sugar, syrup, preserves and wool. He then carried his prize to Ireland and, after discharging her, armed her for his own use. In June he captured the *Concord* of London, 'a tall shippe, and verie well fitted with ordinanunce and municion', along with the *Philip Bonaventure* of Dover, reinforcements which augmented his fleet.

These 'very great shipps' had by now attracted the attention of the Dutch, who armed a squadron to mount a punitive raid. Their actions also led to vociferous protests by the merchants of London whose trade was so wantonly interdicted. Such was the lawless state in his own home waters and the supine state of his navy that King James, following a commission of enquiry into the extent of piracy, had been moved to offer a general pardon on the principal that 'if his Majesty's mercy give them life they may prove able and honest subjects'.

In August 1611 this pusillanimous expedient was carried to the pirates upon the Irish coast by Roger Middleton, a naval officer. However, such were the seductions of being 'on the account,' that Middleton encouraged several pirate chieftains to cruise for further prizes before submission. Since the terms of the offered pardon allowed them to retain all their booty, Middleton could mulct those wishing to trade their freebooting ways for respectability at a better rate for himself. By November 1612 the Privy Council received a petition 'conteyning sundry informacions of frauds and notorious abuses supposed to be done by Captaine Roger Middleton, when hee was employed to carry his Majesties pardon to the said Easton and his consorts'.

Despite his corrupt inducements Middleton enjoyed only a partial success, a dozen or so notorious blackguards responding to the royal appeal to their better nature. Easton, however, eluded him. Returning from a raid on the Newfoundland fisheries the pirate admiral cruised off Morocco in late 1612, seeking news of the pardons. Leaving half his ships off Safi he proceeded towards Villefranche and the Duke of Savoy's dominions with four ships and 900 men, arriving on 20 February 1613. His subsequent assistance as an artillerist in the duke's war on Mantua earned him a marquisate and with his fortune made, he retired to a life of luxury and ease, dubbed by the Savoyard court *Il Corsaro Inglese*. Before being called to answer for his sins, Easton had 'married an heiress, converted to Catholicism and died in the odour of wealth and sanctity.'[11]

Easton was succeeded as 'admiral' by Henry Mainwaring, a man destined for even greater glory who, according to a friend, 'had been a terrible pirate in the flower of his youth, consorting with the King of Morocco … carrying into his ports all prizes captured by him from English, French, Spaniards and Flemings indiscriminately'. Something of an anachronism harking back to the days of Good Queen Bess, Mainwaring had a xenophobic hatred of Spaniards in particular, perhaps for their Catholicism. He was born in 1587, graduated from Brasenose College, Oxford, and may have abandoned a military career for the sea. In July 1612 Mainwaring purchased the *Resistance* from the king's own ship-designer, Phineas Pett. Intending a voyage to the West Indies he sailed in mid-1613 with the *Nightingale* in company, but soon after clearing the Lizard he 'altered his course and fell to takinge and spoylinge of shipps and goods', a practice he continued for two years.

Having made a fortune in cahoots with the Sultan of Morocco through some artifice involving the agents who processed the ransoming of Christian slaves, Mainwaring succeeded in contacting James I to seek a royal pardon. Whether money or some other form of the required 'loyal submission' acted as catalyst with the ambivalent James is uncertain, but Mainwaring may have been moved to act following the Dutch raid on Crookhaven in 1614 which rattled the pirates' sense of security. Whatever his springs, he received his pardon in 1616 to become a devoted loyalist, rising high in the King's favour. Two years later he had been knighted, appointed lieutenant-governor of Dover Castle and then entered Parliament. In 1623 he was appointed flag-captain to the Earl of Rutland, taking part in an abortive naval expedition against Spain. By 1629, as the scourge of Barbary pirates became ever more acute and increasingly occupied the attention of their fraternity, Sir Henry Mainwaring was himself an Elder Brother of Trinity House, deliberating upon the extirpation of his former accomplices.

Whether by Barbary corsairs, or opportunist English thieves wading out at low water to a Dutch merchantman aground off Gravesend at low water, piracy was rife everywhere. Irishmen operated from Bardsey Island off the Welsh coast, Lundy continued to be useful, so too was Milford Haven. James I's general pardon of 1612 had been intended to end at least that part of this curse that was home-grown in both his kingdoms.[12] Even the servants of the state were embroiled, for Middleton was not alone. Others quietly and profitably acted as fences for stolen goods, or as filtering money launderers, warehousemen and general agents. As one report from North Wales dated as late as 1634 stated:

> It will be in vain for his Majesty to set forth ships to sea to apprehend pirates, if they on the coast through the connivance of Vice Admirals [those holding local maritime legal office as deciders of maritime disputes rather than naval officers] find so easy a way to sell their stolen goods and to supply themselves with provisions to support their lewd way of life.

Like Mainwaring, one Robert Walsingham 'stepped directly from his pirate ship to the command of one of the king's' but it remained a time when, as Nicholas Rodger says, even 'Captains of warships enjoyed ambiguous relations with pirates, if not actually engaging in piracy themselves.' But the outbreak of the Thirty Years War in Europe in 1618 began an economic depression that reduced trade, triggering a decline in the piratical activity of the English in the North Atlantic. It was far from the end of piracy, however, for the Barbary corsairs were as active as ever and many Englishmen continued to gravitate to their service. At the seizure of the *Susan Constance* of London off Cadiz in June 1615 by six Algerine corsairs, five were commanded by Englishmen.

But what should be done? It did not help that, from time-to-time, the state itself connived. The Protestant banner-waving and patriotic privateering of the Tudor mariners had been subsumed into the nascent Elizabethan navy; their self-serving, debased and brutal successors of the Stuart era are less easily sanitised. Robert, Second Earl of Warwick, led a mixed force of seven privateers and three men-of-war in a sweep into the Atlantic against Spain in 1627. Although a man thought sufficiently forward-thinking to be chosen afterwards to command the Parliamentary navy, Warwick bestrode the changing nature of the times. One of a circle of men who invested in colonisation, he also put money into privateering and interloping ventures in the East Indies, 'which nearly wrecked the East India Company's trade'. As Rodger points out, his slaving expeditions between Africa and Virginia 'split the Virginia Company,' but that was not all. In association with John Pym and other Puritans, in 1629 Warwick had founded the Providence Island Company. Intending to settle the island of Santa Catalina off Nicaragua, otherwise known as Providence Island, the island lay well within the Spanish Pale. However, colonists were drawn from Bermuda and England and arrangements made with Dutch merchants to buy their produce. Warwick and his associates were Hispanophobes to a man and it was quickly clear that a secondary motive allowed advantage to be taken of Spanish weaknesses in the area. Ships were sent to Tortuga, already a lawless base from which freebooting buccaneers plundered Spanish shipping. In 1635 a Spanish force descended on the island and massacred the inhabitants. In 1641 they fell upon Providence Island and expelled the settlers, ruining the company.[13]

Commanding a squadron of privateers in the Mediterranean the following year, the dashing and 'most accomplished cavalier of his time', Sir Kenelm Digby defeated a Franco-Venetian squadron at Scanderoon, taking three French prizes and sinking another. The concussion of the guns shattered crockery ashore and, according to Digby's own account, even caused the eggs of the English consul's carrier pigeons to crack. But his attacks on Turkish vessels enraged the Porte and the Sultan's threats to stop the Levant Company's trade compelled it to pay compensation against Digby's piracy: What was sauce for the Barbary goose was not considered sauce for the English gander.

The news of a large fleet mustering at Algiers, which prompted the alarm of 1633, came to nothing and the policy of redeeming captured Christians by means of ransoms continued with varying degrees of success. Such demonstrable weakness invited trouble and matters came to a head three years later. In 1636 Barbary raiders, operating from Lundy, landed along the coast of west Wales and further east, near Cardiff. Most insulting to the honour of the kingdom's second city, they swept ashore within twelve miles of Bristol.

> It is certainly known that there are five Turks in the Severn [i.e. five ships in the Bristol Channel], where they weekly take either English or Irish; and there are a great number of their ships in the Channel, upon the coast of France and Biscay. Whereby it is come to pass that our mariners will no longer go to sea, nor from port to port; yea, the fishermen dare not put to sea, to take fish for the country. If timely prevention be not used, the Newfoundland [fishery] fleet must necessarily suffer by them in an extraordinary manner.

With the Mediterranean trade under threat, coastal shipping and the fisheries immobilised, England was in a state of virtual blockade. This was a rich irony for James I of England and VI of Scotland, in adapting a concept brought from Scots law to establish national rights over coastal waters, made the assertion of the crown's 'Sovereignty of the Narrow Seas', mentioned earlier as a matter of policy dear to the perverse heart of his successor. The irony was compounded by James's neglect of the navy and further augmented – given the money being spent on the Royal Navy – by the attempts of King Charles and his Government to build it up, but this was the year after John Hampden had begun his agitation against Ship Money.[14]

The public failed to understand the problem, seeing only the plight of Christian slaves 'in miserable bondage in Barbary' and remaining ignorant of the wider economic implications as they affected trade. This was understandable; religious suffering – even martyrdom – and the widely quoted statistic of two thousand suffering Christians resonated with the temper of the times. As the day of the 'Christian' pirate drew towards a close in European waters the so-called 'Turks' of the Barbary coast were feeling their own muscular strength. Despite the many renegades in their ranks, the Algerine and Sallee corsairs were no longer reliant upon 'Christian' expertise.

Moreover, following Murad Rais's raid on Iceland they roved father afield, attacking Madeira and taking twenty vessels off Newfoundland in 1611, and throughout the 1620s they regularly fell upon the Newfoundland fishery. Carrying large crews, the Newfoundland fishing vessels deployed these men into small boats to catch cod by long-lines, making them perfect and vulnerable individual targets for slavers, 200 of them in 1625. It was this 'white gold,' rather than booty, that the Barbary pirates were interested in, and Algiers alone could annually put about one hundred ships to sea for this wholesale traffic in humanity.

> Between 1613 and 1621 the Algerines brought in 447 Dutch, 193 French, 120 Spanish, 60 English and 56 German prizes, not counting those sunk. Another source suggests that they took not less than 446 English ships between 1609 and 1616.[15]

In September 1620 King James finally bestirred himself and attempted a naval expedition against Algiers under Sir Robert Mansell who was sent with six of the king's ships and a dozen armed merchantmen. Although Mansell attempted a blockade after his arrival off the port on 27 November, the Algerines avoided action at sea while still slipping in and out of the harbour. Algiers itself was impregnable. In any case James had forbidden outright war and Mansell resorted to some fruitless negotiations before his position on a lee shore compelled him to withdraw to Alicante for the winter. He resumed his station in May and on the evening of the 24th he sent fireships inside the mole, but to little effect. Impotent, Mansell was relieved by being recalled.

While European ships might trade with Algiers and maintain a certain commercial and civil intercourse in defiance of the spectre of enslavement, the 'Sallee Rovers' were an entirely different matter. The displaced *Hornacheros* had fetched up in the ruins of Rabat, once 'a great and famous towne' which had become 'desolate' and 'abandoned by the Arabs'. Situated on the bank of the Bou Regreb river that debouched into the Atlantic opposite the port of Salé, the ruins of the ancient *kasbah* – or fortress – of Rabat were restored to become the pirate stronghold of 'New Sallee'. This semi-independent city-state attracted the interests of others, men like Danser and Janszoon – or Murad Rais – who joined the 'Sallee Rovers' and augmented their forces while adding to their know-how. Uncaring of the fates of others, the Christians saw them as 'a bad-minded people to all nations'. Elsewhere, throughout the Islamic world, they were known as *al-ghuzat,* in imitation of the warriors who fought with The Prophet, and they took upon themselves a sea-borne *jihad*. One, Amurates Rayobi, commanded no less that 10,000 men with whom he made war along the hated Spanish coast and all seemed to operate under the shady authority of a Muslim holy-man, mysteriously known as 'The Saint of Sallee'.

The numbers of enslaved men resulting from the activities of all these piratical seizures amounted to thousands. Some 7,000 Englishmen were believed to be in the hands of the Moors, most from the west-country, that home of Drake, Hawkins and the old Elizabethan heroes. But it was not the taking of ships at sea that troubled the English body politic, though it worried the merchants of London, Bristol and else-where, but the wholesale abduction of civil populations. The raids of 1625 and 1626 had at least advertised the plight of coastal communities, raising 'pitiful lamentations' from 'wives and children' who suffered at the hands of the 'ugly onhumayne creatures ... with their heads shaved and their armes almost naked, [who] did teryfie ... exceedingly.' Murad Rais's descent upon Baltimore in 1631 added fuel to the flames of rising discontent. Despite petitions that 'we are assured would move the same passion and grief in your noble hearts as it does in us', the kingdom, for all its manifest puissance, seemed powerless.

Unwilling or unable to subscribe to raise ransoms at between £45 and £250, other expedients were suggested. An exchange of 'harlots and the idle and lascivious portion of the female sect' was proposed, but proved as unappealing. Meanwhile the 'distressed wifes of neere 2,000 poore mariners ... [who] for a longe tyme continued in most wofull, miserable and lamentable capituvitie and slavery in Sally' petitioned the Privy Council. Their husbands were undergoing 'most unspeakable torments and want of foode through the merciless crueltie of theire manifolde masters'. They added the desperation of their own plight and besought 'Your Honours, even for Christ Jesus sake ... to send some convenient messenger unto the Kinge of Morocco ... for the redemption of the saide poore distressed captives.' Although many of these wretches were made to work for the Sultan, many more were incarcerated for indeterminate periods in 'a dungeon under ground, wher some 150 or 200 of us lay, altogether, havinge no comfort of the light, but a little hole,' one of them named Robert Adams later reported. Here they lay in their own filth, fed 'a littlell coarse bread and water' and 'full of vermin ... and, not being allowed time for to pick myself [clean of them] ... I am almost eaten up ... [being] every day beaten to make me turn Turk.' Beatings were most commonly *bastinados* on the soles of the feet.[16]

But although his reputation for *hauteur* was growing, the new king, Charles I, had not proved indifferent to the privations of these enslaved subjects. In fact shortly after succeeding his father in 1625 he had despatched a secret agent, John Harrison, on a mission to Salé. Harrison landed at Tetuan and proceeded 'on a most desperate journey ... the greatest parte on foote, bare-legged and pilgrime-like'. He had orders to contact a holy-man, or *marabout*, named Sidi Mohammed el-Ayyachi, who claimed to have killed thousands of Christians. This was no less a person that 'The Saint of Sallee' himself. Harrison engaged in negotiations with this wily but skilful politician. Aware that his own position was uncertain and the allegiance of the *Hornacheros* to the person of the sultan was uncertain, Sidi Mohammed agreed to an accommodation. He would satisfy his turbulent neighbours across the Bou Regreb by initiating a war with their principal enemy, Spain, and embroil the importunate English. He therefore told Harrison that he would release all English slaves in exchange for cannon, powder, shot and assistance in attacking the hated Spanish, still resident on the shores of North Africa in the fortress of Ceuta.

Returning to London with Sidi Mohammed's terms, Harrison was told that the English would dissemble: only a few cannon and ammunition were sent, while prevarication would be the weapon opposed to Spain. Returning to Salé in the spring of 1627 Harrison informed Sidi Mohammed that King Charles was himself preparing for war with Spain but presented a mere four brass guns, though with all due ceremony. Sidi Mahommed's situation had by now changed, for the *Hornacheros* were in rebellion. The *marabout* declared himself overjoyed and ordered the release of all the slaves, taking the four cannon – he had asked for fourteen – into his arsenal while Harrison found himself paid in reciprocal coin: only 190 of the anticipated 2,000 slaves were released. In truth few remained in Salé, many having been moved inland to serve the Sultan at Meknes, or had been sent to the slave-market in Algiers. Most had died in an epidemic of the plague that had broken out the previous year and remained a danger throughout that summer.

Arriving home again, this time with his pitiful companions, Harrison was followed by a further petition from men remaining in captivity who pleaded with the king to consider their 'distressed estate', reminding Charles that they were 'Your Majesty's poor subjects, slaves under the King of Morocus' and emphasising the length of their ordeal: 'some twenty years, some sixteen, some twelve and he that hath been the least, seven years in most miserable bondage'. But the weak and vacillating king had other more immediate matters increasingly thrust before him. As there seemed to be a short abatement in the descents of 'the Turks' upon the English coast, probably attributable to the political turmoil in Salé, it was sufficient to deflect royal attention.

Having cast off the imperial yoke, this brief hiatus was followed by the spectacular raids of the early 1630s by the Sallee pirates prompted, as seems likely, by Charles's failure to declare war on Spain. While this weakened Sidi Mohammed's power, it also had an effect in England as it was given colour by more news of enforced circumcisions preceding the torture of captives to 'turne [them] Moores'. In the end the king summoned the Levant merchant Giles Penn[17] and William Rainsborough, who had written a memorial upon the subject. Both men were opposed to further placatory plans to redeem the slaves. The cost of arms and ransoms would amount to more than £100,000 and would only encourage the practice for further profit. What was required was a blockade, maintained until the pirate ships were worm-eaten and useless, whereupon such success would be 'very much to the King's honour in all the maritime ports of Christendom'.

The two men were encouraged to go further and in January 1637 Rainsborough presented a memorial of recommendations for royal approval. Consent was given for the sending of an expedition and funds were set aside for the purpose. The fleet was to consist of ships and men who were neither entirely of the King's navy royal, nor entirely merchant ships. Though it is incorrect to assume that this was an expedition of armed merchantmen operating under Letters-of-Marque, for all its ships and their commanders operated under commissions from King Charles, but it was a combination of both the mercantile and naval sea-services. The squadron comprised two thirty-six-gun men-of-war, *Leopard* and *Antelope*; two well-armed merchantmen, *Hercules* and *Mary*, both of twenty-eight guns; and two fast naval pinnaces each of fourteen guns, namely the *Providence* and *Expedition*.[18] The commanders were all – with one exception, the vice admiral George Carteret in the *Antelope* – experienced mercantile ship-masters from the Thames who were, either then or later, Elder

Brethren of Trinity House and thus had the local knowledge of Mainwaring at their disposal to advise them of conditions on the Moroccan coast. Though some, like Rainsborough, had seen naval service, most were seamen whose expertise grew out of their mercantile employment. Rainsborough himself was appointed admiral – by this time the title of the senior officer in command – and, accordingly, on 20 February:

> Captain Rainsborough, an experienced and worthy seaman, took his leave of His Majesty, and goeth instantly to sea with four good ships and two pinnaces to the coast of Barbary, with instructions and resolution to take all Turkish frigates he can meet, and to block up all the ports of Sallee, and to free the sea from these rovers, which he is confident to perform.

The ships assembled in the Lower Hope, a reach of the Thames below Tilbury, and then moved to The Downs where Rainsborough joined his flagship, the *Leopard*, and they weighed and sailed on 4 March. A week later on the passage south they ran into a south-westerly gale and the *Hercules* lost her mainmast, putting in to Lisbon to refit and rejoining Rainsborough's flag on the 18 April, by which time the admiral was at anchor off Salé.

Rainsborough had arrived off Morocco on 24 March, just in time to prevent the enemy's 'frigates' from sailing on their annual piratical cruise north to Ireland and south-west England. More than fifty vessels 'had made ready' and, as the English officers later learned, they were intending to descend on the English coast 'and fetch the men, women and children out of their beds'.[19] But few slaves actually awaited liberation in the dungeons of Salé, 'All that I could heare is that many English have been transported to Algiers and Tunis,' he wrote. He did learn that as a consequence of their revolt from the sultan, the corsairs and the *Hornacheros* had divided the twin towns of Old and New Salé that bestrode the river estuary of the Bou Regreb. The loyalists remained led by the *marabout* Sidi Mohammed el-Ayyachi.

The rebel faction, which largely consisted of the active pirates, was under Abdullah ben Ali el-Kasri, a man described by Rainsborough as 'an obstinate fellow [who was] puffed up with his luck in theeving'. The *Hornacheros* and their allies had refortified the ancient *kasbah* of Rabat, making it the citadel of 'New Sallee'. It was here that Ali el-Kasri held court and where he retained 328 Englishmen and eleven women in conditions of 'great misery'.

Rainsborough anchored with the guns of the *Leopard* and *Antelope* commanding the sand-bar across the entrance to the Bou Regreb River. While his other vessels, especially the shallow-draughted pinnaces, were sent to harry any vessel attempting to break the blockade, Rainsborough set about exploiting the divisions ashore. Though admitting to the King that 'I am not skilled at making articles of peace…' he appeared adept enough to Sidi Mohammed with whom he knew Harrison had had dealings. His timing was fortuitous; 'The Saint' needed help to reassert his master's authority and retain his own position and agreed to an alliance with the English.[20] Through an interpreter – probably an English merchant – Sidi Mohammed gave Rainsborough a personal indication of his goodwill by releasing seventeen of his personal slaves and negotiations opened on 5 May. By the 20th Rainsborough was able to report a degree of success to London, and to seek royal ratification. This arrived by mid-July, along with the reinforcement of two ships, including the frigate *Swan* with two-months' victuals and money for the squadron to purchase fresh meat from Tetuan.

With Rainsborough's ships offshore and Sidi Mohammed's levies on land, the pirate stronghold was besieged. Writing of their exploits Rainsborough's flag-captain, John Dunton, stated that:

> We shot at the castle and into it, and over it, and through it, and into the town, and through the town, and over it, and amongst the Moors, and killed a great many of them… Our men did sink many of their ships and shot through many of their houses…

Dunton's enthusiasm for this destruction was understandable. A ship-master himself, not a naval officer, he had been held captive in Algiers and had been redeemed the previous year. Moreover his only ten-year-old son remained enslaved at Algiers, with little hope of release. Such personal baggage was widespread in the English fleet, reflected by the furious temper of the attack: the effect of the bombardment surprised Ali el-Kasri and his soldiers.

Lying at anchor on a lee shore with the open Atlantic at his rear often rendered Rainsborough's situation near untenable, but he stuck – literally – to his guns: 'We did so torment them by sinking and burning their ships that they were stark mad and at their wits' end,' he wrote. The resistance of several vessels was met by extreme force; the English 'did heave fire pots … and did burne three men of them to death, and did kill fifteen men of them outright'. Meanwhile Sidi Mohammed's troops 'hath beleaguered' New Salé 'with twenty thousand men, horse and foote and burnt all their corne.'

The English ships began to receive a trickle of escaped slaves, including Frenchmen, Spaniards and Dutchmen, swept up by the pinnaces scouring the shore, or finding their own way out by swimming or local boat. These rapidly increased to a flood as resistance caved-in and parts of New Salé fell, while pressure upon the besieged compelled them to seek their own terms as the intense bombardment continued. Eventually, after three weeks, an assault was made on the *kasbah* and finally, towards the end of July, Ali el-Kasri sought terms. He surrendered on the 28th.

Rainsborough now entered negotiations with the distant Sultan through the intermediary of Sidi Mohammed. More slaves were released as these progressed and by 8 August the squadron was over-crowded with almost 350 hungry men and a score of indigent women seeking food and accommodation. With the season of equinoctial gales approaching, Rainsborough now ordered Carteret to embark all the released captives in the *Antelope*, *Hercules*, *Providence* and *Expedition* and withdraw north, to lie off the Spanish coast west of Gibraltar for as long as his stores permitted, before returning home and advising the Lords of the Admiralty of his arrival. While so doing, Carteret was to intercept any corsairs that came in sight. 'I pray God bless you,'

Rainsborough wrote cordially to his vice admiral, 'and cause some Algiers men-of-war or their prizes to come foul of you'.

Soon afterwards, off Salé the weather interrupted contact with the shore but on 12 August Rainsborough had received further reinforcements with the arrival of the *Mary Rose*, a king's ship under another mercantile Elder Brother, Captain Thomas Trenchfield, and the little 80-ton pinnace *Roe Bucke* under Master Broad of Rotherhithe. Trenchfield had been ordered into the man-of-war because her naval commander, Captain Lewis Kirke, had refused to serve under Rainsborough and had instead, been turned out of his man-of-war and sent to Trenchfield's own hired armed merchantmen, the *Margaret*, 'to his greate discontent'. There was clearly a peevish resentment by the naval gentlemen to serving alongside merchant officers raised at a stroke of the king's pen to high commissioned status. Sadly Carteret had been party to it, in a secret correspondence with Admiral Sir John Pennington who in turn had passed the tittle-tattle on to the Admiralty Secretary, Edward Nicholas.[21]

Rainsborough seems unaware of Carteret's attitude. His letters to the vice admiral were cordial and he had himself asked that Carteret be appointed to serve his deputy. Moreover he had detached Carteret on an independent task, clearly confident in the latter's abilities, if not his loyalty. Carteret had stood on and off in Cadiz Bay to protect any English ships homeward bound 'in the vintage time' with cargoes of wine until, having taken in water on the 21st, he sailed for England, sighting four 'Turks' but failing to capture them. Some of the bad-blood that clearly permeated the squadron seems to have leached out on the homeward passage of the detached squadron. 'Notwithstanding strict orders not to leave my company...' Carteret reported to the Admiralty, Captain Harrison in the *Hercules* and Thomas White in the *Expedition* reached Falmouth on the 20 September, having been separated on 'the night of the 16th about 100 leagues off Land's End, which might have proved very prejudicial, for I then had little hope to recover the English coast so soon as I have done, and I had but 11 days victuals left'. This, as Captain Chaplin points out, was clearly a 'somewhat petulant' complaint, for Carteret's plea that he was in difficulties is a fabrication, set at nought by the outcome. On their arrival at Plymouth on the 20th, Harrison reported he thought Carteret was already at Plymouth, a port east of Falmouth. In fact the vice admiral made moan from St Helen's Road, an anchorage off Portsmouth, where he had arrived on the 21st, clearly having outrun the possibly slower *Hercules*.

Back off the Moroccan coast the indefatigable Rainsborough secured, through Sidi Mohammed, an undertaking that the Sultan of Morocco would forbid his subjects to trouble the English coasts again – 'a promise very soon broken' – after which he had left Salé. Flying his flag in the *Leopard* with the *Mary*, *Mary Rose* and *Roe Bucke* in company, he headed south for Safi, the port for Marrakech. Here he hoped to treat for the release of a further thousand slaves who had been sold on to the *mastabas* of Tunis and Algiers. Shortly after anchoring he received on board an ambassador sent by Sultan Moulay Zidan, along with an Arabic-speaking English merchant named Robert Blake. Blake had settled in Safi and so conducted himself as to have come to the notice of the sultan. Moulay Zidan had accordingly appointed Blake the Farmer of Customs for all his ports. On 19 September, having embarked an entourage including other merchants and 230 liberated slaves, Rainsborough's ships weighed anchor and headed back along the coast, departing from Morocco on the 21st.

The ships arrived in The Downs fifteen days later, Rainsborough, Blake and the ambassador landed at Deal while the *Leopard* and her consorts worked round to the Medway. The embassy was received 'with much display and trumpetting'. 'Though it was night, the streets were almost as light as day'. The Moroccan ambassador, Blake and the merchants all rode into London on Arab steeds, richly dressed and wearing gold chains, to be met by the robed Lord Mayor and Aldermen. Behind came a large number of the freed slaves dressed in white, some of whom had been captive for thirty years. On Sunday 5 November the ambassador was received by King Charles and presented to the king several saker falcons and four Arab stallions, led by red-liveried Moorish grooms. Richly caparisoned, they were 'the choicest and best in all Barbary, and valued at a great rate, for one horse was priced at fifteen hundred pounds'.

Rainsborough's achievement was noteworthy, not least because he had maintained a blockading force off an exposed coast for five months but, while it might indeed be 'a happie turn for all Christendome', it failed both in terms of the numbers of prisoners released, and as a means of 'keepinge this towne [of Salé] from ever haveinge any more men of warre'. In the end the treaty with the sultan proved worthless largely because it was unenforceable. Besides, though the depredations of the 'Sallee Rovers' might have been laid in temporary abeyance:

> The activities of the Algerines more than made up. The Irish Sea was so dangerous that it became acutely difficult to send money to Dublin to pay the King's little [naval] squadron there. In 1640 Algerine pirates captured the English ship *Rebecca* with £260,000 in Spanish silver on board, badly damaging the English reputation as well-armed and reliable carriers in a dangerous world.[22]

By 1642 Parliament was debating means by which ransom money could be raised and in 1646 the members commissioned the merchant Edmund Cason to Algiers to ransom as many of the 3,000 men, women and children as his purse allowed. After prodigious enquiries he located about 750, but those who had been 'turned Turkes through beatings and hard usage' fell into the black hole of irredemption. Enormous sums were demanded of Cason; while £25 might free a fit man, women came a great deal more expensive. As Giles Milton points out Sarah Ripley from London cost £800, Alice Hayes of Edinburgh £1,100 and Mary Bruster of Youghal 'a staggering £1,392 – more than thirty-six times the average'. Cason liberated 244 slaves, leaving the others in states of absolute anguish. 'Deny us not your prayers,' wrote Thomas Sweet, 'if you can do nothing else'.

The problem of wholesale abduction was not confined to England and her ships. Spain was especially targeted, the town of Calpe being sacked in 1637 with the loss of 315 women and children, while the corsairs continued to raid as far north as Norway and west to Newfoundland. Nevertheless England, with her growing merchant ship-ping, was particularly vulnerable. In 1645 the first vessel from Massachusetts was attacked and later the newly appointed Governor of Carolina, Seth Southwell, was taken by 'Sallee Rovers'. Fortunately King Charles II soon afterwards arranged for his exchange, but the problem was not to go away for many, many years yet.

Nor were the Barbary pirates the only problem, for while they were largely clear of the North Sea, on the east coast of England they were replaced, as Rodger points out, by 'the Dunkirk privateers and the Armada of Flanders…' Such horrors were, many Puritans thought, divine judgement against the 'Great Malignant', a just punishment for the crimes of King Charles and a mockery of his magnificent fleet, most of whose seamen went unpaid and improperly fed. Problems of international piracy were to be set aside as England descended into bloody civil war.

The divisions that would shortly rend England affected the lives of Rainsborough and his captains. Although Rainsborough accepted a gold chain, a medal valued at £300 and his pay as an admiral at £2 *per diem*, he declined the knighthood the king offered. Was this an indicator of his politics? Perhaps; with the exception of Carteret, most of his captains declared for Parliament when it came to push-of-pike in 1639, while Carteret went on to distinguish himself as an ardent royalist.[23] Ironically, since he attacked English shipping during the Civil War, he was ultimately admitted as an Elder Brother and, in 1664, did not disdain to be elected Master of Trinity House, but all this lay in the future. In 1639, the majority of the brethren of Trinity House sup-ported the Parliamentary cause, not least because the first two Stuarts had 'whittled away' at some of its rights and privileges.

In general 'The maritime class was in sympathy with the general climate of opinion in London' and in January 1642 after the king's attempt to arrest the rebellious five members in the Commons, 'the port [of London] and the riverside rose, and seamen came flocking to the City to pledge their support for the Parliament'.[24] The Royal Navy mutinied, an action, in Clarendon's words, 'of unspeakable ill consequences to the King's affairs'. In 1642 Parliament wished for a loan from Trinity House and this was resisted by the then Master, another irony, for it was that old pirate Sir Henry Mainwaring. He had been elected Master of the Corporation in 1642 but at the instigation of Parliamentary hard-liners, he was soon removed from office for his roy-alist sympathies.[25] Many of the brethren had, like Rainsborough and his colleagues, been active in the service of the state and continued thus under the new regime. One, Captain Richard Swanley, captured a ship laden with Irish soldiers loyal to King Charles and on their way to serve him; they were thrown overboard to drown.

As Trinity House itself was caught between the warring factions of the rebel side, Parliament and the New Model Army, its members found their own salvation. The span of their varied careers is of interest, ably demonstrating the professional and technical accomplishments of master-mariners of the day. Brian Harrison, who in addition to having been master of merchant ships had commanded a privateer, served the Commonwealth Navy as captain of the *Vanguard* and the *Rainbow*. Despite this, he was re-elected to Trinity House when it was reconstituted at the Restoration. Trenchfield was also a privateer who took several rich prizes and in 1640 he was appointed by the Council of State as the Trinity House member on a commission formed to survey Dover Harbour as an anchorage for the king' ships. On his death four years later Trenchfield, who had recorded 'that he had commanded good ships for thirty years and never made a voyage that was not prosperous for all concerned,' endowed four new almshouses on the Corporation's Deptford estate.

Captain George Hatch of the *Mary* remained in command of armed merchant-men. The two pinnace commanders, Thomas White and Edmund Symons, served the Commonwealth Navy in armed merchantmen, one of which took part in the action with the Dutch off Leghorn on 4 March 1653, when White's *Sampson*, was captured. He later commanded the *Centurion* and the *Old James* after the return of the king, becoming Admiralty Agent at Dover and a surveyor for the Navy Board.

As for Rainsborough himself, he was named captain of the *Sovereign of the Seas* just after her building in 1638, a most prestigious appointment given the contro-versy surrounding the opulence of her decorations, her extreme size, armament and expense, but the ship was not commissioned in time for operations that year and he appears to have then retired ashore to manage merchantmen in which he had an interest. He was part-owner of the 200-ton *Confidence* of London, which after due certification was allowed twenty iron guns, and in April 1638 he sailed for Massachusetts with settlers. He was among the petitioners who unsuccessfully sought to set up the Poor Seamen's Fund to be administered by Trinity House mentioned earlier and he submitted a paper recommending that 10,000 pieces of ordnance should be held in store ready to arm a force of colliers and other coastal craft as a naval reserve, urging the superiority of these small but solid ships, a point of view endorsed by James Cook 130 years later. As the country endured the hor-rors of civil war Rainsborough was made MP for Aldeburgh, holding the seat until his death in early 1642, prior to which he been involved with the provision of transports to support army operations.

Sadly, in December 1640, he had also been confronted with stark evidence of the failure of his expedition against the Sallee Rovers. Rainsborough was one of two men chosen to 'represent to the King that 10 sail of Turkish pirates were harassing our Western coasts, and to urge upon the King that two ships... should be forthwith sent to scour the seas'.[26]

When England emerged from the chaos of Civil War it was under the Commonwealth. Trade had suffered during the hostilities but had, nevertheless, con-tinued. The commerce between England and colonial America and the West Indies had done well and consequently continued to attract the attention of pirates who were now augmented by both a naval force claiming legitimacy from the exiled claimant to the throne, Charles Stuart, and the Dutch. Of these three, the Dutch were the greatest danger.

Relations between the two countries had been strained since the friction of competition in the East Indies and the events at Amboina. The final independence of the United Provinces from Spain in 1648 – at the end of the Thirty Years War in Europe – made the Dutch less eager to conciliate with England, while independent economic survival increased a very necessary Dutch maritime activity. Curiously, the newly republican Dutch were appalled by the execution of King Charles I in January 1649; for their part the English, with good reasons, were suspicious of the political motives of William of Orange, the future Dutch *Stadtholder*, who was related by marriage to the displaced Stuart dynasty. Civil strife in England had resulted in the seizure of Dutch ships by both sides and a continuing insistence on the part of the Commonwealth navy to stop and search Dutch merchantmen only worsened relations.

Application of theoretical economics, arising from the intellectual turbulence of the times, only exacerbated the nation's problems. Amongst a torrent of promulgators, the pamphleteer Thomas Mun advanced arguments in favour of the management and manipulation of foreign trade and currency, a theory that became known as Mercantilism. Mun expounded the attractive notion that the world's trade was relatively stable in quantitative terms, but that in order for a nation-state to secure its own well-being it was axiomatic that it could do so only at the expense of another. It followed, therefore, that the regulation of trade, of the flow of money and of both agricultural and industrial production, was a vital responsibility of Government. To ensure this dynamic favoured a particular country, military intervention was consequently if intermittently necessary, an argument lent weight in England by the acknowledged results of James I's neglect of a navy and the ensuing commercial disasters. In such a climate any attempt to make some sort of a union between Europe's two leading Protestant states broke down, and in 1651 the English 'Rump' Parliament revived the ancient Navigation Act of 1381.

The First Dutch War broke out the following year. Despite the maritime competence and martial valour of the Dutch, it was a victory for the English. Driven to trade outside Europe following their break from Spain, the geographical position of England astride their homeward trade routes rendered all Dutch shipping vulnerable to English interdiction. The complexities of the Dutch system of provincial admiralties complicated their ability to field a cohesive feet and, moreover, the shallow home waters of The Netherlands prevented them from building ships of sufficient size to meet the weight-of-metal flung by the broadside of a larger English battleship operating in the line-ahead that was now established as the orthodox deployment for naval engagements.[27]

On the opposing side, the so-called Ship-Money fleet that the late Charles I had unpopularly laboured to build-up, came into its own under the ruthless centralisation of Parliamentary control. One of the reasons men of Rainsborough's stamp and family – men from mercantile backgrounds – rose in the Commonwealth navy was to replace the loss of royalist officers, like Carteret. While in 1642 the Parliamentary navy was initially put under the control of the Earl of Warwick, who as noted had himself had experience at sea as a privateer-commander, fighting squadrons were commanded by men who converted as readily to flag-officers as Rainsborough and company had converted to army officers. Soldiers both, Robert Blake and George

Monck became 'Generals-at-Sea' and what they lacked in nautical skill was supplied by merchant commanders – who all understood the crude tactics and weapons of the day – like Rainsborough and his son Thomas, who in 1747 briefly commanded the entire Parliamentary navy. The war with the Dutch ended in 1654 when Oliver Cromwell, as Lord Protector, in proclaiming that there was 'a sufficiency of trade' for both Dutch and English economies flew in the face of Mun's philosophy. The truth was, though it was not to be resolved until two further wars had been fought with the Dutch, that the success of Parliament's Generals-at-Sea had aggrandised the English position considerably. Indeed the English were poised to supplant the Dutch as a major maritime power.

Of immense importance to the subsequent history of the English, and later the British, merchant marine was the resurrection of the English Navigation Act. This stipulated that the only cargoes that could be brought into English ports in foreign ships were those originating in their own countries. As international carriers it effectively put the Dutch out of business. A secondary and cumulative but, in the short term highly significant advantage accrued by the English as a result of three Dutch Wars, was the acquisition of a number of Dutch *fluyts*. These capacious cargo-carriers were easily handled by small crews and, moreover, could be adapted in different configurations for various trades. The number of variants on the type, whose origins were attributed to one Pieter Janszoon Liorne of Hoorn (after which port Van Schouten named the feared cape on the far side of the world), had long excited envy among English seamen. Seven men and a boy could handle the smaller *fluyt* of 150 tons burthen in the Norwegian timber trade and as early as 1603 Sir Walter Ralegh complained that where thirty English sailors were required to man a 100-ton ship, ten Dutchmen could do the same in a *fluyt*.

Fluyts were built as large as 800-tons for voyages to the East Indies, but the lower tonnages of 200–500 were the most viable, the *Noortsvaeders* and *Oostervaeders* trading to Norway and the Baltic. Armed as *Straetsvaeders*, they made Mediterranean voyages, but were also fitted as whalers for the Spitsbergen fishery. They and their derivatives, the capacious *boeijrs* and *busses*, were also snapped up enviously as useful prizes by the English. In time English shipbuilders built their own version, the 'pink', but *fluyts* were copied and, anglicised as 'fly-boats', and they rapidly increased the size of the English merchant fleet.

This expansion was aided by rebellion in Spain and France, and by war between the two, all of which allowed the newly constituted English navy a hitherto unprecedented freedom of action. Cromwell, who well understood the uses of sea-power pursued an aggressive policy, using the fleet not merely as an instrument of brute force, but as a means of intimidation. In particular he sent Blake to scour the Barbary coast. On 4 April 1655 the General-at-Sea cut up the shore batteries at Porto Farina, some 20 miles east of Bizerta and, carrying a light sea-breeze into the harbour, destroyed a squadron of nine Tunisian corsairs without loss. Blake went on to blockade Cadiz and here he received warning that the *flota*, the annual Spanish treasure fleet from South America, was at sea. This news was brought to him by Captain David Young, the master of the *Catherine* which was then returning from a voyage to Brazil. Young had previously served as a lieutenant aboard the man-of-war *Amity* and knew the value of his intelligence. On 12 April confirmation arrived when William Saddleton, commander of an English privateer, reported the Register ships at Tenerife where they were compelled to await the raising of the blockade by Blake's force. On 20 April 1657, Blake's squadron swept into Santa Cruz de Tenerife and annihilated the entire Spanish force.[28]

Cromwell's consolidation of power stabilised the fiscal uncertainties that had prevailed during the struggle between king and parliament. Parliamentary victory also challenged the rights that derived from the crown's authority, all of which greatly assisted the emerging commercial aggression of English merchants and their active proxies, the masters of their vessels. As touched upon earlier, failure went hand-in-hand with success and the cost in the lives of seamen is now incalculable. The pushy London merchants under Maurice Thompson made a disastrous attempt to found a colonial settlement in Madagascar – an idea successfully copied later by pirates displaced from the Caribbean – however the burgeoning slave-trade, of which more later, had created stations along the Gold Coast at Anomabu in 1639, at Takoradi in 1645, 'Cape Coast' in 1650, and in the fever-ridden Bight of Benin.

In addition to the powerful mercantile communities in London and Bristol, the Scots were also active, though only partially successful in the Scottish Guinea Company, which had been founded in 1634, and less so in Nova Scotia, where a grant of land had been made by King James to Sir William Alexander in 1621. Although touched by the Cabots, the French were already present, naming it Arcadia, and they were granted possession by the Treaty of St Germaine-en-Laye in 1632, but constant quarrelling and interference with the fisheries, persuaded Cromwell to send a force to retake the peninsula in 1654, though Charles II was to return it to France by the Treaty of Breda of 1667. In 1713, under the terms of the Treaty of Utrecht, Nova Scotia again became British, though colonial quarrels were to trouble the territory until in 1763, under the Treaty of Paris, the French renounced all title.

Despite Drake's assertion of having claimed New Albion which lay just beyond the Appalachian Mountains and a mere ten days march from the head of the James River, such imperial pretensions were barely acknowledged at this time, for the emerging 'First British Empire' remained chiefly a matter of the total domination of the British archipelago. It was upon the assumption of title to Ireland that the parliament at Westminster arrogated to itself the cognomen 'imperial', though the colonies in North America would soon be seen as encompassed within the empire. As for immediate preoccupations nearer home, Cromwell turned to the mercantile marine for the military transports needed to transport the New Model Army to Ireland and Scotland. For this merchants, largely orchestrated by the Trinity House and the policies of Rainsborough and his colleagues, fulfilled their old role of supporting the state, though less with auxiliary men-of-war, as with logistical support. 'Taking ships up from trade' for military purposes would become a feature of imperialism as the empire expanded.

The death of Cromwell in 1558 and the failure of the Government of his son, Richard, created a constitutional crisis. The old schism between the army and parliament re-emerged, producing a period of utter confusion. This was largely resolved by an exasperated former General-at-Sea, George Monck, who had reverted to his original trade of soldiering. In November, Monck famously marched south from Coldstream on the Scottish border. Such was the vacuum of power and Monck's reputation that, without fully revealing his intentions, he stabilised parliament, refused the post of Lord Protector for himself and opened negotiations with the exiled Charles Stuart. A wiser man than his father, Charles made an astute and conciliatory declaration from the Dutch city of Breda in April 1660, which was unconditionally accepted by parliament. Charles was declared king on 8 May and landed in Kent on the 29th. Monck was rewarded with the dukedom of Albemarle and soon afterward hoisted his flag as admiral in the Second Dutch War.[29]

Ever since its passing, the Dutch had resented the English Navigation Act, a situation made worse by a second act in 1660 and a third in 1663. These limited amounts of colonial produce, confining their carriage to English vessels, while forbidding the colonies to import cargoes in foreign ships. Although angering and further displacing the Dutch as international carriers, the Navigation Acts did tend to encourage English colonial shipping, subsequently a matter of some moment, as we shall see. Fuelled by rivalry, fighting broke out between the English and Dutch in West Africa in 1661, where it lasted intermittently for two years, and on the other side of the Atlantic the English captured New Amsterdam in 1664. Mercantile lobbying secured the interest of the king's brother, James, Duke of York, but Charles was not eager to go to war with his quondam hosts – who had made both him and his brother the handsome gift of a brace of yachts – until it was forced upon him in 1665. The involvement of France, and also of Denmark, whose ancient rights over the passage of the Øresund, inhibited English trade with the Baltic, complicated the issue, while defeat at sea augured ill. Ashore the plague of 1665 was followed by the burning of much of London the next year; meanwhile Dutch incursions into the Thames estuary, fears of invasion, heavily increased taxation, growing opposition and a decline in trade, drove the near-bankrupt Charles to sue for peace in May 1667. Lack of money compelled the immediate laying up of the king's fleet in the Medway, whereupon the Dutch fell upon Sheerness and the men-of-war moored in the river. The humiliating destruction of many of his most important warships and the subsequent enforced blockade of the Thames forced Charles to sue for a peace that was concluded at Breda in July.

One consequence of this humiliation was to enable Louis XIV to build up a formidable navy that would, in other hands, pose a threat for the next century and a half. Of more immediate importance was Charles's conclusion of an alliance with Louis at Dover in 1670, binding England to France's support against the Dutch. Although Charles cunningly avoided a promised conversion to Catholicism that would, he knew, cost him his throne, his fleet failed to avoid naval humiliation after he was obliged to support his ally in March 1672. In a series of brilliantly conducted defensive actions, the Dutch held the advantage while anti-Catholic agitation in England removed James, the Catholic Duke of York, from office as Lord High Admiral.

Dutch fortunes rose along with those of the House of Orange whose Prince Willem became *Stadtholder* and soon secured alliances with Spain, Brandenburg-Prussia and Denmark, the last two of which again affected English trade and naval supplies. Meanwhile Dutch propaganda resonated with continuing anti-papist sentiment which played upon a pervading sense that the restored monarchy was leading the English to a betrayal of Protestantism. Charles II was rumoured to have converted to Catholicism on his death-bed in 1685 and his lack of legitimate issue had placed his brother, the Duke of York, upon the throne as James II. Such was the indignation that this and the imposition of all the evils that war thrust upon the middle and mercantile classes, that parliament refused the king further funds. England swiftly made peace with the United Provinces at Westminster in 1674.

Although one of James II's bastard half-brothers was to have an effect upon the history of the mercantile marine, of more immediate consequence was James's unwavering Catholicism. This provoked the Glorious Revolution of 1688 that brought his distant relative by marriage, the Dutch *Stadtholder* Willem, to the English throne as William III. Jointly regnant with his Stuart wife Mary, sister of Charles I and the deposed James II, William ensured both the Protestant succession and a defusing of the commercial hostility between England and the United Provinces of The Netherlands.

While James's deposition fuelled further fires in Ireland, the embers of which yet burn, he had made a contribution. His service as sea was noteworthy: he was a competent seaman, a talent not always possessed by flag-officers of the period, let alone royal dukes, and an enthusiastically competitive yachtsman.[30] In addition to the naval reforms he had overseen and in which Samuel Pepys had such a hand, was the granting of a new charter to Trinity House, further strengthening the position of that institution and increasing its influence over merchant seafarers, pilotage, beaconage and ballastage, if not merchant shipping itself.[31] Having somewhat cynically and briefly appointed Pepys a captain in the Royal Navy for the purposes of his sitting on a court-martial – a matter which much tickled the diarist's self-conceit – James had ensured his protégé's installation as Master of the Corporation.

Despite the turbulence of these years and notwithstanding the national humbling of the late two Dutch Wars, once the Baltic had been reopened, English commerce bounced back. Elsewhere too, trade picked up. West Indian sugar was by now a widely available and modest luxury, and in 1670 Charles II had granted a charter to Governor and Company of Adventurers trading into Hudson's Bay. This had followed a submission by two French adventurers, the brothers-in-law Médard Chouart and Pierre Radisson, who had been heavily penalised by the French royal customs officials for their presumption in taking furs and not passing through the toll-exchanges of the St Lawrence River. In 1665 the two men appeared in London and so impressed

King Charles with the notion that the French corridor of the St Lawrence could be avoided by using Hudson's Strait that he gave them two ketches and an allowance of £2 per week for a speculative voyage. In a single season Chouart and Radisson made £1,400 from the sale of pelts in London, attracting the subsequent support of London speculators. By 1668 a trading treaty had been agreed with the Cree Indians and Fort Charles had been built on the southern shores of James Bay. Besides furs the charter granted to the new Hudson's Bay Company a monopoly to 'all Mynes Royall as well discovered as not discovered of Gold, Silver, Gemms and pretious stones'. In emulation of the powers granted to the East India Company, the additional authority was granted to 'make Peace or Warre with any Prince or people whatsoever that are not Christians'. From this incorporation grew a small fleet of smart ship-rigged vessels whose officers wore a distinctive uniform and who in time of war attracted naval escort as far westwards as the 20th Meridian.

The Royal Navy itself took longer to recover. It was to be involved in further fighting in the War of the English Succession, otherwise known as King William's War (1689–97). Action was mainly in the Channel where, following a serious reverse, it would emerge victorious over the French.[32] But such glories lay in the future. Beyond the Narrow Seas new challenges were arising, not least in Barbary where, in 1672 Sultan Moulay Zidan died, to be replaced by Moulay Ismail. This prince was to conceive the conceit of constructing a palace of such vastness and complexity that it would require the services of thousands of slave labourers, an ambition which led to an upsurge in piracy. Another attempt to suppress piracy was made by Rear Admiral Sir John Narborough when, between 1674 and 1677, he commanded an English squadron in the Mediterranean. His task was trade-protection, particularly of the Levant Company in the Eastern Mediterranean, but also that with southern Spain and other ports in the western basin from which dried fruit and wine were brought, and to which dried fish from the Newfoundland fisheries was carried. Trade with southern Spain was important for the mixed nature of its imports, but in particular for the value of its exported woollens. Periodic attacks on the Barbary coast were made, but with little effect. Six pirate vessels from Algiers were driven ashore near Cape Spartel by an Anglo-Dutch squadron in 1670, while seven more fell to Sir Edward Spragge off Bugia (Bougie) in 1671. Spragge burnt them, making 'lovely bonfires, which … was the most glorious sight…' Narborough concluded a quasi-treaty with the Bey of Tunis in 1675, but at the usual price of guns and ammunition that would only be turned upon the shipping of other Christian nations. In the following January Narborough made a daring attack on Tunis, and in this and subsequent operations succeeded in destroying eight pirate vessels. He also reached an agreement with Moulay Ismail, curtailing the activities of the 'Sallee Rovers' to such an extent that a delighted Pepys considered that the 'thorn is out of our foot'.

Pepys was overly optimistic. Although the acquisition of Tangier as part of the dowry of Catherine of Braganza, Charles II's queen, ought to have given the English an ideal forward base for such operations, the problem was too great and, like the Hydra, the lopping off of one head only guaranteed the speedy growth of another. Tangier was exposed, usually besieged and in augmenting its pathetic harbour by an enormous mole, expensive to maintain. Unsurprisingly it was abandoned altogether in 1682.

Unfortunately too, English success against the Barbary corsairs – although modest – was persuading many other Europeans to claim English nationality for their shipping, a subterfuge that so enraged the Algerines that in 1675 they overset the treaty concluded in 1672 and attacked not only English merchantmen, but English warships. Narborough's campaign culminated off Algiers where, in 1674, he succeeded in securing a large sum in compensation for two illegally seized English merchantmen. With this he liberated 'a great number of Christians of foreign nations', including 128 English slaves.

Narborough was followed by Arthur Herbert who in 1682 finally achieved an agreement with the Dey of Algiers which would last for over a century. This was not binding on the other Barbary states, however, and to a greater or lesser extent British merchant shipping ran in and out of the Mediterranean at some risk until the Royal Navy readdressed the problem after the defeat of Napoleon. Nevertheless, one remedy found in the 1670s was that of convoy as recommended by Trinity House. Introduced to cover the passage of merchant ships along the Barbary coast, convoy work became an unpopular but important naval obligation, necessitating the co-operation of merchants, shipowners and masters on the one hand, and the Admiralty and naval commanders on the other.

The varied fortunes of the naval service during the turbulence of the seventeenth century, the frequent rottenness of its ships, the indifference of its manning, the deficiencies of its officer corps and the failures in its administration – tackled eventually by Pepys – tends to obscure the fact that these were simultaneously being offset in no small measure by the mercantile sector.

Waller's claim that the English had made the sea their abode rings somewhat hollow if applied only to the navy, but not so if the full span of merchant shipping is taken into account. Apart from the contribution of merchant sea-officers – not to mention the co-opted skills of merchant seamen – to naval operations throughout the 1600s, and the eastern enterprises already alluded to, the English were increasingly powerful in the Atlantic. The Dissenting colonies of New England had followed the founding of Virginia by Sir John Smith in 1607 and rapidly expanded, both geographically and economically (and by 1692 the governor of Massachusetts was Sir William Phipps who had been a shepherd, then a ship's carpenter and had, for a while, run a shipyard on the Sheepscot River in what is now Maine). Maryland was established in 1632 by means of a proprietary land-grant from Charles I to Sir George Calvert as a refuge for displaced Irish Catholics; the colony was soon second only to Virginia in tobacco production. Under the Commonwealth, conflict with the Dutch had delivered Manhattan to the English state and the financially desperate Charles II had made grants of land to repay his debts to his supporters, even before his restoration, following the practice initiated by his father.

After the execution of Charles I in 1649, the exiled Prince of Wales had visited St Helier, on the Channel Island of Jersey, where Sir George Carteret – Rainsborough's former vice admiral – was an effective governor and raider of Parliamentary English shipping. As an earnest of his gratitude Charles gave Carteret a grant of land in the Americas, but there was little Carteret could do about claiming it until after the Restoration in 1660 when he and Lord Berkeley became proprietors of part of a general settlement of the lands acquired from the enemy in the Second Dutch War in 1665. Charles also conferred proprietorial status on his brother James, the Duke of York and future James II, thus New Amsterdam became New York, as did the adjacent territories, while Carteret's joint grant with Berkeley became New Jersey. The large territory of the Carolinas, named for the king and following the failed experiment at Roanoke, was also established in 1660. Rapidly undertaking the cultivation of rice, tobacco and indigo, the colonists spread southwards so that by 1670 a distinct colony of South Carolina had emerged.

Soliciting repayment for the loan of £20,000 that Admiral Penn had given the Stuart cause, the admiral's son, the Quaker agitator William, was reimbursed in 1681 by a land-grant on the Delaware River. In founding his Peaceable Kingdom of Pennsylvania, William Penn supervised the first building of Philadelphia which, within a century, had become the British empire's third richest city after London and Bristol. Originally part of Pennsylvania, Delaware itself was not to separate with its own legislature until 1704, acquiring its own executive six years later.

By the end of the century English colonies therefore extended from Penobscot Bay to the Savannah River, and although a no-man's land of seasonal fishery settlements along the Arcadian – or Nova Scotian – shores created constant bickering they, with Newfoundland to the north-east, provided a northern buffer with French Canada and the vast hinterland beyond. In the south the no-man's-land of a future Georgia kept the colonists distant from the Spanish territory of Florida, northern mandible of the Hispanic Caribbean.

These new lands of opportunity were rapidly populated by English and Scots settlers, some of their freewill, some displaced by rebellion, upheaval and enforced migration, such as the highland clearances following the Jacobite rebellions of the following century. These new economies were based largely on the production of large quantities of tobacco and rice. The use of tobacco had attracted disapproval from the start, copied as it was from the native Americans. James I had condemned it roundly, taxing imports heavily from 1604, and in some places smoking and chewing tobacco were flogging offences, but its use rapidly gained ground from its assumed therapeutic qualities. Tobacco was found to grow in southern England but local production was quashed by Government edict in order to protect Virginia from the threat of economic failure. By 1614 exports of Virginia leaf were an increasing component of east-bound cargoes and by 1700 some 17,000 tons of imported tobacco raised huge sums in excise duty for the crown. Of this about two-thirds was re-exported to European markets, thus further adding wealth to the carriers, while the subsidiary cottage-industry of cigar-rolling provided work for women on both sides of the Atlantic.

Although comfortably off families, from the losing side in the Civil War and after the Restoration those of the winning, migrated willingly, neither their numbers nor their inclination led them to the plantations unless as owners or overseers. Expansion of the plantation economies of tobacco, sugar, rice and cotton that were to dominate the American littoral from Connecticut to the Caribbean depended heavily upon vast numbers of manual labourers. This could only be provided for by imports of humanity. Although John Hawkins had embarked upon collecting slaves in 1583, these were shipped to the Spanish colonies and, long after the establishment of English settlements in North America, the main markets for English slavers remained those of the Caribbean. While the import of black African slaves would shortly underpin the economic viability of the middle and southern colonies of British North America, the horrors of this have largely obscured the first of the four great phases of wholesale movements of populations that were to provide employment for British shipping over the following two hundred years.

A desire to escape from the enormous religious, political and economic upheavals of the seventeenth century in the British Isles – as elsewhere – became commonplace among the young. Relief from poverty and intolerance could be found by engaging themselves as indentured labourers overseas. This legally binding but freely entered state, attracted thousands of young men and women who contracted to serve a term of between three and seven years in exchange for free passage, maintenance and, eventually, a small grant of money. Needless to say the system was abused; most of these hopeful aspirants finding themselves cheap labourers on plantations, or menial servants to the established colonial families who in many places thereby aggrandised themselves. In time, however, those completing their indentures were free to form a skilled or semi-skilled labour force that tended to migrate into the growing towns of the expanding provinces. The utility of such an expedient proved capable of extension and its economic success created a greater demand for labour, articulated by plantation-masters and their supervising overseers. This fed on a 'conviction that in England there were more men than jobs or land, while in the colonies there was more land than men to work it'. This was answered from England by the deportation of felons and ne'erdowells, paupers, vagrants, whores, schismatics and, following the rebellion of the Duke of Monmouth, Charles II's bastard, hundreds of wretched and misled West-Country rebels. But even these failed to satiate the demand and, in increasing numbers, black African slaves appeared on the quays of Savannah and Charlestown, South Carolina.

It is clear that such an upsurge in traffic, both human and commercial, created an enormous demand for shipping too. And not just home-provided ships from London, Bristol and the smaller but active ports of Devon and Cornwall: all along the colonial coasts grew a profusion of forest providing timber for shipbuilding. Shipbuilding, ship-owning, ship-broking and ship-mastering, soon became a feature of colonial life, not least because the production of commodities necessary for shipbuilding constituted those 'naval stores' of which the Royal Navy was in constant need, and encouraged native-built bottoms in which to derive further profit.

Inshore fishing and coasting was quickly superseded in importance by deep-water cargo and passenger carrying, with whaling following soon afterwards so that a vig-

orous colonial mercantile marine thrived under the English ensign, much as the
'Country-trade' was thriving on the other side of the world in the Indian seas. Such
a growing shipping industry combined with a new and indigenous economy. Having
sprung from a soil distant from England, this sought its own markets and looked south,
where in contrast to its own increasingly settled stolidity, the waters of the Caribbean
– theoretically the lake of Catholic Spain, but one whose waters were troubled by the
winds of change – sparkled with the sunlit glitter of seduction.

The chaos of the West Indies from which the English – and perhaps here we must
start to encompass Scotland in the greater entity of Britain – were to derive such a
bad name and also much material benefit, was caused largely by the Portuguese and,
more successfully the Dutch. For years before the English appeared in the West Indies,
New Spain and the so-called Spanish Main, those vast areas under nominal suzerainty
of the Spanish kings, had suffered a constant nibbling at His Most Catholic's dignity
by his enemies and rivals. The Portuguese first prised the oyster open by making
slave-smuggling into the Hispanic dominions a matter of some ease. Others followed,
bringing not only slaves, but manufactures and luxuries not obtainable directly from
Spain. Among these were the Dutch who had a slave station at Gorée in West Africa
and access to the manufactories of Germany and France.

 The rigorous enforcement of regulations to control their own prerogatives and privileges and prevent incursions by foreign interlopers was undertaken by anyone with an
interest, from the mercantile monopolists in Seville, to the viceroys and their subordinates in the Indies. These restrictions only resulted in disaffection among the colonists,
rendering them disposed to treat with whom they pleased and from whom they might
best reap advantages. This opportunist contempt by the king's own subjects weakened
the royal authority and encouraged the admittance of the eager, interloping traders.
Such a spiralling of cause and effect led to economic chaos. Thus, in their rebellion
against Spain, the United Provinces of The Netherlands found in the West Indies a
target much to their taste and talents. They also discovered vast reserves of salt at Araya,
near Cumaná in Venezuela which, having been denied their traditional source in
Portugal, they urgently resorted-to for their extensive fish-preserving industry. Largely
under the aegis of the Dutch West India Company, Dutch military operations in the
West Indies against Spain, and in South America against the Portuguese, were complex,
but their cumulative effect of undermining of Spanish hegemony was simple.

 Successive Dutch fleets carried out sweeps in the Caribbean which practically drove
 the local Spanish shipping from the sea; and in 1628 Piet Heyn, ablest and most
 celebrated of the company's admirals, in command of a fleet of thirty-one sail, surprised and intercepted the homeward bound *flota* off Mantanzas Bay, and captured
 the whole sailing almost without firing a shot. This triumph, achieved for the first
 time and not to be repeated for thirty years, yielded booty worth fifteen million
 guilders; enough to pay a dividend of 50 per cent to the company's shareholders…
 It ruined Spanish credit in Europe. In the West Indies it paralysed for a time both

communications and defence… Spain still possessed the power to make occasional counter-attacks … but she could no longer dispossess other powers or prevent their acquisition of the islands which she had neglected to occupy.[33]

Nor to any great extent did the Dutch, though other European nations gained toe-holds in the Indies.[34] Instead the great archipelagos of the Greater and Lesser Antilles were to become a cockpit for the British and French. First into the power-vacuum were the English, whose steps thither had at first been accidental. In 1609 the flagship of Admiral George Somers had been blown off course by a gale and ran aground on the uninhabited island of Bermuda. The survivors escaped in boats to Virginia where their accounts of the island's fecundity persuaded sixty colonists to abandon their ailing settlement on the mainland and head for the island.[35]

In 1624 John Powell, on a voyage home from Brazil, landed at Barbados and was so struck with the uninhabited island's beauty that he claimed it in the name of James I. In London he secured the backing of the merchant Sir William Courteen who, with some Dutch colleagues, supported a settlement from which further claims were made in the Virgin Islands. That same year Thomas Warner arrived at St Kitts with a party of would-be settlers and, although they found themselves sharing the island with like-minded French, the two parties agreed upon their own enclaves in the face of Carib threats. The Spanish dislodged them in a savage attack in 1629, but they soon afterwards returned to stay. In 1628 Nevis was colonised from St Kitts, followed by Antigua and Montserrat, although the settlement of Tobago and Lucia around 1640 was initially frustrated by Carib attacks. It is worth noting that at this time Cardinal Richelieu, in forming *Le Compagnie des Isles d'Amérique*, established Guadeloupe and Martinique, both devoid of Carib inhabitants.

Such, however, was the disorder at home that the legal grants of title were made with little proper consideration. 'The West Indian islands, before they fell into the planting of sugar canes, were in those early times thought so little of,' one commentator wrote, 'otherwise the grants would not have been so readily made'. What followed was a disaster for Courteen, who lost all his investments when Warner's backer, the Earl of Carlisle, had himself made 'Lord Proprietor of the Caribbee Islands'. Widespread disorder followed this feudal outcome and while Carlisle himself took little interest beyond the receipt of his dues, further confusion arose in 1650 when Lord Willoughby arrived as governor of all the islands under a lease from Carlisle and a commission from the exiled Charles Stuart.

All early attempts to turn the islands into productive entities met with frustration. In 1631 beautiful Barbados attracted fierce criticism from Sir Henry Colt for the slov-enliness of its farming. 'Your ground and plantation shows what you are, they lie like ye ruines of some village lately burned'. At the time about 4,000 inhabitants toiled at a mixed agricultural economy of subsistence-farming and cash-crop production. On small farms from 'five to thirty acres' in size, maize was grown for food, tobacco and cotton for export. The vast increase in Virginian tobacco, however, reduced its price to an unviable level and the fall in income had its effect on the settlers and their miserable indentured servants, particularly as they relied upon imports of salt-fish from Newfoundland. Meanwhile the population soared, rising eight-fold by 1640. Thereafter: 'White population in all these islands reached its peak in the middle of the sixteen-forties. Thereafter it declined rapidly and has never since recovered'.

English attempts to benefit from the acquisition of the islands began badly. The Dutch dominated the carrying trade 'not unnaturally, since trade was the whole life and livelihood of the [Dutch] state ... [and] Amsterdam was a great city of warehouses from which all Europe was supplied.' As in the case of the *fluyt*, fiscally and technically the Dutch were well ahead of the English.

> Their capital was more fluid ... their ships better designed for cheap and easy han-
> dling... They offered European goods at Lower prices, longer credit and cheaper
> freight rates. It was said, too, that they understood the problems of stowage better
> and took greater care of their cargoes ... and when tobacco became a drug upon
> the European market it was the Dutch who put the West Indians in the way of
> growing sugar instead.[36]

With particular relevance to tropical voyaging the Dutch were attempting to resolve the problem of *teredo navalis*, the wood-boring ship-worm.

However, this domination did not long outlast the consolidation of Parliamentary power in England. Indeed, it was largely to counter-act it that the Navigation Act of 1651 was invoked and, as we have seen, led directly to the first conflict with the Dutch. Thus the religious union of the two Protestant allies foundered, ruptured by the pragmatic matter of trade. But there were other, political and military consider-ations concerning the practical Cromwell. The Dutch were not the only forces at sea hostile to English trade. While Willoughby's rule was judicious, in London the Lord Protector worried not just that the islands might fall to the Dutch, but that they would succour the small royalist navy under Prince Rupert, or worse still, become a base for royalist operations. In fact, the islands were held to be in rebellion, their inhabitants clinging to their links with the Dutch not least to preserve their economy. Sir George Ayscue was accordingly despatched in 1652 and, on his arrival in the Indies, Rupert was compelled to seek help from the French. Cromwell also sent out gubernatorial officers who, while they did not expel all the royalist administrators for fear of chaos, did drive Willoughby to the so-called Wild Coast of Guiana where he founded a colony at Surinam, afterwards ceded to the Dutch by the Treaty of Breda.[37]

But beyond the immediate strategic considerations Cromwell perceived in the arguments of mercantilism an emerging rationale of a compelling nature capable of ruining the Dutch and reducing their economic power. Warwick's adventure was held to be in the Elizabethan tradition and aimed essentially against Spain. Now Puritan ambitions sought to further humiliate the Spanish, while dominating the 'Caribee Islands', discomfiting the royalists and further incommoding the Dutch. This policy became known as the 'Western Design', a grand plan different from anything that had gone before, a war of colonial acquisition financed and organised by the English state.

While it consisted of 'a combination of cupidity, religious fervour, and national vanity' worthy of Drake, 'Cromwell's project was entrusted to an ill-led, ill-armed mob, and its planning was largely based on inaccurate and prejudiced intelligence … and neither Admiral Penn nor General Venables was a Drake'.[38]

Arriving at Barbados in early 1655 and seizing eleven Dutch merchantmen anchored in Carlisle Bay, the expeditionary force then languished 'eating up the island'. Venables illegally augmented his forces by conscripting the island's militia and indentured men to the tune of 4,000. They were to make up half of his force. 'The Barbadians … were being punished for their contumacy' while the men so raised were 'so loose as not be kept under discipline, and so cowardly as not to be made to fight'. However, blaming the quality of the troops did not excuse military incompetence. Landing on Hispaniola in April this motley army found themselves ashore with a 30-mile march to their objective, the city of Santo Domingo. They also found themselves without water. Attacked by a smaller force of Spanish cavalry supported by infantry made up from local cattle-farmers, Venables was only saved from a rout by a force of the fleet's seamen landing to cover their embarkation.

That this disaster was reversed by a brilliant success resulted solely from the inability of Spain to hold her wide possessions in sufficient strength. Again embarked, Venables and Penn needed to make amends and serendipitously decided to make for Jamaica. Jamaica was a curiosity of Spain's empire, a marquisate under the nominal rule of the hereditary 'Admirals of the Indies', the descendants of Columbus. It had attracted the attention of English rovers before now: what was known to the English as 'Spanish Town' had been pillaged by Sir Anthony Shirley in 1596 and in 1642 it was raided by the privateer William Jackson, sent by Warwick and armed with a Parliamentary Letter-of-Marque. Attracted by these easy successes, Venables landed at Hunt's Bay and marched on Spanish Town: it fell with hardly a struggle. The Spanish governor Cristóbal Isasi took to the northern hills and, with the help of a handful of soldiers and a body of loyal slaves, maintained a long guerrilla war against the new garrison sustained for some years by occasional supplies from Cuba. The Spanish naval forces from the Indies had been hit so hard by the destruction of their heavy men-of-war by Blake at Teneriffe two years later that Isasi was on his own. The gallant Spaniard gave up the struggle in 1660 and Spain formally recognised Jamaica's loss in 1670, but Isasi's loyal slaves, brought to the island after the extermination of the native Arawaks, 'remained in the fastnesses of the Cockpit country and formed the nucleus of the redoubtable maroons'.

While Venables and Penn returned to face the Lord Protector's wrath, some members of the invading force were given land-grants. Most settled in the fertile valley of the Rio Minho but Jamaica – its name derives from the Arawak noun for the land of high winds – failed to attract colonists in the manner of earlier, pre-Civil War West Indian settlement. Unsuccessful attempts were made to encourage resettlement of Nova Scotians to Jamaica, an irony given the eventual and reciprocal deportment of the maroons, after periodic insurgencies, to that damp province at the end of the eighteenth century. Instead the island was systematically inhabited by 'a large influx of soldiers and of undesirable refugees, neither of whom made good settlers'. In fact it was soon as notorious as Tortuga as a refuge for harbouring buccaneers whose moral turpitude was far from the stiff morality of Cromwell's Puritan England and better reflected the licentiousness of the subsequent court of the restored Charles. That pragmatic and wily monarch set the reformed and knighted buccaneer Sir Henry Morgan to rule as lieutenant-governor over his unruly quondam brethren of the coast.

Morgan, the abominable doyen of these rogues, we shall come to presently. It was the vulnerability of the Spanish Empire in the Americas that attracted the rootless adventurers from England in particular, many of them outcast by virtue of their religion, politics or bad-luck. Coincidentally the growing British colonial settlements in North America – largely settled by men of similar robust stock – provided ready markets for cheap goods, or facilities for money-laundering. The early American colonists under proprietary or other forms of arbitrary Government, with their own courts and assemblies, remote from the control of parliament in London and *de facto* independent in mind and action, were the catalyst which provided the means by which was generated the heyday of piracy.

In the Caribbean, England's other colonies, particularly Jamaica, lying on the rim of a war-zone, found the temporary licensing of freebooters an evil necessity for self-evident reasons of defence. This cloaked those minded to eke out an existence by preying upon Spanish trade with a legitimate privateering commission, creating a class of sea-faring man who was a patriot in time of war, but a pirate when peace revoked his Letter-of-Marque.

Both London and certain provincial governors woke up slowly to the fact that piratical depredation might annoy an enemy, but when the enemy faded from view the gentlemen concerned became more of an embarrassment. Their continuing existence reduced customs dues, obstructed fair trade and made no merchant's investment safe. Some pirates, perhaps following the precedent of Sir Henry Mainwaring, bowed to the inevitable or seized the opportunity of pardons to reinvent themselves as gentlemen. Morgan was one such, but others chose to ignore the warnings to change with the times, ending up on the gallows like Avery and Kidd by way of a creaking legal system that sought to come to grips with what many regarded as an intractable problem.

In time of peace many of these drop-outs settled in a louche confederacy in what were claimed by Spain as the colonial provinces of Honduras and Campeachy. Here they sustained a loose style of life in logging encampments that supplied shipping with cargoes of logwood. This red-coloured timber grew in swamps and had been found first in Jamaica where its ability to produce a dark indigo dye enabled those clearing ground for use as plantations to offset their costs. It quickly became 'an article of necessity to the woollen manufacturers of Europe' and other sources were located in the Yucatan peninsula, near the creeks and inlets around Cape Catoche. As Richard Pares explains:

> The Spaniards … cut and sold it in the seventeenth century. The English seem to
> have come to the trade from buccaneering: first they plundered the logwood ships,

then they seized upon the piles of wood which lay ready cut near the creeks. Finally they settled down to cut it for themselves, especially after the serious attempts of the English Government to suppress buccaneering forced them to change their career. It was a life of hard work, up to the knees in swamp half the time, and heavy burdens to carry; but it was beguiled by drinking bouts and native women, and recommended itself to those who had been accustomed to live outside the pale of law and order, such as those young men who had escaped irksome indentured labour, religious persecution or the noose wielded by Judge Jeffries and the Bloody Assize.

The wholesale deportation of young men following Jeffries' more humane judgements of young rebels arose from the rebellion of Charles II's illegitimate son, the Duke of Monmouth whose ill-conceived attempt on the English throne was savagely put down at Sedgemoor by John Churchill, the future Duke of Marlborough. The plantations of the New World became a dumping ground for many rebels and it was from this colourful and lawless *milieu* that William Dampier (see Chapter Three) emerged to make his reputation as a 'pirate and hydrographer'.[39] Such young men repudiated authority and drifted into piracy in a kind of grand and meaningless delinquency, coining the name buccaneer from the original French *boucanier*, meaning cattle rustler and referring to their original habit of stealing beef on the hoof, butchering it and selling it to passing ships. From these buccaneers there arose natural leaders with nothing to lose, men who, like John Avery and John Ward, found they could become 'kings of a sort'. A few were psychopaths and like Edward Teach, who is better known as 'Blackbeard', gained notoriety; others, such as Kidd, reputedly made fortunes from raids on Spanish colonies. Most came to bad ends: Kidd was, like John Avery, hanged in about 1696 and Teach we shall meet later.[40]

With the Caribbean a paradise for piracy, most freebooting leaders obtained their ships by barratry, a fraud practised on a shipowner by stealing his ship. A plea of 1622 expressed anxiety on this point: 'Barratrie of the Master and mariners can hardly be auoided, but by a prouident care to know them', i.e. having an attachment between owner and master. Thereafter a buccaneer chieftain might improve his chances by taking over a prize if she were better suited to his ambition, creating a threat to all owners sending their ships to the Caribbean where, from about 1625, sugar began to be imported and a regular trade began. The problem persisted in the Caribbean owing also to the proximity of the Spanish colonies that beckoned with a brimming and illicit temptation. Moreover, freebooting operations retained that specious aura of glamour cast over random attacks on Catholic Spain ever since the days of Drake, and further encouraged by the examples of Warwick and Digby, attracting feckless and footlloose youths like Henry Morgan.

Morgan had arrived in the Indies as an indentured servant but soon escaped his bondage to join a group of buccaneers under Edward Mansfield. He was in command of a privateer by 1663 and took part in Mansfield's brief recapture of Providence Island and his raid on the San Juan River. When Mansfield died three years later, Morgan was elected 'admiral' by his colleagues. Attracting the notice of Jamaica's first governor, Sir

Thomas Modyford, in 1668 he was next commissioned to reconnoitre the Spaniards in Cuba, after which he was ordered to make an attempt to take Puerto Bello from whence had come rumours of a Spanish force intending to recover Jamaica. By a surprise attack on the fortifications, Morgan's men took the place by advancing at night through the surrounding swamps. They then blew the fortifications up, took an immense booty, fought off a counter-attack and tortured their prisoners. Morgan returned to Jamaica where Modyford was compelled to upbraid him for exceeding his commission. A sulking Morgan retired to Port Royal with his unruly men where they indulged in 'all sorts of vices and debauchery, according to their common manner of doing, spending with huge prodigality what others had gained with no small labour and toil'.

The following year Morgan fitted out a fleet of ten sail and made a demonstration before Cartagena, after which he headed for Maracaibo on the Spanish Main. Gaining little here or along the coast of the lake, he encountered three Spanish men-of-war on his way through the narrows. They had not only been sent to destroy Morgan's raiding force of *corsarios*, they bore a quantity of silver specie. In a furious engagement Morgan defeated the squadron, acquiring the silver loot with which he cunningly bought off Modyford's censure.

In 1670, following an ineffectual Spanish raid on the Jamaican coast, Modyford again commissioned Morgan, sending him to the Isthmus with a mixed and polyglot force of about 1,500 men. They sacked Rio de la Hacha, Santa Marta and again struck at Puerto Bello after which, in December, Morgan began a nine days march inland, took the castle of Chagre and boldly and brazenly attacked Panama City itself. The inhabitants resisted, sending herds of bullocks stampeding through the enemy lines, but this tactic only ensured a complete and vengeful destruction of the city after a two-hour assault. This was followed by the brutal massacre or torture of its citizens.[41]

Morgan returned to Jamaica to a vote of thanks from the island's council, but was summoned to London in 1672 'to answer for his conduct'. The raid on Panama had taken place after the formal conclusion of the Treaty of Madrid by which all Letters-of-Marque-and-Reprisal were revoked. Consequently Morgan's treatment of his prisoners was strongly disapproved of and he was subjected to official disgrace. But he had contributed to a shift in the state of affairs in the West Indies by which Charles II had acquired a firmer grip upon 'all the lands, regions, islands, colonies and dominions, situated in the West Indies or in any part of America, that the said King of Great Britain and his subjects at present hold and possess'. It was to prove rather more than the king could cope with.

Morgan's disgrace did not last long; he returned to Jamaica with his knighthood – granted in 1675 – intact, an appointment as lieutenant-governor of Jamaica, senior member of the ruling council and commander of the island's armed forces. Modyford had also been recalled, to be lodged in the Tower for form's sake, but his successors Lynch, Vaughan and Carlisle could do little to prevent the lawless elements in the island from alternately pursuing trade or rapine, according to their inclination. Nor could Morgan, for all his honours and titles, restrain his brethren. Six Jamaican privateers sacked Santa Marta again in 1677. The next year Captain Coxon, an old chum of Morgan, took several ships along the Honduran coast and appropriated quantities of cochineal, indigo and cacao. Refitting in Port Royal under Morgan's very nose, Coxon went on to sell his cargoes in Rhode Island.

Such beneficial links with the North American colonies were rapidly developing.[42] Transit times were far less than with Europe, the prevailing winds favoured regular traffic in both directions, while customs duties and other regulatory inhibitions were more easily minimised or tacitly avoided altogether. What started as a contraband activity was transformed into respectable trade, numbering the buccaneers' days and converting many to gentility, but they were far from extinct. Emboldened by success, Coxon and another pirate named Sawkins, crossed the Isthmus and, seizing some Spanish ships in the Pacific, raided southwards down the coast, returning by way of Cape Horn – an epic voyage of sorts. The outrage this provoked even Morgan to sit up and take notice and he attempted to stamp out the growing nests of outlawed seamen spread among the islands, but it took a naval squadron to appear in the Caribbean in 1685 to begin their final extirpation. Christopher Monck, the second Duke of Albemarle, arrived at Jamaica as governor in 1687, to find Morgan close to his end, drunk and dropsical, attended by quacks. Albemarle sent his own physician, Sir Hans Sloane, to minister to the obese and opulent villain, but it was too late. Morgan died in 1688 and was buried in Port Royal. In 1690 an earthquake destroyed the town, an event seen by many as divine retribution upon a sink of iniquity. But it was not yet the end of English piracy in the West Indies.

In due time, the planting of sugar worked by an immense influx of African slaves would make Jamaica the jewel in the Caribbean crown, for the island lay, as one commentator noted, 'in the belly of all trade' where it was to exert immense influence in the next century. Its shady, opportunist acquisition was about to make the fortunes of countless trading-houses on both sides of the Atlantic, in Britain and in her American colonies, and, in combining with events in the east, would transform the status of the British nation.

'He that is the Lord of the trade of the world is Lord of the wealth of the world,' Sir Walter Ralegh had written at the beginning of the seventeenth century. But while it looked at the time of the old adventurer's death upon the scaffold in the Tower of London as if the ambitions nurtured by the Elizabethan mariners had been abandoned and debased, within three generations the East India Company had consolidated its hold upon eastern trade and the Tudor slaving enterprises had matured into a carrying trade in human beings across the Atlantic. Yet none of this was possible without a growing expertise in seamanship and navigation.

NOTES

1. The relationship between Hudson and Greene is unclear, but is distinctly odd and may have been, in the moral climate of the day, 'unnatural'.
2. It is a perhaps unsurprising curiosity that these ship-names have been so enduring in British maritime history and prefigure the names selected for the ships of James Cook's third voyage.

3   In his mention of the mysterious Hawkeridge, Whitbourne alludes to the former having a curious encounter with a creature who 'did striue to come in to' a boat. This Whitbourne supposed 'was a maremaide'. Hawkeridge was married at St Dunstan's, Stepney, a church with maritime connections, especially with Trinity House, of whose fraternity Hawkeridge may well have been a member. Moreover, in 1643 Hawkeridge was one of two petitioners seeking a royal injunction to prevents foreigners from entering English and Irish ports without a pilot, arguing that this laxity enabled them to carry out surveys, establish channels and thus light the way for any potential enemy – particularly the Barbary pirates. See *The Mariner's Mirror*, Volume 13, Number 1, p51 *et seq*, 927, and Harris, *Trinity House Transactions, 1609–35*.

4. 'Pinnace' was a term used to describe a fast, armed ship until displaced by the Dutch term 'yacht'. Thereafter 'pinnace' was applied to describe a ship's boat which could be sailed as opposed to only rowed, though the noun's root lingered on in the term 'pink' for a small cargo-vessel.

5. Button's chief sponsor, Henry, Prince of Wales, had predeceased his father, James I, and so the old Scots king was succeeded by his second son, Charles I.

6. Verney came from a well-to-do Buckinghamshire family that distinguished itself in the Civil War.

7. Such was its reputation that Crookhaven was subject to a punitive raid by the Dutch in 1614.

8. This circumstance, as the late Captain W.R.Chaplin – himself an Elder Brother – has pointed out, led to the claim that some of these ships were naval, rather than privately owned merchantmen armed for self-defence. See Chaplin, *The Mariner's Mirror*, Volume 31, Number 4, pa 178 *et seq*, 1945.

9. Then a Younger, but afterwards an Elder Brother of Trinity House.

10. In 1654 Wolstenholme's house in Seething Lane became the office of the Commissioners of the Navy, so often mentioned by Pepys.

11. For further detail see Rodger, *Safeguard of the Sea*, Chapter 24, most appositely entitled *No More Drakes*, and Senior, *A Nation of Pirates, English Piracy in its Heyday*.

12. It failed to stop the Scots pirate Herriot who, after cruising unmolested in the English Channel for years, was taken by a Dutch admiral near Falmouth in 1624.

13. Unwisely a Dutch offer to purchase the colony had been rejected in 1639.

14. 'Ship Money' was an ancient tax revived in 1634 to get inland areas to pay money in lieu of the ships that ports provided for the service of the state. It was intended to allow a state navy to be built up and Hampden's resistance failed initially. He was tried in 1636 and served a year's imprisonment but Ship Money was declared illegal by Parliament in 1641 soon after the beginning of the English Civil War.

15. Rodger, *The Safeguard of the Sea*, p350.

16. Harrison afterwards revealed far worse treatment in a book of his experiences. There is little reason to doubt his claims of spectacular cruelties: the dismemberment of living prisoners, the castration of young ship's boys, and all manner of ritual humiliations of white Christians amused the Sultan and his courtiers, just as the reverse has occurred in our own age.

17. Father of Admiral Penn and grandfather to the Quaker William, founder of Pennsylvania.

18. The *Hercules*, commanded by Captain Brian Harrison, rear admiral to Rainsborough, had made voyages to Virginia and had, in 1633, carried settlers to Massachusetts.

19. Rainsborough afterwards remarked: 'The last yeare, by this time, they had brought in 500 of his Majestie's subjects and I verily beleve, had wee not come, they would have taken many more this yeare.'

20. The so-called 'Saint of Old Sallee' is nominated in Dunton's account in the preamble to the agreement reached with Rainsborough as 'the Right Excellent and Renowned Lord

Siddie Hannet Laishi'. In the body of the document he is referred to as 'the Lord Saint Siddie Hannet Laishi'. I have followed Giles Milton. One provision of the agreement of co-operation in an attack on New Salé was that in future that: 'If any ship or vessel of Merchandise by misfortune be cast away upon either of their Coasts [i.e. England or Morocco], that the people shall be intreated as friends, and whatsoever can bee saved of their Ship or Goods, shall freely remain to them … and to suffer them to carry away or sell what shall be saved.'

21. See Chaplin, *The Mariner's Mirror*, Vol. 31, No. 4, p185.
22. Rodger, *The Safeguard of the Sea*, p385.
23. Carteret became Comptroller of the Navy in 1639, succeeding his uncle as Governor of Jersey in 1643, an office he held with great skill. Armed with a commission as vice admiral he attacked English Parliamentary merchant shipping, which earned him a baronetcy in 1645. In December 1651 he was overwhelmed and compelled to surrender the island, personally escaping to join Charles II in exile in France. He returned with the king at the Restoration of 1660, whereupon he was appointed Treasurer of the Navy. In the following year he became MP for Portsmouth, but lost his naval post during the Second Dutch War. However, when the Admiralty was put into commission in 1673 Carteret was one of the Commissioners and remained so until his death in 1680. His name is often mentioned in critical terms by Pepys in connection with the Navy Board. As a colonial proprietor Carteret was a member of the Committee of Trade and Plantations and, his old Barbary connections reviving, was on the Tangier Committee.
24. Harris, *The Trinity House of Deptford, 1514–1660*, p33.
25. Mainwaring followed Charles II into exile but later returned to England to make his peace with the Commonwealth. He died in abject poverty in 1653. He was the author of a Seaman's dictionary.
26. Rainsborough's surviving children all supported the Parliament and the Commonwealth, his sons serving at sea and on land. The eldest, Thomas, having commanded men-of-war, raised troops for the Earl of Manchester's Regiment, largely officered by gentlemen from New England who had returned to support the Parliament. During the temporary halt in hostilities that ended the 'First English Civil War', Thomas was briefly put in command of the Parliamentary navy, but was unpopular owing to his over-bearing manner and radical politics. When Parliamentary schisms plunged England into its 'Second Civil War' Thomas reverted to the land-service. Colonel Thomas Rainsborough fought at Naseby, Bristol and Oxford, rising in Fairfax's favour. He later served ashore at the siege of Colchester but in October 1648 he was surprised at Doncaster and was mortally wounded. Rainsborough's second son William was also a mariner and lived for some time in Charlestown, Massachusetts, before returning to serve in the Parliamentary army. After the Restoration he was arrested and later returned to New England where his sister, Judith Rainsborough, had married Stephen, son of Governor Winthrop of Massachusetts. William later returned to England to serve as a Colonel of Horse, while another sister, Joan, married a captain in the Parliamentary army. The youngest son, Edward, settled for some time in Massachusetts, but also owned land in Middlesex. Owning land on both sides of the Atlantic, Edward was clearly an early and, in the terms of the times, a regular trans-Atlantic traveller.
27. The huge 100-gun *Sovereign of the Seas*, to which Rainsborough was appointed as captain – and which Trinity House said was too large for English waters – had been one of Phineas Pett's most extravagant but effective line-of-battle ships. The first three decked man-of-war she was cut down and much of her decoration were removed under the Commonwealth when she was renamed *Sovereign*. After the Restoration in 1660 she was again renamed, this time as the *Royal Sovereign*. Having served in several actions, she was burnt in 1696 after a candle was overset.

28. The action was one of the most outstanding feats of naval arms. No treasure was taken since it had all been unloaded and moved ashore. Blake died on the way home aboard his flagship, the Commonwealth's State-Ship *George*, as she entered Plymouth.

29. Monck was also made Master of Trinity House on the Restoration, taking over from Alexander Bence, an old friend of William Rainsborough.

30. Both Charles II and James while Duke of York, enjoyed competitive sailing and effectively introduced 'yachting' to England by racing their Dutch-built *stadt-jachts* and ensuring the eclipse of the old English term 'pinnace' as noted above. They also unknowingly began a long etymological confusion as to the English spelling of the word 'yacht'. Phineas Pett wrote 'youathe', but elsewhere there are as many as fourteen variations. In any case the word originally meant 'a light, swift warship', deriving from the verb 'to hunt'.

31. Trinity House, though mandated in its wider responsibilities as, *inter alia*, a General Lighthouse Authority by successive Acts of Parliament, still runs its corporate business under the 1685 Charter of King James II.

32. First at Bantry Bay in May 1689 when a drawn battle was fought with the French, Louis having supported the Catholic James II's Irish campaign which ended in defeat at the Boyne the following year; second at Beachy Head in June 1690 when an Anglo-Dutch fleet, under Herbert, Lord Torrington, was soundly beaten by the Comte de Tourville. Then finally, in May 1692, at Barfleur and La Hogue, Admiral Russell smashed De Tourville, putting an end to James's attempts to reclaim his throne. James was supported by Louis in some state as James III at Sainte Germaine after which his son, the Old Pretender, and his grandson, the Young Pretender, made unsuccessful bids in 1715 and 1745 to unseat the Hanoverian dynasty that followed the last of the Stuarts, the heirless Queen Anne.

33. See Parry and Sherlock, *A Short History of The West Indies*, p50.

34. By the Treaty of Munster of 1648 the Dutch acquired Aruba, Curaçao, Saba, St Martin and St Eustatius. The Danes gained St Thomas (1671) and St John (1719), the Swedes St Bartholomew (1784).

35. Another odd discovery, though one without immediate issue, was made in May 1622 when the English ship *Trial* was wrecked on what became known as the Trial Rocks off north-west Australia. This was the first English contact with *Terra Incognita*.

36. See Parry and Sherlock, *A Short History of the West Indies*, p56.

37. After the Restoration Willoughby succeeded to the Carlisle rights and as governor of the English islands toiled to expand control of them, only to die in 1666 during an expedition against the French at Martinique.

38. See Parry and Sherlock, *A Short History of the West Indies*, p59 *et seq.*

39. For many years this brief, pejorative label adorned Dampier's portrait in the National Portrait Gallery.

40. While displaced and deracinated Englishmen interloped in Campeachy and Honduras, they had a French opposition in the 'filibustiers' of San Domingue.

41. Panama was never rebuilt on its old site.

42. The French islands, though subsequently of great importance, were of slower development than the English colonies, which throve thanks to their rapidly forged trading links with the North American colonies.

THREE

'THE ARTE AND MYSTERIE...'

The Science, Sinews and Society of Maritime Trade

Intellectual endeavour was not far astern of all this commercial aggression, indeed it was in part driven by it, with cosmographers rising like yeast in the ferment of ideas and expeditions that were launched in the succeeding two centuries. The early Tudor English initiatives on the fringes of the Renaissance were occurring against a background of increasing scientific absorption with the problems of cosmography, cartography and navigation. In 1567 the Fleming Gerhardus Mercator had devised a representational projection of the world on a flat sheet of paper which proved suitable for navigation from the Equator up to latitude 60° north and south and three years later his fellow countryman Abraham Ortellius had produced the first folio of sea charts.

Instruments that improved navigational accuracy and the ancillary skills essential to a safe passage were most important. Apart from a simple log, the lodestone and its derivative, the mariner's compass, had long been the almost sole prop to a ship's master, but to this and the impractical astrolabe were now added the cross-staff and more practical backstaff, or John Davis's quadrant. These measured the 'altitude', or angle between a heavenly body and the observer's horizon and by subtracting the result – corrected for refraction, height of eye, dip and so forth – from a right angle, provided the zenith distance, the angle between the observer's zenith and the particular heavenly body. Application of the sun or a known star's celestial latitude, or declination, would with a simple calculation give the observer's latitude. However, it was not until John Hadley, hitherto engaged in improvements in telescopes, refined these basic tools and produced his octant of 1731 that readings of real accuracy were possible. Hadley, by this time a Fellow and vice-president of the Royal Society, exploited the principle of double reflection which made one degree of arc on his octant represent

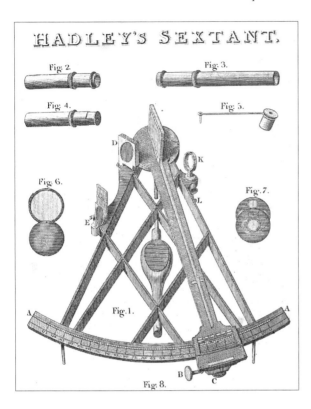

HADLEY'S SEXTANT.

Hadley took up a suggestion by Captain John Campbell RN that great benefit would derive from extending the quadrant's arc to sixty degrees, thereby producing the sextant. From 1757 until its eclipse by satellite navigation at the end of the twentieth century the sextant was an essential component of a navigator's equipment and its importance is often eclipsed by that of Harrison's chronometer. In fact both were required for the accurate determination of longitude. (Author's Collection)

two observed degrees. Hadley's octant quickly gained acceptance but was only able to measure up to ninety degrees. The practice of taking lunar observations for longitude, addressed later, required the measurement of obtuse angles and, upon the suggestion of Captain John Campbell of the Royal Navy, the arc was extended to sixty degrees, allowing observation of double that to be taken on the new sextant, which swiftly found favour among mariners after its introduction in 1757. Even after the supersession of 'lunars' by the method known as 'longitude by chronometer' – consequent upon the perfection of a sea-going time-piece – the extra arc was found invaluable for taking horizontal sextant angles in surveying. The sextant thus became the standard instrument for practical navigation at sea until it was demoted to a back-up role by the commissioning of a constellation of artificial satellites and establishment of an electronic global positioning system in the 1980s.[1]

Among the physicist and instrument-maker Robert Hooke's many achievements as an instrument-maker was the marine barometer, later improved in the nineteenth century by Robert Fitzroy of the Royal Navy. Other devices such as the station-pointer and surveying sextant rapidly improved matters during the nineteenth century when, at long-last, the business of charting the seas was put on a proper footing. Many mariners kept their own detailed notes of seamarks, landmarks, leads, soundings, and so forth in pocket folios and mariners on voyages of commercial exploration invariably sought their employer's approval by so doing. One early example of this is Baffin.

From this source of raw data, volumes of sailing directions and folios of local maps and charts had long been available, particularly for cabotage and pilotage, and were essentially produced for commercial rather than naval use. With an increasing demand for access to such information, not least because it enabled interlopers to penetrate sea-routes hitherto held to be exclusive, improvements in quality and a lowering of price ensured a widening market for these combined folios of maps and instructions.

Such sailing directions went under variety of names. The portolan chart belonging to the Mediterranean, was ancillary to the *portolano*, or comprehensive printed sailing directions, while the rutter, from the French *routier*, Portuguese *roteiro*, and Spanish *derroterro*, were books of navigational instructions and seem to derive from the work of the French mariner Pierre Garcie whose *Le Grand Routier et Pilotage* appeared in 1521. Richard Proude produced *The New Rutter of the Sea for the North Partes*, which consisted of sailing directions for the British Isles. The 'waggoner' was a corruption of the name of the Dutch cartographer Lucas Wagenaer who, in 1584, produced a useful folio of charts called *Spieghel der Zeevaerdt* covering the coasts from Texel to Cadiz. A copy translated and printed in English by Anthony Ashley as *The Mariner's Mirror* had a great impact on British seafaring and was followed in 1693 by *Great Britain's Coasting Pilot* by Greenville Collins. Collins was an English naval officer who, having sailed as sailing master to Sir John Narborough on a voyage into the Pacific, was ordered by Samuel Pepys when that worthy was Secretary to the Admiralty Board 'to make a survey of the sea coast of the Kingdom'.[2] Pepys was disgusted that the Royal Navy had to rely so much on Dutch charts and Collins managed to produce a sufficient number of harbour and coastal charts to earn himself the title of 'Hydrographer to the King'.

This early initiative was not followed up by the Royal Navy and Collins's work was the standard for far too long. Elsewhere, of course, it was a different matter. The Dutch had tackled the problem through the work of Blauw and Plancius, chief cosmographer to the Dutch East India Company, who both produced tables of data for stars of the southern sky useful for navigation in the Indian Ocean on the passage to the spice-islands of the Moluccas. English hydrographic enterprise on a wider scale than the home coast was patchy. Skilled copyists like William Hack reproduced work such as the *derroterro* taken by Bartholomew Sharp out of the Spanish ship *Rosario* which was published in an English version in 1682 as *Waggoner of the Great South Sea*. Bartholomew Sharp, mentioned in Chapter Two, was a buccaneer who served under Morgan in the attack on Panama in 1671 and led a second attack on the Spanish city in 1679. Having crossed the isthmus he seized a Spanish ship and in her cruised in the Pacific. On 29 July 1681, Sharp captured the Spanish ship *Rosario* and the *derroterro* mentioned above, along with 'a young lady about 18 years of age, a very comely creature'. Having 'ravaged the Spanish settlements along the Peruvian coast', he brought his ship round Cape Horn, among the first Englishman to double the promontory. On his return to England he was arraigned on a charge of piracy but was acquitted on Charles II's orders having presented the captured *derroterro* to the king as 'a Spanish manuscript of prodigious value'. Although Charles gave him a commission as captain and put him in command of the *Bonetta*, Sharp's wild inclination got the better of him and he deserted, preferring the command of a nest of buccaneers in the West Indies to command of a king's ship. A second edition of Sharp's *Waggoner* came out in 1685 and in 1699 Hack produced *A Collection of Original Voyages*, detailing the expeditions of Sharp, Cowley and Narborough whose exploits lay in that morally dubious period of late seventeenth century English maritime adventure but which were, nevertheless, of significance for continuing to expose their countrymen's minds to the possibilities of maritime expansion.

Having gone to Virginia as an educated man with a sound knowledge of mathematics and the rudiments of astro-navigation, William Ambrose Cowley volunteered to navigate the privateer *Revenge*, owned by John Cook (see below), from Chesapeake Bay to Haiti. Having left the American coast on 23 April 1683 Cook had decided to make for the slave coast of West Africa. Here he captured a well-armed Danish vessel off Sierra Leone and sold the *Revenge* for sixty black girls. Renaming the Danish ship the *Bachelor's Delight*, Cook sailed south, rounded Cape Horn into the Pacific and joined forces with another English buccaneer John Eaton of the *Nicholas*. The association was unsuccessful in terms of prizes and broke up on 2 September 1684, Cowley transferring to the *Nicholas* for a voyage towards Guam. The crew of the *Nicholas* were reduced by scurvy but recruited their strength in the Marianas Islands before reaching Canton, where they traded with some success before sailing south to Borneo, then through the Celebes Sea to the Moluccas and finally reaching Timor. Here further disputes broke up the company and Cowley and a handful of fellows bought a boat and sailed to Java, finally reaching the Dutch colonial capital at Batavia. Here Cowley obtained a post as navigator in a Dutch East Indiaman. He was successful in assisting the Dutch commander to bring his vessel north-about round Scotland through thick fog to Brill at the end of September 1686. From here he returned home in a yacht, landing in England on 14 October. Having ostensibly been caught up in illegal acts of piracy, his journal was anonymously published, authorship being attributed to 'an ingenious Englishman' and eventually finding its way into Hack's *Collection of Voyages* of 1699.

Although, as we shall see later, the English East India Company undertook hydrographic surveying and the production of charts, and many private cartographers sprang up to supply merchant masters and their naval counter-parts with charts, the availability of such vital aids to navigation was – with the exception of the Indian seas – unsystematic. The indifference of the British Admiralty to see the Royal Navy properly equipped with accurate and comprehensive charts is difficult to comprehend, the more so as it had seemed set to embark on an over-due follow-up to Greenville Collins in 1742. In this year the Navy Board lent a theodolite, plane-table and a twenty-yard measuring chain to the Orcadian, Murdoch Mackenzie, commissioning him to conduct a survey of his native archipelago. Mackenzie laid out a three-mile base line and commenced a triangulation of the islands, the accuracy of which he later checked by two observations for latitude, publishing his results in a folio atlas in 1750. The novelty and accuracy of *Orcades* persuaded the Admiralty that Mackenzie should continue his work and he undertook surveys down the west coast of Britain, round Ireland and by 1770 had reached Pembroke, at which point the fifty-eight-year-old Mackenzie retired, to publish a *Treatise on Surveying* in 1774 which advocated what became a standard form of three-point fix for the precise location of a position using charted landmarks.

These methods were taken up by his nephew, also a Murdoch Mackenzie, and *his* assistant Graeme Spence, who continued the work through the Bristol Channel and along the English Channel. Spence's new survey of the flats east of Walton-on-the-Naze in Essex allowed an anxious Lord Nelson to reach Sheerness in HM Frigate *Medusa* when otherwise pinned in Harwich harbour by easterly winds in 1801, and the channel bears the name of Nelson's least-known flag-ship to this day. By this time the Admiralty had put its house in order and in 1795 Their Lordships had established a properly supervised Admiralty chart office. Even then, however, it was necessary to turn to the Honourable East India Company to find a competent hydrographer capable of collating material in the person of Alexander Dalrymple, whose wider exploits appear in a following chapter. Mackenzie's methods were rapidly taken up by others, for marine surveying along with related 'intelligence' of all kinds – albeit for private advantage rather than public good – had for long been an interest of many ship-masters and mariners worth their salt. Chief among these endeavours were attempts to discover passages through archipelagos which better served a trade, a subject enlarged later. One example will suffice here:

> On the 29 of June, 1793, the [Country-] ship *Shaw Hermozier*, of Calcutta, in company with the *Chesterfield* Whaler, sailed from Norfolk Island, bound to Batavia, with a resolution to explore a passage between New Holland and New Guinea, in which they succeeded; and discovered an island … which they called Tate Island…

This was at considerable cost for in making a closer survey of Tate Island, the master, officers and boat's crew sent in by the whaler were attacked. Several, including Captain Hill, were killed and the subsequent ordeal of the survivors was terrible, but it is noteworthy that such risks were run in the general desire to acquire knowledge.

From its earliest days the East India Company obliged its commanders and masters to deliver four copies – usually each kept by a different officer – of the ship's journal or log-book, along with any useful observations on any matter affecting the navigation of the ship during the voyage. These documents had to be submitted within ten days of arrival in the Thames and were then collated, initially by Captain John Davis who, in 1618, published a rutter for the use of East India Company commanders sailing to the East Indies.[3]

Otherwise there were some notable exceptions to state indifference. Edmund Halley, having connections with the East India Company, had resided on St Helena between 1676 and 1678 where he made astronomical observations, including the transit of Mercury across the sun in 1677. This brought him to the notice of the Royal Society and he was actively engaged on the great scientific debates of the day. Having travelled widely, he was fundamental to Isaac Newton writing the *Principia*, which Halley published at his own expense. In 1682, among a plethora of other scientific observations, including the measurement of height by barometer, Halley begun a long series of lunar observations intended to solve the 'Longitude problem'. In 1698 he was commissioned into the Royal Navy and in the pink *Paramour*, for two years ran the length of the Atlantic studying the earth's magnetic variation and establishing isogonic lines, findings that were published in 1701. He later went on to survey the Bristol Channel before undertaking work abroad and becoming increasingly immersed in astronomy, compiling astronomical tables and making predictions, including that of the reappearance of the comet that now bears his name. He was active in the Royal Society, of which he was Secretary, and he first mooted the utility of observing the forthcoming transit of Venus which would bring James Cook to the fore. Halley succeeded John Flamsteed as Astronomer Royal in 1720 and remained in post until his death in 1742.

British interest in the waters of North America, already stimulated by the Newfoundland fisheries but sharpened by naval operations leading to the acquisition of Canada in 1763, had prompted extensive surveys including that of Newfoundland itself by James Cook. This interest became acute after the stirrings of rebellion in North America in 1775. In 1777 a beautiful folio of charts and coastal views of the eastern seaboard of North America was produced by a team of cartographers working for the Admiralty. Their finished work was the *Atlantic Neptune* and it complements other magnificent surveying done by Cook, his associates and protégés in the succeeding decades. Most notable among these naval paradigms are William Bligh, George Bass, Matthew Flinders, George Vancouver and James Colnett.

Having a chart of a coastline and knowing how to use it was one thing; knowing one's position on the greater surface of the planet, quite another. The so-called 'Longitude Problem' was, of course, a great stumbling block for many years. Although one Gemma Frisius had published a theoretical solution to the problem of longitude in 1530, its reliance upon an accurate timepiece, made it useless to practical seamen. The critical lack of this essential knowledge prompted the British Government to set up the Board of Longitude in 1714 with a reward of £20,000 to foster and encourage the finding of a solution which, eventually, resulted in the successful work of John Harrison. After years of struggle Harrison's chronometer No.4 was tried in 1762 and 1764, but he had great trouble in extracting his just reward from the Board thanks to the difficulty of proving the 'utility at sea' of his time-piece. Nevertheless, a copy by Larcum Kendall proved itself when carried by James Cook in the *Resolution* on his second voyage. At the end of the expedition on 28 July 1775, the error in longitude by chronometer was less than 8 miles, an astonishing accuracy both attesting to the chronometer's 'general utility at sea' and Cook's skill, given the nature of his long voyage.[4]

However, this achievement was not the end of the 'problem', for while it proved the feasibility of producing one reliable chronometer, other hurdles arose: the supply of such expensive items to all ships, both naval and mercantile; and the training of sea-officers to use them. As a consequence standards of navigation in both services, but more-so in the merchants', were patchy and in some cases scandalously lax. Many navigators clung to the lunar method – not least because it was difficult and proved their ability! – while others stuck to a combination of dead reckoning and Parallel Sailing – running down a known parallel of latitude.[5] This apparent purblind indifference to a major improvement has to be set against the expense of both the chronometer and a sextant and, particularly in the North Atlantic, the indifference of the weather and the frequently overcast nature of the sky which rendered astro-navigation such a hit-and-miss business. A master might be happier relying upon other experiential evidence of position: soundings, the nature of the sea-bed, the run of a swell and so forth, rather than upon an astro-solar observation compromised at a vital moment by cloud.

Over time, however, other refinements in astro-navigation were made by numerous contributors, most notably by the French naval officer Commandant Marc St Hilaire in 1785 and the American mercantile master, Captain Thomas Sumner, in 1837. There followed numerous supplementary tables – such as those for observations of latitude ex-meridian – and 'sight-reduction' methods intended to speed up the calculations which were still being promulgated in the second half of the twentieth century.

In 1767 the British Astronomer Royal, Nevil Maskelyne had published the first edition of *The Nautical Almanac*. Having worked out a method of determining longitude by a series of lunar observations while on a voyage to observe the transit of Venus from St Helena in 1765, the new ephemeredes was devised with the taking of 'lunars' in mind. While Arabic astronomy had made many contributions to the knowledge of the heavens, its primary purpose was for astrological divination, though Arab navigators practised a form of astro-navigation as had Europeans when navigating towards parallels of known latitude. Maskelyne's almanac, when combined with Harrison's No.4 chronometer, provided the 'mathematickal navigator' with all he needed to solve the riddle of his more-or-less exact whereabouts on the planet.

After Maskelyne's almanac, such astronomical ephemeris was produced annually not only officially, but also by private companies for use in the merchant service. Private chart-makers, who undertook the public duty of collecting, collating and then publishing the results of surveys as private charts, supplied both the mercantile marine and the Royal Navy where the latter, owing to its dilatory adoption of a Hydrographic Department, was deficient and while naval post-captains were obliged to buy their own charts, where they were available.[6]

In addition to instruments, charts and the ephemeris, navigators required books of mathematical tables and manuals from which to learn their craft. In due course the British Admiralty produced primers and manuals for naval officers and these were used in British training establishments and in some shipping companies, but most were privately produced. Among other tomes, James Hamilton Moore's *The Practical Navigator* was a popular late eighteenth century standard-work for the midshipmen of the Royal Navy and the Honourable East India Company. It was followed in Britain by John Norie's *Complete Epitome of Practical Navigation* published originally for the United East India Company but which ran to several revised editions up to at least 1864; Captain S.T.S. Lecky's *Wrinkles in Practical Navigation* of 1892 and Nicholl's later *Concise Guide to the Board of Trade Examinations*.[7]

One of the most difficult technical problems confronting English navigators of the seventeenth century was locating the entrance to the English Channel, a problem exacerbated by overcast skies which frequently prevented the obtaining of latitude. The 400-ton *Royal Oake*, seen on the stocks by Samuel Pepys in January 1661, made her maiden voyage to Bantam in 1663, but was wrecked on the Scillies on 18 January 1665 when homeward bound and making for the Chops of the English Channel. Sir John Narborough had a lucky escape when returning from his tenure of command in the Mediterranean, narrowly avoiding running aground on the Isles of Scilly. On board was a Lieutenant Shovell who, by 1707 had become both a flag-officer and a knight. Returning from Gibraltar that October, the *Association*, flagship of Admiral Sir Clowdisley Shovell, in company with three other men-of-war drove ashore on the Scillies with great loss of life. Attempts to ameliorate this dilemma, never entirely solved for sailing ships into the early years of the twentieth century, centred on the provision of lighthouses. A lighthouse was erected by Trinity House on Lizard Point in 1619, one on St Agnes in 1690 and a third on the Casquets Rocks off Alderney in 1724. In the days of open coal-chauffers there was, of course, no means of distinguishing one such glow in the night from another, so multiple fires were exhibited, two being shown at the Lizard and three at the Casquets. Unfortunately this did not end disastrous wreckings and frightful loss of life, one example being that of over a thousand men aboard Admiral Balchen's 100-gun flagship *Victory*, which ran into the Casquets on the night of 5 October 1744.[8]

Notwithstanding the increasing provision of charts and sailing directions, buoys, beacons and lightvessels – the first of these being at the Nore in 1732 – and the use of pilots, much depended upon the navigational competence of masters and mates. Given the ambivalent and mixed social standing of the profession as a whole, along with its fearsome reputation for drink and excess, it comes as a surprise to find that at least the opportunities for betterment in mathematical and navigations skills was perhaps easier for a mate in the merchants' service, than for an officer in that of His Britannic Majesty's. Indeed until the abolition of the naval rank of master – by then transmogrified into that of staff commander – in the mid-nineteenth century, by which time commissioned lieutenants had long since become competent navigators in their own right, the Royal Navy looked to its warrant masters to provide them with the necessary navigational skills and the more practical but unscientific knowledge of loading and stowage, stability and trim, skills not quite commensurate with the notion of a naval gentleman's calling. Needless to say such skills were acquired largely in the mercantile service and recruited therefrom by Their Lordships.

While the imperfect efforts of Trinity House began to provide a few adequate seamarks to assist homeward-bound shipping, a general understanding of the world in which English ships were venturing was not considered a matter for the state. And although the Royal Society, founded in the reign of Charles II, was for the betterment of scientific knowledge and the arts, its success relied heavily upon individual thought, experimentation, industry and achievement, a serendipitous substitute for any formulated policy. But this was the age of the English amateur, driven, often very

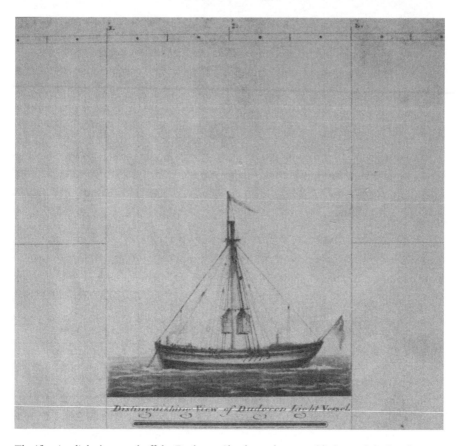

Distinguishing View of Dudgeon Light Vessel.

The 'floating lights' moored off the Dudgeon Shoal was the second lightvessel deployed on station but, unlike that at the Nore stationed off Sheerness, the Dudgeon lay in the open North Sea and was tendered from Wells-next-the-Sea on the Norfolk coast. (Author's collection)

effectively, by enthusiasm and even passion, among whom were a smattering of isolated 'professionals' though outside the strict confines of their daily preoccupations.

One such individual was William Dampier. Born in Somerset in 1652 he was soon orphaned and was bound apprentice to a ship-master, making a voyage to the Newfoundland fishery. Finding the conditions uncongenial, once the term of his indentures were expired, he joined an East Indiaman and found the tropics more to his taste. Returning home in 1672 he joined the navy on the outbreak of the Third Dutch War and saw action in the *Royal Prince* under Sir Edward Spragge's flag. Unsuited to a naval career he was invalided out of the service and offered the job as manager of a Jamaican sugar plantation, but so hated the life that he ran away, enjoyed a drunken debauch in Port Royal and joined a ship bound for the Bay of Campeachy. Here he left her and joined the easy-going, but hard-working and hard-drinking lumber-jacks of the logwood encampments, referred to in the previous chapter, where he spent 1675–76.

The hostility of the Spanish to these unsavoury and unwelcome settlements was reciprocated by the log-wood cutters who frequently metamorphosed into buccaneers. Dampier joined one such group under Bartholomew Sharp, taking part in Sharp's attack on Panama and the subsequent raids on the Spanish coastal settlements in the *Rosario*, but leaving before Sharp made his homeward voyage round the Horn. Returning overland to the Caribbean, Dampier took part in several other opportunistic cruises without much success until in 1683, having arrived in Virginia, he joined Captain John Cook and, with Cowley, embarked on a piratical voyage round the world during which he documented observations on all he saw. He had long cultivated an interest in the natural sciences and seems to have taken part in the raids of Sharp and the cruise of Cook 'more to indulge my curiosity than to get wealth'.

Dampier's experiences in this mad adventure – which began in a small vessel called the *Revenge*, continued in the prize renamed the *Bachelor's Delight* and ended in another called the *Cygnet* – included near-cannibalism, marooning, opium smuggling and a perilous voyage in a native *prau* from the Nicobar Islands to Sumatera. Among the *Cygnet's* varied adventures was a landfall made on the north-west coast of Australia – the second British vessel to contact the mysterious southern continent after an accidental encounter by the *Tryall* in 1622 – near Buccaneer Archipelago.[9] In Sumatera Dampier enrolled as master-gunner in the East India Company's factory at Benkulen. Always individualistic and often unreliable, Dampier was never a biddable man; he and the governor disliked each other and Dampier deserted, taking a position as a seaman in a British ship bound for home. He arrived in England in 1691 with a Malay slave in tow, and began writing the first of his published works, *A New Voyage Round the World*, which appeared in 1697. An illustrated compendium of observations rather than yet another account of a voyage, its charm and detailed illustrations by Dampier himself, attracted wide notice and provoked a second volume entitled *Voyages and Descriptions*, published in 1699.

These books, with their minutely observed drawings and charts, were prototypical of the output of marine explorers in the following century. At the time and, as a direct consequence, Dampier became rehabilitated to such an extent that he was appointed to the Customs service. Given increasing interest in the trade-potential of the West Indies and the Pacific, he was consulted by the Council of Trade and Plantations (forerunner of the Board of Trade) and was asked about piracy and navigation in the Indian Ocean.[10] He was lionised by the Royal Society, to whose president, Charles Montagu, he had dedicated his first book, and upon Montagu's recommendation, the Admiralty misguidedly gave him a commission and put him in command of HMS *Roebuck*, a small pink intended to proceed upon a surveying voyage in quest of *Terra Australis*.

The voyage was not a success, although Dampier conducted a survey of the inhospitable west coast of Australia before being obliged to refit at the Dutch port of Timor. From here he sailed to New Guinea and was embarking upon a survey of the island's coastline when his crew mutinied. The atmosphere aboard the *Roebuck* had been poisonous for many months; Dampier had been at daggers-drawn with his first lieutenant, one George Fisher, a regular naval officer who resented Dampier's parvenu but senior status which caused a deep animus between the two men. Worn down with scurvy and apprehension, Dampier's harsh treatment and mismanagement provoked his crew to extremity. Compelled by these events to abandon his survey, Dampier returned to Timor and then the *Roebuck* set off for England. Unfortunately the little pink was worn-out and foundered off Ascension on 24 February 1701. Dampier and his crew lived for 'some Time; having Plenty of very good Turtle by our Tents, and Water for the fetching'. All was, according to the resourceful Dampier – who seems unfazed by any privations – 'exceeding wholsome'. About a week later they signalled a passing group of ships. Three men-of-war, *Anglesey*, *Hastings* and *Lizard*, with the East Indiaman *Canterbury* in company, anchored offshore and, in due course, Dampier made his passage home in the *Canterbury*.

Dampier was now subjected to a court-martial on the *Roebuck's* loss. As a result of the court's findings and Fisher's damning evidence, Dampier was cashiered with the loss of all his wages. Although this disgrace would have stopped a lesser man in his tracks, Dampier's indifference to the world of wealth seems to have insulated him against opprobrium. Besides, his reputation as a scientific navigator was unimpaired and he was again dined by members of the Royal Society with whom he enjoyed an easy relationship. He was clearly a man of parts, not least of an easy charm upon occasions, which, with his scientific turn of mind, commended him to the membership as an auto-didact.

He subsequently had no trouble in finding employment as master of the twenty-six-gun *St George*, one of two privateers being fitted out for service against the Spanish in the Pacific in 1703. Dampier was also given control of the other vessel, the *Cinque Ports*. Unfortunately his abilities as commander of a privateer – where the crew was paid by results and a commander needed motivating skills – were no better than of a warship. Nor were they helped by his lack of aggression when tempting and profitable targets presented themselves. On the one hand the uncaring Dampier proved irresolute and on the other over-bearing, possessed of a hot temper and mercurial mood swings. None of these circumstances helped when trouble erupted in his consort. At Juan Fernandez, where they took wood and water, the mate and master of the *Cinque Ports* fell out and the latter was voluntarily marooned. His name was Alexander Selkirk and he was to become the inspiration for Daniel Defoe's novel *Robinson Crusoe*.

Having headed off a general mutiny, Dampier's ships failed to capture a French prize, bungled a raid, and effected a single inglorious capture. As Captain Stradling took the *Cinque Ports* south, leaving his chief, Dampier's own crew mutinied. Under the mate of the *St George*, one Clipperton, these ingrates turned themselves over into their prize, abandoning Dampier and twenty-seven of their shipmates in the *St George*. However, with reduced numbers and his own hardihood, Dampier sought to redeem the situation. He might have succeeded had a little more fire burned in his belly instead of illuminating his mind, for he fell-in with every privateer's dream, a Spanish Register ship. The subsequent engagement hardly merited the name. The now rotten *St George* was driven off with ease and several of her disaffected crew deserted when she touched land. Dampier was now reduced to commanding a few desperate loyalists and with these he had a change of heart, attacking the town of Puna and capturing a small Spanish vessel lying at anchor. This he exchanged for the unserviceable *St George* and headed for Batavia in the prize. Here Dampier now found the Dutch ready to arrest him and his ship, but he extricated himself from this impasse and reached home in 1707, only to be confronted by a critical account of the voyage written by one of the *St George*'s company, William Funnell. The battered Dampier responded with a *Vindication* but, though his abilities as a navigator and natural scientist remained admired, his reputation as a commander remained abysmal.

 Within a few months, however, Dampier was engaged in a second privateering expedition, though not in command, but as 'pilot and adviser' to Captain Woodes Rogers in the *Duke*, a twenty-gun frigate-built ship which, with the *Duchess*, was bound for the Pacific. The two sailed in August 1708, when Dampier was fifty-six. Having made some insignificant captures, the vessels doubled Cape Horn and reached Juan Fernandez. Here they liberated Selkirk, who initially objected to being taken off to the *Duke* when he heard that Dampier was aboard. The ships then sacked Guayaquil before engaging a small Register ship, the *Neustra Señora de la Encarnación Desengano*. After a hard action off Cape San Lucas they captured her and transhipped her cargo. In October 1711, on returning to London and selling their booty, the privateers made a handsome £170,000. In the aftermath Woodes Rogers paid tribute to his pilot, suggesting that when not in command, he was better than history has painted him.

Like Morgan before him, Woodes Rogers, was made a colonial governor, being appointed to the Bahamas with instructions to root out piracy, which he did with some effect, driving the most determined pirates out of the Caribbean and sending them to seek refuge in Madagascar. His account of his circumnavigation, *A Cruising Voyage Round the World*, was published in 1712 and he died in the Bahamas during his third term of office as governor in 1729. His navigator, Dampier, was a more prolific author. In addition to his account of his earlier circumnavigation and his other publications, William Dampier was the first student of the winds and, although he confined these to tropical and low temperate latitudes his *Discourse of Winds*, part of his *Voyages and Descriptions*, drew attention to the existence of persistent air-streams – the Trade Winds. In suggesting a global wind-system, the *Discourse* was afterwards printed separately and was for over a century the only analytical study of the subject.

Dampier's disastrous voyage in the *Roebuck*, the substance of which was contained in his 1703 publication *Voyage to New Holland*, was initiated by the growing conviction among the British establishment of the possibilities of new, exploitable lands. Notwithstanding having afterwards been found unfit to command any of Her Majesty's ships, within a year Dampier had been summoned to an audience with Queen Anne and the Lord Admiral, the Queen's consort, Prince George of Denmark. He had dined with Samuel Pepys and John Evelyn and it was Coleridge who later spoke of his 'exquisite refinement of mind'. Not only did his exploits touch upon Defoe's masterpiece *Robinson Crusoe* – thought by some to be the first English novel – but it influenced Defoe's lesser novel *Captain Singleton*. Dampier is considered (along with Fletcher Christian) to have inspired Coleridge's *Rhyme of the Ancient Mariner* and Jonathan Swift referred to his works in writing *Gulliver's Travels*.

That Dampier's character consisted of the virtues enshrined in his works and the vices revealed by the court-martial's findings and Funnel's revelations, should not surprise: he led an extraordinary life and unquestionably possessed a morose and sullen side to his character, but he stood at the dawn of a new age when new ideas were emerging after the religious ferment of the seventeenth century. Dampier can fairly be said to be a torch-bearer to the Enlightenment, 'the Cook of a former age', and a contemporary of the philosopher John Locke, whose own writings were to have a profound effect upon the future. Dampier died in poverty, 'diseased and weak in body, but of sound and perfect mind,' in March 1715.

What Locke argued was to provide the justification for an empire. In his *Second Treatise on Government* of 1690 Locke propounded the theory of *terra nullius*, or no man's land. From this was developed the notion that an advanced society might, indeed ought, to undertake the duty of a civilising mission. From this it followed that such a society, conceiving itself to fulfil the criteria of being civilised, might acquire the territory of an uncivilised society. Thus was born the justification for the acquisition of colonies which, while it might not have impressed those made subservient, was seized upon as a justification by all the maritime nations of Europe and encouraged the competitive acquisition of foreign lands in the name of one or other of the crowned heads of Europe. God, Locke argued, had given the world to 'all Mankind, and commanded Man also to labour, and the penury of his Condition required it of him'. Thus 'God and his Reason' having set mankind on this self-improving path, enabled mankind to 'lay out something upon it that was his own, his labour'. Thus, in order to establish a claim of territoriality in the first place, Locke's logic ran on:

> He that in Obedience to the Command of God, subdued, tilled and sowed any part of it [some land], thereby annexed to it something that was his Property, which another had no Title to, nor could without injury take from him.

If a society was unable to demonstrate it had 'laid out', or invested, something upon it that was its own, a statement taken to mean at its most basic level cultivated land for agriculture, it was said to be *terra nullius*: no man's land, and consequently, and most conveniently, up for grabs. Whatever inhabitants were encountered in this wilderness were logically held to be primitive and if not Christian – which they were not – were therefore outside the Grace of God. In such a case it was, then, the clear duty of the superior, civilised and Christian society to put the matter right, to – in the buzzword of the day – 'improve' it. The first step was to make a claim, by hoisting colours, firing a salute of guns, leaving a cairn of stones or a carved wooden board at a conspicuous landing-place and of making gifts to the non-Christian locals. This planting of the flag, so beloved of the generation of Cook and his protégés, was, however, only one method of initiating a trade – and a very uncertain one which took some years to develop.

Elsewhere trade went on with societies at least as advanced as that of Great Britain, and some which – if the nature and degree of their civilisation was debatable – were of greater antiquity. It did so, and had being doing so for years, without the need to make any territorial claim and it accomplished this by the creation of the seafaring class, a social group whose relationship with trade is analogous to that of the chicken and the egg.

A ship at sea contained two human components: a master and a crew. Once a ship had left port and was bound upon her passage the master stood alone, governor and manager 'under God', a symbol of authority and of the flag-state to which a ship belonged, a representative of her owner, or owners. A man might call himself 'captain' but it was a courtesy-title and carried no legitimacy; neither was his post binding and he carried his fortune upon the back of his reputation. An owner would appoint a master he trusted, a man with the necessary skill but, more importantly a man whose interests coincided in some way with his own or, as was most frequent, the owner and his partners.

The vicissitudes of the merchant seaman's life were such that although a man might rise from relatively humble origins to enjoy a fair prosperity as master of a foreign-going merchantman, the position of master guaranteed nothing. A ship-master might have to seek a ship through an almost grovelling process. Ned Ward – with nautical metaphor – remarked in 1698 upon a powerful merchant walking on the Royal Exchange, pointing out that 'those fellows that come astern [of him] and now and then come up upon his quarter, with their topsails lowered, are commanders of ships who are soliciting for employment'.

Excepting East Indiamen, which were always set apart, a master unrelated to an owner, or not owning some modicum of shares in his vessel, or unable to obtain preference through ability or family connections, would have to prove his worth in order to have security of tenure in his command. One, George Simon, having commanded three foreign-going vessels, was obliged in 1674 to accept a berth as second mate aboard a collier; no naval commander was subject to such indignity. On the other hand, if nepotism secured a master a ship, he might hold the post for many years, losing it only if he was exceptionally incompetent in both fields of commerce and navigation. The position held by a master was one of great trust. He was:

> ...the owners' agent, responsible not only for navigation but also for maintaining their interests, maritime and commercial, while the ship was far removed from their control; able to bind them for debt and render them liable to penalties for his contraventions of the law. [11]

Captain Richard Haddock, trading with Italy in the last quarter of the seventeenth century managed his ship at sea and in port arranged for the recruitment, provisioning and paying of her crew, the maintenance of her fabric, and presented his voyage accounts to the assembled majority of her owners at voyage end. Abroad, he consulted with the trading houses that acted as his owners' agents, helped negotiate freight-rates and the loading, stowage and discharge of cargoes and kept his owners' interests uppermost in his dealings. Occasionally, when necessary, a master might sell his ship, as did Nathaniel Uring in Lisbon when she had become 'perfectly worn out with age'. In an era before classifications surveys, underwriting societies and protection-and-indemnity clubs, the responsibilities of a ship-master were awesome. For this reason, not only were familial connections with owners useful, but so too was the utility of the master having a share-holding interest in his ship.

Often, particularly early in the period under review, or when a trade was starting up, the principle owners or charterers would send out one of their number or a trustworthy associate to handle the sale and purchase of cargo in a foreign port. Increasingly, although not all masters were worthy of the trust or even met the standards of required competency, the majority handled more and more commercial business, so that in many trades it became superfluous for a merchant to ship an agent on the voyage. These men, known variously as 'supracargoes' or 'supercargoes', or even *compradors* from the Portuguese, tended to migrate ashore in the ports of destination to become local agents, facilitating trade and acting both as ship-brokers and forwarding-agents. In such a way enclaves of British ex-patriates developed in such places as Smyrna, for the Levant trade, and Leghorn (Livorno) for the general Mediterranean trade, putting down roots, establishing families and dynasties, founding small but influential ex-patriate 'colonies' around which grew up schools, hospitals and churches all of which linked Great Britain with foreign interests quite divorced from colonialism.

Not until the mid-nineteenth century was shipowning in general anything other than a part-time business, often ancillary to a merchant's main interest. The risks were high and therefore people spread their investments thinly so that a ship might be owned by many share-holders and it was not until the Merchant Shipping Act of 1854 that the number of shares in a ship was actually limited by statute to sixty-four. In the seventeenth century a vessel commonly had a score of owners and large share-holding magnates were rare. They were not unknown, however, one of the greatest being Sir Henry Johnson who, in 1686, was a part-owner of thirty-eight ships, mostly Indiamen many of which he built in his yard at Blackwall. However, although in total he possessed eighty-eight thirty-seconds, in only one of them did he own more than one eighth of the entire ship. In the 1750s a Richard Lascelles had interests totaling thirty-two sixteenths, spread among twenty-one vessels.

Each ship was a separate investment and every voyage a discrete venture; a ship was usually managed by the investor who first put up the proposal to purchase her and the risk was customarily shared with a 'different set of part-owners for each of the ships … managed'. The chief reason for this complexity of mutual yet spread interest was that risk-management could only find its solution in such a web. The risks to which a ship was exposed were many and were not confined to the conduct of a ship at sea when Acts of God – usually extremely bad weather – had to be added to the dangers of fire, grounding, foundering, wrecking, piracy or – in time of war – enemy action. There was always the enemy nursed in the bosom. Owners were liable for losses of cargo by accident or embezzlement, or defaults of fees caused by the malfeasances of a master even when entirely innocent. In 1735, however, an act limited claims against an owner to the value of a ship and her freight. The prospect of meeting such an unlimited claim is a clear explanation of the small fractions into which ownership was divided and why a rich man would invest small sums in many vessels rather than the whole of his capital into just one or two. There was also the question of capitalizing a venture, which did not come cheap, so amassing sufficient funds to freight an outward-bound vessel required a number of investors.

Commenting upon this diversity of ownership in 1725, Daniel Defoe wrote that: 'Almost all the shopkeepers and inland traders in seaport towns, and even in the waterside part of London itself, are necessarily brought in to be owners of ships', an echo of the comment by William Stout of Lancaster, made in 1698. Stout said that, 'being at this time much out of business, I was persuaded by some neighbours to stand a sixth part share in a new ship of 80 tons, now building'. That such a speculation was risky is emphasised by the fact that Stout's ship, the *Experiment*, was lost after four years during which Stout steadily lost money.

In practice one or two, or perhaps a small committee, of the principal share-holders would form a vessel's managing-ownership, dining with the master at a specified tavern at the beginning and end of a foreign voyage when the accounts would be settled. The owners would be headed by their principal, who became known as the 'ship's husband' and the practical personal contact between the master and the owners. The point of contact between the owning group, including the ship-master, and a merchant wishing to ship a cargo by chartering a bottom, was the Royal Exchange. Here, too, one might seek to invest in a ship and there grew up 'on 'Change' another party, the ship-broker, whose functions increased over time. He was a middle-man who: 'Sells Ships or part of Ships by Publick or Private Sale. Lets Ships to Freight, Enters and Clears Ships at the Customs House.' These compulsory procedures at the Customs House of a port required the presence of the master with various documents such as his cargo-manifest, upon the presentation and evidence of which all duties would be calculated by the Customs House officers and without whose 'inward clearance' no cargo could legally be discharged. Likewise, a vessel had to be 'cleared' for outward lading by way of a 'jerque note'.

The Customs House officers and their associates, the Excise-men with their coastal patrols of riding-officers and Revenue-cruisers offshore, acted under the aegis of the Board of Trade and Plantations, a committee of the Privy Council established in 1696. These state officials, although incapable of entirely preventing either smuggling or the wholesale robbery of ships lying 'in the tiers' of the River Thames, had a major regulatory effect upon the conduct of the trading process. The necessary interaction of ship-masters with these proto-civil servants maintained a direct contact with the ship-master and subverted the ship-master as a potential – if part-time – servant of the state.

The ship-broker, on the other hand, unequivocally stood for trade and in the early eighteenth century he grew in importance. He 'Made Insurance on Ships and Merchandise' and in co-operating with others of his stamp initiated an immense source of business and wealth. Improvements in private insuring business, the transactions for which were carried out in a variety of locations in and around the City of London, some in the vicinity of the Royal Exchange and Change Alley, others in Cornhill and elsewhere, led eventually to the centralised establishment of the institution known as 'Lloyd's'. For years shipping deals, from the dinners at which owner and master discussed a proposed voyage, to the buying and selling of ships and goods at auction, had been carried out in taverns and the increasingly popular coffee houses. One of these was Haynes's Coffee House in Birchin Lane which around 1678 significantly changed its name to The Marine Coffee House. Various trades used different establishments, such as the Jamaica or the Virginia Coffee Houses and it was in such convivial meeting places that capacity and passenger accommodation was advertised. Masters seeking cargo 'cruised the city for goods', often pleading the superiority of the sailing qualities of their ships over others. Occasionally they made trips to the growing manufactories at Birmingham, but in tandem with the coffee houses, where they could meet merchants, brokers and owners directly, use was made of newspapers to promulgate information. One, the *City Mercury*, appeared in 1675 purely to carry: 'Notice of all goods, merchandise and ships to be sold... Any Ships to be let to Freight, and the Time of their Departure, the Place of the Master's habitation and where to be spoken with...' Often in place of the master's name and some point of contact, the name of the owner's agent or broker appeared.

Coffee houses existed abroad, particularly in the British colonies of North America. Samuel Kelly was in Philadelphia in 1790 during the crisis with Spain over Nootka Sound and mentions the utility of such institutions:

> The vessels laying here belonging to the Dons began to arm, and a report was in circulation that they meant to intercept all the British vessels on their leaving this port which considerably alarmed us, as we actually saw their guns on board. The *Alert* being now ready for Liverpool, and the master fearing two Spanish armed schooners ready for sea also, went slyly to the Coffee House and entered a notice in the Intelligence Book there, that two British frigates had been seen off the Capes of the Delaware, and trusting this would have its intended effect on the Spaniards, sailed immediately...

Among the most important of these places of rendezvous in London was the Castle Tavern which, after its removal from Broad Street after the great fire of 1666, reappeared in Cornhill. It too changed its name to the Ship and Castle in 1686, perhaps a sign that business was migrating from it, for the last recorded sale there was in November 1688. Thereafter no central venue attracted the various parties until, on 28 July 1692, a Mr Lloyd gave his name to a new coffee house he was opening in Lombard Street. This establishment rapidly became the most popular haunt of all those wishing to transact shipping business. In 1674 the Common Council of the City of London had laid down regulations for persons wishing to practice as brokers and with an increasing number of these men specialising in ship-broking the City declared that:

> ...the persons generally called Shipbrokers who are in the nature of interpreters to masters of ships and assisting them in receiving their freight ... are to be deemed brokers within the meaning of the present Act for restraining the number and ill practice of Brokers and Stock-Jobbers.

In 1718 all these coinciding interests created two powerful bodies, the Royal Exchange Assurance and the London Assurance Companies which began writing new business and encouraging hull insurance, hitherto a burden borne by the owners.[12] Matters prospered. After the death of Edward Lloyd, his coffee house passed eventually to Thomas Jemson, a member of the Shipwrights' Company and he set in train a weekly shipping newspaper that appeared in 1734 and has done so ever since. It was soon afterwards matched by a rival coffee house established by Thomas Fielding, a former waiter of Mr Lloyd's. Fielding set up shop in Pope's Head Alley, off Lombard Street, a 'genteely fitted up' establishment 'for the Reception of Gentlemen, merchants, &c.' Both coffee houses produced their own version of *Lloyd's List*, but Fielding had taken with him the most prominent men in London's shipping circles and in 1771 some seventy-nine of these clubbed together to establish a New Lloyd's Coffee House. On 5 March 1774 the new premises – henceforth to be known internationally simply as 'Lloyd's' – was opened 'over the north-west corner of the Royal Exchange'.

The consolidated *Lloyd's List*, long since a daily paper, collected information from a multiplicity of sources and led to corresponding agents in ports world-wide, twenty-eight being covered by 1792, on the eve of the long war with France. This demand for information would eventually establish a network of Lloyd's Signal Stations linked in due course by the telegraph but even in the Great War with France (1793–1815) the institution of Lloyd's was to work closely with the Admiralty in co-ordinating a convoy system. This was assisted by *Lloyd's Register of Shipping*, which had become available from 1764, giving details of some 1,500 British merchant ships.

Marine insurance, while risky, could also be extremely profitable. Richard Thornton was born in 1776, the third son of 'an impecunious yeoman farmer' in Yorkshire who, thanks to his uncle, another Richard, was educated at Christ's Hospital. In 1798 he joined a consortium at Lloyd's as a marine insurance broker. Family connections with the Russia Company also led him into trade with Russia which during the long war offered him exceptional opportunities for profit. The Government's need for naval stores, especially hemp, became crucial during the period of the Napoleonic Continental System which embargoed trade with Russia between 1807 and 1810. This 'tempted Thornton into daring ventures through the Baltic in his own armed ships'. In 1810, just before the Tsar issued a *ukase* revoking his agreement with Napoleon, this trade was described as 'the most lucrative in the world'. Two years later, by which time Napoleon was embroiled in a bitter war with his former ally, Thornton was secretly informed by his brother and partner Laurence, then in Russia, that the *Grande Armée* was retreating from Moscow. Thornton consequently secured 'large contracts for the forward delivery of Russian imports at their peak wartime prices' before knowledge of the French débâcle became common knowledge. The acquisition of such wealth earned the bachelor Thornton the enduring soubriquet of 'the Duke of Dantzig'. His exploits after the final defeat of Napoleon in 1815, which included shipowning and charitable benefaction, were no less remarkable. Upon his death in 1865 he left a fortune whose probate value at £2,800,000 was the largest ever recorded, and in his vast wealth Richard Thornton pre-figured the great patricians in British entrepreneurial shipowning.

Those who actually part-owned ships during Thornton's boyhood might be merchants requiring their vessel to load whatever they themselves traded in; or owners who sought charters and who 'offered' their vessels for cargoes at freight-rates acceptable to the shipper. They might also be the builders of the ship, or chandlers whose main interest was in providing ship-masters with supplies, foodstuffs and so forth. Such were the constituent parts of the many consortia which might also benefit small investors, including women – particularly widows – who sought modest gains for reasons of subsistence rather than speculative profit.

Notwithstanding the risks inherent in any voyage, partial shipowning appeared attractive, not least to ship-masters themselves who had a powerful incentive to minimise any risk. The opportunity thus offered was equally embraced by their families. A Yorkshire master, Captain Henry Denton, acquired part-ownership because his father, who 'kept asses … by mere dint of starving himself, saved as much as bought his son a share in a ship … and by the success of the share [his son has] risen to be a principal owner'. Captain Samuel Pinder of Whitby systematically bought shares in his own ship and at the time of his death in 1703 owned a thirty-second of eight other vessels. Captain Richard Haddock increased his share-holding in the *Supply* from one sixteenth to one quarter in six voyages; his holding in his next command, the *Bantam*, was one third. Such steady progress in ownership became common and, in the right circumstances and trade, could draw a ship-master into the court of directors of one of the large joint-stock enterprises such as the Levant and East India Companies.[13]

Such a multitude of business connections inevitably led to financial failures of one kind or another. Occasional swindles or the barratry or misconduct of a master led in due course to a proposal by John Bland in a pamphlet of 1659 entitled *Trade Revived* in which he suggested a national register of shipping. The notion fell upon deaf ears but after the Restoration a petition for 'The Erection of an Office to enroll all Bills of Sale' was submitted, followed by similar initiatives in successive years until in 1697 a bill was introduced to the House of Commons 'For Registering all Bills of Sale of Ships and Vessels of Burden in a General Register Book'. However, nothing effective was to be done by the Government for a century.

The cost of ships rose steadily throughout the seventeenth century, as did their size. Around 1610 a tonnage of more than 200 tons burthen was unusual outside the large carrying trades to the eastern Mediterranean or the East Indies and cost around £2,000. This tonnage had doubled by about 1720, the cost rising to about £5,000. Although a variety of rigs from bilanders to brigs were favoured in the coasting trades, most vessels engaged in deep-water commerce were ship-rigged, that is to say three masted, with square yards on all three masts and a lateen mizen 'course'. The four-masted vessel that had appeared briefly in the late 1500s disappeared until the later nineteenth century. Small ships carried courses and topsails, larger bore topgallants and even occasionally royals but the noun 'ship' essentially derives from this dominance of the 'ship-rig' which was to serve – with multiple incremental improvements – until the final flowering of the sailing vessel around 1900. Not until the 1800s were ships known by their rigs, however; hull form, port of registry and trade were the means by which most generic terms were coined, thus 'a Guineaman' was a fast slaver, while 'a Whitby-cat' described a small, versatile vessel with no figurehead that might be employed in the Baltic trade, as a whaler, or a collier on the east coast of England. The term 'East Indiaman' is self-explanatory; such a vessel built in 1750 at around 800 tons burthen, by then a common tonnage, would have cost about £14,000, comparable with the £15,680 paid for the *Charles the Second*, at 800 tons the largest merchantman built in the seventeenth century.

The costs of building a ship, though considerable, were often far less than the value of her cargo and it was this, rather than the carrying bottom, that was insured.[14] This, of course, increased the risks to shipowning investors and while it was occasionally offset by the protection offered to bottomry bonds, the insurance of ships was not common until well into the eighteenth century. The bottomry bond was a form of marine mortgage which, while it protected the borrower if a ship was lost, demanded such a high rate of interest that it was not commonly used for the outright purchase of a vessel. Instead it was useful to a master faced with unexpected and essential repair bills in a foreign port where letters of credit were not available to him and could only be raised for the continuance of a voyage. In such a case the master stood as agent for the owners. An alternative method, if the master could act as agent for the cargo-shipper, was to pledge a part of the cargo, or in the event sell it, a method of fund-raising known as 'respondentia'.[15]

It follows that placing such an investment in the hands of a stranger was unwise. Nepotism, embracing family, friends and fellow investors, became the norm. Masters often, though not invariably, were part-owners or family members, and it was common for seamen – particularly ship's mates – with no prospects and little cash, to marry into shipowning families. In 1665 one John Smart 'came to that imployment [of master] by friends that knew him capable thereof'. Although the system worked tolerably well, it did often placed kinship and obligation above competence. Such incompetence might not embrace a simple lack of seamanship, but might include men able enough in theory, but whose character did not fit them for the task.

Not unnaturally one hears more of those who betrayed their owners' trust than those who acquitted themselves well. Writing in 1685 James Houblon, 'one of the greatest merchants of his day', bemoaned:

…the great and general debauchery and prodigality of Masters of Ships to maintain which both when they are on their voyages and in their families at home they run in debt and render bad and doubtful Accounts to their Owners, waste the Ship's provisions and stores.

While willful criminal acts ranged from the minor fraud of selling stores and provisions, to major offences such as barratry, the most pernicious agent of breakdown was alcohol. In describing Captain Thomas Clarke of the *Constant Elizabeth*, the complainant might have been adumbrating a constant figure in this history. 'A very careless, improvident and riotous person … very quarrelsome, and he is also very much addicted to excessive drinking of strong drinks'. Clarke's persistent failure to return to the ship after bouts of boozing ashore led to his 'neglect[ing] the care of the Vessell wherewith he was entrusted'. Then, as later, such masters were usually both physically and metaphorically 'carried' by their mates. What proportion of the whole body such reprobates were is impossible to say, since most seafarers drank and did so enthusiastically in port. Certainly it occasionally became close to being endemic, even in respectable organisations: 'The Hudson's Bay Company in its early years had endless trouble with incompetent, careless, drunken and dishonest masters'. Such an assertion has to be set in the context of the *mores* of the time; drinking vast quantities of beers, wines and spirituous liquors was part and parcel of daily life and at sea filled the vacuum left by the absence of the consolations of the land, but it is probably safe to say that it was – and is – the single most disruptive agent on board ship. While part-ownership might stimulate a master's duty of care, it occasionally – and usually fired by alcohol – made him cock-o'-the-walk and the author of an entire crew's unhappiness. Alcohol was equally freely used by other members of a crew, though with less deleterious effect upon the outcome of a voyage than its abuse by a master. Nevertheless, most masters were not compulsively and habitually drunken sots; the majority carried out their duties properly and with due regard for their responsibilities both to their principals and their subordinates, notwithstanding the rigors of the seafaring life. Most did their best, often in trying circumstances, and whatever its consequential evils might be, a little alcohol could often stiffen the resolve of a wavering heart without entirely corrupting it.

Most ship-masters undertook their difficult business with ability and probity, though their private conduct might not answer. In 1787 Samuel Kelly sailed as mate in the *Thetis*, part-laden with salt for Philadelphia. His master 'though a civil man and an excellent seaman, had nothing more of a gentleman about him than what was confined to his clothes; his whole delight was vulgarity in the extreme'. Notwithstanding this lack of social graces, the master of the *Thetis* was demonstrably a trustworthy person for: 'Having delivered our cargo, our vessel was chartered to load mahogany and dyewood for Liverpool. Being now laden, we took on board a quantity of dollars privately, as the British agents, for want of procuring Bills [of Exchange] on England, were obliged to make their returns in dollars.'

Preferment went to men who did not take to the bottle, though such were rare-birds. The former black slave Olaudah Equiano found the drinking habits of the

Discharging wine in large casks at Brewer's Quay about 1780. In the foreground the wine is being tested for spoliation during the voyage. (Author's Collection)

Christian whites perplexing. It caused them to behave contrary to the gospel of Christ they preached to their captives and he himself eschewed alcohol when serving in British merchant ships. As a consequence of his continence he rose to the status of mate; as Vincent Carretta points out, competence was more important than colour in the late eighteenth century.

Though hundreds of ships made successful passages between two ports, these were not necessarily efficient in every sense of the word and individual navigation was a hit-and-miss affair in all senses of the cliché. As Sir William Monson hypothesised upon the disparity in results by several working out the mystery of dead-reckoning, or 'the traverse at sea':

> There is no certainty in the art of navigation, in our ordinary masters ... for if there were they would not vary so much from one another as they usually do. For proof whereof, let there be four or five masters or pilots in one ship ... if they be any time in traverse at sea you shall have some of them thirty leagues before the ship, and others as many leagues behind...

This is a slightly unfair criticism and applied equally to men-of-war, for there was no accurate instrumentation available for the recording of distance run beyond the primitive 'log-ship', while the ship-induced errors in magnetic compasses were barely understood in wooden ships, and thus the raw data for course-and-distance-run were wildly variable. Pepys, on his passage to Tangier, famously misunderstood this, blaming 'the master and mate ... [who] are a sort of people, who do all by mechanick rule, and understand nothing, or very little, of the nature and reason of the instruments they use'. In spite of Pepys's animadversion, conditions at sea conduced little to the accuracy of the somewhat primitive instruments of the day which, while they might answer well enough in a class-room ashore, were less effective on a heaving deck. Moreover, such theories as there were, were best learned by rote, then a teaching method widely used. Thus it was necessary for ships to rely upon the basics of log, latitude, lookout and the all important lead, which gave the nature of the seabed and to which might be added the 'smell' of things, that intuitive skill that determines the true 'seaman' from his less competent colleague.

> We hove our ship-to, with the wind at sou'west, boys,
> We hove our ship-to, for to strike soundings clear;
> It was forty-five fathoms, with a fine sandy bottom,
> So we filled the main topsail, and up-Channel steered.

Such were the words of the old sea-song *Spanish Ladies* dating from this period, from which can readily be judged the reliance placed upon experience and the tallow-armed lead-line. In the absence of a chart, it was all there was. Indeed it is clear from the memoirs of Samuel Kelly, sailing as master in the 1790s, that he relied on soundings in a specific latitude, the condition of the bottom and then headed for an identifiable coastline. Thus: 'The Principal thing in a pilot ... of our coast is to know where he is ... the skill ... is to know the land as soon as he shall descry it'. Knowing instantly where upon a coast one had landed-up was, perhaps, the essential key to being judged a competent navigator at this time. It was not uncommon, therefore, to find a merchant ship commanded by a young and inexperienced master supported by an older and more able mate who perhaps lacked sufficient influence, interest or means to fund or find a command of his own. Such a combination might, however, work tolerably well if the master was efficient at securing the business of the ship, leaving much of the handling at sea to his mate, for in many trades a good master had not only to command skills in navigation and ship-handling, but needed a good head at business.

However, there were some spectacular misadventures like that of a Captain Williams who, returning from the West Indies in 1731, took the *Parham* up the Bristol, rather than the English, Channel. The owner expressed his indignation thus:

> How in the world you should commit such a blunder [I] can't imagine now in the Summer when it's not bad weather and near seventeen hours daylight. Can't remember of any such mistake made by anyone in my life at that time of the year. Won't redound to thy credit or reputation.

That it might happen at other seasons wherein it might be less reprehensible is an interesting aside; the truth was, making the Chops of the Channel was, as noted earlier, a matter of some difficulty and Williams was guilty of not having known his whereabouts when he finally sighted land, rather than entering the wrong arm of the coastal seas.

As for a master's duties in port, the acquisition of cargoes, though often left to the supercargo, an agent or a charter-party, might well require his close attention, particularly after the discharge of his outward lading. This could demand considerable time spent ashore in negotiation, expanding an efficient and active master's contacts and thus his influence and power. Of course to a greater or lesser degree, many were corrupted by such inter-action, both as takers and givers, for bribes were an accepted lubricant to business transactions in most parts of the world. Such oleaginous dealings were regarded as mere private extensions to customs and excise duties by those involved – but against which the smuggling of so-called free-traders was set as a more legitimate and 'honest' form of trade. Smugglers, who proliferated throughout the eighteenth century, cast themselves as the true descendants of Robin Hood, whether bringing genever across the North Sea, or silk from India. As for the customary channels of trade, favours were often necessary and, as Ralph Davis points out, they 'were expected in return'. Fundamentally the entire 'mercantile community was in effect bound together in a network of back-scratching'.

This was, however, a most important component in the entire business for, by such means, the man responsible for the care of a shipper's property was bound into that duty of care by something stronger and more persuasive than a mere sense of responsibility. Some cargoes needed little attention while others, like exports of lead and coal, were often shipped as ballast to give weight and therefore stability to a ship laden with a commodity of high stowage factor but little mass. Many commodities required particular and skillful care, particularly coal. If damp and partly smashed up into dust, or slurry, coal can not only become a highly flammable cargo, liable to spontaneous combustion, but shifts like a thick fluid. Rice, shipped in increasing quantities from the Carolinas during the 1690s, if wetted by a leaky hull, swelled to such an extent as to threaten the integrity of a ship's hull. Lime was also dangerous when wet, often causing a fire with fatal effect. There was also loss of value to a 'spoiled' cargo. The most vulnerable in this respect was tea, a cargo upon whose delicate scent its purchase and consumption depended. Tea was liable to damp, taint, or contamination by other, stronger smelling substances. In contrast to the relatively simple considerations applicable to a homogenous cargo, a master would often have to take into account varying and often competing requirements in a 'general cargo' consisting of a variety of goods. Ralph Davis cogently emphasises the arcane nature of the business:

> Merchants, shipowners and ships' officers were familiar with the cubic measurements of a ton of all the principal goods of commerce, and their memories could be aided by lists which were generally available. In ports where a variety of cargo was

to be had, the mixing of light and heavy goods so as to maximize simultaneously the cubic volume and the tonnage of the goods carried, was one of the nicer arts.[16]

Bulky goods had to be handled with care; manufactures such as porcelain and other household wares might become damaged in heavy weather; fabrics could be ruined by damp, not just the ingress of water in bad weather, but simple condensation; other hygroscopic commodities such as salt and gunpowder could prove difficult to discharge if contaminated, while containers such as the plethora of casks of various sizes then in use needed secure stowage 'bung-up and bilge free'. Lashing and tomming – the holding steady by baulks of timber known as dunnage – were subsidiary skills expected of seamen, less obvious than the smarter work attended to on deck or aloft. Although supervision of such tasks was the province of a mate, the master always bore overall responsibility and was 'sovereign aboard his ship'.

In addition to this general concern a master had always to consider the effect of a cargo's stowage upon his ship's stability and trim. The science of the former was complex and not well comprehended in a mathematical sense during the eighteenth and much of the nineteenth centuries, but the basics were understood, for over-setting and capsize were dangers the dimmest seaman could appreciate. A ship had to be able to 'stand up to her canvas' and return to the vertical equilibrium of an even keel at all states of a voyage, notwithstanding the fact that parcels of cargo might be discharged at various ports along the way. To this transverse dynamic, longitudinal trim often made or marred a voyage. A sailing ship performed best at a certain loaded condition, but determining precisely what this was, was a matter of subjective judgement. While varying loads meant that a vessel floated at varying draughts, the degree to which she sat in the water trimmed by the stern – or by the head, for that matter – often affected her sailing and, more particularly, her handling characteristics.

Critical among these was her ability 'to stay', or 'tack', when beating to windward. In square-rigged ships, gaining ground towards the direction from which a wind blew meant making a series of zig-zag 'boards' or 'tacks' at an angle to the wind of usually about seventy-five degrees. It was not a very efficient method of making ground and only employed when absolutely necessary. To make an ocean passage it was better to sail an additional thousand miles under the influence of a favourable wind, than struggle against it, but occasionally – particularly in confined waters – beating to windward was unavoidable. To change from zig to zag, the process of turning the bow of the ship through the wind was called 'tacking or staying' and it had to be done efficiently otherwise the turn could be arrested, the vessel 'caught in irons' and either sent backwards to make 'a stern board' or cast back onto the former tack. If this happened the operation had to be repeated, if there was room. Often there was not and a ship was cast aground on the object she tacked to avoid. The alternative of 'wearing ship' by turning away from the wind and putting the stern through the wind's eye was a safer technique, but it required more sea-room and, most significantly, it lost valuable ground to windward. Being cast off to leeward lost time and time, it was increasingly appreciated, was money.

A badly trimmed ship would not turn into and across the wind efficiently, so such matters preoccupied masters and mates more than calculations of latitude, while anxieties over cargo – upon which the entire viability of a voyage and hence of the ship's company's fortunes rested – were equally worrying. Since 'freight was the mother of wages' the entire business of loading, handling and discharging a ship was a matter of great moment. The ability to make sensible decisions was largely acquired empirically, by experience, trial-and-error and therefore a good deal of what we would consider gross incompetence prevailed. To these grander anxieties other often equally vexatious concerns would be added.

All matters associated with the purchase of food, ship's stores, ropes, sails, spars, paint and the manifold supplies necessary for the maintenance of a vessel were in the hands of the master. In all this he would be in contact with chandlers and might possibly employ ship-yard specialists and tradesmen. He was also responsible for the matter of crew pay and advances. Accordingly, at the end of a voyage, a master had to account for all these disbursements and set them as debits against his voyage accounts. In a small merchant ship, much depended upon the master who needed to be a jack-of-all-trades, as Kelly recalled in 1788:

> On the 12th, having bad weather, we sprung our bowsprit, which our captain repaired with an oak fish, having no carpenter on board; but, indeed, such a man was unnecessary, as our captain was not only one of the most complete and expert seamen I had ever met with, but also an excellent mechanic, being very ingenious. He could make masts and yards, mend a frying-pan, or manage a ship with any man, and I have seen him make good cabinet work, for which purpose he kept various tools.

Nevertheless he might, upon occasion during the voyage, delegate some of these subsidiary duties to his officers.

Below the master in subordination came the mates, two in a small ship, up to six in a large East Indiaman. The senior of these, the man who inherited command if the master died but, until that happened was always kept at a distance, was usually called *the* mate, rather than the first, or the chief, mate. The others bore subordinate names and stood their watch either singly, as was most common, or in pairs in a large Indiaman. If she carried passengers, a vessel might bear a purser on her books, and perhaps a surgeon. Later in the eighteenth century surgeons were mandatory aboard whalers while both surgeons and gunners had long been common in slavers and privateers. Thereafter came the petty officers, led by the all-important carpenter whose practical skills often kept a ship afloat and who was invariably a ship-wright. The leading seaman was the boatswain, responsible for the organisation of the crew and he might be supported by a boatswain's mate or two. Depending upon the trade, duration of the voyage and size of the vessel, the steering might be entirely managed by quartermasters rather than shared by the able seamen. Catering was undertaken by a cook and possibly his boy, while a steward or cabin 'boy' attended to the officers, their daily feeding and accommodation. This was predicated not so much upon class distinctions as upon the notion that the master and mates must, at all times and in all circumstances, put the care of the ship first and that if they were not on duty attending to this, they were off duty eating, sleeping or supervising some aspect of a ship's internal management.

Set apart from the central 'brains' of a vessel at sea was the 'brawn that made it all work; that toiled when work was to be done irrespective of the prevailing conditions'. In many small ships the so-called officers would commonly toil alongside the seamen, the distinctions between a junior mate and a boatswain being almost indeterminate and the duties often combined. The construction of a ship's hierarchy, like so much else about her, depended upon her size, trade and port of origin. A vessel of 180 tons trading to Spain for wine and fruit had, perforce to run the risk of interception by the Barbary pirates and her crew was correspondingly larger than a vessel of similar tonnage trading elsewhere. Such a ship would typically bear a master and two mates, a surgeon, gunner, boatswain, carpenter and eighteen seamen, a similar complement to a slaver. On the other hand, a Baltic-trader of similar tonnage carried a master and one mate, a surgeon, boatswain, carpenter and eleven 'men and boys', about one third in total, though in time of war a gunner was invariably added. Occasionally, and increasingly as time passed, a dedicated cook was signed-on, becoming 'a most necessary member so long as there will be bellies'. As with other senior hands, the cook had a boy as an assistant who came at minimal cost. Such ships stood in stark contrast with the East Indiaman whose voyage was a long and dangerous affair, not least because disease often ravaged an Indiaman's crew. In 1703 a small Indiaman of around 400 tons comprised her commander, five mates and three midshipmen – no apprentices for John Company. Among the officers were a purser and surgeon, the latter with two assistants, or mates, while subordinate to the purser were a steward, a captain's personal steward and two assistant stewards to attend the other officers and any passengers. Each of the chief petty officers, the boatswain, gunner and carpenter, had two to four servants-cum-mates; cook and cooper both had mates and there were besides a caulker and his assistant, a joiner and two tailors. Last but by no means least came the fifty or so common sailors and a handful of wretched boys, whose 'unique function was to stay on board as watchman in foreign ports, when the rest of the crew had gone to taste the pleasures of the shore'.[17] As such a security measure, the provision of 'boys' was often specifically mentioned in charter-parties.

Writing in 1780 the nautical lexicographer and former purser William Falconer wrote:

> The Principle articles required in a common sailor to entitle him to full wages are that he can steer, sound, and manage the sails, by extending, reefing and furling them as occasion requires. When expert at these exercises, his skill in all other matters is taken for granted.

However, he confuses the generic with the specific in prefacing this definition with the remark that a 'Seaman' was 'a mariner or person trained in the exercise of fixing the machinery of a ship, and applying it to the purposes of navigation', which might

Late eighteenth-century merchant ship, from William Falconer's *The Shipwreck*. (From a private collection)

include a mate or master. The ordinary-seaman who had achieved some competence at his business could only be promoted and rated able-seaman, if he could 'hand, reef and steer' to which Falconer adds 'sound', that is handle a lead-line and interpret its readings even in the dark, a responsible task usually given to trusted sailors. By such personal skills and activity did a sailor make his mark within a ship's company; ashore he was perceived very differently.

The sailor was an object of curiosity to the landsman. The entire profession was disparaged, it being commonly believed that 'whosoever putteth his child to get his living at sea had better a great deal bind him prentice to a hangman'. And Matthew Bishop, confronted by landsmen, was told that 'they took the Sea to be fit only for those who could not get Bread by Land'. Much of this prejudice the seaman ashore brought upon himself. Visiting Wapping in the 1770s the novelist and social reformer Henry Fielding remarked that 'a man would be apt to suspect himself in another country' such was the 'idle and dissolute' behaviour of Jack ashore. Earlier in the century another novelist, Daniel Defoe, hammered a pejorative adjective: ''Tis their way to be violent in all their motions. They swear violently, whore violently, drink punch violently, spend their money ... violently ... in short, they are violent fellows, and ought to be encouraged to go to sea...' Here, however, in their element, Fielding conceded that they were 'perfect masters of their business ... always extremely alert and ready in executing it, without any regard to fatigue or hazard'. And herein, of course, lay the psychological spring for all that shore-side debauchery: a seaman was never quite certain whether he would survive a voyage which was, inevitably, filled

Eighteenth-century European merchant ship rigs from Frederik Hendrik Af Chapman's *Architectura Navalis Mercantoria* of 1768. (Author's Collection)

with risk if not outright danger. He enhanced his image by the extravagance of his language, employing a technical argot which added to his appearance as a stranger, and often dressed in an extravagant, beribboned fashion. It was no mistake that a seaman called shore-leave 'liberty' and he made the best of its limited freedoms. Whilst employed at sea, though, he became more generally tractable as the eighteenth century wore on. Querulous to a degree, ready to blame authority in the person of the master for every ill, perceived and real, the early eighteenth century merchant seaman was often not far from mutiny or even turning pirate. Owners warned their ship-masters in no uncertain terms as to the importance of maintaining order. 'You have heard how frequent conspiracies are growne aboard ships, wherefore keep a watchful eye and be very carefull and diligent to prevent such practices in your ship', the owners of the *Samuel and Anna* on a long voyage to Borneo in 1702 instructed her master. Time and marginally more stable conditions improved matters a little so that in her *Journal of a Lady of Quality*, Janet Schaw recorded her impressions of a voyage made in the 1770s. Rough they might be, but she remarked upon 'the warm hearts we generally meet with in sailors'.

His own cloth was more critical. Recruiting a crew for a trans-Atlantic crossing in winter during the Royal Navy's 'Spanish Armament' of 1791, Samuel Kelly recalled that:

As the seamen were now obliged to secret[e] themselves from the press-gang, I had many a weary step after them, but having obtained all but two of the crew I

sent the vessel into the river by way of securing those I had shipped. Towards the
close of Sunday I obtained a promise from two men at an ale-house of the lower
order that they would go with me, but as they had not spent all their money, lately
received from an African voyage, their landlord treated me with an insult ... but ...
I was determined to keep close to them. The next day I hired a boat in readiness and
paid them an early visit, but as seamen are a wavering set of people, I had to follow
them from place to place ... and at last, just at the top of high water, I was under the
necessity of taking two women of their acquaintance into the boat with them, they
little knowing that the vessel was at that moment under sail in the river. As soon as
I got alongside, their chests were handed on board, and as the men entered the deck
the boat was ordered away and we proceeded to sea.

Despite his apparent unruliness and debauchery, the sailor ashore was more sinned
against than sinning. If he had just been paid he was ripe for exploitation by pimps
and whores, by gamblers, tricksters, hucksters, inn and tavern-keepers, brothel-owners,
pawn-brokers and almost all those he came into contact with along the world's water-
fronts – particularly that of the London River. The uncertainty of the sea-life often
prompted lodging-house owners to offset debts left by seafarers departing upon a
foreign voyage by procuring them to make wills in their favour, or to take out powers
of attorney in the seaman's behalf. Other, more suspect practices, such as usurers setting ridiculously high interest-rates on loans, or the forging of claims in the names of
seamen lost on a voyage, were commonplace. Such milking of the wages of seafarers
must have been a powerful inducement to despairing drunkenness and moral dissolution. The seaman's inability to press a matter through the courts owing to his
economically driven imminent departure was a gift to the shark ashore, a far greater
danger to Jack's well-being than the shark at sea.

Among the worst of these was the crimp, whose practices reached a peak as late as
the 1890s, but whose origins were reasonably respectable. A seaman seeking a berth
in a ship might, on his own initiative, find one at the Royal Exchange; but he was far
more likely to encounter a middle-man along the Ratcliffe Highway, in Wapping or
across the river in Rotherhithe. One such, Robert Crispe of Shadwell, was in 1704
'a crimp provideinge mariners for masters' whose business was 'onely to bring the
master and men together. They make the agreement themselves'.

Until as late as 1929 this 'Agreement' was usually made verbally in a tavern, circumstances that rendered matters of detail unclear at a later date. Although, under the terms
of its charter of 1685 Trinity House had sought to secure a proper contract between a
ship's master and her crew this, where it applied at all, affected only vessels plying in
and out of 'the River of Thames'. In 1729, however, the notion of a formal agreement
between the master, as the owner's hiring and managing agent, and the hired hands, was
enforced by law under an 'Act for the Better Regulation and Government of Seamen
in the Merchants' Service (2 Geo II, c36). Although renewable every five years, the
act became perpetual in the following reign. After 1729 a written document had to
be signed by all parties and became known as the Articles of Agreement, or 'Articles'

for short. All seamen, petty officers and mates – and even often ship-masters – signed Articles on a voyage-by-voyage basis. Matters became disputatious if, as often happened in a trading voyage, the planned ports and length of the voyage were changed. Such, the seamen argued, invalidated the terms of the Articles and it became customary to offer inducements such as an advance of wages before a voyage could resume to another port. This was intended, on the one hand to provide a penurious seaman with the means to equip himself with suitable clothes, bedding and comforts for a voyage, and on the other, to bind him into a further and altered term of service. For example, the master of a ship bound to the warm waters of the Mediterranean, receiving a change of orders at Lisbon, advanced 'all the company ... a month's pay, they urging that Newfoundland was a cold countrey and that they should want cloathes'. Nevertheless, after 1729 the seaman – whatever hardships he was compelled to endure – at least enjoyed a legally binding security of employment unknown elsewhere among labouring men.

As was to be expected, a slightly different system appertained in East Indiamen. Seamen in John Company's employ were entitled to a two months advance of wages to provide for their families and to settle their affairs prior to an East India voyage. They were also obliged to appoint an attorney, their wife, family member or a creditor, who was entitled to one months' wages for every six months a man served. With an average voyage length of two years the sailor and his agent would receive a substantial sum prior to a final settlement after the homeward cargo had been landed in the East India Company's warehouses and the freight upon it had been paid to Leadenhall Street. A seaman might receive pay for working a ship in a river where such movements were necessary but separate from the signing-on for a voyage. This was particularly so in Indiamen where they were moved in and out of the East India Dock and rigged and unrigged at the beginning and end of a voyage. Such practices led to seamen being employed in shore-gangs specifically for such purposes. Similarly large advances were paid in slavers, since the crew mortality rate was high, many seamen succumbing to a variety of tropical diseases which their diet and their constitutions left their auto-immune systems ill-equipped to counter.

In general-traders a man's wage was paid by the month at around 24 or 25 shillings for an able-seaman throughout the eighteenth century, a boy receiving half a man's rate. War, however, invariably distorted the matter of pay, often doubling it and therefore making service in men-of-war extremely unpopular. Not all owners paid a monthly wage, however. Ships bound for the Grand Banks off Newfoundland 'to catch and cure fish' received a small monthly payment and since 'it hath been a constant custom used beyond the memory of man to allow them one fifth or one sixth part of the fish, or every fifth or sixth fish they catch or the value thereof in money' they bought into the profitability of the voyage. This sometimes became the only source of remuneration when a powerful attraction was required for a specific purpose, such as privateering. Such were the aggressive qualities required in privateers operating under Letters-of-Marque-and-Reprisal that no wages were offered, but generous proportions of prize-money were agreed to. A less extreme system of part-pay, part-profit sharing pertained in whaling ships after the revival of the fishery in the middle of the century. All the crew of the Liverpool whaler *Britannia*, leaving 'for Greenland or the Davis Straits' in 1762 signed-on for monthly wages, but the master, mates and harpooners received a bonus on 'each half gallon of neat oyl'.

There was also the matter of deductions. During a voyage a master would sell slops, comforts, tobacco and even spirituous liquor to his crew, making a profit out of this much resented form of micro-monopolistic transaction. Seamen might also be fined for 'each and every day or night that they lye ashore without the leave or consent of their master' – a not infrequent misdemeanour in many ports where sex and alcohol were readily available. There were always deductions for loss or damage, particularly to cargo, and in this one must include the 'black gold' of slaves. Often such mulcts were unjustly applied and occasionally they were challenged in court. Indeed, although it had lost much of its power by the mid-1700s, the High Court of Admiralty retained its right to try cases where a ship's company could sue for loss of wages, a particularly popular means of proceeding when a master or owners defaulted in the matter of crew pay. By the process relying only upon the name of one seaman being entered as plaintiff, with the rest being grouped as one company, it allowed the majority to return to sea and earn their living while the case proceeded. Such joint-suits could be had at little cost to the individual and were another unique feature of the seafaring life. Occasionally such cases, of which there were many, were pursued 'to the last plank' since they were made *in rem* – against the inanimate ship – not against a person. If a judgement was brought in favour of the plaintiffs that 'wages are due and ought to be pay'd,' a ship could be compulsorily sold to raise the money. Clearly this required the ship's existence and, as Edward Barlow points out, the case was entirely different if the ship – and her all-important freight – were lost through wrecking or foundering.

> Many times their ships are cast away and perhaps the men saved, and then they lose all they have, small and great: and many times they fall into enemies' hands, and then they lose all and suffer an imprisonment besides.

Indeed such cases proliferated to such an extent that in 1742 a group of merchants were moved to petition the House of Commons to prevent vexatious suits in the High Court of Admiralty. They also wished to restrain increases in seamen's pay in wartime when obtaining seamen became a very difficult business, thanks to the demands of the Royal Navy. Most unpopular of the deductions was that which all merchant seamen were obliged to contribute, sixpence a month to 'the Chatham Chest' so named after its establishment at Chatham for the relief of seamen by Drake and Hawkins in the late sixteenth century. This was deeply resented because, by the mid-1700s, the deduction was not only compulsory but went to the maintenance of Greenwich Hospital. A disabled seamen could only secure a place as a pensioner at Greenwich if he had seen naval service and been injured therein. This was not the only injustice perpetrated at Greenwich. William Spavens, writing about 1763 and himself a pensioner who had served in both merchant and naval ships, in the latter of which he had been disabled, says:

Though none can claim or ought to have admittance into it [Greenwich Hospital] but such as have served in the Royal Navy, yet some time ago, many gentlemen, through interest, gained admittance for their worn-out domestics who had never been at sea in their lives, consequently these had no rights, if a merchant's [sea]man who pays to its support has none or is allowed none; but these abuses are now reformed.

Despite the reform, merchant seamen remained largely excluded, though time moderated this harsh ruling. Writing a polemical book sixty years later complaining – with numerous incidents to back him up – of the appalling state of indiscipline in the British merchant marine in 1830, Captain Christopher Biden, much of whose command-time was in the service of the Honourable East India Company, wrote in a footnote:

A seaman lost his leg in the Honourable Company's ship *Kellie Castle*, when I was chief mate of her, by a fall from the royal yard; he was afterwards admitted to Greenwich Hospital.

This general lack of charitable provision for merchant seamen was addressed in part by the Trinity Houses at Deptford, Kingston-upon-Hull and Newcastle, but these were inadequate to answer the extent of the evil. The richest of these corporations, the Trinity House of London, established almshouses suitable for 'decay'd mariners' and also granted annuities, but such largesse was unequal to the size of the problem. The Court of Elder Brethren attempted to establish a similar system of compulsory deduction to run alongside that of the Chatham Chest for the benefit of merchant sailors, but it failed on the grounds that it was *another* deduction, rather than a *replacement* of the first.

While shipwreck or capture spelled personal disaster in which, as Barlow also points out, 'The loss of a chest and clothes ... are more to him [the seaman] than he can make good again in a twelvemonth time', there were occasional ameliorations. Although seamen from the earliest times until after the Second World War were rarely worth 'more than their wages' and possessed little beyond the clothes and perhaps the tools necessary for their work, in the seventeenth and eighteenth centuries almost everyone on a voyage embarked upon a little private trading. Although many borrowed from usurers, thus placing themselves in hock at punishing rates of interest, in order to make 'a small competence' such an 'adventure' could amount to tidy sums in provident hands. Raisins bought in Alicante could be sold for a profit of 100 per cent in London, similar profits could be made in Indian waters by buying *arrack* in Bombay and selling it elsewhere along the Malabar coast. Despite the terrors of premature death in the slave-trade, many sailors of all ranks did very well out of it. As an inducement to look after their human cargo, they were paid a portion of their wages on delivery in the West Indies. Such payments suited the shipowners since they were made in the slightly debased local currency but such small lump sums enabled the sailors to invest in trade-goods. 'It is customary,' it was recorded in 1719, 'for the mariners to lay out their money in tobacco, whereby they generally make fifty or sixty per cent profit'. Rum was also a readily convertible commodity but its accessibility in small puncheons often proved self-defeating to Jack in search of profit.

Lack of money and space on board restricted private trade within modest limits, but an inventive and persuasive seaman might sail from home with trade-goods provided by others, offering him an opportunity to cheat his investors. Of course masters and mates did best, because they commanded both more space and more capital. They also enjoyed certain rights, particularly in the slave-trade where a master might carry up to three slaves free of freight for his own profit. If it was in any sense 'lucky' to be taken aboard a slave-ship, it was for these few individuals, who were not only better looked after by their owners, but were often taught a trade such as carpentry to enhance their value on the mastaba of the slave-market. The extent of private trade was greatest in East Indiamen, and subject to serious abuses in the packets of the General Post-Office, subjects discussed later. However, it was not only in the ships of John Company that a prudent mariner might grow wealthy and a man who achieved the status and trappings of a ship-master might consider himself 'made', acquiring middle-class status. The former black slave Olaudah Equiano, through thrift and astute dealing made sufficient money to die a gentleman, circumstances that in the late eighteenth century provide perhaps the best evidence of the essential meritocracy that the merchants' service *could* be if a man was patient and played his cards right. Manumitted under the name Gustavus Vassa, Equiano married an Englishwoman named Sarah Cullen in April 1792 and the couple had two daughters. When her father died in 1816, an event which was noted in *The Gentleman's Magazine*, his sole surviving daughter Joanna inherited the considerable sum of £950.

Occupying an ambivalent position in a merchant ship's hierarchy were the wretched apprentices. Apprentices had a raw deal, not least because their parents had to find a premium which varied from £10 in a small, deep-water trader, to £100 in an Indiaman. An apprentice bound himself for four years to a master by an indenture in which he agreed to attend to his master's business, not frequent ale-houses or taverns, 'unless it be upon his master's business', 'nor play at naughty games'. Although, in three hundred years, there was never any obligation for a master to train his apprentices to become navigators, since an apprentice's indentures only committed the master to teaching him the business of a seaman, this was the usual route by which an ambitious lad became first a seamen, then a mate and finally – with the right aptitude and an eye for a modest investment – a ship-master. An apprentice who had completed his indentures – usually of four years' duration – could be rated able-seaman, thus changing officially from boy to man, but could only advance further if he showed promise and possessed the necessary drive and ambition. Thus the onus to 'improve himself' was thrown upon the immature and callow youth, leaving the ship's master to exploit apprentices as cheap-labour, a situation that pertained until the middle of the twentieth century. A young man showing talent might nevertheless attract the favour of instruction by a mate or even the master himself in the 'art, science, mysterie and trade of a mariner'. Most endured years of drudgery and occasional outright tyranny, often left to fend for themselves if a ship was laid up without cargo. One, Gerrard Monger, made complaint against Captain John Ely who 'did never teach or instruct in the art of navigation' but confiscated the 'bookes and mapps touching' the subject with which Monger had been provided.

However, to assist the ambitious there developed from an early period a small number of schools of varying quality but noble intent. Some of these private institutions combined nautical education with instrument-making and the writing and publishing of the first treatises on what Charles II was pleased to call 'the arte and mysterie of navigation,' the derivatives of which have been mentioned earlier. Royal patronage endowed a navigation school at Christ's Hospital in 1673, and the first fifteen Blue-coat boys were obliged to pass an examination before the Elder Brethren of Trinity House in 1675. Charles expressed his royal will, exhorting 'the goodwill and assistance of the principal companies of merchants by their interposition with the masters employed by them' to encourage the education of marine apprentices. Moreover, the king instituted a grant of a seaman's pay for every apprentice a ship-master took up. Other schools where boys could learn the mathematics 'requisite to instruct youth in the Art of Navigation, to fit them for the Sea Service' were opened soon afterwards. Most notable among these were Sir Joseph Williamson's at Rochester (1701), Neale's Mathematical School in Fleet Street (1715) and the Royal Hospital School attached to the Royal Navy's Greenwich Hospital (1716). This last, intended for the orphans of naval seamen, established an enviable reputation and places were sought by those with living parents so that by 1750 it had on its books some 100 boys intended as apprentices to officers of men-of-war or merchant ship-masters.

Elsewhere similar institutions grew up, often over-seen by ex-mariners like Captain Joshua Kelly who ran an establishment at Wapping New Stairs. Another Wapping academy offering a wide curriculum which sensibly reflected the many demands that might be made upon a ship-master in the course of his duties, was that of Cutler and Groom who in 1711 considered themselves:

> Teachers of Writing, Arithmetick, Merchants Accompts, Geometry, Algebra, Trigonometry, Navigation, Astronomy, Gunnery, Gauging, Dialling, Perspective, Measuring; the use of the Globes, and all other Mathematical Instruments, the Projection of the Sphere, on any circle, etc.[18]

There were other London teachers, 'one Mr Atkinson ... on Rotherif [Rotherhithe] Wall,' attended in 1714 by John Cremer; while beyond the capital, Charlton's Mathematical School at Whitby was so efficient that it 'so well ... profited' Francis Gibson in 1763 that 'during his first voyage he made a chart of the coast and harbour at Goldsborough in New England'. The Trinity House of Kingston-upon-Hull was forward in employing a *domine* to instruct a class of boys in navigation, blossoming in 1786 into the Trinity House School, which, like Christ's Hospital, is extant to this day.

There was, of course, no systematic policy of recruitment, no state social engineering to provide the steadily increasing mercantile marine with men. Malthusian determinants provided numbers and, as we have seen, proper training in any professional sense was haphazard. Nevertheless among the pamphlets and publications generated amid the intellectual ferment of the seventeenth century this national necessity is clearly set out and imperfect attempts were made to secure it. It was widely assumed that a supply of seamen for both the merchants' as much as for the king's services would be available if certain maritime trades and enterprises were protected. Chief among these 'Nurseries of Seamen' were the Newfoundland and Iceland fisheries and the Newcastle-to-London coal trade. In *The Trades Increase* of 1615, the latter was:

> If not the only, yet the special Nursery, and School for Seamen. For, as it is the chiefest in Employment for Seamen, so it is the gentlest and most open to Landsmen; they never grudging in their smaller Vessels to entertaine some fresh-men, or learners; whereas, to the Contrary in the Shippes that voyage to the southward or otherwise, far out of the Kingdome, there is no Owner, or Maister, that will ordinarily entertaine any land-men, be he never so willing, as being bound by the Charter-Partie to the Merchant … not to carry but sufficient Men, and such as know their Labour.

It was here that, in the words of Colonel Birch in the Commons on 13 April 1671, 'in the Coal Ships[,] Country Fellows … are made Seamen quickly'. Even the disparaging and scurrilous Ned Ward in *The Wooden World* of 1706 stated that:

> If his breeding has been North of Yarmouth … he is a rare horse that will never fail you in bad Weather, being as insensible to Rain, Cold or Thunder as a Cannon-bullet. He is generally above the common size of other Tars, in Bulk, Strength and Courage, which is mainly owing to his northern Diet…

Unfortunately the state was lazy; it did not always secure the more distant of these, the Iceland fishery going through several periods of boom and bust, while tolerating a continuous French presence at St Pierre and Miquelon, over-looking the Newfoundland grounds, under the terms of several eighteenth century peace-treaties. As long as there remained congruence between the basic requirements of merchantmen and men-of-war, it was always easy for a mobilising navy to poach from the merchants' shipping. Able men could be readily found in merchant ships, men who could be guaranteed to hand, reef, steer, sound with the lead and work a gun: men who 'know their Labour'. Of this subject we shall hear more.

Despite the ties of blood or business that bound men together in commercial interest, the fragmented nature of shipowning in the eighteenth century did not always work in practice. The support a master might expect from an owner was sometimes as unforthcoming as the fragile trust an owner might place in a master. While cases of barratry were not unknown, the specific, if not individual, nature of the crime gave it a more felonious gloss than mere indifference on the part of an owner when the master and crew were in trouble. Whatever privations trouble might mean at a personal and usually physical level to a ship's master and crew, the distant owner was invariably touched by trouble in his pocket, and a man may easily justify keeping the contents of his pocket where they were. No owner willingly paid out for moral reasons and while losses to storm, ship-wreck and other acts of God could be offset by insurance, or the spreading of invested capital, losses of ships to the malice of others was a different matter.

Ships lost to privateers as well as to pirates, for example, often attracted ransoms. Preying upon trade, or practicing *le guerre de course*, was a specialisation at which – whatever their deficiencies were in other forms of maritime warfare – the French were very effective throughout the wars of the eighteenth century. One British master, Captain Anthony Dewstoe, captured by French corsairs in 1704 during the War of the Spanish Succession, was put up for a ransom of £65. Unfortunately the ship's owner, Valentine Enys of Falmouth, initially refused to redeem him from incarceration in Brest. 'No one in the world,' he wrote with a cool pragmatism to the wretched Dewstoe, 'would ever ransom a ship for more than the worth [of it]'. Enys did eventually pay-up but he did nothing to help the crew of his ship the *Francis*, taken by 'Sallee Rovers' whose chief objectives were, as we have seen, the crews aboard merchant ships, which sold well in the *souks* of Meknes and Marrakesh.

Piracy by the corsairs of the littoral states of North Africa was a constant and fearful threat to the merchant seafarer, persisting long after the treaty of 1682 agreed between Admiral Herbert and the Dey of Algiers which was, in the words of the English Secretary of State, somewhat misleadingly stated to have been 'commodious and beneficial for his subjects trading in all those seas'.[19] As observed in the previous chapter, the most intransigent were the Salé rovers, who could sell a Christian into slavery for around £30. The majority of these wretches were put to hard labour, toiling on the construction of the palace of Moulay Ismail, Sultan of Morocco. This apparently endless project – it was the largest edifice of its day, far exceeding the contemporaneous pile of Versailles – stretched for miles over the hills of Meknes and it was voracious of human lives.

The *Francis*, Captain John Pellow, was captured along with the *George*, Captain Robert Fowler, and the *Southwark*, Captain Richard Ferris, in 1715. First to be attacked, Ferris resisted the pursuing vessels 'fighting ten hours, and with a noble resolution' but he was finally overwhelmed by the crews of Ali Hakem and Abdul Rahman el-Mediouni whose men outnumbered the British. In due course the survivors of this action were thrown into the notorious slave pens of Salé and then taken to Meknes to work on the imperial palace. Among the crew of the *Francis* was Pellow's nephew Tom, a boy scarcely in his teens when he was tortured to the point of apostasy and 'turned Moor'.

Only a few of the Christian slaves were ransomed from the clutches of the utterly despotic Moulay Ismail and his successors, while reselling to his neighbours the rulers of Algiers and Tunis continued in spite of the vaunted treaty. But those who renounced Christ, even under the most hideous persecution, became 'renegades' for whom, in that intolerant age of religious certainty, there could be no redemption. The attitude towards such desolate souls was epitomised by the Reverend Cotton

Mather, a Puritan minister from New England – which lost many ships and crews to the Barbary pirates. For their 'consolation' Mather rhetorically asked: 'Who gave thee to the African pyrats?' He then helpfully provided the answer that 'It was the Lord, against who you had sinned'. It is difficult to understand the extent of young Tom Pellow's sins; perhaps they were mere peccadilloes for, in his own words: 'Nothing but the Almighty protection of a great … and gracious God could have carried me through it'. Pellow made several attempts to escape and his final success was most unusual; he finally returned home to Cornwall where his parents failed to recognise him after twenty-three years' enslavement.

These men had nothing to hope for and their only chance of a life of any standard was to fall in with the Sultan's plans. Many escaped the terrible labour of working with lime and soil mortar in raising walls of imposing grandeur, by signing up to the Sultan's immense army and employing their martial skills. One such was an Irishman named Carr, who became Moulay Ismail's artillerist, and it was in arms, particularly muskets, and gun-powder that any trade between the Sultan's subjects and British merchants went on. As we have seen, attempts to mediate and ransom British merchant seamen were bungled on one side, and treated with contempt on the other. Even when an agreement seemed in prospect, the whimsical Sultan would disregard it, usually after sums of money and lavish gifts had been deposited in his treasury. Although a consular official was maintained by the British at Tetuan, he was given insufficient money to maintain any standard likely to impress the Sultan's *kaids*, relying for his very subsistence upon 'consulage' – an inadequate levy on imports of English goods into Morocco. Inadequate for redeeming slaves, this sum kept the consul in a state considered contemptuous by the sultan and his people, an indication of the impoverished state of the distant British kingdom that employed him.

One of these unfortunate diplomats, Colonel Anthony Hatfeild (sic) reported to London that: 'The Salleymen … rove where they please' and noted the capture of four ships and fifty seamen. 'A great many persons are in captivity in Salé,' he wrote, 'where they endure inexpressible calamities'. This included women, a few of whom were captured on board ship and who were taken into the Sultan's immense seraglio. It was no different in Algiers or Tunis. Occasionally, to justify Mather's belief, an act of God delivered a crew directly into the hands of the Sultan. In 1746 the *Inspector* was wrecked in Tangier Bay and eighty-seven survivors were swiftly enslaved. 'Large iron chains were lock'd around our necks and twenty of us were link'd together in one chain,' wrote Thomas Troughton after being one of the few ransomed by the British Government after five years of terrible suffering. Of all of those overtaken by such an indescribable fate, most perished of malnutrition, torture, harsh punishment, capricious execution or utter neglect. Of those who survived by apostasy, we know only that while they might rarely rise in the Sultan's service, they were almost never allowed a status equivalent to naturalisation.

White enslavement was not a problem that had gone away, but one which would continue to vex mariners for years to come.

NOTES

1. Attempts at circumventing the meteorological problems associated with astro-navigation by means of radio waves were initiated before the Second World War. Some of these, such as radio-direction-finding, were for coastal navigation, some for off-shore operations such as the Gee-system (actually designed for bombing but abandoned by the USA and exploited for navigation by the Decca Navigator Company of the UK) and Loran, for Long Range Navigation. The former of these last two used hyperbolic wave comparison, the latter time-base comparison; both were successful and a modernised form of Loran remains in use. A long-range wave comparison system known as Omega was developed in the 1960s but was rapidly overtaken by the Global Positioning System (GPS) using satellites.

2. Narborough had gone to sea in the service of a relative, the naval officer and later admiral and knight, Christopher Myngs. After service in the West Indies, Narborough fought alongside his kinsman at Lowestoft and during the Four Days Battle in the Second Dutch War. After Myngs's death Narborough was promoted captain and commanded the *Assurance* in the West Indies. Although a naval officer, he was sent by Charles II into the Pacific in 1669 in an attempt to penetrate and break the Spanish monopoly on trade in that vast ocean. By the time Narborough, in the *Sweepstakes*, reached the Straits of Magellan, his consort in the *Bachelor* had had enough and returned to the Thames with a report that Narborough had been lost. In fact he had pressed on. An attempt to obtain fresh water at Valdivia on the coast of modern Chile, resulted in the arrest of a party landed to negotiate with the Spanish colonial authorities. With insufficient force to attack and secure the release of his men, Narborough was compelled to abandon them and returned to England without further achievement. Narborough returned to serve during the Third Dutch War when he commanded James, Duke of York's flagship, the *Prince* at the Battle of Solebay. After the war he was promoted to rear admiral and put in command of a fleet in the Mediterranean. His operations against the Barbary pirates have already been mentioned in Chapter Two.

3. Not to be confused with his contemporary, the Arctic explorer of the same name. Both men sailed with Lancaster's 'first voyage' to the east. John Davis of Limehouse was a subordinate pilot but being appointed master of the *Ascension*, sailed as pilot of the *Expedition* in 1608/09, master of the *James* (1611/12), and the *Swan* (1615/16). He was taken prisoner by the Dutch during this voyage at Polaroon in 1617 and his rutter was probably published in his absence, for he was not released until the following year when it would appear that he joined the *James* as gunner on her voyage between 1620 and 1621. How long he served in her seems uncertain, for he died at Batavia (Jakarta) in 1622 and probably never completed her voyage.

   John Davis the Arctic explorer, sometimes called Davys (*vide* the DNB), was Pilot Major to Lancaster and one of the most accomplished seamen of his age. Devon-born, he went to sea as a boy. In 1583, along with Adrian Gilbert and Dr John Dee he was an advocate of the exploration of the north-west passage, persuading Sir Francis Walsingham to back a venture thither. He made three voyages north in the *Sunshine*, with other ships in company and in 1587 he discovered the strait west of Greenland which today bears his name, penetrating what is now Baffin's Bay. He commanded the *Black Dog* in the defeat of the Spanish Armada and sailed with Cumberland on the duke's expedition to the Azores in 1589, taking the galleon *Uggera Salvagnia*. In 1591 he accompanied Thomas Cavendish on the latter's second privateering expedition. This fiasco ended in the Strait of Magellan, when the fleet turned back and Cavendish was lost. Davis continued westwards until driven back by contrary storms, whereupon he fell in with the then undiscovered Falkland Islands. Mentioned earlier as an inventor of the backstaff and double-quadrant, Davis also wrote two works of navigation, the treatise *The Seaman's Secrets* of 1594 and a global rutter, *The World's Hydrographical Description* of the following year. In 1596/7 Davis was master of Ralegh's flagship on the expedition to Cadiz and the Azores. At the instigation of the Earl of Essex he joined a Dutch voyage to the Spice Islands in 1598 as pilot of the Dutch East Indiaman, the *Leeuw* (*Lion*) and narrowly escaped with his life after attack by treachery. There followed his service with Lancaster and then in 1604 he joined Sir Edward Michelborne in the *Tiger*. Michelborne was an 'interloper', outside the legitimised trading organisation of the East India Company, one of a long tradition of merchants seeking to circumvent the Company's monopoly. Unfortunately in 1605 the *Tiger* ran foul of Japanese pirates off Singapore and in the ensuing affray Davis was killed.

4. French chronometers produced by Berthoud and Leroy were proved ship-compatible in 1767. It is worth noting that in the last years of the daily use of astro-navigation at sea by skilled professional navigators in the 1980s, instrumental, observational and tabular interpolational errors and inexactitudes could not *guarantee* practical accuracy greater than two miles, though comparison with GPS-derived positions often showed a closer conformity.

5. Indeed the naturalised American but Nova Scotian born Captain Joshua Slocum used it in his first solo-circumnavigation in the yacht *Spray* as late as 1895–1898.

6. In the Nelson era the Royal Navy's most experienced professional navigators were its 'masters', warrant officers not to be confused with the commanders of merchant ships, though this was often where they came from, most having learned their trade in merchantmen. They were obliged to provide their own charts, which at that time almost invariably came from private suppliers.

7. There were many refinements published by others, and many celebrated works by navigators and nautical scholars other than Britons, most notably perhaps the splendid *American Practical Navigator; An Epitome of Navigation*, the original edition of which appeared in the early nineteenth century from the pen of Nathaniel Bowditch. A fine, two-volume 1984 edition sits beside me as I write.

8. This ship was the predecessor of Nelson's famous flagship of the same name. The two towers at the Lizard and three on the Casquets are still extant, though only one at each station is today lit.

9. The second of the East India Company's ships to be sent towards Java, the *Tryall* ran aground and was wrecked on 25 May 1622 with heavy loss of life. Captain John Brookes and his mate, Thomas Bright escaped the wreck with forty-three men and reached Batavia. Bright accused Brookes – whose longitude was woefully inaccurate – of incompetence and of abandoning the *Tryall* precipitately, leaving many seamen to drown. Rumours circulated that he had got away with silver intended for trade. He was later given command of the *Moone* which sank off Dover in suspicious circumstances, resulting in a prolonged court-case during which Brookes was imprisoned but nothing was proved.

10. One unfortunate consequence of Dampier's in-put was the ill-fated Scottish trading-settlement on the Isthmus of Dairen mentioned later.

11. Davis, R., *The Rise of the English Shipping Industry*, p127.

12. Another great institution ancillary to this history was founded at this time. In 1694 the Bank of England was incorporated. Until 1640, when they were seized wholesale by Charles I, private deposits of bullion had been left by London merchants in the Tower of London under crown protection. Although returned to them, the City merchants henceforward mistrusted the king and left their monies with the Goldsmiths' Company who had acted as bankers for country gentlemen and others for many years. In addition to taking money on deposit, upon which they paid interest (against the extant laws

against usury), the goldsmiths acted as money-changers and took charge of rents. In exchange for money they gave 'goldsmiths' notes', the first form of bank-note and the means by which large transactions were carried out. The goldsmiths acted as financiers for the Protectorate Government of Cromwell – who had, incidentally, removed the strictures about the Jews living and money-lending in England. After the Restoration the goldsmiths advanced sums to the impecunious Charles II, charging him 12 per cent interest, whilst only paying about 5 per cent to those private persons investing with them.

In 1672, however, came national bankruptcy with the suspension of Exchequer payments. Charles II owned the goldsmiths £1,300,000, a bad debt which ruined both them and their depositors. This crisis and the desperation of the state prompted the establishment of a proper national bank with security of deposits, a safe and underwritten form of bank-note, and a lower and thus more generally beneficial rate of interest on loans. Other than the goldsmiths, and in some cases arising from them, a number of private banks had grown up in London and in other cities such as Bristol, Hull and Nottingham. These proved successful, but the best examples of viable banking came from Amsterdam. Following the representations of several influential City merchants, including the Scotsman William Paterson, an Act was passed on 27 July incorporating 'the Governor and Company of the Bank of England', initially for twelve years. Subsequent acts arising from the extremities to which the Government's finances were reduced, extended the bank's life and capital, reduced interest to 6 per cent and protected it as a semi-monopolistic institution by restricting the ability of other banks to issue notes. In 1722 the Bank's reserve was set up and in 1751 it took over the administration of the national debt. New charters were issued in 1764 and 1781. Following a fiscal crisis in 1793, in 1795 £5 notes were first issued and in 1797, the increasing cost of the war with Revolutionary France – and to some extent mutiny in the Royal Navy – created a crisis during which cash payments were suspended by the Bank Restriction Act following a run on gold coin. From this time onwards bank-notes effectively became legal tender.

13. See Davis, *The Rise of the English Shipping Industry*, p84 *et seq*.

14. There were some exceptions to this, notably the Norwegian and Baltic timber trade which in 1695 was considered 'more profitable to the Ship and Men than to the Merchant'.

15. Selling a cargo was often undertaken for a number of reasons. It might be necessary to remove the lading to a place of safety to get at a damaged part of the hull, in which case its storage would incur charges. Occasionally cargoes were subject to seasonality, either because of their perishable nature, or the temporary nature of the market for a commodity. A quick sale was always better than no sale if a ship was delayed in reaching her planned destination.

16. Davis, p180. The balancing act between capacity and deadweight was a continuous brainteaser to all parties and it was not until industrial methods adapted some commodities for shipment that some of the problems were resolved. A particular example of this was cotton, an extremely light and voluminous cargo which filled a ship's capacity without conferring any weight to stabilise her until it was capable of being massively compressed into heavy bales by steam-plant.

17. See Davis, p113.

18. 'Dialling' had several meanings, one of which was the constructing of sun-dials and other inscribed instruments, some having maritime applications; another was the art of using a dial or compass in surveying. 'Gauging' was the method of determining by actual measurement – rather than the estimation which is meant today – the capacity of a vessel or the amount contained in it.

19. They continued to be a problem until late in the nineteenth century. One 'solution' to the mystery of the *Mary Celeste*, found bereft of a crew in November 1872, was that her company had been abducted by Barbary pirates. During his solo-circumnavigation in the *Spray* which began in 1895, Captain Joshua Slocum was chased off the Moroccan coast after leaving Gibraltar. Piracy thrives in many parts of the world to this day. Merchant ships' crews are at best terrorised and not infrequently murdered, even in the twenty-first century.

PART TWO

'The Danger of a Seafareing Life'

British Shipping in the Atlantic Ocean 1550–1807

'Beware, beware the Bight of Benin,
For few come out,
Though many go in.'

Anonymous

'I own I am shocked by the purchase of slaves,
And fear those who buy them and sell them, are knaves,
What I hear of their hardships, their tortures and groans,
Is almost enough to draw pity from stones.
I pity them greatly, but I must be mum,
For how could we do without sugar and rum?'

William Cowper (1731–1800)

FOUR

'A GREAT NUMBER OF USEFULL PERSONS KEPT IN BEING'

The Atlantic Slave Trade, 1550–1807

Gold first lured Europeans to the 'Guinea coast' of West Africa. In 1325 King Mansa Musi of Mali arrived at Mecca with a train of camels each carrying gold. The news spread fast; the king's entourage also included five hundred black-skinned slaves, but this did not yet register with avaricious Europeans who heard of unlimited wealth lying somewhere in the south of Africa, perhaps attached to the fabled kingdom of a great Christian prince called Prester John.

Ready access to this paradise was barred by the Sahara desert and the 'Moorish' states of the feared Barbary coast of North Africa, linked by Islam and united against the inroads of infidels. During the second half of the fifteenth century Portuguese navigators, however, stretching south along the coast of Mauretania and beyond Cape Verde, began trading with Arab merchants, fetching back to Lisbon gold, pepper and ivory. In these dealings the Portuguese discovered a secondary source of income in the coastal carriage of slaves on behalf of their Arab associates, who employed black African porters on the trans-Saharan trade routes and sold men and women into captivity throughout the Arab world. This sea-borne traffic proved quicker and less mortal than overland marches through inhospitable terrain, and became a lucrative business for the Portuguese.

By 1482 the Portuguese had built the fort of São Jorge de Mina – later known as Elmina – on what they called the Gold Coast (Ghana), from which they ventured beyond the Muslim lands, passing the Bight of Benin and reaching Ngola (Angola) by the end of the century. By now the Portuguese had discovered another even more exploitable opportunity among the native peoples of the African coast, namely an existing traffic in human beings. By the time Vasco da Gama had reached India, the

Atlantic archipelagos of the Azores, Canaries and Cape Verde Islands had been colonised and insular sugar plantations had begun to create a demand for cheap labour. To the bodies being shipped north on behalf of Arabs traffickers and a handful taken to Europe as servants, a steady number of slaves condemned to serve under the colonial lash was carried to labour at the production of sugar on these mid-Atlantic islands.

Although prevented from actually trading for slaves in Africa by the Treaty of Tordesillas, the Spanish created a ready market for shipments of 'negroes' in their own equivalent and expanding plantations in the Indies. Thus the first African slaves crossed the Atlantic around 1502, carried thither by the Portuguese but under Spanish control and for a Spanish market. By 1595, so great was the demand for slaves that Madrid consented for the entire trade by means of the *Asiento*. Economic benefits to Spain from the unification with Portugal were not only brief, the Portuguese breaking away again in 1640, but were complicated by the Dutch who both rebelled against Spain and acquired colonies in the Caribbean. Now they interloped into the slave-trade, under-cutting the official Iberian cartel. Further incursions were made by the English and French, both of whom were, as we have noted, settling in the Caribbean. They too took up 'live cargoes' from West Africa and sold them to eager Spanish colonial buyers.

As remarked, the English had long since turned envious eyes upon the riches of the Spanish Indies and they quickly grasped the commercial possibilities of this new 'trade'. Several speculative voyages were made, the first being that of Thomas Windham, who left Portsmouth in August 1553 bound for the Guinea coast and the Bight of Benin. The participants brought back stories of what was perceived as a debased form of sub-human life, and thereby cleared any moral scruples out of the way at an early and formative stage. Reporting on his voyage to 'Guinea' in 1555 Captain John Lok not only described the indigenous population as 'a people of beastly living,' but added the presumption that they were 'without a God, lawe, religion, or common wealth, and so scorched by the heat of the sunne, that in many places they curse it when it riseth'. At the later date of 1734, Captain William Snelgrave wrote in *A New Account of Some Parts of Guinea and the Slave Trade*, that he had traded at:

> Old Callabar, where, in the year 1704, I saw a sad instance of Barbarity. The King of the Place, called Jabrue, being fallen Sick, he caused by the advice of his Priests, a young Child about ten months old, to be sacrificed to his god, for his recovery. I saw the child after it was killed, hung on the bough of a tree, with a live cock tied near it, as an addition to the ceremony.

Such narratives sustained the well-rooted prejudices established by early speculators, among who had been the Hawkins family, kinsmen of Drake.

In 1562 Captain John Hawkins broke into the Iberian monopoly by shipping a cargo of slaves to Spanish Hispaniola (Haiti), Columbus's landfall in the New World. The fury aroused in both Lisbon and Madrid at this incursion induced Queen Elizabeth to lend Hawkins a royal ship, the *Jesus of Lübeck*, for his second voyage of

1564–65. Undercutting the official prices agreed by the principals, Hawkins sold his cargo to the indifferent Spanish colonists, indifferent at a handsome profit, inducing Hawkins and his royal backer to repeat the process in 1567. Hawkins was joined on this new expedition by his cousin, Francis Drake, who had made a voyage to Africa under John Lovell in 1566. On the coast of Sierra Leone Hawkins assisted three African kings in a war, besieging the walled town of Conga, after which: 'We took and carried thence for traffique to the West Indies five hundred negroes'. Job Hortop, the writer, added further evidence of the contempt for which life was held in West Africa: 'The three kings drove seven thousand Negroes into ye sea at low water, at the point of the land, where they were all drowned in the ooze, for they could not … save themselves'. Out of such tales of a profligate waste of humanity grew the conviction that transportation to the West Indies was actually beneficial to its victims.

Hawkins's fleet consisted of nine vessels besides the *Jesus of Lübeck*. One, *The Grace of God*, was commanded by a Frenchman, another, the little *Judith*, by Drake. Trading with the Spanish proved difficult; the governor of New Andalusia – as the portion of the Spanish Main now known as Venezuela was then called – was Don Diego Ponce de Leon who refused to treat with men who threatened to destroy his royal master's monopoly. Hawkins tried to force the issue by attacking Rio de la Hacha, and consequently sold some of the enslaved black men and women for £7,000, but by now the coast was in a state of alarm; Hawkins was rebuffed, his attack on Cartagena failed and he was assailed by bad weather. He ran before the wind, the *Jesus of Lübeck* labouring badly:

> On either side of the stern-post, the planks did open and shut with every sea … and the leaks so big as the thickness of a man's arm, the living fish did swim upon the ballast as in the sea.[1]

Having been blown north-east the wind veered and blew the fleet back towards the Yucatan peninsula. Only the *William and John* broke away to beat to windward and so head home while Hawkins, anxious for the fate of the Queen's own ship whose loss would fall entirely upon Her Majesty's account and invite her personal displeasure, took refuge off San Juan de Uluá in the Bay of Campeche. This was near Vera Cruz and the eastern end of the over-land route to Mexico City, capital of New Spain, and the Pacific beyond. It was where the Spanish Register ships loaded silver and the *flota*'s arrival from Spain was expected within days, bearing the new Viceroy, Don Martin Enriquez. Hawkins's battered fleet with its hungry seamen refitted their ships as best they could, fortified an offshore island set amid the reefs of the bay, while the coast armed against them. All awaited the outcome of an inevitable conflict that would almost certainly precipitate war between two countries for so long at each other's throats.

As the Spanish ships entered the increasingly crowded anchorage, Enriquez – wishing to see his galleons safely moored – opened a negotiation with Hawkins that he intended breaking at the most advantageous moment. Hawkins sent Robert Barrett, his Spanish-speaking master of the *Jesus of Lübeck*, to remonstrate over some details, only to have Barrett seized and confined.[2] Meanwhile, aboard the *Jesus of Lübeck* a Spanish prisoner was found with a dagger hidden in his sleeve, at which a cry went up and the fragile truce was broken. Where men had been fraternising, they now fought. Alongside the *Jesus of Lübeck*, the *Minion* was taken by the Spanish and retaken by a furious Hawkins who roared an invocation to 'God and Saint George!' The *Minion's* broadside next detonated a powder-barrel on the deck of an adjacent Spanish galleon, the explosion of which only added to the confusion and the mutual lust for blood.

As the battle raged, the Spanish ignited one ship and sent her into the anchorage as a fire-ship. The French commander of *The Grace of God*, set fire to his own vessel for the same purpose, but in losing the mainmast his vessel became unmanageable and all hands took to their boats. English losses mounted; the *Angel* was sunk, the *Swallow* captured and Hawkins was forced to sacrifice the *Jesus of Lübeck* and flee in the *Minion* and *Judith*. The expedition thus ended in disaster, the remnants arriving home starving. Drake was accused of having deserted Hawkins in his own struggle to save the 50-ton *Judith* in bad weather that had cast the larger *Minion* upon a lee shore and from which Hawkins had only escaped by fine seamanship. Drake arrived home on 20 January 1568, Hawkins on the 25th.[3]

War with Spain was a consequence of this inexcusable adventure which, by attempting to force trade upon – and then fight – the subjects of King Philip II of Spain, all but throttled English participation in the slave trade. By default this contraband traffic remained largely in Dutch hands, encouraging the equally illicit homeward carriage of the products of the Spanish Indies: sugar, tobacco, cacao, hides, cochineal and, of course, silver. Such a lucrative flow of goods excited envy, while an increasing demand for slaves in the English colonies encouraged a colonial trade with the Dutch, in contravention of the English Navigation Acts. The English bestirred themselves in their own interests.

As mentioned earlier, English trading-posts had been established at Anomabu in 1639, at Takoradi in 1645 and at Cape Coast in 1650 where English ships began trafficking in slaves, but it was not until after the Restoration, in 1662, that matters got into their amoral stride with the founding of 'The Royal Adventurers of England Trading into Africa'. This joint-stock company enjoyed exclusive rights to ship slaves to the English sugar plantations and initiated a rich trade whose imports of gold caused Charles II to mint a new coin to the value of 21s, known as 'a guinea'. However, the company soon ran into financial difficulties, largely as a result of an attack by the Dutch under De Ruyter who captured the company's forts and a number of its ships. The company suffered a loss of £200,000 and was compelled to relinquish its charter.

In 1689, however, creditors and some share-holders of the old company were reincorporated as 'The Royal African Assiento Company' which extended operations and 'entered into a contract to supply the Spanish West Indies with slaves' by means of the *Asiento*, or at least part of it. All began well, exports of woollens, cotton cloth and iron bars opening 'a considerable market for Sheffield wares' which provided utensils for washing, shaving and cooking. Exported cloth was used not only for clothing but to press palm-oil, while the bent soft-iron bars known as 'manilas' were forged into weapons, domestic and cultivating tools. Other articles also found a ready market:

> Muskets, firelocks and cutlaces [sic] they use in war. Brandy is most commonly spent at their feasts. Knives to the same purposes as we use them. With tallow they anoint their bodies … and even use it to shave their beards… Venice bugles, glass beads … serve all ages and sexes, to adorn their heads, necks, arms and legs, and sarsaparilla is used by such as are infected with the venereal disease.

Such were the trade-goods brought to the Guinea coast by the slavers. What was borne outwards was more important to the shipowners. Gold, ivory tusks – known as elephant's teeth – and redwood for dying were important, but although such importations caused the minting of batches of up to 50,000 guineas at a time, it was the shipping of slaves to the westward that earned the greater profits. The contract with Spain was for 3,000 slaves a year at about £17 a head, giving a valuation of 'one ton of sugar, per slave' each of whom was acquired for about £3. At Kingston in Jamaica the company built a large house 'for the accommodation of factors, who were stationed there to conduct the business, and for the reception of the human cargoes which survived the horrors of the "middle-passage" '. Such was the vigour of this revived interest in the potential of the slave-trade that the company's monopoly was soon under attack and in 1694, as a consequence of intense lobbying, the trade was opened to independent ships provided that they obtained a license from the Royal African Company. The company had exposed itself to this attack largely because, like its contemporary, the United East India Company, it preferred to charter the ships of others but, unlike John Company, it failed to comprehensively bind-in the full interest of owners, ship's husbands and ship-masters, so that pleas for *laissez faire* continued unabated, interlopers proliferated and the company was cheated by its own agents who overloaded the ships, causing high-mortality while setting the losses off against the company's account. At this time the English trade in slaves was dominated by the highly capitalised merchants of London and Bristol.

> Liverpool adventurers with a small capital were unable to equip vessels and purchase goods specially adapted to the African market …, nor could they afford to await the uncertain results of round voyages, sometimes prolonged to more than a year, and subject to terrible dangers unknown to any other description of trading… Early in the eighteenth century, however, a successful rivalship with Bristol, in exporting provisions, and coarse checks and silk handkerchiefs of Manchester make, to the West Indies and the continent of America, eventually enabled the merchants of Liverpool to participate in the more lucrative slave traffic.[4]

This stiff competition started a commercial war between London, Bristol and Liverpool. For the last named it 'stimulated the industrious and enriched the enterprising, multiplied the ships in her docks, and filled her warehouses with sugar, rum, and other West India produce...' While Bristol was to send almost sixty ships a year to Guinea between 1701 and 1709, forcing London's contribution to decline, this supremacy was not to last and Liverpool rose in importance while Bristol slowly declined.

The competing interests of the English and Spanish markets which the slavers exploited by selling where the higher market price obtained, led the government to favour an expansion of the trade which would allow the price to level. To achieve this, diplomatic moves began to secure the entire *Asiento* but these were frustrated and the tempting commercial plum fell in 1702 into the hands of the French. Wresting the *Asiento* from Louis XIV became a subsidiary war-aim – after that of denying the Spanish throne and Empire, plus The Netherlands, to Louis and his family – during the War of the Spanish Succession (1702–1713).

Meanwhile at home, renewed pressure to dispense with the Royal African Company's advantageous position was resisted, but this success was short-lived. At the conclusion of the war the terms of the Peace of Utrecht concluded in July 1713 granted significant advantages to Great Britain, emerging for the first time as a major European state with the capability of influencing the balance of power. Under its provisions Britain acquired from France its territories of Acadia, Newfoundland, territory around Hudson's Bay, and St Kitts in the West Indies. From Spain came Gibraltar and Minorca and with these gains came the full *Asiento*. This conferred upon Great Britain for a term of thirty-three years the monopoly of supplying 4,300 slaves annually from West Africa to the Spanish colonies in the Caribbean, along with which went the concession of one large ship of 500 tons being sent to trade formally at Portobello, a concession augmented by two accompanying 'tenders'. It would turn out to be a bad bargain: the annual trading voyage was subject to restrictions, one quarter share of the ship's cargo and a levy of 5 per cent on the rest going to the King of Spain, while the sale of slaves was subject to controls that threatened profits. The activities of interlopers who remained vigorous were not so constrained, all of which depressed the market-price of slaves. Under-cutting occurred elsewhere: the North American colonists bought their sugar and molasses at cheaper rates from the French, all of which encouraged mercantile indulgence in a continuation of contraband trade with the Spanish colonists. However, realisation of these multiple disadvantages lay in the future: in 1713 euphoria seized those for whom the monopoly of the *Asiento* had represented a grand objective. Not all of these people had an interest in the Royal African Company.

For some time before the signing of the treaty at Utrecht, Robert Harley, the Lord Treasurer, had been among those seeking a more legitimate way of breaking into the source of riches exploited by the Spaniards through their South American possessions, other than the skulduggery of smuggling. In 1711, in anticipation of this hoped-for success, he had founded the South Sea Company, nominally a joint-stock enterprise to trade with South America, the west coast of America and all Spanish colonies. As its first governor Harley contrived to establish a board of political appointees whose real objective was to rival and provide an alternative banking mechanism to that of the Whig-dominated Bank of England, to rival the United East India Company as a means of enriching its directors, and to oust the Royal African Company from its notional domination of the slave-trade.

To achieve his objective Harley established an alliance between the government and South Sea Company which persuaded the many holders of government securities, amounting to about £10 millions sterling, to exchange these at par value for stock in the new enterprise. Great returns were promised to investors since, in exchange, the government guaranteed paying in perpetuity an annuity of £576,534, equivalent to 6 per cent on the £10 millions invested. The prediction of vast riches seemed accurate when the acquisition of the *Asiento* under the terms of the Treaty of Utrecht was passed to the South Sea Company to carry out, much to the chagrin of the Royal African Company for whom the subsidiary role of wholesaler – as the supplier of the human commodity – was reserved.

The value of the South Sea Company's stock now began to increase, despite the failure of the company to carry out a single trading voyage to South America until 1717 – and that with little success – and the fact that relations with Spain deteriorated in the following year. These had never been good and provoked intermittent hostilities, but other concerns emerged not the least of which was the failure of the Royal African Company to produce sufficient enslaved Africans. The South Sea Company complained it gained nothing by the *Asiento*, Madrid complained that the king's share was inadequate, while 'The Company's steady refusal to produce its accounts for inspection lent some colour to this suspicion.' This inhibited neither the directors of the South Sea Company nor the government in London. Having effectively gulled the public into underwriting the national debt once, the government did it again in 1719 when the South Sea Company proposed a scheme under which it would issue more shares and acquire more than half of the national debt. This was reckoned at about £31 millions, though in fact with irredeemable annuities and other sums the total was nearer £50 millions. For its part the government guaranteed a return of 5 per cent until 1727 and 4 per cent thereafter, thereby converting high interest debt, which was all but impossible to trade, into a low interest debt readily marketable in South Sea shares. At the time the Bank of England held £3.4 millions of the national debt, with the East India Company holding a similar amount which together amounted to about two thirds of that already held by the South Sea Company. The Bank then made a rival bid which was turned down, largely because the South Sea Company dispensed over a £1 million in well-placed bribes. In April 1720 the South Sea Company's bid prevailed with the strong support of many prominent people, including the enthusiastic Chancellor of the Exchequer, John Aislabie.

The company talked-up the value of its stock with 'the most extravagant rumours', appealing to the cupidity that is the least attractive quality of the English character but which was more than just a fostering of national gullibility. There was then abroad a mood of post-war patriotic optimism, for the nation was on the brink of the great era of exploration and had, since Drake's day, been fed with notions of vast wealth in the Spanish Indies, the Spice Islands, Cathay and elsewhere. It was also – as we shall see shortly – assailed with what were largely urban myths of piratical wealth being taken by sheer British boldness in the face of the despised and 'Dago' Spanish, all of which nonsense provoked a boom. As a consequence of these false and subtle influences, other joint-stock companies, known as 'Bubbles', were floated on promises of high returns on foreign ventures and other bizarre ideas. One of these advertised a prospectus for a company 'carrying out an undertaking of great advantage, but of which no-one [yet] knows'. With matters getting out of hand, the Bubbles Act was passed in June 1720, declaring that joint-stock companies must have a royal charter, which, while it stifled a proliferation of such speculative notions, only focussed greater attention on the South Seas Company, which received its own royal charter at this time. The 'speculating phrenzy' that followed was fuelled by greed and all sort of double-dealing, as the share price rose from £128 in January, to £175 in February and £330 by May.

Shares were 'sold' to politicians at the market price and swiftly sold back to the company as the price rose, the vendor receiving the profit of the increased valuation. The holder never actually paid in the first place and the method, though it deceived some of the best brains on the country, appealed to the great and the greedy in the land, from politicians to the King's mistresses. It also bound their interests to the company's fortunes, encouraging a further driving-up of share valuation and, by adding the names of the illustrious to the enterprise, in turn seduced medium and small investors by an endorsing aura of legitimacy.

On the granting of the company's charter in June the share-price reached £890, which encouraged selling, whereupon the company's directors ordered their agents to buy, propping up the price at around £750 until it gained further momentum. In August the share-price reached £1,000 at which point it was impossible to stem the flood of sales and the value dropped sharply. This was complicated by the fall in value coinciding with instalment payments on subscriptions, for which the company offered loans, but a lot of shareholders buying on credit could not pay and what would become a torrent of bankruptcies began. Worse, similar speculations were ending badly in Amsterdam and Paris and an international scramble for liquidity caused the South Sea bubble to burst. The ruin was pandemic: by the end of September the stock had fallen back to £150. Thousands of individuals, and hundreds of private banks and companies were ruined. No sector of society escaped: King George I himself, many aristocrats, politicians and financiers were embroiled with smaller investors in a financial catastrophe. Some of those regarded as insiders close to the company fled abroad, suicides became a commonplace and, after losing £20,000, Isaac Newton lamented that: 'I can calculate the movement of the stars but *not* the madness of men!'

Parliament was recalled and an investigation followed. Reporting in the following February, it accused the South Seas directors of fraud, leaving the mess for one of the scheme's original opponents, the new First Lord of the Treasury – and effectively the first British prime minister – Robert Walpole, to clear up. The South Sea Company remained in existence until the 1850s, still managing part of the national debt, but in the short period in which it did what it was set-up for it had only made eight voyages to Portobello – the last of which was in 1733. In all it made only ninety-six authorised slaving voyages, ending these in 1739 when it relinquished the *Asiento* for the sum of £100,000. Most of the trade had been effectively contracted-out, an expedient that, at the very least, enabled a measure of licensed control to set standards in the trade insofar as it was carried out under the British flag. It did, however, throw open the licit traffic to others.

With no possessions in Africa and interference with that continent barred to them by the Treaty of Tordesillas, deprived of Portuguese support and French co-operation, the Spanish had been compelled to agree to the pragmatic solution to their labour shortages by allowing the hated 'English' to carry slaves across the Atlantic on their behalf. With the granting of the *Asiento* the Spanish thought that they could put an end to British smuggling and illicit trading with both their colonies and their colonists, and thereby contain British ambition. In this they had proved as mistaken as the British in their own assumptions. Two brief wars in 1717 and 1727, followed by the larger conflict over Captain Jenkins's ear which in turn escalated into the War of the Austrian Succession (1739–1748) were indicative of the poor relations between Great Britain and Spain.

Rising English ambition was marked in Liverpool, drawing the port into the slave trade, for which the city has since become notorious. At the time its chief exports were cloths of various sorts, 'Manchester checks … French and Scotch osnaburgs…' which were in great demand in the Spanish Indies. Direct Spanish exports of these commodities, under monopoly, attracted a duty of 300 per cent which the Liverpool merchants were happy to undercut by a contraband trade using Jamaica as an entrepôt.

> A growing demand resulted in ample returns in specie to Liverpool and Manchester, and in spite of the vigilance of the Spanish Guarda Costa, which were continually cruising between the south-end of Jamaica and the Spanish Main, this trade flourished for about twenty years, and gave the Guarda Costa some excuse for the cruelties they practised in boarding and plundering British vessels, under the pretence of searching for contraband goods.

This opportunism would continue provoking the Spanish *Garda Costas* – largely composed of 'rapacious and venal irregulars' – to harry British shipping, a circumstance that would require the permanent deployment of men-of-war on the Jamaica station almost on a war footing which, according to Richard Pares, 'subjected trade to some of the nuisances and expenses of war, and sometimes came near to causing more serious hostilities.' The gradual decline in Anglo-Spanish relations led, in 1739 on the thirty-third anniversary of the acquisition of the *Asiento*, to the alleged assault carried out upon Captain Jenkins and precipitating the war known by the worthy ship-master's ear.

When the subsequent War of the Austrian Succession was concluded at the Peace of Aix-la-Chapelle in 1748, the *Asiento* was renewed for four years but it lasted only two, the rights being sold out again in 1750. By this time, however, the British were heavily involved in a trade from which their clutch would only be removed by a huge change in moral values and an act of their own Parliament. But this is to run ahead.

The acquisition of the *Asiento* by the South Sea Company was, as noted, a disaster for the Royal African Company. Although its name lingered on and received a revival much later, in the early eighteenth century it declined, the joint-stock was dissolved in 1750 and two years later the company's forts along the African coast were all transferred to the Crown. The first of these had been on James Island in the Gambia River and it was here that British slavers originally arrived. The pattern of what became known as 'the triangular trade' was established early. African chiefs, anxious to acquire arms and ammunition, rather than be palmed off with worthless trade-goods created a situation where open trade was impossible. The amassing of quantities of small-arms caused the creation of forts, rather than factories, along the Guinea coast. There were, of course, other reasons. The security of arms and of the company's agents was one thing, another was the security of cargoes. These forts, backed up by staked barricades, were effectively warehouses for human lading, garnered as the slavers – or 'Guineamen', as the ships became known – ran in from the Atlantic to barter their cheaply made muskets, balls and black-powder, along with the iron manilas, cowrie shells and bright glass trinkets that still commanded a portion of the market.

In the mean time the Royal African Company's displacement by the South Seas Company led to a decline in interest in the slave-trade by the London merchants who had almost relinquished it by 1720, when the South Sea Bubble burst. Liverpool was late engaging in the slave-trade. Between 1709 and 1730 only a single Liverpool vessel crossed the Atlantic with slaves, but thereafter the exploitation of the *Asiento* remained a matter between Bristol and Liverpool, from which the latter emerged pre-eminent, dominating the trade until its abolition for British ships in 1807.

The Guineamen of this early period were substantial vessels. The *Hannibal* was acquired on behalf of share-holders by Captain Thomas Phillips in 1693 and measured 450 tons burthen and thirty-six guns. Phillips's principals were Sir Jeffrey Jeffreys and his brother John, Samuel Stanyer 'then sub-governor of the African company, and some other eminent merchants'. As master he was given a share in the ship which was then placed under charter to the Royal African Company.[5] On the passage south Phillips fought off a spirited attack by a French frigate which, after pursuing them for some time, 'struck his false colours and hoisted the French white sheet'. He went on:

> I was extremely glad that by God's grace we defended the ship, though she was most miserably shatter'd and torn in her mast and rigging, having had eleven shot in our main mast, three quite through him, and several lodg'd in him … eight shot in our fore mast, two quite through; our main-top shot to pieces; our main-topmast splinter'd half away; our mizzen yard shot in two pieces; our sprit-sail, top-mast jack, and jack staff, shot away; our ancient (ensign) staff shot by the board, so that [we] had

no colours flying most part of the ingagement [sic] but the king's pendant, which, by authority of my letter-of-mart, I fought under; we had several shot through our yards, with much more to long to insert. As to the rigging, I know not how to begin … it was so torn by long bars of iron they fired… We had not above thirty shot placed in our hull, four of which were under water; he fired very high for the most part … to bring our mast[s] by the board … but it was our good fortune to have little wind … until we had opportunity, by stoppers, preventers, knotting and splic-ing, to secure them… We fired low into his hull, and loaded our low [main-deck] guns (which were all demi-culverins) constantly with double and round shot and all our quarterdeck guns with round shot, and tin cases full of musket bullets, so that we must certainly have killed him a great many men; our three boats … were shot through in many places; and we had a suit of sails quite spoil'd, some being shot through like strainers. We had five men kill'd outright, and about thirty-two wounded; among the last was my brother, my gunner, carpenter, and boatswain; the carpenter had his arm shot off, and three others their legs; five or six of my best men were dreadfully blown up by their carelessness in laying lighted [slow] matches among some cartridges of powder; our harper had his skull fractur'd by a small shot; the rest are but slight small shot and splinter wounds, and bruises… The fight lasted six hours, from four till ten o'clock [at night], being all that while within pistol shot … and firing as fast as both sides could load… I judged him to be about 48 guns, and a man of war…

With his ship's harper wounded in the action, Phillips gave the retreating Frenchman 'a levet with our trumpets'. Afterwards 'our bag-piper's leg was cut off a little below the knee' by 'our surgeon, Mr William Gordon … a diligent man'. For three days they lay-to unmolested, repairing the damage, by Phillips's account a matter of no very great moment, though extraordinarily inconvenient, before pushing on to the Cape Verde Islands where they careened the ship with assistance from the shore and effected fuller repairs. Phillips went with some of his officers 'to pay my respects to the [Portuguese] governor at St. Jago town, having our trumpets in the pinnace's head'. This was all done in formal style, the *Hannibal's* musicians cutting something of a dash. During his trip ashore at São Iago, Phillips encountered:

> …negro women, who talked to us many smutty English words, making lascivious undecent [sic] gestures with their bodies, which were all naked, excepting a little clout about their waste [sic]…

The island provided him with all his wants as, having stopped the leaks, 'our car-penters spliced a piece to the main-yard, and clap'd two good iron hoops and two wooldings up it…' and so forth. Phillips purchased 'fifteen goats, ten sheep, four hogs, sixty hens, five hundred oranges, and five hundred lemons…' which was bought for 'three pounds in Spanish money which I had picked up among my officers, and the rest in muskets, coral and painted linen'.

Arriving on the African coast, Phillips began general trading, picking up a 'pepper-spice' called 'malagetta' and related to cardamom in exchange for iron bars and 'two-pound pewter-basons.[6] The reason of our buying this pepper is to give it to our Negroes in their messes to keep them from the flux and dry belly-ach [sic], which they are very incident to.' A few days later Phillip's brother died. 'He had been sick of a malignant fever about eight days, and many of my men lay ill of the same distemper'. Phillips buried his brother from the ship's boat. 'Then the *Hannibal* fired sixteen guns … which was the number of years he had lived in this uncertain world'.

During this slow coasting progress Phillips constantly met local people in canoes with whom he either traded or sought to open negotiations for slaves. It is clear from his account that both sides mutually sought the traffic, the indigenous population for the artefacts that the *Hannibal* bore. 'The goods they most covet,' he remarks, 'are pewter basons, the larger the better, iron bars, knives, and large screw'd pewter jugs, which they did much affect'. One afternoon, there:

> …came a four-hand canoo [sic] aboard us from Bassam, assuring us of good trade of gold and slaves in the morning, if we would anchor, and that they would stay with us all night, which we permitted them, hoisting up their canoo in the tackles, and let go our anchors in fourteen fathom water. In the morning those aboard fell to trade, of whom I took thirty-six achies of gold in fatishes for pewter and iron bars.

Further trade in gold followed, but not in slaves and Phillips was by now unwell 'with a violent racking pain in the right side of my head … a dimness in my eyes … [so bad] that I could not stand or walk without assistance'. The *Hannibal* kept company with another Guineaman, for there were pirates rumoured on the coast, including 'Long Ben' as Avery was known. A few days later Phillips 'went ashore to our castle at Succandy, where we found the factor, Mr Johnson, in his bed raving mad, cursing and swearing most wretchedly at us…' This ill usage arose from a jealous passion at having a young mulatto girl taken from Johnson whom he had been keeping 'using much kindness and tenderness' until 'she was of age fit for matrimonial functions'. However: 'When she was grown man's meat and a pretty girl', a Dutch rival seduced her and 'soon cracked that nut which Mr Johnson had been so long preparing for his own tooth'. The duties of the indisposed and lovelorn factor were undertaken by 'his second (who was a young lad, and had been a blue-coat hospital boy)'. Later Phillips learned that the wretched Johnson had been 'cut to pieces' by his rival who, with the connivance of the Dutch governor, 'surprized and seiz'd the fort … and plundered all the goods and merchandise'. Eventually the *Hannibal* anchored off Cape Coast castle, firing a salute of '15 guns which they returned'.

> The merchandise and stores we brought for the castle, we sent in our longboat as near the shore as she dare go, and the canoos came and unlade her; which being flat bottom'd, play upon the sea until they perceive a smooth, then with violence run themselves ashore, take out the goods and launch off again. We landed … thirty sol-

diers for the company, in as good health as we received them aboard … but in two months they were near half dead, and scarce enough of the survivors able to carry their fellows to the grave.

In addition to the trade good brought hither to barter for slaves, Phillips also unloaded 'on account of the African company, muskets …' cottons, carpets, lead and tallow, 'none of which did answer expectation…' He now began to load maize – 'ordered us for the provision of our negroes … about four bushels for every negro' – two chests of gold for the company and two 'canoos' before proceeding directly for 'Anamaboe' (Anomabu) where, having saluted the fort with seven guns, Phillips called upon the factor, Mr Searle. The *Hannibal* thus made a leisurely progress eastwards, from one post and its factor – each with his mistress – to the next, acquiring stores, trading and unsuccessfully seeking the readiest supply of slaves.

On 20 May 1694 they reached 'Whidaw' or Ouidah. Here the native 'canoos' purchased at Cape Coast Castle that would assist them in loading the slaves were hoisted out. These were dugouts made from the hollowed trunk of a cotton tree, 'the largest being not above four foot broad, but twenty-eight or thirty foot long … of which each ship that buys many slaves ought to carry two'. They came with their own crews, one of whom acted in charge 'and steered them by a steering oar'. The crews were paid an agreed fee, half advanced in gold 'and the rest in goods when we have done with them'. They were also allowed one of the canoes in which to return to Cape Coast, the other being broken up on board for firewood. On purchase, each boat was strengthened by the ship's carpenters and they were indispensable, for 'without them there is no landing or coming off of goods'.

Still in company with the other English ship, Phillips and his men, both crew and hired boatmen, now began the serious preparations for the Middle-passage. Hereabouts lay:

…the pleasantest country I have seen in Guiney, consisting of champaigns and small ascending hills, beautified with always green shady groves of lime, wild orange, and other trees, and irrigated with divers broad fresh rivers, which yield plenty of good fresh fish; towards the sea-shore it is very marshy, and has divers large swamps.

Our factory … stands low near the marshes, which renders it a very unhealthy place to live in; the white men of the Africa Company send [sic] there, seldom returning to tell the tale; 'tis compassed round with a mud wall, about six foot high, and on the south-side is the gate; within is a large yard, a mud thatch'd house, where the factor lives, with the white men; also a storehouse, a trunk (compartment) for slaves, and a place where they bury their dead white men, call'd, very improperly, the hog-yard; there is also a good forge, and some other small houses… The factory is about 200 yards in circumference, and a most wretched place to live in, by reason of the swamps adjacent, whence proceed noisome stinks, and vast swarms of little flies, call'd musketoes, which are so intolerably troublesome, that if one does not take opium, laudanum, or some other soporifick, 'tis impossible to … sleep…'

It cannot have been that pleasant for the *Hannibal* had arrived at the onset of the rainy season and Phillips was tormented by the 'musketoes'. All hands succumbed to fever and flux which 'quite ruined' Phillips's health. Nevertheless, the work went on. Now the slaves began to arrive by an arrangement undisclosed by Phillips but probably due to the industry of the unnamed factor. The factory proved useful as a holding pen when the slaves could not be shipped off directly to the *Hannibal*, for delays arising from a heavy surf along the shore were common and could last for some time, adding to the long period of incarceration for those being first shipped on board. The captives were brought to the fort by 'cappashiers', the native dealers, whereupon:

> …our surgeon examined them well … to see they were sound [in] wind and limb, making them jump, stretch out their arms swiftly, looking in their mouths to judge of their age; for the cappashiers are so cunning, that they shave them all close before we see them, so that let them be never so old we can see no grey hairs in their heads or beards; and then having liquor'd them well and sleeked them with palm-oil, 'tis no easy matter to know an old one from a middle-aged one, but by the teeths decay. But our greatest care is to buy none that are pox'd, lest they should infect the rest aboard; for tho' we separate the men and women aboard by partitions and bulk-heads, to prevent quarrels and wranglings among them, yet do what we can they will come together, and that distemper which they call the yaws, is very common here, and discovers itself by almost the same symptoms as the *Lues Venera* [syphilis] or clap does with us; therefore our surgeon is forced to examine the privities of both men and women with the nicest scrutiny … what can't be omitted.[7] When we had selected … such as we liked, we agreed in what goods to pay for them, the prices being already stated … how much of each sort of merchandize we were to give for a man, woman, and child, which gave us much ease and saved abundance of disputes … then we marked the slaves we had bought in the breast, or shoulder, with a hot iron, having the letter of the ship's name on it, the place before being anointed with a little palm oil, which caused but little pain, the mark being usually well in four or five days, appearing very plain and white after.

Purchase at this time was by cowrie shells which are still in some places known as 'Guinea-money' with the going rate being 'about 100 pounds [weight of shells] for a good man-slave'. Next in demand were thin brass basins, which were cut-up to make bracelets and collars, followed by 'cambricks' or lawn cloth, chintzes, coral, iron bars, gun-powder and brandy. The value of these goods to the slavers varied, the average outlay per slave being about 'three pounds fifteen shillings a head' but 'if a cappashier sells five slaves, he will have two of them paid for in cowries, and one in brass, which are dear slaves; for a slave in cowries costs us above four pounds in England; whereas a slave in coral … or iron, does not cost fifty shillings.' Interestingly, the cappashiers would not yield to accepting other commodities until they had exhausted all the cowries and copper-ware that the ship had to barter, so these items would bring slaves 'as fast as they could be purchased'. As for the negotiating ship-masters, Phillips has this to say:

…where there are divers ships, and … separate interests, about buying the same commodity they commonly undermine, betray, and out-bid one the other; and the Guiney
commanders' words and promises are least to be depended upon of any I know who
use the sea; for they would deceive their fathers in their trade if they could.

The cappashiers assisted the *Hannibal's* crew in taking the branded slaves down to the
shoreline for ferrying off to the ship in batches 'of 50 or 60' by the 'canoos' which
bore them through the surf to the longboat waiting offshore. Occasionally the canoe
crews lost trade goods in the surf, sometimes by design and sometimes by accident.
While the canoe-crews ferried the slaves to the longboat, others in the ship's crew
rafted off small barricoes of fresh water to keep the large casks in the hold topped up,
and to purchase livestock where and when available. Sometimes such ventures inland
proved dangerous, the white seamen risking ambushes.

From the Bight of Benin it was customary for the ships to sail south, in order to
pick up the trade winds and 'recruit' at the Portuguese island of São Tomé, or occasionally Prince's Island. The delay extended the middle-passage but was to enable
the sick to be taken ashore 'for the benefit of the air and also replenish their stock of
fresh water'. São Tomé 'abounds with wood and water and produces Indian corn, rice,
fruits, sugar and some cinnamon' while Prince's Island also offered 'Black cattle, hogs
and goats … but [was] infested with a mischievous and dangerous species of monkeys'.[8] Such a stay was not always useful. Surgeon Falconbridge:

> …landed upon the island of St Thomas with nearly one hundred sick Negroes who
> were placed in an old house taken on purpose for their reception. Little benefit,
> however, accrued from their going on shore, as several of them died there and the
> remainder continued nearly in the same situation as when they were landed, though
> our continuance was prolonged for about twelve days…

From here began the middle-passage proper. The slaves were far from tractable, not
even after the die was cast, many leaping into the sea far from shore where the sharks
which followed the slavers seized them. They had, Phillips says, 'a more dreadful
apprehension of Barbadoes than we have of hell,' adding with a weary condescension
'tho' in reality they live much better there than in their own country; but home is
home &c.' During the middle-passage the *Hannibal* 'had about 12 negroes [who] did
wilfully drown themselves, and others starv'd themselves to death; for 'tis their belief
that when they die they return home…'

Details of the shackling, routine and diet, which changed little throughout the
trade, is given in a later account, but Phillips makes the point that although the slaves
were most likely to rebel at mealtimes 'being all upon deck', the seamen not engaged
in distributing food stood 'to their arms; and some with lighted matches at the great
guns [the demi-culverins] that yaun [sic] upon them'. However, once they were
divided into their messes of ten slaves each 'they will readily run therein good order
of themselves'. Phillips put great faith in the slaves' helplessness once out of sight of

land, in a strange environment and unable to understand the workings of the ship. But the *Hannibal* also had among her 700 unwilling passengers:

> ...some 30 or 40 Gold Coast Negroes ... to make guardians and overseers ... and sleep among them to keep them from quarrelling, and in order, as well as to give us notice, if they can discover any caballing or plotting among them, which trust they discharge with great diligence. They also ... make the negroes scrape the decks were they lodge every morning very clean, to eschew any distempers that may engender from filth and nastiness.

These 'Gold Coast Negroes' were therefore fundamental in keeping the slave-decks clear of ordure and thus preserving the live cargo as far as possible, but the *Hannibal* was over nine weeks on the passage to Barbadoes from São Tomé, and her losses were prodigious. Of his own crew Phillips lost fourteen men; of his slaves – including the suicides – he lost 320, almost half. Each loss, he lugubriously points out, at a cost of £10 to the Royal African Company and ten guineas to the owners of the ship – of which he was one. The total loss approached £6,500, the cause of death being 'the white flux'. This contagion – which spread from the crew to the slaves – Phillips attributed to 'unpurg'd black sugar, and raw unwholesome rum' bought by the crew at São Tomé and made into punch. Such had been their excesses that Phillips had been obliged to chastise several of them by flogging. Surprisingly an outbreak of small-pox, which was also carried by the whites and transferred to the susceptible blacks, was contained to about twelve deaths among one hundred cases, but it was the financial aspect of his losses that deeply affected Phillips who bemoaned the fact that the trade obliged him to endure 'much misery ... [It was by] slaves' mortality [that] our voyages are ruined, and we pine and fret ourselves to death ... and take so much pains to so little purpose'.

The *Hannibal* delivered only 372 slaves at Carlisle Bay, Barbados, at an average price of £19 per head, and soon afterwards began loading for London. Seven hundred hogsheads of muscovado sugar was her main freight, with cotton and ginger completing her lading and she sailed with about thirty other merchantmen under the convoy of HMS *Tiger*, Captain Sherman, and HMS *Chester*. Seven of the merchant ships bore more than twenty-eight guns and Sherman ordered these to form line of battle if they met with an enemy. Phillips was pleased to be appointed to lead one division if they went into action, but no enemy was met and instead of repeating his valorous conduct on his outward passage, Phillips spent most of the voyage in his cot, seized 'with violent convulsions' and 'a vertigo'. He was all but helpless. Having lost the hearing of one ear on the Guinea coast, he now found that of the other impaired. Moreover, the *Hannibal* had lost her worthy surgeon, William Gordon, who had died in Carlisle Bay. Thus it was that once home Captain William Phillips was obliged to submit to be:

> ...tormented by the apothecaries, with does of nasty physick every day, for four or five months time, and butcher'd by the surgeons with blisters, issues, setons, &c. and spent about 100 guineas among them, without receiving one farthing benefit;

wherefore I did conceive it more prudence to bear my deafness as contentedly as I could ... accordingly I shook hands with the doctors, and being rendered unfit for my employment by my deafness, I settled my affairs in London, took my leave of it, and came down to Wales...

It is difficult not to sympathise a little with the wretched man as he fades into obscurity among the Black Mountains of his native 'Brecknockshire', for a trail of death lay in the wake of his career, a substantial number of his crew – including his brother – and almost 400 black Africans from the voyage of the *Hannibal* alone.

Quite how many enslaved black Africans were transported across the Atlantic in the notorious 'middle-passage' is impossible to say. No accurate figures exist and conjecture is more emotive than helpful: estimates range from 10 to 40 millions. The British contribution to this seems to be around 7 millions, something like the population of today's London.[9]

This hideous and wholesale 'export' of human-beings was caused by a number of factors, first of which was the opportunity so clear in Phillips's account. The initial origins of the traffic have already been adumbrated, but encouragement gathered momentum over time. William Snelgrave 'a slaver of great experience' explained that from a perspective of the early 1700s:

It has been the custom among the Negroes, time out of mind ... for them to make slaves of all the captives taken in war. Now, before they had an opportunity of selling them to white people, they were often obliged to kill great multitudes [as Job Hortop had witnessed], when they had taken more than they could well employ in their own plantations, for fear they should rebel and endanger their master's safety.

Most crimes among them are paid by mulcts and fines; and if the offender has not the wherewithal to pay his fine, is sold for a slave. This is the practice of the inland people, as well as of those on the sea side.

Debtors who refuse to pay ... or are insolvent, are likewise liable to be made slaves ... I have been told, that it is common for some inland people to sell their children for slaves, tho' they are under no necessity for so doing... But I never observed that the people near the sea coast practise this, unless compelled thereto by extream [sic] want and famine as the people of Whidaw (Ouidah) have lately been.

Now by these means it is that so many Negroes become slaves, and more especially by being taken captives in war. Of those the number is so great, that I may safely affirm, without any exaggeration, that the Europeans of all nations, that trade to the coast of Guinea, have in some years exported at least seventy thousand...

This annual harvest, Snelgrave explains, was drawn from a coastline 4,000 miles long, from Cape Verde to Angola where polygamy and promiscuity 'means the countrys [sic] are full of people'. Opposition was raised against the trade as early as 1734, Snelgrave remarking that:

Several objections have often been raised against the lawfulness of this trade, which I shall not here undertake to refute. I shall only observe in generall [sic] that tho' to traffic in human creatures, may at first appear barbarous, inhuman and unnatural, yet, the traders herein have as much to plead in their own excuse, as can be said of some other branches of trade, namely, the advantage of it…

Ah yes: 'the advantage of it'; that universal justification of all enshrined in the acquisition of money by one party at the expense of another! Naturally, Snelgrave goes on to attest to the positive advantages, first to its victims and then to their overlords:

First, it is evident, that abundance of captives, taken in war, would be inhumanely destroyed, was there not an opportunity of desposing [sic] of them to the Europeans. So that at least many lives are saved, and great numbers of usefull persons kept in being.

Secondly, when they are carried to the plantations, they generally live much better there than they ever did in their own country; for as the planters pay a great price for them, 'tis their interest to take care of them.

Thirdly, the English plantations have been so much improved, that 'tis almost incredible, what great advantages have accrued to the [British] nation thereby; especially to the Sugar Islands which, lying in a climate near as hot as the coast of Guinea, the Negroes are fitter to cultivate the lands than white people.

Then as to the criminals amongst the Negroes; they are by this means effectually transported, never to return again [to Africa]; a benefit we very much want here [in Britain].

In a word, from this trade proceed benefits far outweighing all, either real or pretended mischiefs and inconveniences, and let the worst that can be said of it, it will be found, like all other earthly advantages, tempered with a mixture of good and evil.

Much the same would be written a century later in its defence by Captain Frederick Marryat, the popular novelist and naval officer whose father, a Lloyd's 'name' and London agent for Grenada, also supported the trade. Marryat wrote his defence of the system when slavery – as opposed to the slave-trade itself – was finally outlawed throughout the British Empire, regretting its passing and predicting dire economic consequences.

However, as has been observed, it was not true, as was popularly believed by 'some people in England [who] think we hunt and catch the slaves ourselves'. Having divested themselves of their human cargo in the West Indies, the masters of slave-ships would load the produce of the sugar islands for the homeward passage. This was, however, one of those compounding benefits that ensured the success and growth of this odious trade. The initial purpose of the voyages of Hawkins and his successors was for the valuable produce of the West Indies, specifically the logwood and indigo colourants, the hides, silver, pearls and that other dyestuff of which the Spaniards had had the monopoly, but which was highly prized for the scarlet cloth it produced: cochineal.[10]

These were the commodities whose value seduced Queen Elizabeth and her subjects to dabble in a forbidden commerce with the Spanish Indies, but the increasing demand for the importation of sugar, rum and molasses on the third leg of the triangular trade temporarily absorbed shipping into the new and lucrative slave-trade, postponing for a generation the collision with Spain over other sources of cargo and wealth.

Setting aside the immorality of the slave-trade, in a history of British maritime endeavour it is important to see it as it was regarded by Snelgrave and his ilk, and set it within the context of its times. The trade involved the carriage of a high-value cargo and while, as we shall see in more detail, the conditions under which thousands of frightened, deracinated and abused humans were mercilessly borne across the ocean to a life of servility were invariably appalling, such a vast traffic was not carried out without a degree of expertise and some care. That this was a reprehensible industry does not mean it was an incompetent one, and some measures to mitigate the hardships – if only to preserve so valuable yet fragile a commodity as human life – were put in place. Indeed, the slave-trade under the British flag was to be an early form of carriage by sea that found itself regulated. Losses during the middle-passage were usually attributable to the 'bloody flux' – or amoebic dysentery – which took between twenty and ninety days to incubate. This caused grave concern, not for the loss of human life, but for the loss of monetary value, the overall average loss in British slavers being estimated at 5.7 per cent. Respect for property, for it was as property that the Guineaman's 'live-cargo' was viewed, was a hall-mark of the Georgian Age and provoked legislation. In 1788 an Act introduced by Sir William Dolben provided for the carriage of surgeons in slaving ships, laid down minimum qualifications for slaving commanders and drew up a scale of maximum lading of humans based on a ship's tonnage. Both the master and surgeon were induced to make every effort to preserve the lives of the enslaved by a bonus scheme granted if their losses were less than 3 per cent of the numbers shipped. This, however, inevitably led to overloading and double-entry book-keeping. In short, the relentless nature of 'the iron hand of commerce' cut both ways and while the enslaved suffered, those investing in a slaver's voyage did not want their human harvest ruined by poor diet, maltreatment, disease or – worst of all – an uprising. All who trafficked were likely, power tending to corrupt as surely aboard ship as it does ashore, 'to get corrupted' by the trade, but not all Guineamen were entirely hell-ships, and most were designed with a degree of spaciousness in their slave-decks which is, admittedly, difficult to appreciate from the propagandising literature of the abolitionists. Only later, when the trade was declared illegal by the British parliament, did slavers have to become fine-lined and speedy, intended to outrun the Royal Navy's pursuing cruisers. These minor regulatory mitigations actually did little or nothing to ease the suffering of the enslaved, though they did help – however ineffectually – to preserve the spark of life.

About 1795 a Doctor George Pinckard, 'administering to a curiosity' boarded 'a Liverpool Guinea-man … fitted out expressly for the trade, with a sufficient number of hands and guns on board to protect her against the enemy's privateers and calculated for a cargo of five hundred slaves… [The] ship was kept remarkably clean…'

But slavers, even when well-run, possessed no comforts for their cargo, and stank vilely despite the liberal use of vinegar and other concoctions. Sanitary arrangements in eighteenth century ships were barely adequate for their crews, let alone several hundred slaves and thus the preservation of health was difficult during the middle-passage in an age which did not understand sepsis and infection. Nevertheless, better provisions were made for the carriage of slaves than for troops, and the attendance of the surgeon and his mates was more assiduous than in other ships, particularly if we recall from an earlier chapter, Edward Barlow's rant against his ship's quacks. James Barbot, part owner and supercargo in the *Albion* as early as 1699, noted that:

> ...our surgeons, in their daily visits betwixt decks, finding any [slaves] indisposed, caused them to be carried to the *lazaretto* under the fore-castle ... a sort of hospital, where proper remedies could be applied. [But he admits that: t]his could not leisurely be done between decks because of the great heat that is there continually, which is sometime so excessive that the surgeons would faint away and the candles would not burn...

As for the slaves themselves, far from being Godless and unsophisticated, they were only fazed by the utter unfamiliarity of their surroundings. As Olaudah Equiano afterwards wrote:

> At last, when the ship we were in had got in all her cargo, they made ready with many fearful noises, and we were all put under deck, so that we could not see how they managed the vessel. But this disappointment was the least of my sorrow. The stench of the hold while we were on the coast was so intolerably loathsome, that it was dangerous to remain there for any time, and some of us had been permitted to stay on the deck for the fresh air; but now that the whole ship's cargo was confined together, it became absolutely pestilential. The closeness of the place, and the heat of the climate added to the number in the ship, which was so crowded that each had scarcely room to turn himself, almost suffocated us. This produced copious perspirations, so that the air soon became unfit for respiration, from a variety of loathsome smells, and brought on a sickness among the slaves, of which many died, thus falling victims to the improvident avarice, as I may call it, of their purchasers. This wretched situation was again aggravated by the galling of the chains, now become insupportable; and the filth of the necessary tubs, into which the children often fell, and were almost suffocated. The shrieks of the women, and the groans of the dying, rendered the whole a scene of horror almost inconceivable.[11]

In addition to confinement in mephitic air, the slaves were exposed to sufficient pathogens and imposed barbarities to make substantial losses among a human cargo inevitable.

Those opposed to the trade did not entirely ignore other 'evils attendant on this inhuman traffick,' remarked slaving surgeon Alexander Falconbridge in 1788, the year of the Dolben Act.

[T]he sufferings of the seamen employed in the slave trade from the unwholesome-
ness of the climate, the inconveniences of the voyage, the brutal severity of the
commanders, and other causes, fall very little short, nor prove in proportion to the
numbers, less destructive to the sailors than the negroes'. [12]

Losses among seamen were also about 6–7 per cent.

Although an approximately proportionate mortality was experienced by a slaver's
crew, as occurred in the *Hannibal*, this tended to the profit, rather than the losses of a
voyage, for a dead sailor made no demands for pay. Again, quantifying such losses is
impossible, but a notion of the extent of such deaths may be gained from the fact that
between 1720 and 1744 the Royal African Company actually owned and ran forty-
four vessels and that during this period twenty-two of their ship-masters perished in
their service. In short, it was a brutally dangerous trade for all concerned and some
notice of the death-rate among its seamen and the native auxiliaries hired on the
Guinea coast had, by the 1790s been taken by Parliament. An act provided for the
proper employment of natives – the so-called 'Pull-away boys' – to help man the oars
of a ship's boats as well as the purchased 'canoos' in which the slaves were brought
offshore to the waiting Guineamen.

Increasingly the ships themselves were owned by small consortia or single owners
rather than being in traditional multi-ownership. This was in part owing to the
specialised nature of the business which raised the bar so that owners, needing to
conform to legislation, required trust-worthy and competent masters and mates who
themselves often regarded their status as higher than those in ordinary general-cargo
vessels trading in the Western Ocean. Like the privateers into which they often turned
in wartime, they frequently described themselves as 'commanders' and 'lieutenants'
rather than the plainer 'masters' and 'mates', having gunners and armourers subordinate to them in ships that were, after all, well-armed.

The so-called 'Slave-Coast' lay between the Senegal and Congo Rivers, much of it low-
lying, consisting of sandy beaches upon which the relentless breakers of the Atlantic roar,
occasionally pierced by rivers by which the interior might be penetrated, but which
flow to their sand-barred deltas through malarial swamps. Dotted at intervals along this
dreary littoral, each commanding an open anchorage, lay the forts of the slaving nations:
Goree, the Gambia, the Sherbro, Anamboe, Accra, Ouidah, Elmina, Old Calabar, Benin
or New Calabar, Bonny, and Cape Coast Castle which became the principal British
settlement on the now Ghanaian coast. In the course of the eighty years following the
first granting of the *Asiento*, the British forts increased to fourteen of the total of forty
on the coast. These were governed and garrisoned, populated by agents, factors, clerks
and company soldiers whose lives were short and who sought consolation for this tem-
poral brevity from concubinage, excess and drink. Most suffered quotidian disease, if
not worse; many perished swiftly. For the majority it was a half-life that transposed itself
into a lingering death; only a remarkable few adapted and survived. For some, however,
it was better than being at sea: Nicholas Owen who resided as a slave-dealer on the

Sherbro River around 1750 wrote that he 'must be contented with my lot without complaining' for 'The help of patience and God's assistance ... [had] miracllously [sic] preserved us from the danger of a seafareing [sic] life'.[13]

No one of course realised that the bites of mosquitoes was the cause of malaria – the observations of that sixteenth-century master having been ignored – nor that the whites imported their own diseases to infect the blacks, but all Europeans feared the 'unhealthy miasmas' that rose in the mists rolling over the swamps and rivers, bringing in their clamminess the 'marsh-ague' of malaria. Under such conditions the seamen were required to work the boats up-stream if anchored in the Gambia or Sherbro Rivers, to handle the slaves when they were mustered for boarding and no power on earth could stop a lusty young seaman from indulging himself with an eager local girl – let alone the slaves once they were on board – which was another constant source of trouble and disease. John Barbot, who became the Royal African Company's agent at Cape Castle on the coast of the Fanti and Ashanti kingdoms, warned against such behaviour:

> I have often represented to some of the principal men [ship's officers and factors alike] how to live more regularly, viz., to abstain from the black women, whose natural and hot and lewd temper soon wastes their bodies, to drink moderately, especially of brandy, rum and punch; and to avoid sleeping in the open air at night, as many, when heated with debauchery, do, having nothing on but a shirt, thinking thus to keep cool, but, on the contrary they murder themselves; for nothing is more pernicious to the constitution of Europeans, than to lie in the open air...

Keeping their crews content, healthy, willing and obedient, taxed many an anxious commander to the limits of his own abilities.

The practices involved in the trade varied between one place and another. Depending upon location, dealing was done with the senior local Arab *alkaid* or merchant, or the local African king. Harbour dues or anchorage money was paid in the form of soft iron 'manilas', liquor or firearms, a greater quantity going ashore a few days later as customs dues to the local chieftain. In some places a number of persons would greet the incoming Guineaman, among whom could be found two interpreters, locals who had a smattering of English and were not always men, many being 'ladies of colour' and probably maintained on board as mistresses to the commander or other officers. These, especially the males, were often characters of considerable distinction to their peers and ridicule to the seamen, often bedecked in cast-off, adapted and inappropriate English finery. They were, nevertheless, crucial to the success of the traffic. One would remain on board to facilitate the commander's conduct of his business, while the junior would accompany the ship's boats as they collected slaves. Accompanying the linguists were messengers who carried dockets or notes, acted as runners and nursed ambitions to become interpreters themselves. There might also be a gang of 'butlers' who undertook to service the ship's domestic needs and so preserve the health of the ship's company from over-exposure to the sun or excessive contact with disease, thus was built-up a supporting infrastructure comparable in a minor way to that on the waterfront at home.

1 William Dampier, 1652–1715. Buccaneer, navigator, hydrographer, privateersman and failed naval commander, Dampier's tattered reputation is belied by his devotion to the observation and recording of the natural world. In this he is a pre-cursor of the era of exploration exemplified by James Cook, demonstrating that trade and opportunism preceded the flag. (© Courtesy of the National Portrait Gallery)

2 Sir William James, 1721–1783. Born of humble stock in Pembrokeshire, Commodore of the Bombay
Marine in the service of the Honourable East India Company, Captor of 'Sevendroog' in 1755 and took
part in that of Gheriah in 1757, afterwards created first baronet, served as MP for Looe, as Chairman of the
Court of Directors of the East India Company and from 1775 as Deputy Master of Trinity House.
(© Courtesy of the Corporation of Trinity House)

3 William Money, 1738–1796. A respected member of the East India Company's Marine Interest, seen here in the undress uniform of an Elder Brother of Trinity House. (© Courtesy of the Corporation of Trinity House)

4 Schematic diagram of a late eighteenth-century merchantman from William Falconer's *The Shipwreck*. Although dated 1803, the images depicted shows a merchant ship of *c.*1770, the date of the first publication of Falconer's epic poem. The author of a *Marine Dictionary* in 1760, Falconer died in a shipwreck in 1769. (From a private collection)

5 Side elevation of interior of a frigate-built Privateer and plan of (top) upper-deck, and (bottom) gun-deck (no guns shown). This vessel's build and fittings are indistinguishable from a naval frigate of similar size and tonnage with an accommodation deck separate from the main gun-deck. From Frederik Hendrik Af Chapman's *Architectura Navalis Mercantoria* of 1768. (Author's Collection)

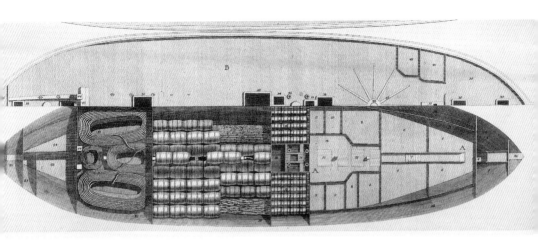

6 Plan of (top) berth-deck and (bottom) the cable-tiers, lower hold, magazine, store-rooms and sail locker of a frigate-built Privateer. From Frederik Hendrik Af Chapman's *Architectura Navalis Mercantoria* of 1768. (Author's Collection)

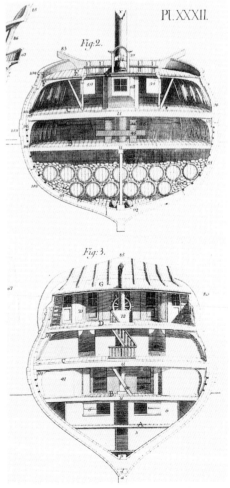

7 Top: cross-section looking forward from forward of main-mast of a frigate-built Privateer. Note on the upper-deck the cat-heads and belfry, on the gun-deck the window to the brick-lined galley, and on the berth-deck the cable bitts. Bottom: cross-section looking aft from abaft main, after capstan. Note the store-rooms in the hold, the berth-deck accommodation, the gun-deck entrance to the ward-room, the wheel and great cabin on the upper, quarter, deck with the poop above. From Frederik Hendrik Af Chapman's *Architectura Navalis Mercantoria* of 1768. (Author's Collection)

8 The Whaling Fleet of Sir Charles Standidge consisting of the *Berry*, *Britannia* and *British Queen* in the Arctic, 1769, with their boats out in pursuit of the Greenland Right Whale. From a painting in the Ferens Art Gallery, Hull. (© Courtesy of the Bridgeman Art Library and the Ferens Gallery)

9 Judging by the small number of men shown in this painting by Thomas Luny, dated 1800, this is a merchantman of some 400 tons burthen. Her relatively few hands are having difficulty shortening sail in a strong wind and the vessel is typical of a small East Indiaman or a West Indiaman of the last decade of the eighteenth century. (© Courtesy of the N.R. Omell Gallery)

10 A Liverpool slaver of about 1780 approaching the coast of Africa. Sail is being reduced, among preparations made for anchoring and hoisting out a boat. Note the broadside of eight guns, the swivel-gun on the knightheads and the hammock nettings and commanding elevation of the poop. Notice also the ventilation ports just above the black strake, admitting air into the slave-deck, and the canoes coming out to meet the ship. This reminder of local collusion had been painted over prior to acquisition of the painting, by William Jackson, by the Merseyside Maritime Museum. (© Courtesy of Liverpool Museums)

11 A well-armed merchantman of the late eighteenth century, the West Indiaman *Antigua* is shown off the South Foreland, with Dover Castle in the background. She appears to have just lowered a boat and, judging by the activity on the foredeck, is preparing to anchor in The Downs off Deal. A detail of a painting by Thomas Luny. (© Courtesy of the N.R. Omell Gallery)

12 Shipping on the Thames off Rotherhithe, 1756. The vessel on the left is a plain-headed, ship-rigged cat shown drying her sails while discharging sawn timber. She is typical of the general trader of the mid-eighteenth century of perhaps 200–250 tons burthen. Such vessels ventured from Britain to the White Sea, the Levant, North America and the West Indies. Plain and robust, James Cook selected one for his first circumnavigation. The cutter on the right with a lion-figurehead could be either a small naval cruiser or a revenue-cutter. From a painting by Samuel Scott. (© Courtesy of Richard Green)

14 (Right, bottom) A larger vessel than that depicted in Plate 13, this similarly brig-rigged cat lying hove-to off Liverpool with a gig alongside is armed and is probably trading with a Letter of Marque, as opposed to being a fully commissioned privateer, and is in the West India or North America trade. She flies the 'Blue Peter' at her foremasthead, indicating imminent departure to seaward. From a painting by Robert Salmon. (© Courtesy of the N.R. Omell Gallery)

13 *(Above)* A typical brig-rigged coasting and short-sea trader, this anonymous brig is shown here off Whitehaven. Despite this west-coast location, she was typical of the many hundreds of collier-brigs and Baltic traders of the period 1770–1840. From a painting by Henry Collins. (© Courtesy of the N.R. Omell Gallery)

15 A large, 800-ton East Indiaman of about 1685, such as Edward Barlow would have been familiar with. The ship flies the 'gridiron-ensign' of the Honourable east India Company, along with the English flag of St George and other East India Company striped flags. The magnificence and heavy armament of the vessel conveys the power of John Company, even in these early days, the globular stern lanterns a potent signal of aspiration. From a painting by Isaac Sailmaker. (© Courtesy of the National Maritime Museum)

17 *(Right, bottom)* East India House in Leadenhall Street, London, headquarters of the world's first powerful company. Originally an Elizabethan mansion, by the end of the eighteenth century the company's court-room, sale room and administrative offices had been housed in neo-Classical splendour. Trade goods were never displayed, although the library and a museum contained oriental works of an intellectual, rather than commercial nature. From an engraving by J.C. Stadler after a painting by T.H. Shepherd. (From a Private Collection)

16 (Above) A convoy of East Indiamen anchored off Anjer on the Javanese coast in the Sunda Strait, from a painting by William Daniell. The ship flying the blue ensign and firing a signal gun is an escorting man-of-war. Anjer was at this time no more than a watering place. (© Courtesy of the National Maritime Museum)

18 HCS *Earl of Abergavenny*, commanded by Captain John Wordsworth, the poet's brother. Built in 1796 at 1,460 tons this large East Indiaman was wrecked on the Shambles Bank off Dorset on 5 February 1805 while outward bound on her fifth voyage. Owned by William Dent, she was built by Pitcher at Northfleet on the Thames. From a painting by Thomas Luny, showing her entering Spithead prior to joining a convoy. (© Courtesy of the British Library, India Office Collection)

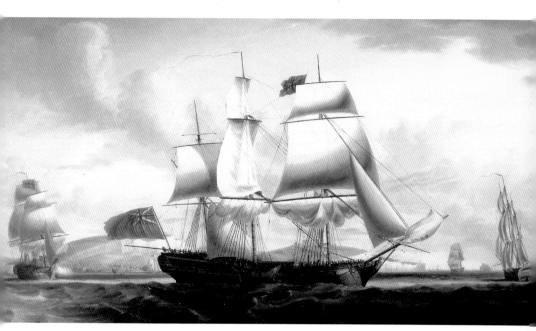

19 The Honourable East India Company's ship *William Pitt* shown in three positions off Dover by Robert Dodd. The first of three ships bearing the same name, the *William Pitt* of 1785 was a medium-sized Indiaman of 798 tons burthen, launched from Perry's Blackwall yard to the account of Robert Preston, later Sir Robert and a Deputy Master of Trinity House. She was commanded by Captain Sir Charles Mitchell and made six voyages to the east. In 1805 Captain Boyce took over and made a voyage to Botany Bay and China, after which the ship was employed as a troop-transport and West Indiaman. She was sold for breaking-up in 1809. (Private Collection/© Courtesy of Richard Green)

20 A cutter running ahead of a merchantman off Sheerness. The merchantman is possibly a West Indiaman or a medium-sized East Indiaman and is outward bound. The cutter has a number of turbaned figures on deck, with an officer and may well be an East India Company hoy being used as a tender to Indiamen in The Downs. She is typical of the small craft used to chase smugglers, carry out surveys or attend buoys, beacons and 'floating lights'. From a painting by Thomas Luny. (Private Collection/© Courtesy of Richard Green)

21 Thomas Luny's painting of shipping off Gravesend on the Kentish bank of the lower Thames shows a variety of small craft, including an open fishing boat in the right foreground, about 1780. The small hoy in the centre may well be one of those belonging to the East India Company and used to tender to the East Indiamen, one of which is outward-bound on the left of the painting, (© Courtesy of the N.R. Omell Gallery)

22 The Trinity House Yacht of 1788 off the Casquets lighthouses near Alderney. The Elder Brethren carried out many of their duties in this handsome yacht which was one of a number of vessels at their disposal. From a painting by Thomas Whitcombe. (© Courtesy of Trinity House)

23 Although built under patent from Trinity House, Henry Winstanley's lighthouse of 1698 was a private speculation. It was destroyed in the great storm of November 1703 during which Winstanley himself, as well as his lighthouse keepers, were killed. Artist unknown. (© Courtesy of Trinity House)

24 John Rudyerd's wooden lighthouse was erected in place of Winstanley's and was lit in July 1708. Although Rudyerd was a silk-merchant, his design was sound and based on ship-building principals. He was funded by Colonel John Lovett who was granted a 100-year lease following an Act of Parliament gained by Trinity House. Lovett expected a return of £700 per annum from an investment of £5,000 – his wife's dowry. Weakened by ship-worm, the tower caught fire in December 1755 and burnt down; the two keepers escaped. Artist unknown. (© Courtesy of Trinity House)

25 John Smeaton, the father of English civil engineering, erected his fine, granite tower in three years, lighting it in 1759. Although the candles providing its light-source were weak, this was improved with Argand burners. The upper three quarters of the tower was removed and re-erected on Plymouth Hoe when a much larger lighthouse was built on an adjacent rock in the 1880s. Trinity House assumed direct responsibility for the lighthouse in 1806. From a painting by Admiral Beechey. (© Courtesy of Trinity House)

26 The lighthouse on Bidston Hill on the Wirral from which a lookout was kept and the arrival of ships in the offing was signalled to their owners in Liverpool (in the right background) by means of signal flags and shapes hoisted above the adjacent out-building. (© Courtesy of Liverpool Museums)

The Queen of Naples of London, Capt. George Grey, coming in the Naples 1791

27 The brig *Queen of Naples*, of London, Captain George Grey, coming into Naples, 1791. A regular trader to the Mediterranean, the *Queen of Naples* is shown in Naples Bay with Vesuvius in the background. Note the pre-1801 red ensign. The Grey family served in both the Royal Navy and the mercantile marine from the eighteenth to the twentieth centuries. (© Courtesy of Michael Grey)

From Fort James and other estuarial stations the ships would often work further upstream, increasing the likelihood of malarial and other infections and there barter for gold and goods other than slaves. However, the tract of coast with which British slavers mostly sought their cargoes lay far south and east of Fort James and the Gambia River, covering some 1,500 miles between the Sherbro River a little south of Sierra Leone, and the Benin River, or New Calabar, just west of the Niger Delta, with Old Calabar beyond. Although the Sherbro was an exception, elsewhere there were few creeks or rivers and the 'entire shoreline, almost in every part, is difficult of access, because of the heavy surf that breaks upon the beach and it is only possible to land in a light canoe and even in that way it is frequently impractical for many days together'.

For a ship-master embarking a cargo of humans in such conditions there were additional problems attached to their feeding and watering. He must lay in a store of maize, fruit, corn, yams and, for himself and his officers, some palm wine. Water was always a problem and might be had from the river in which he lay if it was not excessively brackish, otherwise there were other sources.[14] At Cape Coast, William Richardson recalled:

> Thse Castle has a lofty wall around it and stands on rocky ground near the sea, but has no fresh water except what they save in a very large tank during the rains, and which supplies [both] the garrison and shipping. In order to destroy the Guinea worms in it we put two or three spoonsful of quick lime into each [water] cask [filled from the cistern].

Elsewhere the slaves were held in baracoons, stockaded like livestock and, once examined and accepted by the surgeons, branded as sound with the shipper's mark to avoid substitution by physically sick or inferior persons. At Calabar and Bonny, regular numbers of slaves were brought down-stream by the native traders in twenty or thirty canoes every fortnight. Once within reach of the sea they would be stockaded, fed and rubbed down with palm-oil to improve their appearance. The confinement in the forts or baracoons might last for weeks when a high surf was running and the slavers lay in an exposed road as on the 'Slave Coast' of the Bight of Benin. Here negotiations with agents of the King of Dahomey could also be protracted and there were, as we have seen, additional costs involved with the hire of native canoes to bring off the slaves, the ship's boats being inadequate to handle the surf. 'The preliminary costs of lading a slave ship, on this coast, around the year 1790, amounted to a value of some £368; and about the same time slaves were costing five ounces of gold, or £10, apiece'.[15]

The trade was surprisingly well controlled, communications between owners and commanders facilitated by other merchant ships and the regular mail packets run by the General Post Office to the West Indies. The written orders given to the commander of a slaver were comprehensive, those to Captain Ambrose Lace of the *Marquis of Granby* of Liverpool in April 1762 being typical. Of his outward cargo which had been found and shipped by his owners, Lace was 'to have the usual Commission of 4 in 104 of the Gross Sales, and your Doctor, Mr Lawson, 12 pence per Head on all the slaves sold'. It being war-time Lace was to sail in company with another slaver:

> ...as you are both Ships of Force, and we hope Tolerably well-mann'd you will be better able to defend yourselves against the Enemy ... should you be Fortunate enough to take any vessel or vessels From the Enemy, we recommend you sending them Home or to Cork ... so as not to Distress your own ship.

Lace was to concert his offer for slaves with the masters of any other Guineamen treating for cargo on the Guinea coast 'so as not to advance the Price...' and he was expected to purchase 550 slaves. He was abjured:

> to be very Choice in your Slaves. Buy no Distempered or old Ones, But such as will answer at the Place of Sale and stand the Passage and as Callebar is Remarkable for great Mortality in Slaves we desire you may take every Prudent Method to Prevent it, viz. – not to keep your Ship to[o] Close in the Day time and at Night to keep the Ports shut as the night Air is very Pernicious. The Privilege we allow you is as Follows: yourself ten Slaves, your first mate Two, and your Doctor Two, which is all we allow except two or three Hundred w[eigh]t of screveloes [small elephant's tusks of less than 20lb weight], but no Teeth [full sized tusks] ... as we will not allow anything more.

He was then directed to proceed to Barbados where he would 'Find Letters lodged ... at the House of Messrs. Wood & Nicholas...' which would direct him to the most favourable market at 'Guadaloupe or Martinico or any other of the Leeward Islands...' Instructions for his homeward cargo were no less specific. It was to consist of:

> ...about One Hundred Casks of good Mus[covad]o. Sugar for the Ground Tier [i.e. the lowest layer of casks in the hold], the Remainder with First and Second white Sugars, and Betwixt Decks with good Cotton and Coffee, and the Remainder of the neat Proceeds in Good Bills of Exchange at as short Dates as you can.

However, should Lace not find favourable prices, he was – with as little delay as possible – to 'proceed for Jamaica and ... there apply to Messrs. Cuthbert & Beans, Messrs. Hibberts, Messrs. Gwyn and Case, or any other House you think will do best for the Concern...' In case he had to load at Jamaica he was to pick up:

> ...as much Broad Sound Mahogany as will serve for Dunnage, the Hold fill'd with the Best Muso. Sugar and Ginger and Betwixt Decks with good Cotton and Pimento and about Ten Puncheons of Rum...

The balance of his 'neat Proceeds' were to be converted into Bills of Exchange as before, while his dealing with whichever of the two 'House[s] you are to sit down with must Furnish you with what money you want for Payment of wages and other necessary Disbursements of your ship which we recommend the utmost Frugality'. Lace's instructions concluded with how he was to sell slops to his crew and the recommendation that he should keep 'Good Rules and good Harmony amongst your Crew and a good watch, Particularly whilst you have any Slaves on Board...'There was some advice about precautions in the handing of powder and then a sobering conclusion, 'in Case of your Mortality (which God Forbid) your First Mate, Mr Chapman, must succeed you in command...'[16]

Among the eight signatures of the *Marquis of Granby*'s owners was that of William Boats, himself a former slaving captain who in 1758 had fought a smart engagement with a French corsair when master of the *Knight*. Boats acquired his odd surname from being discovered, Moses-like, a waif afloat in a boat. His benefactor had had him educated at the Blue-Coat School and he went to sea in Guineamen, rising rapidly to command and then to shipowning, by which he prospered, marrying well and dying rich at the age of 78. By Boat's day the trade was dominated by Liverpool Guineamen, as an anonymous publication of 1795 explained:

> The reason that the port of Liverpool could undersell the merchants of London and Bristol, was the restriction in their outfits and method of factorage. The London and Bristol merchants not only allowed ample monthly pay to their captains, but cabin privileges, primage and daily port charges; they also allowed their factors five per cent. on the sales, and five per cent. on the returns, and their vessels were always fully manned at a monthly rate. The Liverpool merchants proceeded on a more economical but less liberal plan, the generality of their captains were at annual salaries, or if at monthly pay, four pounds were thought great wages at that time, no cabin privileges were permitted, primage was unknown amongst them, and as to port allowances, not a single shilling was given, while five shillings a day was the usual pay from Bristol, and seven and six from London... The factors ... [also] had an annual salary, and were allowed the rent of their store, negro hire and other incidental charges...if the consignments were great or small, the advantages to the factor suffered no variation. Their portage was still more economical, their method was to take poor boys apprentice for long terms, who ... became good seamen, were then second mates, and then first mates, then captains, and afterwards factors on the islands.

In 1730 Liverpool owners had sent fifteen vessels south; seven years later there were thirty-three. In 1750, the year the *Asiento* was officially and finally given up, Liverpool had its own 'Company Trading to Africa' established by Act of Parliament and consisting of 101 merchants and eighty-seven vessels. Of these, five traded with Benin, eleven with Ngola, fourteen with New and Old Calabar, thirty-eight with the Gold Coast, eight with the Gambia and a dozen with Bonny. Occasionally the insalubrious nature of the places of embarkation affected the rights of the sailors and costs to the owners of their crews. The men of the *Lucretia* signed on at 25s a month but 'in case of slaving at Senegal to increase the wages to 28 per month'.

Like all Guineamen, the Liverpool bottoms took their human cargoes to the West Indies or the North American plantations 'from Maryland and Virginia southwards, after which they returned to Liverpool, with cargoes of sugar, rum, and other colonial or tropical produce'. Some brought a few slaves home, usually those retained on board by the master and by this time possessing some useful domestic skill. With smaller overheads Liverpool slavers sold their live cargoes of 'prime negroes' some 12 per cent cheaper than their competitors yet obtained equivalent returns. Captain Jenkinson reported his arrival at Jamaica in the *Fanny* in November 1756 stating that he had had 'a tedious passage of 13 weeks and 4 days' but his 110 slaves had sold from between £48 and £50 per head'. On the other hand the *Priscilla* of Liverpool was reported to have lost ninety-four of her normal shipment of 350 slaves, 'a shocking rate of mortality'. Boats himself, on the voyage he fought off a privateer in 1758, lost thirty-eight of his original shipment of 398 'Coromantee, Ashantee, Akin and Whydah negroes'.

The price received for black slaves varied according to the current demand, which in turn depended upon the location of the sale and the perceived 'quality' of the product. Being considered tractable and hard-workers the Ibo people sold best, averaging some £40 each, but prices of well over £50 per head could be obtained if the market favoured the vendor. The best return recorded by a Liverpool Guineaman is that of the *Vine*, Captain Simmons, in 1766. The ship bore 400 slaves from the Bonny River to Dominica and returned to Liverpool in seven months and ten days, realising about £13,000 in the sale of her live cargo.

Apart from exposure to tropical disease it was far from plain sailing for the crews of Guineamen. The slave-trade excited much envy, and losses of slavers occurred during hostilities with Spain and France. In 1746 the *Fortune* of Liverpool, Captain Green, with 354 slaves on board was captured by a Spanish vessel, while the resistance put up by Captain Tristram and his crew aboard the *Ogden* the following year was so fierce that the ship and all but one seaman, five ship's boys and nine slaves were killed and the *Ogden* was sunk by the Spanish privateersmen. Nor were the Spanish and French the only enemies, for the snow *Clayton* was taken off Fernando Po by pirates from Liverpool itself. These men attacked opportunistically, having earlier deserted from the *Three Sisters* in the ship's boat. Most of the *Clayton*'s crew, including Captain Patrick, were turned adrift in their own ship's longboat, but four voluntarily entered as rovers, and the chief mate and two boys were impressed into the pirates' service. The rest of the crew were twelve days in getting into the river Bonny, where the king seized their longboat, and the seamen had to enter on board different slavers trading there in order to get home. The pirates carried the *Clayton* to Pernambuco, where a Portuguese man-of-war retook her and escorted her to Lisbon. The *Three Sisters* herself was wrecked on the coast of Wexford where most of her crew perished.

The piratical scourge of the Guinea coast had been Bartholomew Roberts, himself originally an officer in Captain Plumb's slaver *Princess*. In April 1721 Roberts was back on the coast in the *Royal Fortune* where, as Robert Carse points out, he 'plundered and burned with his habitual success'. Such was the impact of Roberts and his men that after lobbying by anxious shipowners, the government were obliged to send out HMS *Swallow* and on 10 February 1722 Roberts was caught off Parrot Island by Captain Chaloner Ogle. While skilfully manoeuvring his vessel, Roberts was cut down by grapeshot, the *Royal Fortune* fell off the wind and Ogle fell upon his quarry. 'But Roberts's men … lowered his body over the side into the sea … before they surrendered. Most of them were weeping, and none of them attempted to fight'.

Occasionally the slavers themselves behaved in a despicably lawless, piratical manner. When the local chief with whom several slavers were dealing in the River Bonny in 1757 would not treat with the commanders in – or so it was believed – an attempt to drive up the price of slaves, they took drastic and high-handed action. The persistent delays in supplying slaves were resulting in a rising mortality among the waiting crews so, after taking counsel together, the commanders agreed on a concerted plan. While Captain Jones of the *Marquis of Lothian* and Captain Baille of the *Carter* remained at anchor with their guns trained on the town, Captains Nobler of the *Phoenix* and Lievesy of the *Hector* moved into a creek – 'it being nigher the town' – with the intention of opening a bombardment. But the intimidating tactic misfired, for the local chief and his men were armed with muskets and some cannon, and although Nobler 'plied his carriage guns for some time' he was obliged to strike his colours. This, however, 'did not avail, for they kept a continued fire upon him, both of great and small arms'. Nobler, his shattered ship stuck in a narrow creek under a competent and heavy fire, was obliged to abandon her and to retire in a boat towing astern, to reach the *Hector*, in which he and his surviving men escaped. 'The natives soon after, boarded the *Phoenix*, cut her cables, and let her drive [go aground] opposite the town,' where they began plundering the ship until setting her on fire 'by which accident a great many of them perished'. Shortly afterwards, however, trade opened as normal, 'all things … [having been] made up … but very slow, and provisions scarce and dear'. The *Marquis of Lothian* was later taken by the French off Martinique.

Many slaving captains were unfortunate during the Seven Years War, both in terms of encounters with the enemy, and in terms of losses through the odious vicissitudes of their trade. The presence of the trafficking slavers on the Guinea coast attracted the enemy and on 28 March 1757 two French men-of-war arrived off Melimba wearing false British colours. The *Ogden*, *Penelope*, *King George* and *Black Prince* were all loading slaves when the sixty-four-gun *St Michael* and the frigate *Leviathan* approached. Immediately realising they were cornered by an enemy force, several of the slavers fired at the *Leviathan* as she led her larger consort in, although their guns were far lighter than their opponents'. When the *St George* approached and opened fire with 24-pounders, the four commanders ran their ships on shore to avoid capture, but two launches from the men-of-war chased them into the shallows and attempted to cut off the rearmost, the *Black Prince*. Captain Creevey's men fired their stern chase guns loaded with musket balls, deterring the attack and the boats made instead for the *Ogden*, boarding and taking her, later burning the other grounded slave-ships. Having:

> …allowed 70 of the [local] natives to plunder the *Ogden* … [the French] fixed
> a fuzee to the powder magazine, which blew up the ship and all the black men

on board. This wanton cruelty so exasperated the natives that they threatened to take revenge… The blacks behaved extremely kind [sic] to all the Englishmen, and assisted them with what they wanted.

Jackson of the *King George* lost '390 slaves, who ran away and were for the most part taken by the natives'. He had twenty left which he had 'got on board the *Wolpenburg* of Flushing and with them crossed the Atlantic to Surinam. Creevey of the *Black Prince* had been obliged to ship himself home via Rotterdam, Wyatt of the *Penelope* 'we left at Melimba, with some slaves that he had saved', while Lawson of the *Ogden*, with his surgeon, 'was carried away by the French men-of-war'.

A greater danger came from French corsairs. In 1758 Captain Joseph Harrison of the *Rainbow* wrote to Messrs. Thomas Rumbold, his Liverpool owners, that he had beaten off a French privateer with the considerable loss of three men killed and six wounded, the latter including both his first and second mates. During the voyage he buried all his officers except his first and third mates, and his gunner.

Having lost since [we] left Liverpool, 25 white people and 44 negroes. The Negroes rose on us after we left St. Thomas's (São Tomé); they killed my linguistier whom I got at Benin, and we then secured them without further loss…

Captain Parkinson of the *Hazard*, laden with 411 slaves, beat off two attacks by privateers in 1758, as did Captain Lievesy of the *Hector* the following year. Captain William Creevey, back on the coast in the *Betty*, fared less well. Having been 'out-carried' in convoy by the escorting men-of-war, the *Betty* crossed the Bay of Biscay only to run into a convoy of French East Indiamen escorted by the '*Fortune* of 64-guns … one of their best sailing frigates, who sunk your Snow *Betty*, with the greatest part of her cargo'. Creevey bemoaned his fate and:

…the shocking prospect that's before me, in being carried to the Indies, where I have neither money nor credit … it being the unhappy event of war, in which I have been … twice taken in less than twelve months.

When a slaver was captured carrying her live cargo the predators sold the slaves. This occurred to Captain Timothy Wheelwright of the *Molly*. Captain Christopher Carus of the *Achilles* was also taken by the French after one of his guns, a 4-pounder which had been re-bored to fire 6lb shot, burst and killed his third mate and wounded eight of his seamen. Captain Edward Cropper of the slaving snow *Mac* struck to the French privateer-brig *Mars* mounting fourteen carriage guns and twenty swivels and manned by ninety men. Cropper had fought a gallant defence of an hour and a half and surrendered with only six men capable of fighting. Many other slavers were taken by French corsairs or French men-of-war, Liverpool alone having almost one hundred ships taken by the enemy during the Seven Years War (1756–1763).[17]

Despite the horrors of capture by the enemy in wartime, the most feared event was an uprising of the slaves. This was not always suppressed and the most danger- ous time for such a revolt was while the slaver was completing her lading, lying at anchor with only part of her crew on board, her captives unreconciled to their fate and within sight of the shore. Captain Potter of the *Perfect* was killed in such circum- stances in January 1759, along with his surgeon, carpenter, cooper and a ship's boy. Henry Harrison, one of the *Perfect's* men, had been ashore and managed to get off to another slaver, the *Spencer*, but was unable to persuade Captain Daniel Cooke to attack the *Perfect* with sufficient vigour to prevent the hundred or so slaves from run- ning her ashore and setting her alight.

A similar event took place in January 1769 when the *Nancy* of Liverpool lay at New Calabar with 132 slaves on board. About eight in the morning the slaves rose and wounded several of the crew. Captain Williams had only five fit men on board at the time and was obliged to draw his sword to defend himself but the noise of pistol shots brought off the locals in canoes. They swarmed aboard:

> …took away all the slaves, with some ivory … plundered the vessel … stripped the captain and crew of books, instruments, and cloathes, afterwards split the decks, cut the cables, and set the vessel adrift. Captain Labbar, who was lying in the river, sent his boat, and brought Captain Williams and his people from the vessel, which was then driving with the ebb, a perfect wreck.

This was not an act of liberation on the part of the inhabitants, but one of aggran- disement, for the local chiefs and their people seem to have been nothing if not opportunistic and as bad at enslaving their neighbours as the slavers. The removed slaves doubtless found their way onto another ship, resold to the profit of their handlers. Indeed the entire traffic that took place between the slavers and their local suppliers was tainted by compromise and all-too-often outright pitiless indifference.[18]

That such conduct might lead to consequences back home is given credence by an account by Samuel Kelly, a ship-master who was no friend to the slave trade. Witnessing the arrest by bailiffs of a shipmaster at a boarding-house Kelly's curiosity was aroused:

> On enquiry I found that this captain and another, on the coast of Africa, having had some altercation with the natives, the crews of both ships were sent on shore, armed, at night with their faces blacked and attacked the village, doing much injury. The natives, being aware of their enemies, repulsed them and found means to cut off one of the ships. The other captain, who lost his ship, afterwards returned to Liverpool, and being the principal transgressor, the present arrest was at the suit of the under- writers for the recovery of their loss. This captain was liberated after examination and was afterwards blown up in his ship whilst engaging a French privateer, and I believe most, if not all, of the crew and cargo if slaves perished. How awful!

Indeed, when invited to take a position as mate in a Guineaman, Kelly refused:

…the law not allowing the appointment of masters, unless they had previously been either a surgeon or mate on two voyages. This proposal I declined, being well aware of the iniquity practised in that trade.

Later, lying off Kingston, Jamaica, Kelly found his own vessel, the *Thetis*, 'surrounded by slave ships from Africa, the stench from which about daylight was intolerable and the noise throughout the day very unpleasant…'

The most serious and discreditable affair in this dubious intercourse took place at Old Calabar in 1767 when a number of Guineamen lay awaiting slaves. They consisted of the *Edgar* of Liverpool, the *Canterbury* of London, and the *Indian Queen, Duke of York, Nancy* and *Concord* of Bristol. In negotiating with the local chiefs the commanders had encountered a rivalry between two towns, Old Town and New Town as the British called them. Pretending a conciliating friendship, but actually by arrangement with the headmen of New Town, the ships' commanders invited the principal grandee of Old Town, known to them as Ephraim Robin John, to come on board under their protection while they sought mediation. The chief sent his three brothers, led by Amboe Robin John, who were treacherously seized while aboard the *Duke of York* and although some of their entourage jumped into the river, they and their canoe crews were massacred in the shallows. Caught between musketry from the ships, the pursuing ships' boats or the inhabitants of New Town, some three hundred wretches were cut to pieces.

This concerted work done, the warriors of New Town boarded the *Duke of York* and demanded the person of Amboe Robin John:

> The unfortunate man put the palms of his hands together, and beseeched the commander of the vessel that he would not violate the rights of hospitality by giving up an unoffending stranger to his enemies. But no entreaties could prevail. The commander received from the New Town people a slave … in his stead, and then forced Amboe Robin John into the canoe, where his head was immediately struck off in the sight of the crew, and of his afflicted brothers. As for them, they were carried off, with their attendants, to the West Indies, and sold into slavery.

Gomer Williams withholds the names of the ship-masters involved, adding that:

> The action of the captains has never been defended; but we must not forget that they were dealing with a shifty, greedy, and treacherous lot of rascals, who made a practice of selling their countrymen into slavery. The delays and subterfuges resorted to by the native chiefs to enhance the price of slaves … must have been extremely exasperating to the slave commanders, whose lives and cargoes were imperilled by a prolonged bargaining, owing to the climate, and the possible outbreak of disease among the slaves cooped up in the hold, before they left the coast and entered upon the horrors of the sea passage.

He goes on to say that 'papers belonging to the commander of the *Edgar*, show that the chiefs were in his debt … [and] prove that they held him and his family in high esteem…'

While disreputable and lawless incidents marred the conduct of slavers on the African coast, the relationship between the English dealers and their middle-men is of interest. There was a rich correspondence between the local leaders, the 'Grandee Kings' who assumed English-style names for the purposes of trading, and the many merchants of Liverpool and London whom they had known previously as slaving-commanders. While not attempting to justify the conduct of these men, it is likely that Williams has a point insofar as emphasising that the only inducement the Grandees understood was main-force – which is not to condone anything. In July 1773 Robin John Otto Ephraim, one of the Grandees of Old Calabar wrote to Ambrose Lace, the former slaving commander who was by now a merchant in Liverpool. The chief writes a torrent of pidgin which reveals much about the relationships that could develop between these men:

> Sir, I take this opportunity to write to you I send [you] Joshua 1 Little Boy By Captain Cooper [.] I been send you one Boy by Captain faireweather I ask Captain Cooper wether Captain faireweather give you that Boy or not he told me Captain faireweather sold the Boy in the West India and give you the money[.] I desire you will Let me know wether faireweather give you money or not[.] my mother Send your wife one Teeth [elephant's tusk] by Captain Sharp… I want 2 Gun for every Slave I sell[.] Send me 2 or 3 fine chint[zes] for my self and handkerchief… Send me some writing paper and Books[.] my Coomey [the duty levied by the local head-men from the slavers] his [is] 1600 Copper[.] Send me 2 sheep … Sir I am your BEST friend Otto Ephraim.[19]

It is clear from the foregoing that not only were many implicated in the slave trade, but that it was a complex matter, steeped in the contrariness of human nature. Clearly, not all of the trade's beneficiaries were white, but in terms of enrichment it was white men who profited most. Between 1783 and 1793, when war again broke out with France, Liverpool alone cleared 878 ships for the coast of Guinea, carrying to the West Indies and America an estimated 303,737 slaves. Their value was some £15,186,850 which, after deductions for factors' commissions, fees at sale, charges on bills of exchange and so forth, remitted to Liverpool a net return of £12,294,116, that is in excess of £1 million sterling per annum.

By the time of the abolition bill in 1807 Liverpool had entirely displaced Bristol in importance and was developing its own system of wet-docks. Not only had it benefited from the slave-trade, but also with the enormous growth of commerce with both Canada and the now independent United States. Moreover, at the conclusion of the Napoleonic War in 1815 when the East India Company's monopoly of Indian trade ended, Liverpool was poised to seek greater status. The success of a steam-powered industrial revolution in its very hinterland opened new opportunities for its entrepreneurs and they were not slow to take advantage of this.

On the eve of the 'Great War with France' (1793–1815) the slave-trade, though by now under scrutiny and attack, remained a flourishing enterprise and it is worth noting that Liverpool was not the only port sending slavers to the Guinea coast. William Richardson joined the slaver *Spy* of London in 1790 at the time of the 'Spanish Armament' that followed the confrontation of British and Spanish in Nootka Sound. The *Spy* was 'a fine ship ... with a tier of gun ports and copper bottomed, a rare thing for a merchantman in those days'. There was a hot press out owing to the imminent possibility of war and Richardson was lucky to evade it. Captain Wilson engaged him as fourth mate among a crew of forty-five. After loading trade goods and:

> ...having got our powder in, we sailed down to Gravesend, and ... received our river pay and a month's advance [of wages], the seamen having £2 5 shillings a month. We had a letter-of-marque commission to permit us to capture the Spaniards in case of war, and I was well satisfied with my situation...

This was not to last and Richardson's account is as frank and revealing as Phillips's a century earlier. The first intimation of trouble came when the *Spy* anchored of Anomabu where 'a great many ships' lay at anchor. The men in a visiting boat from a Liverpool slaver recognised the *Spy*'s chief mate, Mr 'Cummins', as Mr Thorsby late of the Guineaman *Gregson* of Liverpool from which ship he had been imprisoned for maltreatment of the cook. Thorsby had escaped, changed his name and sought a berth with Wilson who was:

> ...a sharp hand [who] had been many years in the Guinea trade out of Liverpool, and had paid some hundreds [of pounds] in course of law for bad treatment to [his crews]... Mason, our second mate was one of the same stamp, and had impudence to do anything, if encouraged.

The *Spy* eventually sought her cargo off the Bonny Bar, anchoring under a murderously hot sun. After a few days she passed upstream and re-anchored off the town of Bonny. Receiving King Pepple on board with a salute from his cannon, Wilson 'broke trade', giving the king an old iron gun and a suit edged 'with something like gold lace'. *The Spy*'s crew now began to prepare the ship for receiving slaves. The sails were unbent and stowed away, the spars lowered on deck and the top-masts struck. Using the longer spars and an abundance of palm leaves, a roof was constructed over the deck as an awning so that the ship looked 'like a great barn'.

> This roof stood firm against the tornadoes, which occasionally come on here, and generally on a calm hot day ... [and are] known by a small black cloud rising in [sic] the horizon... As the cloud gets larger it soon draws near, roaring like a hurricane, accompanied with thunder and lightning and torrents of rain; this continues generally three or four hours, then clears up, and the weather becomes finer and healthier.

The next thing to do was to … [build] a barricade … across the main deck near the mainmast about ten feet high … [from behind which to] fire among the slaves if necessary and a small door to let only one man through at the time. When the slaves are on deck in the day-time the males are all kept before the barricade and females abaft it.

Platforms were then erected on the cleared 'tween decks upon which the slaves would sleep. Lengthwise the space was divided into four by 'strong oak palings'. This was to separate the slaves, the women occupying the after compartment, the boys the next, with the largest reserved for an anticipated number of Ibos – 'a harmless people' – and to be segregated for those in the foremost room, 'the Quaes, a savage kind of people, who have their teeth filed sharp … and ('twas said) were cannibals'.

For two long months the *Spy* took in her human cargo a few at a time until about two hundred had been embarked. The slaves were terrified, apprehensive of the consequences of every unfamiliar situation they were confronted with. 'One of … [the females] went out of her mind; we did all we could to comfort them, and by degrees they became more composed.' The ship still required more slaves but the routine began:

In the mornings, when the decks were all washed and dried, the slaves were all ordered up on the upper deck; the men were all arranged in line along both sides of the main deck; they were shackled together two each by the legs and then a long chain on each side was rove through a ring at each shackle and secured at both ends, so that the poor fellows could only sit or stand; in the evenings the chains were unrove and they were sent below, but still having their shackles on; the females were never shackled, nor [the] boys, for they assist the cook to get up wood and water and to peel the yams; when all were got below in the evenings the gratings were put over and well secured and the watch set. In regard to victualling them … they had two meals a day, one in the forenoon consisting of boiled yams, and the other in the afternoon of boiled horse-beans and slabber sauce poured over each; this sauce is made of old Irish beef, and rotten salt-fish stewed to rags, being well seasoned with cayenne pepper; the Negroes are so fond of it that they pick out the little bits and share them out, but they don't like the horse-beans. Their allowance of water was small, and they suffered much from thirst...

One feature of the diet was its 'binding quality' which was very necessary to deter diarrhoea, that 'inveterate distemper that most affects them, and ruins our voyages by their mortality'.

It was now that Captain Wilson revealed his character assuming:

…as much consequence as if he had been captain of a line-of-battleship: all we four mates had to attend him with hats off at the gangway in going out or coming into the ship; he flogged a good seaman for losing an oar out of the boat, and the poor fellow soon after died.

In contrast Wilson now revealed another side to his character, for a black woman appeared dressed in English clothes to soothe the anxieties of the slaves by sitting with them and telling them of the good life to which they were going. She was Wilson's trump-card, a slave he had befriended as his mistress and whom he had kept concealed in his cabin all the while; she was now used as a live palliative to subdue his cargo. The soothing of the women's anxieties ended their keening lamentations and was thought to remove an incitement for the men, kept forward out of sight, but not out of hearing of their women.

In the extended hiatus while they waited to complete their lading, and while boat parties under the mates went away to gather provisions, the crew fell sick by degrees. Several men 'got the blind fever' and Cummins/Thorsby died of some form of malady, followed by three other men. At this point 'King Pepple, whose wisdom the negroes have great confidence in (and indeed he deserves it), advised our captain to remove the ship farther from the land, which we did and the fever soon left us'. Less fortunate were two women slaves who slipped quietly overboard and began swimming ashore one evening. 'But before the poor creatures had got a few yards from the ship the sharks had torn them in pieces...'

One morning the *Spy's* crew went aboard a French slaver to assist in the suppression of a slave rising, Wilson ordering them not to fire among the slaves or they would face a lawsuit for damaging the French commander's property. In the event fourteen were killed but the rising was put down largely through Wilson's cunning initiative. The slaves on the upper deck were soon overcome, but those below were:

> ...knocking off their irons as fast as they could; our captain, who had probably experienced such work before this, knew how to manage them with the least danger to us. Seeing an old sail on deck that the Frenchmen had been repairing, he ordered us to cover over the gratings with it and then knock the [ventilation] scuttles in close on each side of the ship to prevent the air from getting into the 'tween-decks to the slaves; this done, we loaded our muskets with powder, but instead of shot we filled the barrels with cayenne pepper, which is plentiful here; then fired them off through the gratings into the 'tween-decks, and in a few minutes there was stench enough from the burnt pepper to almost suffocate them. This was the finishing blow; they cried out for mercy, which was granted, the sail was taken away, the scuttles opened, and the slaves let up two at a time and properly secured again.

Wilson was now desperate to complete his loading. In five months he had only bought three hundred slaves and the cost of keeping them all was prohibitive. He remonstrated with King Pepple, negotiating with arms and ammunition until the king sent an expedition inland. Pepple's war canoes returned and 'we soon after this got our number completed, near half of them females and boys'. There were now 450 slaves aboard the *Spy* and the process of preparing for sea commenced. The temporary roof was torn down, the topmasts sent up, along with the yards upon which the sails were re-bent.

> The hold was full of yams and water and wood; under the tops were hung large
> branches of the palm tree full of nuts like cherries in colour. The negroes are fond of
> palm oil, which they rub over their skin which softens it and makes it shine; we used
> to fry with it instead of butter.
>
> The ship being ready we discharged the pull-away boys and got under way …
> our own ends served. After passing the bar we steered to the southward for what
> is called the Middle-passage to the West Indies. It was pitiful to see the poor slaves
> with their eyes full of tears, looking to the land as long as … it was to be seen; the
> females wept bitterly.

It was now necessary to take steps to maintain order and six of the 'most tractable'
male slaves were appointed:

> …boatswain's mates, each with a cat-of-nine-tails to show their authority. Strange
> to say, they assumed more severity over their fellow slaves than any of us would do,
> and all this for only being allowed to go about unshackled and a little more victuals
> given them occasionally.

Boys and girls helped prepare the food and a few trusted slaves were allowed to wait
at the cabin table. Each officer had a defined area of the ship under his close scrutiny
during the daytime and after dark, when all the slaves had been confined below, the
officers, including Wilson, were on doubled watches.

Richardson observed the good behaviour of the female slaves in his charge. They
were encouraged to dance 'to keep them cheerful and healthy' but, although not
one died on the passage, Wilson savagely flogged a woman found to have stolen and
secreted a knife. Beneath Wilson's vicious repressiveness one can see the captain's ruthless professionalism. Within the context of the time his regime was not of itself cruel,
though it was undoubtedly cunning, but he was heartless at the slightest infringement
of it, and brutalised a culpable slave as an intimidating example to the others just as he
had flogged a sailor for losing an oar.

The *Spy* was a fast ship, capable of 9 knots, and she soon made Carlisle Bay,
Barbadoes, where she received orders to proceed to Montego Bay, Jamaica, to sell her
slaves. Here Richardson:

> …was sent on shore with a hundred of our healthiest males to give them an airing,
> but more with the intent of giving the planters see what fine slaves we had got. The
> poor fellows were glad to have their feet on shore again, and followed me about the
> town like a flock of sheep after the shepherd, and met with several Negroes whom
> they had known on the coast of Guinea. At the farther end of the town there was a

pond of fresh water, and as soon as they saw it they gave a shout which startled me, until I saw them run into it and, having their shackles off, begin to plunge and jump and shout, quite delighted, and tumbling one over the other like a set of wild men; after they got a good washing, we went down to the boat and then on board, not one missing. I was much pleased with this excursion…

It now remained to sell the slaves, though not by open auction. At this time in Jamaica a procedure had been adopted whereby the slaves were admitted to a darkened room into which the planters followed knowing that the slaves were offered at a flat rate. Each planter carried a number of tallies indicating the number of slaves he wished to purchase and, in the darkness, each planter groped their quarry, secured his tallies round the necks of the appropriate number of slaves, after which all were let out. The *Spy*'s male slaves sold at £44 each, a considerable profit if to the outlaid cost of £10 per head a small victualling allowance of a few pence per day for what was usually a four or five-week passage is added. Although no women had died, one male slave had been lost after being struck by Mason who, thanks to Thorsby's death, had been promoted to chief mate. The dead slave 'was opened by the doctor on the quarterdeck, where a black spot was found on the liver which the doctor said caused his death'. Consequently Mason was discharged in Jamaica, as was the other mate (Richardson's immediate superior), for no discernible reason other than the fact that he was 'not much of a sailor'. Clearly Wilson tolerated no incompetents.

The ship was thoroughly cleaned and the slaves' sleeping platforms stripped out prior to loading a cargo of 'sugar, rum and mahogany, and got away near about the middle of March 1791, and headed for London'. But irony was now to strike the crew of the *Spy*:

Off Beachy Head we were brought to by the *Nemesis*, frigate, (Captain Ball), who pressed all our men except four Germans (sugar bakers whom the captain had shipped in London to do the drudgery of the ship). Some of the poor fellows shed tears on being pressed after so long a voyage and so near home. The frigate sent an officer and a party of her men to take us into the Downs, and bore up with us, where we both came to anchor.[20]

Next day an officer came on board with our men to get their clothes and notes for their wages … [after which] we got ticket men from Deal (called so by having tickets to keep them from being pressed), and when we got to Gravesend our captain left us and went up to London [a common practice], leaving the pilot and me in charge of the ship… Two days after our arrival, as I was busy in getting a derrick up to get out the cargo, a galley came alongside, and the [naval] officer in charge of her told be to get my things ready to put into her and go along with him. I told him I had charge of the ship, and he must be answerable for what happened. He said he knew that but I must go; so I got my things into the … press-boat, and in rowing to the *Enterprise* receiving-ship, lying off Tower Stairs, they let me know that the doctor of our ship had informed against me by telling them that I was only acting as chief mate, and had no protection, which was true.

Richardson secured his wages and was eventually put aboard the *Nemesis* 'where I got among my old shipmates again. He was later transferred to HMS *London* which paid off that September, after which Richardson returned to London and secured a berth aboard Captain Anthony Calvert's *Surprise* as fourth mate. The *Surprise* was another Guineaman, a large, coppered ship, and Richardson confessed that: 'Although I had said I never would join such a barbarous trade again, I was now obliged by necessity to it, for poverty compelled me'.

Calvert, who we shall encounter again, was a hard-headed owner, allowing Richardson only 2s a day whilst he rigged the ship. Richardson gave up his boarding house to save himself from further debt, but found a cook-shop near the *Surprise*'s berth which furnished him with 'a good leg-of-beef soup for two-pence, and a pennyworth of bread' with which he expressed himself 'satisfied'. Calvert, who dwelt nearby in The Minories was among those 'owners of ships, [who] though floating in wealth, were very hard on poor sailors at this time not shipping them till the last minute, and then giving them low wages'. Richardson's complaint, though by no means confined to his time, was sharpened by the fact that the partial demobilising of the Royal Navy flooded the market with unemployed seamen and instead of the 45s paid on the *Spy*, the rate for seamen was now no more than 30s, not much more than the 24s allowed a naval able seaman and over the inadequacy of which the Royal Navy's men would mutiny six years later when a hot war with Revolutionary France was in progress. But fate had another twist for Richardson. The *Surprise* was bound for Ostend 'to take in spirituous liquors for trade, as part of the cargo' when, in approaching the port, she was caught on a lee shore in a rising gale.

The pilot we had brought from London, was afraid to run the ship into the harbour, though the wind was fair for it; so we hauled on a wind to keep her off; but the gale increasing, we drove nearer the land, and on the 24th [December 1791] there was a danger of the ship going on shore that night; so to save our lives the captain thought it best, as the harbour was under our lee, to run her in haphazard.

So everything being prepared, with one of the anchors hung under the bowsprit to bring her more on an even keel, we bore away under close-reefed fore and main topsails, while the lofty waves and broken water all along shore looked dismal, and gave poor hopes of saving our lives. There are two wooden piers running out from Ostend seaward … and though … high-water, she soon struck on the bar, but the roaring wind and waves forced her along, and the next stroke she gave unshipped our rudder; but still the wind and waves drove her along, until the want of the rudder caused her to sheer to port, and, having by this time entered the mouth of the harbour, she ran against the easternmost pier with such force that she stove in her larboard side and soon went to the bottom: this was about the dusk of the evening, Christmas Eve.

Fortunately in shallow water the *Surprise* sat on the sea-bed and after a miserable, freezing night of strong gales, sleet and snow, they secured her to the pier and received some gin and cheese from a Dutch boat that ventured out to them. In the days that followed they discharged some of the cargo to lighten the *Surprise* then, 'getting at the broken part of our hull' they 'patched it up with tarpaulin and plank … and then we got her into the basin'. Calvert soon afterwards 'came over from London in his yacht, and finding the ship too much damaged to pursue the voyage … discharged all hands'. 'Being in poverty, and no wages to receive, next morning we officers waited upon Mr Calvert to see what he could do for us'. He offered them another ship, a slaver, which Richardson declined, to make his voyage to India in the *Prince of Kaunitz* mentioned elsewhere. He was not to serve in the merchant service after that, but ended his thirteen years as a mercantile seafarer by being impressed into the Royal Navy where he rose to be a warrant gunner. On his superannuation in March 1819 he acquired his own little sailing boat in which for fourteen years he enjoyed pottering about the waters of the Solent.

Richardson was not alone in disliking the slave-trade and had joined the *Spy* under a misapprehension, having been told she was 'going on a voyage of discovery'. The Abolitionist's most famous convert was Captain John Newton. A complex man, unreliable and fractious in his youth, the son of a ship-master whose mother died when he was only seven, Newton settled to nothing. Having been given an opportunity in his father's ship he was found a position in a trading house in Alicante. His behaviour earned him dismissal whereupon he was offered a post in Jamaica. Having fallen in love, he missed his ship only to go back to sea as a common seaman. Here he fell foul of the press and even after his father had negotiated elevation to midshipman aboard HMS *Harwich*, he overstayed his leave and was later flogged and disrated. At Madeira he exchanged out of the *Harwich* into a Guineaman from which he gravitated to a beachcomber on the Guinea coast. In due course, however, he joined a slaver in which he survived a near-overwhelming tempest. It was a Damascene moment in which he felt the first stirrings of religion. Despite this conversion, Newton was to continue serving in slavers, rising in due course to master of the *Duke of Argyle* in 1750. In 1752 he was in command of Mr Manesty's *African*, introducing Sunday worship and pacifying his cargo into a wonderful docility which, in his changed state, he piously attributed to Almighty God, but it was some time before the air of sanctity about the head of Captain Newton settled into a conviction that he was employed in an evil trade.

> During the time I was engaged in the slave trade, I never had the least scruple as to its lawfulness. I was, upon the whole, satisfied with it, as the appointment Providence had marked out for me… However, I considered myself as a sort of gaoler or turnkey; and I was sometimes shocked with an employment that was perpetually conversant with chains, bolts and shackles. In this view, I had often petitioned, in my prayers, that the Lord (in his own time) would be pleased to fix me in a more humane calling…

Upon the eve of joining Manesty's new ship, the *Bee*, as master, Newton was seized with a fit. He resigned his command and, after recovering, was appointed tide-surveyor at Liverpool, a task that 'requires pretty constant attendance, both by day and by night' on alternate weeks. 'I have a good office, with fire and candle, fifty or sixty people under my direction, with a handsome, six-oared boat and a coxswain to row me about in form'. In due course Newton was to take holy orders and become first the curate and later the vicar of Olney, in Buckinghamshire, where he befriended the poet William Cowper. He lost all his savings when Manesty went bankrupt, but found consolation in his marriage and his friendship with Cowper. Between them they produced the Olney Hymns, including Newton's *Amazing Grace*. Newton was later the incumbent of St Mary Woolnoth in Lombard Street, and in 1787 his experiences, set down in a pamphlet, were of use to the increasingly vociferous Abolitionists.

Although the redemption of such a sinner as Newton had undoubtedly been in his youth was held to be a wonder, most men were caught up in the trade from economic necessity and remained because – provided they survived – it paid well. James Irvine began his career as a surgeon and made five voyages in this capacity, commenting frequently in his letters home on the deaths of his shipmates. In December 1786 he wrote to his wife that 'I'm nearly wearied of this unnatural accursed trade and think (if no change of station takes place) ... I will at least look around me'. He received his change of station in due course, being appointed master of Baker and Dawsons's slaving schooner *Anna*, in which he had the misfortune to be ship-wrecked on the Moroccan coast and was himself enslaved.

One who at first disapproved of the trade, but afterwards prospered in it was the Manxman Hugh Crow who spent two years boat-building before going to sea as a bound apprentice to 'a Whitehaven merchant'. His career was not typical, but is certainly remarkable as an illustration of what was possible to an ambitious and capable man. He manifested these qualities early, securing a berth as second mate before he was out of his indentures. To take it up, however, meant deserting his ship and he was dragged from hiding aboard his new vessel by his old master accompanied by a bailiff, constables and a patrol of infantry. After cooling his heels in 'a noxious prison, amongst a number of dirty, runaway negroes' he returned to his ship. He had acquired a quadrant early in life, but unfortunately lost an eye, though this disability did not hold him back. At the end of 1787 he 'sailed as a passenger on board a ship bound from Cork to Kingston, Jamaica, paying one penny, as was the custom, otherwise a sailor (although a passenger) might claim wages'. Crow served as second mate in the *Elizabeth* trading to the West Indies, during which he was made a grant of cash for assisting in getting the ship afloat after she had grounded. The money enabled him to buy 'the first respectable suit of clothes he ever possessed'.

In due course, however: 'His repugnance to the slave trade was at length overcome' and he joined Dawson's Guineaman *Prince*. After this he was second mate in Boats's *Jane* before being made mate of the *Gregson* in June 1794. Under the command of Captain W. Gibson this 'fine ship' mounted eighteen 6-pounder guns, which proved inadequate for, after loading spirits in Guernsey on her way to Cape Castle, the *Gregson* was attacked by the French man-of-war *Robuste*. The Frenchman was better armed and manned, with twenty-four 12-pounders and 150 men, but it took an action of two hours to compel Gibson to strike his colours, whereupon the *Gregson* and her company were carried a lawful prize into L'Orient and joined other prisoners-of-war. The experience compelled Crow to compare his situation with that of black slaves:

> Often our indignation at this partiality, and indifference to our fate, did we wish that our colour had been black, or anything else than white, so that we might have attracted the sympathy of Fox, Wilberforce, and others of our patriotic statesmen.

By the autumn 2,000 prisoners had died and in the following February those survivors capable of it were marched across country to Pontoise. Here an English merchant officer and fellow prisoner coached Crow in mathematics, while he picked up a smattering of French. One morning in May he fixed a tricoloured cockade in his hat and escaped, only to be stopped the following day when he ran into a detachment of troops on a bridge. Crow's French proved inadequate to the task of answering the officer's questions so he lapsed into Manx and was taken for a Breton. After a series of adventures he reached Le Havre where he slipped aboard a Danish merchantman where a generous master not only took him to Deal but paid his onward fare by coach to London. Crow next joined the Guineaman *Anne*, bound for Bonny under Captain Reuben Wright, taking only three weeks to complete her lading of slaves. Approaching Barbadoes with a brig from Lancaster in company, they beat off an attack by a French corsair which 'left the *Anne* much damaged, and with several white and blacks wounded'. On their arrival at Carlisle Bay they had 'a galling reception', being stripped of men by the Royal Navy.

Presumably Captain Wright rounded up some local sailors, for the slaves were sold at Santa Cruz before the *Anne* departed for Liverpool. Crow was next mate of the *James* which not only grounded in the Mersey estuary on sailing in October 1796, but ran aground in the Bonny River when leaving for the West Indies with 400 slaves on board. The ship was leaking badly and the slaves were transferred to other Guineamen, whereupon the locals boarded the stranded ship to loot her. An affray ensued in which 'many whites and blacks were wounded' and Crow defended his property until King Pepple arrived to quell the rabble. This did not stop the ship herself from 'literally being torn to pieces' in the next few days, Crow and the survivors being lodged in the native town. Here they were obliged to take part in a ceremony of thanksgiving for the gods' gift of the *James*. In due course Crow returned to Liverpool where his diligence in refloating the *James* on her initial departure had attracted the notice of his owners and their underwriters, as a consequence of which he was made master of the *Will*:

> …belonging to Mr. W. Aspinall, one of the most generous merchants in Liverpool. She was about 300 tons burthen, carried eighteen six-pounders, besides small arms, and was manned by fifty men. The instructions I received were most liberal, and as a young man on my first voyage as master of a ship, I could not but be highly grati-

fied by the friendly and confident language in which they were conveyed. We sailed for Bonny, in July, 1798, and arrived safely, after a fine passage... We soon procured a cargo, and after a pleasant run arrived at Kingston in good health and spirits. Our voyage proved to be most successful. I sold nearly £1200 worth of return goods, which I had saved from my outward cargo, and received the bounty allowed by government for the good condition of the slaves on their arrival. We sailed for England with the fleet [i.e. a West Indies convoy], from which we parted in a gale of wind; but ours was, nevertheless, the first ship that arrived at Liverpool.

Thus blithely did Crow enjoy his first voyage in command of a slaver. The second was to be somewhat different. Outward-bound in July 1799 he fought off a French schooner-privateer off Cape Palmas; while in the Bonny River the *Will* was one of several Guineamen that drove off an attempt by three French frigates to capture them on 16 December 1799. Then, when approaching Tobago on 21 February 1800 an eighteen-gun privateer gave chase and ranging up alongside fired two broadsides into the *Will* before attempting to board. Crow responded with 'such a destructive fire from the *Will*'s guns, loaded with round and broken copper dross, that she sheered off, and fired from a greater distance'. The exchange of gunfire went on for two hours during which:

My officers and the ship's company conducted themselves ... with the greatest coolness and determination, and we found a young black man, whom we had trained to the guns on the passage, to be both courageous and expert.

The corsair made another approach, demanding surrender, which Crow vociferously rejected. He was then compelled to undergo an ordeal as the French commander took pot-shots at his person with a musket as he ordered his men to board and sheered alongside with a wild yell. The *Will*'s men poured three rapid broadsides into the Frenchman, which again fell astern to knot and splice the damage before making a final attempt to close with her quarry. A further two-hour fire-fight followed, by which time the French commander had had enough. The *Will* continued her voyage with one gun burst and three of her crew wounded. Enemy shot had passed into the hull among the male slaves, wounding twelve, two mortally and two seriously with broken thighs. Crow took great satisfaction from the gratitude of 'the black women who ... gathered round me, and saluting me in their rude but sincere manner, thanked their gods, with tears in their eyes, that we had overcome the enemy'. This creditable defence met with the worst possible reception when the *Will* – having refitted at São Vincente – arrived off Port Royal. 'We had scarcely let go the anchor ... when no fewer than eight men-of-war boats came alongside, and took from us every man and boy they could find.' One wonders about the fate of the brave young slave and what had prompted Crow to absorb him into the crew. It is implied that he too was pressed, manumitted by service in the Royal Navy but compelled to enslavement of another kind about which Crow was quite as clear as over other injustices.

The impressments of seamen I have always considered to be, in many points of view, much more arbitrary and cruel than what was termed the slave-trade. Our great statesmen, however, are regardless of such evils at home, and direct their exclusive attention to supposed evils aboard.

Crow's unrepentant attitude was probably typical, yet he appears to have been something of a *beau ideal* in this filthy commerce, for yet again his 'blacks were so healthy, and so few deaths had occurred amongst them, that I was, a second time, presented with the bounty of £100 awarded by government'. Whatever scruples Crow had were thus swept away by wealth and approbation and much of his inveighing against 'our great statesmen' was undoubtedly against the wealth-closing noose of abolition. Notwithstanding this naked self-interest, Crow was intelligent enough to deploy certain manipulative skills in his management of his live-cargo for in addition to 'keep[ing] the ship in a state of readiness to receive any enemy we might meet' he 'selected several of the finest of the black men' to join in exercises at the guns 'in passing along the powder' and with small arms. 'The blacks, who were very proud of the preferment, were each provided with a pair of light trowsers, a short jacket, and a cap...'

After this successful trip, Aspinall fitted out a second ship, the *Lord Stanley*, into which Crow's mate, Mr Kirby, went as commander and both were placed under Crow's direction. On this voyage he did not lose a man and it is telling that his rather sickening encomium refers to his crew as well as his cargo: 'Indeed my friends at Kingston used to say – "Crow has come again, and, as usual, his white and blacks are as plump as cotton bags" '.

The *Will's* return passage with sugar and rum was in a convoy of 164 ships which left Port Royal on 21 May 1801 and 'when under full sail presented a most beautiful appearance'.[21] During the passage one ship foundered and the *Will* rescued her company, Crow thereby further distinguishing himself. His star was in the ascendant for on his return to Liverpool he was made a gift of silver plate by the merchants and underwriters for his gallant defence in the Bonny River in December 1799, while for his action against the French corsair off Tobago the underwriters of Lloyd's Coffee House presented him with a gift of money and 'a handsome silver cup' valued at £200.

Crow went on to command the 400-ton frigate-built *Ceres* and by 1 December 1806, upon the eve of abolition, he was master of the 500-ton *Mary* as the ship ran down towards Tobago on her middle-passage. Familiar with the likelihood of meeting French cruisers in the vicinity, Crow called his crew aft when two men-of-war were seen approaching in chase under a cloud of canvas. Crow addressed his men, warning them of the consequences of a French prison and encouraging them to defend the ship. As the twilight darkened to night Crow sent his men to quarters and at ten o'clock the headmost of his two pursuers ranged up close and hailed in English. This was 'an old French trick' and Crow maintained his course and speed, soon after which the stranger opened fire, exchanging broadsides for over an hour until the second strange sail loomed alongside in the darkness of the night. There then commenced an unequal action.

The *Mary* was well armed with twenty-four long 9-pounders, and four 18-pounder carronades – short-barrelled, heavy calibre, short-range weapons – upon her quarter-deck. She also had a crew of about 70 experienced seamen in her crew. Nevertheless this was no match for two men-of-war, notwithstanding the fact that it was now night-time. At one point the helmsman was winded by a passing ball, while at the same moment Crow fell to the deck, wounded by a splinter. He and the quartermaster soon recovered, whereupon Crow left his mate, Mr Scott, on the quarterdeck to manage the running ship while he animated his men from every part of the vessel. The hours passed in a storm of projectiles, the darkness stabbed by the flames of gunfire. Men fell wounded and killed, the boatswain's legs were shot off at the thigh; balls smashed their way into the slave rooms, killing five males and wounding many more. After almost six hours one of the pursuing ships dropped astern and Crow thought he had triumphed, until, having knotted and spliced, she made sail and the *Mary* was once again hotly engaged on both sides.

The first streaks of dawn spread across the eastern sky as Crow was knocked senseless by a second splinter. The man at the wheel called out the captain was killed and as Crow revived, he found the *Mary*'s ensign struck: his men had lost heart. He ordered the colours hoisted again, but it was too late and Crow was carried below as one enemy ship ran alongside. To the intense chagrin of all involved it was now discovered that the *Mary*'s two opponents against whom she had so stoutly maintained her defence were the British sloops *Wolverine* and *Dart* whose officers had mistaken their quarry in the darkness for a French corsair.[22] Learning of this tragedy Crow 'in his anguish and vexation, struck his head several times against the cabin floor, until the blood started... Friendly hands restrained his phrenzy, and a flow of tears relived his grief...' Crow had in fact put up an incredibly spirited fight; William Laird Clowes says 'The conflict was a close and terrible one, each side displaying the utmost tenacity. After seven hours of give and take, the *Mary* was at last overpowered, and one of the warships boarded her'.[23] Such tragic errors in identity were not common, but neither were they unknown. The casualties are uncertain, but six men of the *Mary*'s crew were killed in the action or mortally wounded, while havoc was wrought among the wretched slaves. Commander Joseph Spear of the *Dart* was obliged to give Crow a certificate exonerating him from the damage to his ship and cargo, and recording the gallantry of his action. Gomer Williams remarks that 'It is worthy of note that from the afternoon before the action, until it was over, the crew of the *Mary* had not a single glass of spirits, nor did a murmur arise on that account'. The one benefit this awful incident produced was a protection against pressing which arrived from Admiral Dacres, the Commander-in-Chief, when the *Mary* anchored at Kingston.

It is perhaps not out of place to record that, according to Crow, while he was lying in his cot on the first Sunday forenoon after his arrival at Kingston, Scott the mate came below and asked if Crow would receive a deputation of 'a great number of black men and women' all of whom had come on board 'dressed in their best'. He readily agreed, sprang up, drew on his clothes, whereupon:

They all rushed into my cabin, and crowding round me with gestures of respect, and with tears in their eyes, exclaiming – 'God bless massa! How poor massa do? Long live massa, for 'im fight ebery voyage' – and similar expressions of good will and welcome. I soon recognised these kind creatures as having been with me in one or other of the actions in which I had been engaged on former voyages, and though my attention to them when on board was no more than I had always considered proper and humane, I was deeply affected by their mark of grateful remembrance. Poor Scott shed tears … and observed, 'How proud, sir, you must be to receive this … tribute of regard! And how few captains can boast of a similar proof of their good treatment of the blacks under their charge.' Indeed, I could not refrain from shedding tears myself, when I reflected that the compliment came from poor creatures whom I had brought from their homes in Africa. The women were neatly dressed… The men appeared in white shirts and trousers … and I was glad from my heart to see them.

This passage is of interest for several reasons. Firstly that 'a great number' of the enslaved were free to visit their old captor on a Sunday; second that they wanted to; third that Scott made an observation that for all Crow's patronising self-congratulation, not many slave captains had earned such approbation; and fourth that Crow expressed a degree of contrition. That Crow was one of the better Guinea commanders – perhaps business-like is the correct way to express his *modus operandi* – is epitomised by a song about 'Cappy Crow' said to have been popular among the enslaved black inhabitants of Kingston town. The song recalls that the governor of Jamaica had been on board the *Mary* after her fight with the men-of-war which, Crow himself remarked, 'was a compliment seldom known to be paid to the master of a merchant ship'.

The *Mary* arrived home from her tumultuous voyage on 2 May 1807 where Crow learned from Thomas Aspinall that the Abolition Bill had been passed. Hereafter, had the *Mary* met the two sloops her fight would have been for real – well not quite, for there were yet some tricks of the game to play. 'The abolition,' Crow rants with his own emphasis, 'was a severe blow for England, and particularly as it affected the interests of the *white* slaves who found employment on the trade,' meaning, of course, the seamen manning the ships. He then gives his opinion that 'Providence' ordained the traffic 'as a necessary evil' and castigates 'these pretended philanthropists' for worsening the condition of the enslaved Africans by causing others less humane than Englishmen to carry it on, a nice flourish! In fact Crow was to make another slaving voyage, but not in the *Mary* whose slaving days were over. Instead he transferred to Mr Henry Clark's 300-ton *Kitty's Amelia* of eighteen guns. This ship had been cleared outwards at the Customs House prior to the passing of the bill through Parliament, which permitted her to be sent out on one last slaving voyage so that, despite abolition, business went on and Crow's reputation had never stood higher. His insurance brokers in London, Messrs Kerwen, Woodman and Co., who insured his commissions from Liverpool to Africa at 15 guineas per cent – considerably less than the norm – added that:

…we have never heard greater praise bestowed on any commander than the under-writers in general have expressed in consequence of your very gallant behaviour, which will always procure their decided preference to whatever vessel you sail in.

Clearly the Royal Navy did not extend the same courtesy to a gallant officer. The *Kitty's Amelia* sailed on 27 July 1807, four of her men being pressed by Captain Tobin of HM Frigate *Princess Charlotte* in defiance of their exemptions. On the outward passage of seven weeks Crow, with three Letters-of-Marque in his possession, 'chased and boarded several vessels, [but] he took no prizes' before arriving in the Bonny River. The *Kitty's Amelia* was immediately visited by King Holiday demanding to know the truth behind the rumours.

[A]ll captains come to river tell me you[r] King and you[r] big mans stop we trade, and 'spose dat true, what we do?'

It was a pertinent question, for the King complained – among other things – that he had too many wives. He concluded that he did not think the trade would stop, a speech that Crow considered shrewd and, in the event, prophetic.

But this last voyage was to be dogged by ill-fortune, as if Crow's 'Providence' had turned against him. The haste with which the *Kitty's Amelia* had been fitted-out to clear before the passing of the bill and before Crow had been appointed master, had resulted in part of her cargo being spoiled. When the casks were opened the unspeci-fied goods were found to be rotten and, although the contents were dumped, the action marked an outbreak of dysentery. This was not helped by rain storms and the fact that, with a dozen ships eager for slaves, the *Kitty's Amelia* had a long wait. Although Crow left Bonny with 'as fine a cargo of blacks, as had ever been taken from Africa,' he began losing both his crew and his cargo, for 'the disease baffled the skill of the [ship's] two doctors, and he was deeply afflicted to see both whites and blacks dying round him at an alarming rate'.

Crow put into São Tomé and waited until the sick had recovered, only to find that within days of the ship's departure the disease broke out again. Thus Crow's last voyage was his worst, with all the attendant horrors familiar to so many slavers during the middle-passage. Crow lost his mate and then:

One afternoon when we were ten or twelve hundred miles from any land, and were sailing at the rate of seven or eight knots, the alarm was given that the ship was on fire … springing upon deck the first persons I saw were two young men with their flannel shirts blazing on their backs; at the same time I perceived a dense cloud of smoke issuing from below… I was determined … to extinguish the fire, or to perish in the attempt. When we got below we found the fire blazing with great fury on the starboard side, and as it was known to the crew that there were forty-five barrels of gunpowder in the magazine, within about three feet only of the fire … a thrill of despair ran through my whole frame… We paused for a moment, struggling, as

it were, to determine how to proceed. Very fortunately for us our spare sails were
stowed close at hand. These were dragged out, and by extraordinary activity we succeeded in throwing them over the flames which they so far checked, that we gained
time to obtain a good supply a of water down the hatchway, and in the course of ten
or fifteen minutes, by favour of the Almighty, we extinguished the flames...

The fire had been started by the two young men Crow had first seen on deck. Its
cause was a common one: they had been drawing off rum from a cask, with an
unguarded candle.

Crow lost both his surgeons in the middle-passage but by the time they approached
the West Indies the sickness had burned itself out with the loss of thirty of his crew
– about half – and fifty of the enslaved black people. At Kingston Crow found the
market glutted in the face of the imminence of abolition. The haste with which merchants had tried to profit before the trade ended produced a coda of death. Sixteen
slavers lay at anchor, some of which had been there up to six months, their slaves
unsold and dying daily in their appalling confinement. 'It appeared,' wrote Gomer
Williams, 'that the Liverpool slave trade was doomed to come to an end amid death
and ruin on a large scale'.

Not for Crow, for in all respects he was the exception that proves the rule in this
sordid and reprehensible traffic and now his luck turned.

His friends inserted a paragraph in the newspaper stating that Captain Crow had
arrived with the finest cargo of Negroes ever brought to Kingston. The puff did
its work, and in five days the cargo of the *Kitty's Amelia* had been sold at auction at
higher prices than those obtained by any other ship.

This achieved, Crow handed the *Kitty's Amelia* over to his mate, remaining himself
in Kingston to transact some business before taking command of the schooner *King
George* for the homeward passage. During his sojourn ashore he was often greeted by
slaves in a friendly fashion, and he clearly regarded himself as a caring ship-master
whose interest was beneficial to his live-cargoes. He remained steadfast in his condemnation of abolition, which he considered 'pernicious to England' because:

...it destroyed her nursery of seamen, and drove her young men, whose prospects
at home were blighted, into the American service, where they afterwards fought
against their own country [in the war of 1812–1814].[24]

The now wealthy Crow retired to the Isle of Man in 1808, becoming a member of
the House of Keys, but returned to Liverpool in 1817. He removed to Preston ten
years later where he wrote his memoirs and died, aged 64, in 1829, to be buried at
Maughold in his native Man. It does the slave-trade little credit that it produced at
least one humane, if unrepentant ship-master, but Crow's life was full of adventure
and in the end it was marked by private tragedy.[25]

While Crow's career demonstrates that a degree of compassion could be applied to the carriage of human cargoes, the horrors of the middle-passage cannot be glossed over. One compilation of 7,904 purchased slaves notes that 2,053 perished; another states a mortality rate of 20 per cent. In some ships it was much higher, in others considerably lower, as noted. Among the abolitionists the Rev Thomas Clarkson garnered statistics and details of the manifold horrors of the trade, the branding, the terrorising, the dreadful over-crowding, the effect of manacles, the general abuse – particularly of women – the appalling effects of the highly contagious bloody flux and other noxious distempers that caused micro-epidemics within the confines of the ship. Others assisted, some less well known than Clarkson and Wilberforce and his parliamentary friends. A Captain Parrey was sent by the government to survey the exact dimensions of slavers in Liverpool, reporting the illegal carriage of 351 men, 127 women, 90 boys and 41 girls, amounting to 609 people in the *Brooks*. This frigate-built slaver of twenty guns and 320 tons by measurement, was licensed to carry only 450 slaves. During fine weather on the middle-passage of forty-nine days she lost ten men, five women, three boys and a girl, but during a gale when the slaves were confined under hatches with the tarpaulins over for eighteen hours, fifty of the 140 below died of asphyxiation, terror, sea-sickness … who knows what?

'The mind cannot realise,' Gomer Williams says:

> …language cannot paint the sufferings of one day, nay, of one hour, passed under such circumstances, by the tightly wedged human cargo in the hold of the best managed slaver. Dreadful must have been the agony under the most favourable conditions, with a humane captain … an able surgeon, fine weather and a short passage, but what a circumscribed hell were they tormented in when, after several months spent on the coast to complete the cargo, they experienced, during a long passage to the West Indies, lasting from six to eight weeks, rough weather, inhuman treatment, and scanty rations of bad quality!

Perhaps worse for a sensitive individual was to come when, after the appalling privations of such a passage, the enslaved Mandingo, or Ibo, or Ashanti, was offered for sale. Private treaty was arguably the least humiliating, better than the scramble-sale held in the dark aboard the Guineaman, or ashore as recounted earlier. On such occasions all went at a fixed price and therefore the buyer sought a bargain with the utmost inconsideration to the individual. Often the slaves broke free and jumped overboard during such a ghastly ritual. The last method was the public auction – known as a 'vendue' – at which the 'refuse and sickly' were disposed of. Here the prices might fall far below the top whack of £40 to £50; perhaps a dollar, or even, in the case of a poor blind male brought in by Thomas Leyland's aptly named *Lottery*, Captain Whittle, simply given away. At such vendues 'the slaves were exposed to public view, naked … regardless of age or sex, and the slave-merchants and planters viewed and handled them as a butcher handles the cattle he is about to purchase for slaughter'.

Agitation to abolish the trade had begun as early as 1770, initiated by books and pamphlets such as Adam Smith's *Wealth of Nations* and John Wesley's *Thoughts on Slavery*. Both the established church and dissenting sects such as the Quakers, who were much involved on both sides of the Atlantic in shipowning, began its denuncia- tion. Abolition was first raised in parliament by David Hartley, MP for Hull, in 1776, the year that slavery lost legal recognition in Scotland. Matters at first seemed to play into the Abolitionists' hands. In 1783 a case was heard in London's Guildhall in which a number of underwriters sued the owners of the Guineaman *Zong* of Liverpool for attempting to defraud them. The case against the *Zong*'s owners, Gregson & Co. and Captain Collingwood, the ship's master, was that Collingwood and his offi- cers had thrown overboard 132 live slaves in order to claim the insurance on the cargo, deposing that the slaves had died in the 'customary way' by disease during the middle-passage. The allegations, however, were proved and evidence was produced to tell of the appalling events. During the middle-passage sixty slaves died and the surgeon reported many more to be sick. Alarmed by the losses which threatened the viability of the voyage, Collingwood proposed to his mate, James Kelsall, and others, that if they disposed of a number of the slaves overboard and logged that they had died naturally the loss would fall upon the underwriters, whereas if they continued to expire from sickness – what was perversely called 'a natural death' – the loss would have to be borne by the ship's owners. The conspirators callously agreed and 132 of the sickest were selected for disposal, fifty-four of whom were flung overboard that day, followed by forty-two the next. A few days later the remainder were brought up on deck and sixteen were consigned to the deep, whereupon the remainder 'with a noble resolution, would not permit the officers to touch them, and leaped overboard after their companions'. The case, once the circumstances were made known, pro- voked widespread disgust and condemnation.

In 1787, The Society of Friends, or Quakers, petitioned against the trade follow- ing the case of a slave named Somerset. The successful declaration of Somerset being free of bondage by virtue of being on British soil thrust the issue before the public at large. The case had been espoused by the Rev. Thomas Clarkson and Granville Sharp, the latter of whom headed the extra-Parliamentary campaign and founded the Society for the Abolition of the African Slave-Trade. The Society's Committee, excepting Sharp, Clarkson and one other, was composed entirely of Quakers. The year of 1787 also saw other reforms: a statute that *naval* seamen must be fed at no charge to themselves and that the food must be wholesome, also provoked legislation two years later extending this right of free victualling to slave-ships and their human cargo. This inadequate but humanitarian extension of the Naval Victualling Act of 1787 had been prompted by the first attempts by William Wilberforce to press for a bill on the abolition of the slave-trade.

Reaction was inevitable. Vested-interest linked shipping, West Indian plantations and the production of sugar and rum with political power, while the perceived threat to a trade worth something like half the nation's wealth, fed fears of abolition as much as the arguments of Captain Crow and his ilk. The lobby for the *status quo* found high-born and vociferous advocates, not least that royal naval officer the Duke of Clarence who declared the abolitionists either 'fanatics or hypocrites'. A young naval colleague and friend of the equally young duke, Captain Horatio Nelson, with his experience of the West Indies, was pro-slavery, and the Liverpool slave-merchants found a literate defender in the person of the Rev. Raymond Harris. Harris had been born in Bilbao and was a Jesuit who had settled in Liverpool where he officiated at the Catholic Church in Edmund Street. Harris published a counter-blast with a pamphlet entitled *Scriptural Researches on the Licitness of the Slave Trade, showing its conformity with the principles of Natural and Revealed Religion, delineated in the sacred writings of the Word of God.* This dissertation began with the admonition of God to the escaped slave Hagar and so delighted were the Liverpudlian slave-merchants that 'the reverend sophist' was presented with a gratuity of £100. Lord Hawkesbury, afterwards Lord Liverpool, 'actually condescended to distribute some of Harris's "Researches," recommending them ... as containing unanswerable arguments in favour of the slave trade'.

It seemed for time that the reactionaries had the upper hand. Successive attempts made annually to introduce an Abolition Bill lost momentum as parliamentary defeat followed defeat. This conservatism and reaction was entrenched by the French Revolution with its 'death' of Christianity, the horrors of The Terror and the appalling consequences of the high-sounding principles of '*Liberté, Egalité et Fraternité*'. But there were contrary stirrings, most significant of which was the great slave-revolt in San Domingue, when Toussaint L'Overture overthrew the French and established a black state. Although the temporary cessation of hostilities with Britain enabled Napoleon to send his brother-in-law, General Leclerc, to suppress the revolt and capture L'Overture, the French could not hold the entire island and first under Dessalines and then King Christophe, the independent – and black – state of Haiti emerged into the modern world.

Amid this turbulence, Wilberforce persisted, believing that abolition of the trade was the first step in the universal emancipation of slaves. There were some nasty moments, as when a Captain Kimber was acquitted of the murder of a slave-girl and later accosted Wilberforce in an unpleasant confrontation, but finally, on 25 March 1807, after twenty years of struggle, the slave-trade was finally to be 'abolished and prohibited and therefore to be declared unlawful' and received the royal assent.[26]

The end of the British slave-trade was, as Crow had written, a bad blow for the crews of the slavers. Its rewards to those who survived it were better than in many other trades and it had a certain specious glamour arising from its inherent hazards. The risk of the enslaved rebelling against their captors had been a perpetual threat to a Guineaman's crew, no-doubt in many cases crushing all sentiments of humanity and encouraging harsh and tyrannical regimes.[27] One of the worst of these uprisings had occurred aboard the *Thomas* of Liverpool, owned by Thomas Clarke and commanded by Captin Peter M'Quie. The *Thomas* was carrying 375 slaves from Loanga towards Barbados when, on the morning of 2 September 1797, the armourer left the arms chest unlocked. Subsequent events hint that M'Quie's regime might have been more relaxed than was customary, in which case it was an error as fatal as that of his armourer whose folly was discovered by a pair of the unfettered women slaves while the majority of the crew were at breakfast.

> They got into the after hatch-way and passed the arms through the bulkheads to the men-slaves, about two hundred of whom immediately ran up the fore-scuttles, and put to death all of the crew who came in their way. The captain and a few of his men fought desperately with the arms remaining in the cabin; but they were eventually overpowered, the slaves gaining complete possession of the ship. Captain M'Quie and many of his crew perished, being either killed in the conflict, butchered afterwards, or driven overboard. Twelve of the hands, however, escaped in the stern-boat, and after enduring the most dreadful hardships, two only survived to land in Barbadoes. A few were kept alive to steer the vessel back to Africa. Four of these escaped in the long-boat, and after being six days and nights without food or water, reached Watling's Island, one of the Bahamas... Five of the crew still remained on board the *Thomas* ... to steer the vessel... After forty-two days of misery and dread an American brig, laden with rum, came alongside, of which the Negroes made themselves masters, her crew escaping in their boats. Rum casks were opened, and a scene of drunkenness and confusion ensued, during which several of the blacks were drowned. The remaining crew of the *Thomas* took immediate advantage of this occurrence and recaptured the brig – the boatswain' with the captain's cutlass, having first killed the ringleader of the Negroes – set sail for the nearest land, and reached Long Island, Providence. The *Thomas*, with the surviving Negroes, was afterwards recaptured by HM Frigate *Thames*, carried into Cape Nicholas Mole [Haiti], and sold there.

Despite all these vicissitudes: the dangers of disease, of death at the hands of rebellious black Africans, or of ambushed in hostile country, the trade outlived abolition. The profits for both owners and crews induced some to continue under the cover of foreign flags, especially that of the United States, and this provoked a further Act of Parliament in 1811, making the carriage of slaves by British nationals a felony. Conviction attracted a sentence of fourteen years' transportation; but it also exacerbated the declining relations between Great Britain and America over the Royal Navy's right to search American ships for British seamen which ultimately provoked the War of 1812. A further act in 1824 declared the shipment of slaves to be piracy, thus making the offence capital. Despite this, slave-owning itself was not outlawed in British colonies until 1833, and even that is not the end of the tale. The direct consequences of this are dealt with in a subsequent volume.

NOTES

1. Quoted G.M. Thomson, *Sir Francis Drake*, p29.
2. Barrett commanded the ship as master, Hawkins, in charge of the entire fleet occupying the post of 'General', then a term more favoured than admiral which, after the Spanish

fashion and the word deriving from an Arab root, was usually given to an expedition's second-in-command. Barrett was burned by the Inquisition and Job Hortop endured twenty-three years of captivity, half of which was chained to the oar of a Spanish galley.

3. Hawkins, like Drake, from now on became a naval officer. Both men fought in the attack on the Spanish Armada, Hawkins in the *Victory* being knighted by the Lord High Admiral, Lord Howard of Effingham, during the long battle. He is widely regarded as 'the architect of the Elizabethan Navy' though his joint-command with Drake of an expedition to the West Indies in 1595 was not successful. The two men fell out and Hawkins died of dysentery off Puerto Rico on 12 November. His son, also Sir John, served under Drake and commanded the Queen's ship *Swallow* during the attack on the Armada. In 1593 he sailed on an intended circumnavigation and rediscovered the Falkland Islands first found by John Davis (see Note 3, Chapter 3). After passing the Straits of Magellan he attacked the Spanish at Paita, was captured and ransomed in 1603. He later joined Sir Robert Mansell in an unsuccessful naval attack on the Barbary coast and died in 1622, apparently an apoplexy caused by the refusal of the government to pay his seamen.

4. See Gomer Williams, *History of the Liverpool Privateers and Letters of Marque, with an Account of the Liverpool Slave Trade*, pp466, *et seq*.

5. Among the *Hannibal's* passengers were a number of the Royal African Company's soldiers one of whom fell sick. When the surgeon's mate attempted to apply a glister, it was discovered the soldier, known as John Brown, was female, 'about twenty years old, and a likely black girl'. The account of Phillips's voyage is given in full in *Slave Ships and Slaving* by Dow and is abstracted from Churchill's *Collection of Voyages*, Vol.6, London, 1746.

6. Malagetta, or *Amomum Meliguetta*, was used as a spice and a medicine and known colloquially as 'Grains of Paradise' or 'Guinea Grains'.

7. Before the age of the Wassermann reaction the symptoms of yaws and syphilis were virtually indistinguishable, while the difference between the two diseases was not understood. Those of clap, or gonorrhoea, are very different, but more obvious on such an intimate examination.

8. Slavers often picked up monkeys as pets, Captain Hugh Crow telling several yarns of these in his memoirs, including that of a monkey with decidedly homicidal tendencies. It is from these acquisitions that the monkey on the shoulder of the sailor entered British culture.

9. According to Paul E. Lovejoy, *Transformations in Slavery*, Cambridge University Press, 2000, the total number of slaves actually accounted for between 1500 and 1900 is 11,151,000 souls. The figure between 1701 and 1800, which approximates to the period when the trade was dominated by the British – though the participation by other nations such as Spain, Portugal, the United States and others, must never be forgotten – is said to be 6,090,000. Even after the Abolition of the Slave Trade Act of 1807, after which no British ship legally bore slaves and the Royal Navy actively suppressed the trade, the total remains high at 3,466,000 for the period 1801–1900. By this time, however, the illegality of the trade probably obscures the reality, unlike the figures for the preceding century when a measure of regulation, howsoever imperfect, probably created a more accountable system and consequently conveys a more accurate 'feel' for the number.

10. See Amy Butler Greefield, *The Colour Red, Empire, Espionage and the Quest for the Colour of Desire*, Doubleday, 2005.

11. O. Equiano, *The Interesting Narrative*, 1789. In his preface to the Penguin edition of 2003, Vincent Carretta points out that Equiano may not in fact have been born in Africa but there is little doubt that his voice – taken here from page 58 of this edition – is authentic. Equiano is mentioned in Chapter 3 but it is of some interest that he signed

on the British Admiralty's Arctic expedition of 1773 under Captain Phipps, sailing in the *Racehorse*, while the future Lord Nelson was in the *Carcass*.

12. Falconbridge wrote an *Account of the Slave Trade on the Coast of Africa*, published in London in 1788.

13. See Owen, N. (Edited by Eveline Martin), *Journal of a Slave-Dealer*.

14. Richardson tells of the practice aboard the *Spy* of not rationing water, but allowing it to be sucked from the scuttlebutt through a stripped musket barrel. To deter over-frequent recourse to the scuttlebutt, the musket barrel was kept at the mainmast-head from which it had to be fetched and returned, another example of the wily Captain Wilson's expertise in his vile trade.

15. Dow, G.F., *Slave Ships and Slaving*, p11.

16. Lace survived the voyage and seems to have gone into business on his own account some time later for he is addressed in letters dated 1773 as 'Marchant Lace, Sir...' By Grandy King George, the king of Old Town, Old Calabar.

17. There were also, of course, the usual risks inherent in seafaring: the second mate of the outward-bound *Francis*, Captain Thomas Onslow, falling asleep on his watch and drowning twenty-three of his fifty-eight shipmates when the *Francis* piled up on Fuerteventura in the Canaries; the *Charlotte*, Captain Lowndes, blowing up while handling powder with only a solitary survivor. The *Othello*, Captain Christian, also blew up, as did the *Parr*, both ships catching fire when lying at Bonny.

18. The casual nature of these dialogues is epitomised by a letter to Captain Brighouse, dated Sunday 30 December 1777: 'Friend William Brighouse, I have sent you one woman and girl... I will come tomorrow to see you. Suppose you Some Coffee to spar[e]. Please send me a Little. I am your Friend, Egoboyoung Coffiong.'

19. A similar letter from 'Grandy King George' to Lace requests a whole inventory, including 'six Chears for my house and one two arm Schere for my Salf to sat in and 12 Puter plates and 4 dishes 12 Nifes and 12 forcks and 2 Large table spoons... Send Plenty of Puter Jugs for trade send me two Large brass beasons and puter ones for trade... Send me one gun for my own shuting 5 foot barril and two pueter piss pots[.] Send me one good Case of Rezars for my S[h]aveing...' and so on in a remarkably competent command of English given the contemporary vagaries of spelling and the fact that the Grandy's initial encounter with English words would have been from direct speech.

20. Captain Alexander Ball paid HMS *Nemesis* off later that year, so the ordeal of the *Spy's* pressed men was not long. Upon their impressments Captain Wilson had attempted to fine them £3 each for the loss of the two women eaten by sharks off Bonny. The men protested and were supported by the naval lieutenant who was intent upon enslaving them in His Majesty's navy – albeit temporarily – and Wilson 'was obliged to give it up and give full wages'. Richardson, p66.

21. The convoy was escorted by several warships led by HMS *York*, sixty-four guns, 'Commodore John Ferrier'. Ferrier was a post-captain at the time, carrying the title 'commodore' while commanding the escort to the convoy. He was made rear admiral in 1810 after twenty years' service as post-captain and died a full admiral in 1836. It was clear that Ferrier was aware of Crow's reputation and abilities for: 'The *Will* was appointed a pennant ship [i.e. a column leader], and at the same time, one of the whippers-in of the fleet'.

22. The *Dart* was an experimental vessel built to the unorthodox design of Brigadier-General Samuel Bentham, brother of the philosopher. She carried thirty guns, all but two of which were 32-pounder carronades, throwing an exceptionally heavy ball over a short range and therefore a powerful opponent for the *Mary*. The *Wolverine*, Commander Francis Collier, was a *Cruizer*-class, eighteen-gun brig-sloop, one of the most numerous classes of warship ever built for the Royal Navy. The class of over 100 vessels was

intended to protect trade and to cruise against the numerous enemy privateers attacking British merchant shipping in the post-Trafalgar period.

23. Laird Clowes, *The Royal Navy, A History*, Vol. 5, p394.
24. Gomer Williams, p655 *et seq*. He goes on to quote Crow who thought the Abolitionists, those 'pretenders to humanity' should 'look to Ireland which is in a most deplorable state of slavery and disaffection, for which no politician has yet discovered an adequate remedy'.
25. Crow obtained a position for his fifteen-year-old son aboard HM Frigate *Arethusa* under Captain Robert Mends. Towards the end of the Napoleonic War the lad was captured while in the frigate's boats cutting out a ship from a French port. Imprisoned in Verdun, Crow junior escaped but had been 'contaminated with the wickedness and debauchery of the prison. On the way to [re]join the *Arethusa* ... the lad fell into bad company, and enlisted in the 9th Light Dragoons. This nearly killed his father' who procured his son's release but the youth died in Lisbon 'thus blasting the captain's fondest hopes'. Quite what the young Crow fell foul of in Verdun, Williams does not reveal, but the euphemistic inference is clear and probably directly caused the lad's early death, the 'broken-heart' being unconvincing.
26. Wilberforce's triumph was only partial and he was subjected to endless frustration, lamenting ten years later, after the end of the long war, that he had yet to achieve full emancipation.
27. Such rebellions were invariably wrongly referred to as 'mutinies', no doubt because they occurred aboard ship. It is incorrect to name them thus, since a mutiny can only be an insurrection against lawful authority by those contracted to submit to that authority.

FIVE

'HIS FREEDOM WAS A SHAM'

Private Trade and Private Warfare in the Western Ocean, 1707–1763

In the century between 1700 and 1800 the British merchant fleet expanded from 3,281 vessels to 20,893 under the influence and protection of the English Navigation Acts which stipulated that all imports had to be carried in British ships or bottoms belonging to the country in which the cargo was produced and which had been reinforced by new legislation in 1786. By 1790 this usually meant British-flagged vessels, since most imports came from colonial sources, except those from the newly independent United States. Colonial imports were similarly restricted while all exports from Britain had to go in British vessels. Colonial commodities which had first to be sent to Britain before re-export were known as 'Enumerated Goods' and originally consisted of sugar, tobacco, cotton, indigo, ginger, fustic and logwood; later coffee, raw silk, naval stores, pig and bar iron were added. Rice was included between 1706 and 1730 and sugar was removed in 1739, but the effect of this regulation was to ensure a cheap and reliable supply to the home and strategic market, whilst simultaneously protecting customs dues, then the principal source of state revenue. This colonial trade mainly concerned that between Britain and the West Indies and North America, but re-exports extended this to Europe. Until 1776, of course, all 'American' shipping was British-flagged and it is worth noting that by 1751 an estimated one million people of British origin lived in North America.

Trade-routes other than that across the North Atlantic were of great importance. Chief among these if we except the East Indian Company's monopoly, was the rich and vital import trade with the Baltic States which handled the timber and so-called 'naval stores' mentioned elsewhere but upon which both the nation's men-of-war and her merchantmen depended. This had subsidiary connections, maintaining a thriving trade with the North Russian ports of Archangel and Murmansk, much of which was conducted from Scottish ports like Dundee, but the main centres of the Baltic trade were Newcastle, Sunderland, Scarborough, Whitby, Hull and Great Yarmouth, six places which also dominated the coastal trades of England and Wales. On a lesser scale the Cumbrian port of Whitehaven, like Newcastle and Sunderland a source of coal exports, was to be the place of origin of Britain's longest surviving shipping company, that of Brocklebank & Co., which soon migrated to Liverpool, the rising international port in this period. At the same time Glasgow grew in importance.

After coal, grain and other agricultural products dominated cargo-manifests and enabled the smaller ports to thrive, places like Hartlepool, Berwick-on-Tweed and Alnmouth. Among other commodities carried were such items as soap, casks of salted pork and dried beef, smoked hams and cured bacon, clothing, linen and woollen goods, honey, pickled-cod, lime, general iron-mongery, lead, sail-cloth, rope and cordage, tallow, butter; while much that did not lend itself to baling or being cased, came in a variety of wooden barrels that enjoyed names such as firkin, barricoe – pronounced 'breaker' – casks, hogsheads and leaguers, each of which was of an increasing capacity.

There were other important commercial connections other than these, in which an immense number of merchant ships were involved in a complex web of inter-woven trading patterns which could take a modestly sized vessel of around 200 tons outwards to the Baltic or the Mediterranean, from thence to Philadelphia and back to Liverpool, London or Newcastle in a voyage of many months, several cargoes and a considerable turnover in money. In the five years between 1781 and 1786 the *Forrester* of Shields on the River Tyne carried coal to London, Kronstadt, Marseilles, Gibraltar and the Barbary coast, and Lübeck; she returned from the Baltic ports with iron, hemp, timber and tallow; she made one voyage in ballast to Archangel, return-ing with 1,600 barrels of tar, then sailed in cross-trades from Cadiz to Königsberg with salt, and from Memel to Coruña with spars, making intermediate short passages in ballast between discharge and loading. She carried wheat, sheep and beeswax to Gibraltar from Barbary and came back from Marseilles to London laden with cotton and sarsaparilla.

The importance of the trade in so-called 'naval stores' is emphasised elsewhere but by the mid-eighteenth century it had migrated from the Norwegian ports of Bergen, Drammen and Christiana (modern Oslo) which were ice-free throughout the year, into the Baltic itself. Ships loaded iron, pine resin, and deals – long sawn planks of vari-able length and width but up to 6 metres in length – in the port of Gothenburg. Riga exported huge mast-timbers floated thither from Byelorussia; from Dantzig (modern Gdansk) came more mast and spar-timber, deals of oak and pine; more timber, iron, tar, flax and hemp was shipped from Memel and St Petersburg. Ships iced out of the Baltic in the winter were redeployed in the coastal coal trade, as the demand rose in 'the Great Wen' of London.

Although made later in the century, Captain Samuel Kelly's voyages as master of the brig *John* of Liverpool, were typical of the period. Kelly left Liverpool on 17 July 1789, bound for Philadelphia with a cargo of coal, salt and unspecified bales. At

Philadelphia he loaded wheat and flour for Barcelona, passing Gibraltar thirty-eight days out, and taking a further three weeks to reach his destination. Having discharged, he received orders 'to load sea-salt at the most eligible part of the Mediterranean'. He accordingly ballasted the *John* sufficiently to carry him over to Ibiza where he took in a full cargo of sea-salt and left for Philadelphia, taking sixty-nine days to reach the Delaware. Here he took on a cargo of pig-iron, tar, red cedar and barrel-staves for Liverpool, arriving in George's Dock basin after a thirty-six-day passage. Such commodities were dispersed inland by way of a growing network of canals, early evidence of Britain's Industrial Revolution and upon which steam-power had already appeared. In 1736 a steam-tug had been built for canal use by Jonathan Hull using Newcomen's steam engine.

Despite their proliferation – often the fate of the commonplace – few iconographical images of the deep-water merchant ship of the period survive. Often the best descriptions we have derive from advertisements for the disposal of one, usually 'by the candle' at a tavern, shop or coffee house. Such a document giving notice of a sale on 10 March 1760 in Liverpool describes the ship-rigged *Planter*:

> [B]urthen about 200 tons, square sterned, Lyon-[figure] head, takes the ground well, mounts two six-pounders on slides in the cabin, three new four-pounders on deck, four swivels and is pierced for 16 carriage guns, being deep waisted with iron stanchions and double netting fore and aft, and suitable for the African or American trade; being 10 feet dep in the hold, 4 feet 9 inches between decks, from the mainmast forward, and from the mainmast aft, 6 feet 2 inches, with her materials, 2 new cables, one new anchor, and all her stores as she arrived lately from London...[1]

At 200-tons burthen she would have been a very typical deep-water merchantman of her day, one of hundreds working out of London, Bristol, Glasgow or Liverpool.

The history of the mercantile marine in the eighteenth century is intimately connected with the port of Liverpool which prospered to eclipse Bristol and rival London, largely because its situation rendered redundant the windward passage down Channel and lent itself to the growing trans-Atlantic trade. This put Liverpool in the forefront of port-management and by the 1770s it boasted a talented and pioneering principal water bailiff, harbour and dock-master, Captain William Hutchinson, who made the first parabolic reflector for lighthouses, carried out extensive tidal observations, surveyed and opened channels in the Mersey approaches and initiated a buoyage system to mark them.[2] Not content with keeping their own house in order, the Liverpool shipowners also challenged Trinity House's right to erect lighthouses, arguing with some justice that the Elder Brethren had been dilatory in establishing seamarks proper to safe navigation on the west coast of England. When lighthouses were mooted on the Isle of Man in an act of defiance they successfully petitioned to have these placed under the management of the Commissioners for Northern Lighthouses, based in Edinburgh; other lighthouses covering the outer approaches to Liverpool they built themselves.[3]

At one of these, set atop Bidston Hill on the Wirral peninsula and fitted with Hutchinson's first parabolic reflector, they also established a signal station, described by Samuel Kelly:

> My owners had been appraised [sic] of my arrival by signal, which gives information long before the vessel enters the river, and before she can be seen from the town. This is managed on a hill in Cheshire opposite Liverpool, on which the merchants have each flagstaffs. On this eminence there is also a lighthouse kept by an old seaman who had been (I think) fourteen voyages to Africa in the slave trade. This man and his wife manage all the signals. When a Liverpool vessel approaches the north-west buoy at the entrance of the dangerous sands and shoals lying without the mouth of the Mersey a signal is made by the vessel that she belongs to such a merchant. The man residing at Bidston Lighthouse hoists the flag on that merchant's pole, and at the same time displaying a blackboard on one of three poles erected on the lighthouse, certifies whether the vessel making her signal is either a snow, brig or ship.

He might equally have brought a cargo home from the West Indies, for it was not only slavers who completed their triangular trade by carrying home West Indian sugar; a regular and direct traffic in coffee and sugar was established in ships that came to be known as 'West Indiamen'. The trade was of immense importance for domestic consumption and for re-export to markets in Europe and the customs levies placed upon its import and re-export made it crucial to the nation's revenue stream. Thus the merchants and plantation-owners themselves assumed political influence. There was also a subsidiary traffic between the British American colonies and the islands, though the independently minded colonists, while keen to seek the protection of the English Navigation Acts when it suited them, did not mind ignoring them either. These opportunists traded openly – and usually for sugar – with the French colonies, particularly Martinique and Guadeloupe which, although captured several times during the wars of the eighteenth century, were invariably restored to France at each succeeding peace. Not only were the British West Indian islands hampered by a 4.5 per cent export duty, but the French islands produced sugar of better quality and at a cheaper rate than Jamaica, ready access to virgin land enabling them to avoid the heavy cost of manuring, while the by-product of molasses and rum were almost unsaleable in a France addicted to brandy and could be had in Martinique for knock-down prices.

North American exports included salt-fish, grain and barrel staves for hogsheads which were sold for cash or bills of exchange drawn on London in the British colonies, but for sugar and molasses in the French islands. This was in contravention of the Molasses Act and was but one step towards the inevitable confrontation between New England and London that would eventually provoke the colonists to declare independence. Occasionally British slavers partook of this cross trade, 'turning their triangular trade into a quadrangular one; and undoubtedly some of the French sugar carried to New England in this way was re-exported to England as British grown'.[4]

Throughout the 1700s sugar production costs rose in the British islands and a serious drought in 1764 combined with several hurricanes had a dire effect. In some islands losses could be offset by growing and exporting other commodities, such as cacao, cotton and ginger. Coffee, which had been transplanted to the Caribbean around 1730 to be grown commercially in sufficient quantities to export, was increasingly important until the collapse of the German coffee market in 1773. Barbados and the Leeward islands depended almost entirely upon sugar while Jamaica was in no markedly better position, consequently the economies of the British West Indian islands inevitably depended upon the policies and largesse of the government in London. For this reason when the rupture with the Thirteen Colonies came, only Bermuda sent a deputation to the Continental Congress at Philadelphia. The West Indian political lobby secured some small victories: in 1775 the Royal Navy abandoned its contract with the French for brandy for the Royal Navy and went over to rum, used by ships on station in the Antilles for many years. There was also a loosening in the former strict regulations over West India merchants obtaining credit and a limited emulation of the successful Dutch and French expedients of the free-port system, initiated by the Free Ports Act of 1766. Four such ports were opened in Jamaica, and two in Dominica where foreign merchants could buy and export slaves or any British goods except naval stores and tobacco. There were certain restrictions and exceptions to this, but the effect was to encourage trade.

Meanwhile at home the demand for sugar continued to rise and this created another lobby: 'Grocers, refiners and distillers wanted cheap sugar and molasses' and did not much care where these came from, while the rising class of industrial manufacturers were anxious for large markets with free and affluent populations anxious to buy their products. Thus: 'Interest was beginning to shift from the West Indies to Continental America, North and South; from the Caribbean to the Atlantic as a whole'. It was this, of course, that swiftly re-established commerce between the new United States and Great Britain upon the recognition of American independence by the latter in 1783.

Although all these economic strictures affected the planters badly, there was plenty of work for merchant shipping serving the West Indies. There was, however, little reward in it beyond that of subsistence. As late as 1790 Captain Samuel Kelly summed up his lot:

> My wages while mate of the *Thetis* was three pounds per month, and on being ship-master, was raised to five pounds per month, but I do not think during the whole time I commanded a vessel (except my last voyage) that I ever made more in wages and perquisites than barely seventy-five pounds per annum. From this income I had to assist three of my relations.

If the lot of the ship-master was unsatisfactory, that of the common seaman was worse and the century had begun with a wave of piracy that would extend into the Indian Ocean. Daniel Defoe attributed to the freebooter Bartholomew Roberts the explanation that:

> In an honest service [i.e. a legitimate merchant ship] there is thin Commons, low
> Wages, and hard labour; in this [as a pirate], Plenty and Satiety, Pleasure and Ease,
> Liberty and Power, and who would not ballance [sic] Creditor on this Side, when
> all the Hazard that is run for it, at worst, is only a sower Look or two at choaking
> [i.e. hanging].

Since death must come to all and the seaman's life was full of hazard and the likeli-
hood of sudden death, better to spend it living out Roberts's alleged motto: 'A merry
Life and a short one'. Another justification for turning pirate is given by Charles
Bellamy who, according to Defoe, harangued a merchant thus:

> …you are a sneaking Puppy, and so are those who submit to be governed by Laws
> which rich Men have made for their own Security, for the cowardly whelps have
> not the courage to defend what they get by their Knavery; but damn ye… They
> vilify us … when there is only this Difference, they rob the Poor under the Cover of
> Law, forsooth, and we plunder the rich under the protection of our own Courage.

With a few exceptions such as John Avery, Edward England and Roberts himself,
the British pirates active in western waters during the first two decades of the eighteenth century were confined to the Caribbean and the southern coasts of the British
American colonies where they received a certain amount of support. The Bahamas,
ungarrisoned by the crown, became a base for hundreds of these freebooters and complaints from the merchants of the American colonies led to George I's government
taking action. At first, in 1717 and 1718, the king issued an amnesty, but the results
were disappointing, several well-known pirates accepting the pardon and then resum-
ing their former 'sweet trade'. Faced with such blatant and contemptuous recidivism,
Captain Woodes Rogers was appointed as the islands' governor with a commission
to dislodge the pirates from the archipelago.[5] Soon after his arrival in 1718 Rogers
succeeded in driving the pirates out, causing many to disperse to the cays of the West
Indies, the inlets and creeks of the southern colonies and the rivers of the Guinea
coast. It also created the wider disapora of the more competent pirate commanders to
Madagascar and the Indian Ocean, with consequences we shall shortly encounter.

Once the British government and the Royal Navy had adopted a policy directly
attacking piracy with the Third Piracy Act of 1721 – which made receivers of pirated
goods culpable – the menace began to diminish in the Atlantic. Roberts's demise
off Africa has already been related, others, including Stede Bonnet and the women,
Anne Bonny and Mary Read, got their due come-uppance.[6] The most notorious of
the pirates of this period was Edward Teach, who had gone to sea in a privateersman
in the War of the Spanish Succession. Familiar with the waters of the Caribbean,
he turned pirate when peace deprived him of his chosen living. In 1717 he seized
a large French merchantman, refitting her as a formidable armed ship of forty guns
and renaming her *Queen Anne's Revenge*. A crew was raised from waterfront layabouts
while tacit support, obtained by bribes and shared plunder, was allegedly secured

from the governor of North Carolina, Charles Eden. A large and forbidding figure, Teach prosecuted a ruthless interdiction of legitimate trade, enhancing his fearsome reputation by wearing a long black beard – by which he was also known – and plaiting smouldering slow-matches into his long dark dread-locks. Among other ships, he took a large and well-armed merchantman named the *Great Allen* and escaped the pursuit of the man-of-war *Scarborough*. For a while he sailed in alliance with Stede Bonnet, but the two fell out and Bonnet was subsequently captured by William Rhet and hanged at Charleston on 28 October 1718.

Teach's actions so aroused the venom of the merchants of the coast that they petitioned the governor of Virginia to take action and he ordered that a small naval force of two sloops be mustered and placed under the command of Lieutenant Robert Maynard of the Royal Navy. Maynard, in the *Ranger*, discovered Teach's ship at anchor on Ocracoke Inlet on 21 November and, running the *Ranger* alongside, boarded her. After exchanging pistol fire, Maynard engaged Teach hand-to-hand. A deft swordsman, Maynard inflicted twenty-five wounds upon his larger opponent before the notorious 'Blackbeard' fell dead, whereupon Maynard had Teach's head cut from his body and returned to Charleston with the grisly trophy secured to the extremity of the *Ranger's* bowsprit.[7]

Nevertheless, the appeal of piracy remained potent among seafarers. John Archer, who had sailed with Teach, admitted before his execution in 1724 that it was hard usage that had driven him and many like him to turn pirate. 'I could wish that Masters of Vessels would not use their Men with so much Severity, as many of them do, which exposes us to great Temptations'. William Fly, on the scaffold in 1726 exonerated himself with an old and familiar complaint:

> I shan't own myself Guilty of any Murder. Our Captain and his Mate used us Barbarously. We poor Men can't have Justice done us. There is nothing said to our Commanders, let them never so much abuse us, and use us like Dogs.

To the New England cleric Cotton Mather, the seafaring community was, after witches, beyond redemption.[8] In 1718 he confided in his diary that:

> If I begin with Seafaring, Oh, what an horrible Spectacle have I before me! A wicked, stupid, abominable Generation; every Year growing rather worse.

The truth was that seafarers, whether the allegedly oppressive masters or the much put-upon seamen, were but wage-slaves and their relationship epitomised and prefigured the troubles that would dog the struggle between capital and labour in the coming centuries. In the very long run the constant chafing of this exacerbation would have a major effect upon the British mercantile marine. As was so often to happen, however, a short-term stability calmed matters down as trans-Atlantic shipping undertook increasing bulk cargo carriage, and North America and – to a lesser extent – the Caribbean became consumers of manufactures as well as mere producers of raw materials. As time passed, credit became more readily available and bills of exchange multiplied with improvements in the postal packet service, an increased number of banks and insurance brokers, along with a complex but supporting infrastructure of other incidental services. British shipping employed an increasing number of seamen whose wages, though remaining low, rose slowly above the level of basic subsistence until, by 1750, some 60,000 seamen sold their skills for wages, and underpinned the rise of British and colonial North American capitalism across the Western Ocean. Even the state had become marginally involved, passing an Act for the Better Regulation and Government of the Merchants' Service in 1729 as was mentioned in Chapter Three.

All this was in the teeth of opposition, both French and Spanish, the latter being at this period the more important. The British encroachment begun by the buccaneers in the Bay of Campeachy and consolidated by the acquisition of Jamaica continued. In 1723 James Oglethorpe had founded the thirteenth 'English' colony in North America in the no-man's land between South Carolina and Spanish Florida, naming it after the king. It had been intended that Georgia would eschew the use of slaves, but with its economy based upon rice-production slaves were found to be indispensable, increasing the demand for black African labour while the new colony only fuelled Spanish ire. With the slaving *Asiento* including an annual trading voyage or two, breaches of the agreements by British interlopers constantly provoked Spanish hostility and the privilege was at the least threatened, at worst withdrawn. Despite protests neither the South Sea Company, nor its sub-contractor, the Royal African Company, could stem the invasion of their fellow countrymen or their cousins from North America and were left fulminating impotently as the former headed towards ruin. Preying upon these genuine if illegitimate trading ventures as well as muddying the blue waters of the Caribbean, the swarm of pirates only exacerbated relations with the Spanish. This in turn was worsened by British possession of Jamaica and the occasional presence of the Royal Navy. The arbitrary and irregular conduct of the colonial Spanish and their agents, the *guarda costas*, brought frequent confrontation and intermittent states of local warfare, as already remarked.

Matters moved inexorably to a head. In 1730 Spanish privateers from Porto Rico seized the *Mary* of Liverpool in the West Indies and Rear Admiral Stewart was ordered to make a reprisal. However this was opposed by the South Seas Company directors who dissuaded the Admiralty from such rashness which would have lost the Company's 'Annual Ship' as a counter-reprisal. The Admiralty backed down but this perceived pusillanimity upset other merchants and shipowners. Such Spanish seizures became increasingly common, intervention by the *guarda costas* being attracted by the cargoes lifted in British vessels.

The export of logwood and braziletto wood, a source of orange dye, were among the contraband cargoes that attracted the hostile notice of the Spanish authorities and led to the celebrated mutilation of Captain Jenkins, master of the *Rebecca*. Jenkins' brig was boarded on 9 April 1731 off Havana, by Spanish *Guarda Costas* led by Capitano Juan de Leon Fandino, 'who had a widespread reputation for cruelty'. When Jenkins protested at being boarded, Fandino drew his sword and sliced off Jenkins' left ear, after which he plundered the brig. Rear Admiral Stewart, compiling a long list of such incidents in his official protest to the governor at Havana written on 12 September 1731, stated that Fandino left the *Rebecca* 'with the intent that she should perish on her passage'. The brig did not perish, reaching the Thames on 11 June, soon after which Jenkins – who had pickled the ear in spirits – is said to have made a statement 'before the king'. Although only one among many interferences with British trade which reached a peak in 1737, the captain's lost ear resonated with public xenophobia and the outrage was raised again by the opposition to the Duke of Newcastle's government in an agitation of 1738. In June Jenkins appeared before the House of Commons where he was asked what his feelings were when he found himself 'in the hands of barbarians'. Not lost for a reply, Jenkins declared: 'I committed my soul to God and my cause to my country'. Coinciding with disputes over the borders of Carolina and Georgia with the Spanish province of Florida, Jenkins' conduct in the Commons became a *cause celebre* that in 1739 transmogrified itself into a *casus belli*, propelling Britain into a full-blooded war with Spain. Whether or not the British master lost all, or only part of his ear lobe is uncertain. 'If they had looked under his wig', Richard Pares quotes, 'they would have found both his celebrated ears on his head; Alderman Beckford said so, and he might very well know'.[9]

The War of Jenkins' Ear soon escalated into the War of the Austrian Succession (1739–1748). In 1739 Admiral Vernon captured Porto Bello 'with six ships only' but this was followed by a disastrously unsuccessful attack on Cartagena in the following year and a bungled landing in Cuba in 1741.[10] The sense of struggle, of adversity and perhaps of not quite being up-to-the-mark, inspired James Thomson to write *Rule Britannia* as a work not of triumphalism, but of determination that Britons 'never, never, never *shall* be slaves'. An ironic triumph of sorts was achieved by Commodore George Anson who was sent into the Pacific to attack the Spanish in the ocean they regarded as *mare nostrum*. Anson's badly organised squadron suffered terribly, he lost all but one of his ships by the time he had passed Cape Horn, and scores of his men – many of them pensioners – who fell victim to scurvy.

Anson might have avoided this curse of seafaring, caused by a lack of Vitamin C in his men's diets. Although the root cause was to elude scientific discovery until the early twentieth century, the remedy had been known long before the work of James Lind and Sir Gilbert Blane improved matters in the Royal Navy. Thirty-four years before Lind took his medical degree in Edinburgh in 1748, George Cheyne had published *An Essay of Health and Long Life*, a best-selling book which ran through many editions between 1724 and 1827. In it Cheyne stated unequivocally that scurvy could not only be avoided, but reversed:

> A vegetable diet for a few weeks or months together with drinking water of unfermented liquors (such as tea, coffee, teas made of oranges or other seeds or plants) will fasten the teeth when dropping out, cure any cutaneous foulness or eruptions and even any spreading ulcer.

Others, as has been related earlier, had come to much the same conclusion.

However, having attacked and sacked the city of Payta with his enfeebled force, Anson also engaged and captured one of the fabulous Spanish Register ships, better known as Manila, or Acapulco, galleons that crossed the Pacific to Manila laden with silver from the mines of Potosí in order to pay for Chinese silks, pearls, jade and ivory-ware and other oriental luxuries loaded in the Philippines. Thereafter the galleons returned eastwards in higher latitudes to Acapulco and the goods were transported overland for transhipment to Cadiz.[11]

During the war attacks upon British shipping were frequent and successful. Notable among these were two heroic defences of merchantmen against powerful French privateers carrying overwhelming numbers. In 1744 the ship *Yarmouth* distinguished herself in this way, and two years later the *Ann Galley* of Liverpool, a Guineaman owned by Messrs Whalley & Co. and commanded by Captain Nehemiah Holland, did likewise when off Antigua. Such gallantry was offset by considerable losses of merchant ships to enemy cruisers and corsairs, again raising questions about the competence of the Royal Navy to protect the nation's trade. Although less affected than the merchant houses of Hull, London and Bristol, for the merchants of Liverpool – whose rising trade was immediately affected by the war and who resented the inability of the state to honour its obligations – what was sauce for the goose, was also sauce for the gander. If they were to be frustrated in exporting their chief manufactures of 'blue and white earthenware, which at present almost vie with China (large quantities are exported for the Colonies abroad), and watches, which are not to be excelled in Europe...' they would turn to other means of making a profit. In consequence a few began fitting out privateers.

After four years of war Liverpool possessed only four: the *Old Noll*, Captain Powell, and *Terrible*, Captain Cole, both of twenty-two guns and 180 men; the twelve-gun *Thurloe*, Captain Dugdale and 100 men, and the *Admiral Blake*, of which only her commander, Captain Edmonston, is detailed. These performed some useful service. Between 1744 and 1746 the *Terrible* recaptured the *Joseph* of Bristol, laden with logwood and tar which had been taken by a Spanish corsair and sent her prize into Waterford. Cole also retook another Bristol ship, the *Bromfield*, which had fallen to the French when homeward from St Kitts, and also captured *L'Amiable Martha* on her way from St Domingue to Bordeaux. She yielded a valuable cargo 'of 370 hogsheads and 44 barrels of sugar, 57 casks of coffee, 11 hogsheads of indigo, one hogshead white sugar, 1,270 pieces of eight and five cobs [a rounded lump] of gold' and finally the *Terrible* captured a vessel from Martinique. In July 1744 the *Thurloe* seized a wine-laden Frenchman and, with the *Admiral Blake*, engaged and overcame the *Vulture*, a corsair from Bayonne mounting fourteen guns and flush with 118 men, taking her into Cork. These ships worked in company for, after taking a Martinique ship, Edmonston joined Dugdale and they jointly took another prize into Cork, the deeply laden French merchantman *Amiral*, from Martinique for Bordeaux. On her own and with another Martinico prize in company, the *Thurloe* was herself captured in August by a French corsair, but afterwards fell in with Captain Powell in *Old Noll*,

who engaged the French privateer – said to have been of thirty guns and 300 men
– and drove her off. Having thus overwhelmed the captor and the *Thurloe's* prize
crew, Dugdale was restored to his own quarterdeck. Powell's successes were considerable; he took the *Providence* from Martinique to Bordeaux, retook the British
vessels *Hannah* and *Sarah* – the former from Jamaica and the latter from Carolina,
captured the *Ville de Nantes* ' a very large ship', seizing besides several lesser prizes.
Unfortunately Powell fell foul of the French navy and in November 1745 news
reached Liverpool that the *Old Noll* had been sunk, possibly driven ashore 'by the
Brest squadron'. Encouraged by these largely successful voyages other Liverpool privateers joined in, notably the *Warren* and the *St George*.

Although this account is imperfect, it gives some idea of the extent of the success
of Liverpool privateers, which was competent, but modest. That few were in action
before 1744 – the year in which war with France broke out – is eloquent testimonial
that their commissioning was in reprisal for injuries received in more than the legalistic meaning, for losses to French and Spanish corsairs far exceeded the modest total of
Liverpool's private martial enterprise. Given that London, Hull and Bristol lost more
vessels than Liverpool, the tally for the last port is bad enough: during the period 1739
and 1748 at least 104 Liverpool vessels were seized by the enemy. Although a handful
was, as noted, recaptured, most were not, and of these the vast majority were engaged
in trade with the West Indies or North America.

The War of the Austrian Succession produced no naval heroes: there was no equivalent to George Rooke, the captor of Gibraltar in the War of the Spanish Succession,
no Hawke harrying the enemy to destruction on his own coast as he did de Conflans
at Quiberon Bay in that 'Year of Victories', 1759. But Hawke himself had a hand in a
minor drama, for there was one man – a merchant master – who, despite his ultimate
fate, enjoyed a degree of fame: the misnamed Fortunatus Wright.

Wright was a Liverpudlian privateer captain operating in the Mediterranean.
His first command was the *Fame*, fitted out by the merchants at Leghorn in which
Wright took about a score of prizes after her commissioning in 1746. In taking these
Wright acquired a notoriety better aimed at the practices of the times, which allowed
merchantmen to carry goods owned by their enemy – usually itemised personal
effects – covered by a pass. Thus in taking a couple of Frenchmen, significant among
which was the capture of the *Hermione* on 26 February 1747, Wright found he had
unwittingly violated passes issued by George II for the carriage of personal baggage
belonging to an Italian prince and to the Ottoman Porte. Wright defended his actions,
deposing to the English Consul at Leghorn that:

> The two ships named ... hoisted French colours and struck them to me; nay ...
> [one of them] engaged me for a considerable time under these colours. For these
> reasons I brought them to Leghorn, and have had them legally condemned in the
> Admiralty Court [as legitimate prizes], by virtue of which sentence, I have disposed
> of them and distributed the money.

The upshot of this spat was to cause the Turkey Company in London to petition the British Government to issue instructions on 30 March 1747 that Turkish property even when on board French vessels was not lawful prize. Understandably Wright objected to this ruling being imposed retrospectively and, following a flurry of diplomatic activity, the Tuscan authorities arrested and imprisoned him on 11 December 1747, refusing to deliver him to the British consul, Mr Goldsworthy. In due course and after about six months, the Austrian court at Vienna instructed the Tuscans – whom they ruled – to hand Wright over to the Turks, an order which was countermanded by another stating that he should be set free having given bail. The lawsuit rumbled on for years and its end is uncertain, but in taking sixteen prizes, Wright had made about £400,000 which he had, perforce, to share with his principals. Wright's position at the war's end is not clear, but about 1749 he entered into a partnership with William Hutchinson, later the harbour-master at Liverpool. The following year, with Wright resident with his family at Leghorn, the two master-mariners bought a redundant naval frigate, the former twenty-gun *Lowestoffe*, and fitted her for trade. Under Hutchinson's command she made several voyages to the West Indies.

In the middle of the war and encouraged by the French, the Young Pretender, Charles Edward Stuart landed in Scotland, marching south to claim the throne of his grandfather, James II. Intelligence of his disembarkation was provided by a merchant master, Captain Robinson, who had put into the Isle of Skye on a north-about passage from the Baltic. The news was conveyed to London by 'an express' when Robinson arrived at Liverpool.

For the British the outcome of the War of Austrian Succession was disappointing. Having captured the great French fortress of Louisbourg on Cape Breton Island, it was relinquished at the peace in exchange for Madras which had fallen to the French.[12] Equally frustrating was a lack of success in breaking Spanish domination of the Caribbean. In an action off Havana on 1 October 1748 Rear Admiral Charles Knowles, Commander-in-Chief at Jamaica had sought to intercept the Spanish treasure fleet but had instead been met by a squadron under Vice Almirante Reggio. Though several Spanish warships were lost, the outcome was inconclusive and, following a court-martial, Knowles was reprimanded. However, after the peace, insofar as trade was concerned, matters continued much as before.

British traders and hence British shipping were active in many places. Interloping in defiance of protective legislation by other nations was as endemic among the commercially enterprising as insistence upon the protective imperatives of the Navigation Acts was applied by the British Government. Such, for example, was the dependence of the Portuguese economy upon British markets and manufactures that it was not difficult for agents of British trading houses in Lisbon to be sent to Brazil and build up a contraband trade, and not only in slaves. Such were the perceived riches in the South Americas that, early in the next century, they were to embroil Sir Home Riggs Popham, who induced an expeditionary force to be sent from the Cape of Good Hope to prise open the opportunities even further which in turn led to the disastrous defeat and surrender of a British army under General Whitelocke at Montevideo in 1807.

Commercial jealousy of the monopolies of the old joint-stock companies continued to move the ambitions of restless minds, particularly when this was excited by that other old English envy: that of the Spanish. Unquenched by war it would obtrude again. There lingered still the unsolved riddle of the whereabouts of the North West Passage. Undeterred by the disappearance of James Knight in 1719, eager to wrest commerce from the Hudson's Bay Company and fired by crack-pot assertions about the complex tides in Hudson's Bay 'proving' a western – and therefore Pacific – outlet, the project enjoyed a revival in 1737. Arthur Dobbs, sometime member of the Irish Parliament, began an agitation to mount a new expedition. His motives were not entirely disassociated from his ideas of diverting the fur trade from the Hudson's Bay Company and unfortunately the Admiralty fell in with his suggestion, not least because Dobbs's notions of ending Spanish control of the Pacific seemed so credible an outcome as to appeal to King George II. Dobbs moreover suggested Christopher Middleton as expedition leader. A commander in the service of the Hudson's Bay Company, Captain Middleton was a distinguished mariner and a Fellow of the Royal Society, having been elected on the strength of his observations on magnetic variation and his work on determining longitude by astronomical means using Hadley's quadrant.

In March 1741 Middleton was persuaded to seek the elusive passage, being commissioned master and commander in the Royal Navy. He was not enamoured of his naval crew who were 'a set of Rogues, most of them having deserv'd hanging before they enter'd with me'. In the bomb-ketch *Furnace* with the accompanying sloop *Discovery*, commanded by William Moor, a cousin who appears not to have been commissioned, Middleton made his way into Hudson's Bay where the ships over-wintered. Scurvy struck the ill-disciplined crews and the expedition returned to the Thames in October 1742 having discovered the Churchill River and Wager Inlet, but no passage westwards. Disappointed in his protégé, Dobbs accused Middleton of covering up the discovery of a passage in order to protect the Hudson's Bay Company's monopoly. As a consequence Middleton was unfairly condemned, though a fellow Hudson's Bay Company master, Captain Coats, backed him up. Ignored by the Admiralty who might have made use of him sooner, since the War of the Austrian Succession was in progress, Middleton was eventually put in command of HM Sloop *Shark* in the North Sea, but languished neglected for years after the war's end until his own death.[13]

Dobbs was so successful in blackening Middleton that he persuaded the Government to further invigorate the project in 1745 by an Act of Parliament offering a reward of £20,000 to the successful explorer. Having agreed with his cousin that no passage existed, Moor now came forward to lead a two-ship expedition consisting of his own ship, the *Dobbs Galley*, with a Francis Smith in command of the supporting *California*. The two vessels endured a terrible winter and excited suspicions among the Hudson's Bay officials who encountered them. They too failed to find any westwards passage, due entirely, according to Dobbs, to 'the Timidity, ill Conduct or bad Inclination,

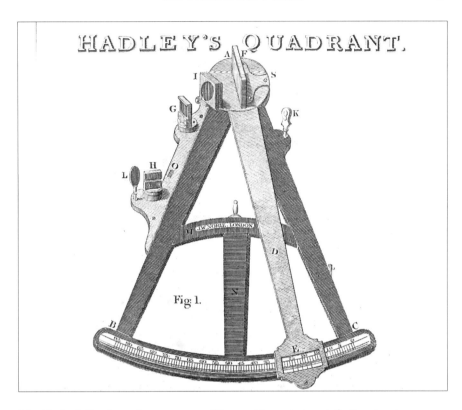

John Hadley's Quadrant of 1731 was one of the most important contributions to astronavigation, which greatly improved the accuracy of determining latitude and longitude. Its principal disadvantage was the limitation of its arc, which could only measure up to a little over ninety degrees. Hadley was a Fellow of the Royal Society and had, up until producing his quadrant, been an instrument maker specialising in telescopes. (Author's Collection)

of some of the Commanders'. He gave it up, diverted his attention to bee-keeping, accepted appointment as governor of North Carolina and passes from our history.

In fact such expeditions proved nothing beyond a growing geographical awareness in Great Britain which, by the time of Middleton's death in 1770, saw scientific enquiry, as opposed to commercialism taking over as the principal motive for exploration. The Royal Navy moved in, dispensing with mercantile officers: in 1775 Captain Constantine Phipps – afterwards Lord Mulgrave – was sent with HM Ships *Racehorse* and *Carcass* due north to discover the supposed ice-free sea at the North Pole – with the infant Nelson as a nominal coxswain in his train as well as Olaudiah Equiano; later James Cook was despatched upon his third voyage in the *Resolution* and *Discovery* to penetrate the strait discovered by Vitus Bering and come at the Atlantic from the Pacific. Both Phipps and Cook discovered impenetrable ice, sowing doubts as to the accepted wisdom that sea-water did not freeze. In 1776 the British government offered a prize for the first ship to sail beyond 89° North, unconsciously initiating what became in time a race for the pole.

British mercantile and maritime endeavour was active in the most obscure places. In 1743 The Russia Company sent the young Jonas Hanway – later a founding-father of The Marine Society and advocate of Christian mercantilism – into Persia by way of St Petersburg and the Caspian Sea. Here he was helped by Captain Thomas Woodroofe, master of the ship *Empress of Russia*, which Woodrooffe had had constructed on the Caspian's shores and in which he maintained a prosperous trade until Russian expansion squeezed him out. Nevertheless it was Woodroofe and a colleague, Captain John Elton, author of *Elton's Quadrant*, a treatise on navigation, who produced a chart of the Caspian, thanks to Woodroofe's three years of surveying and information-gathering.

The unsatisfactory nature of the peace left Britain restless. Equally restless were her colonial citizens in North America where a deteriorating situation along the loose borders between French Canada and the Thirteen Colonies was coming to a head. The more enterprising colonists – including one George Washington – wanted to push west, over the Allegheny Mountains and into the Mississippi/Ohio valleys beyond. But this vast territory, at least in the imagination of the French, busy intriguing with the Amerindians, linked Louisiana and Canada. The French despatched ships and troops to reinforce Louisbourg and Quebec and in face of this supposed 'aggression' a weak British Government played an over-strong hand. In April 1755 Vice Admiral Edward Boscawen was sent with a powerful squadron to intercept and detain any French ships carrying troops. In the poor visibility of the Grand Banks Boscawen found three, and after a smart action took two, one escaping in the fog. By the following year full scale war had broken out and, at the start, it went almost disastrously wrong for the British.[14] However, the Seven Years War (1756–1763) was to end with Great Britain as a world power, triumphant over the Spanish and, in particular, the French who were ousted from Canada and, as we shall see, all but a tiny portion of India.[15]

Even before hostilities broke out formally, the Royal Navy began to press seamen and in June 1755 HMS *Winchelsea* entered the Mersey for this purpose. On the 30th the merchantman *Upton* sailed up-river and a boat put off from the *Winchelsea* under the command of a lieutenant to board the *Upton* whose crew were soon aware of the approaching threat. They immediately ran aft in a body and seized the *Upton's* master and mate and bundled them below into the cabin before manning the ship's guns and laying them on the naval party. As the naval boat retired to seek reinforcements, the *Upton's* men lowered their own yawl, tumbled into it and pulled heartily for the shore, only to find the Royal Navy in hot pursuit.

A fierce encounter took place, shots being fired on both sides, the struggle ending by the yawl being upset. Two of the crew swam ashore, 15 others were captured, and two were drowned. The officer commanding the barge was shot in the cheek, the ball passing clean through his mouth. Several seamen on both sides were mortally wounded.

When war actually broke out in the following May, the short period of the peace had done nothing to erase memories of the previous conflict, or of the unsatisfactory protection Their Lordships afforded merchant shipping. 'Swift and well-armed French privateers found their way into the North passage [Channel] and the Irish Sea, and kept Liverpool blockaded for many weeks'. Similar humiliations were visited elsewhere and privateering rapidly became a more popular method of employing ships and men than before. The *Revenge, Anson, Brave Blakeney* and *Mandrin* (sic) left Liverpool and were soon sending in prizes.

The *Anson*, Captain Edward Fryer, seized a French West Indiaman valued at £20,000, followed by the *Brave Blakeney*, Captain George Fowler, which took two similarly richly laden vessels. These successes further encouraged Liverpudlians to invest in privateers. Not all were shipowners, others such as the ironmongers Messrs Edmund Rigby and Sons 'advertised that they had contracted with the proprietors of Birsham Foundry for the delivery of a large quantity of good swivel and carriage guns'. Ammunition was also available while gun powder was 'manufactured by Messrs Cunliffe, Stanton and Craven, at their mills at Thelwall, the powder being stored at the Black Rock Magazine in Cheshire'. The same company also recycled the stuff, offering 'damaged gunpowder wrought over again fit for service, at 20s[hillings] per barrel'.

Fryer was especially successful in the fast sailing 150-ton *Anson*. Owned by George Campbell, she mounted '16 carriage guns (four, six and nine pounders) 24 swivels, and 100 men'. In the summer of 1756 she sailed on a cruise towards the Bay of Biscay, took the 400-ton *Alexander*, valued at £5,000, and engaged *La Juno*, a twelve-gun French corsair, in an action lasting four and a half hours, ending with Fryer victorious and his prize on her way to Kinsale. On 20 September, Fryer fell in with the fourteen-gun *Artabonetta* from St Domingo to Nantes and fought her for two hours until she too capitulated. She was homeward bound loaded with sugar, coffee, indigo and 'superfine San Domingo cotton'. Both the *Alexander* and the *Artabonetta* were sold 'by the candle' in Liverpool and the *Anson* was said to have made 'above 5,000 per cent of what was expended in fitting her out'. Fryer now transferred into the eighteen-gun *Hope*, Captain Gersham Speers taking over the Anson. Speers sailed for the Mediterranean with Fowler in the *Brave Blakeney* in January 1758 and on 28 May 'boarded a French polacca, freighted with Turks and their effects ... whom they ransomed for 1,000 Barbary dollars'. A second French coaster was ransomed for 600 sequins, initiating a string of similar successes. Other Liverpool privateers and merchantmen bearing Letters of Marque enjoyed similar triumphs. Notable among these were the *Hawke*, Captain Hewston; the *Prussian Hero*, Captain Day; the *Catherine*, Captain Augustine Gwyn; the *Revenge*, Captain John Gyles; and the *Mandrin* commanded by Captain Mackaffee. When the *Revenge*'s crew came ashore they 'made a handsome appearance, each man having a clean French ruffled shirt on'. However, Gyles and Mackafee who were instructed to act in concert, were rumoured to have fallen out, and on their return to Liverpool stories of the latter acting in a cowardly manner began to circulate. Fortunately Mackafee exonerated his colleague, Gyles having engaged a French ship of superior force until Mackafee could bring

the *Mandrin* up to his assistance. Gyles went on to command the larger, sixteen-gun
Mercury in which he chased a twenty-two-gun French ship – thought to have been
the *Bristol* of Bordeaux – in the Bay of Biscay on 16 December 1756. A furious action
ensued lasting two and a half hours during which the *Mercury* had her rigging shot to
pieces and sustained a shot below the waterline which caused her to fill. With seven
feet of water in the hold Gyles struck his colours. However, by his own account to
Messrs John Hulton & Co., his owners:

> …the enemy kept up a continued fire into us, which determined us to throw all our
> guns overboard… Soon after the Frenchman hove out a signal of distress, but we
> could not assist one another, and I believe never were two ships in a more shattered
> condition, for they appeared as much disabled as ourselves. If it had not been for
> that fortunate shot, I believe we should have taken her. Four of my men are killed
> and thirteen wounded. I have received a shot in both legs, and have not been able to
> turn myself in my hammock since. I am more concerned for the loss of my cruise
> (and therefore Hulton's loss of earnings) than my own wounds; and if it please God
> to spare my life, and one leg, I will have the other knock at the French.

Incredibly Gyles reached Kinsale, three more men having died of their wounds
while the commander himself was in a serious condition, 'two of the four wounds
he received in his left leg being very dangerous'. With Gyles and his ship patched-up
they returned to the Mersey on 20 January 1757, the one to be properly repaired, the
other to recover from his wounds. In the spring both Gyles and the *Mercury* were
off again, retaking the ship *Liverpool*, Jamaica to London with a cargo of sugar, rum,
ginger, pimento, cotton and mahogany, on 25 March.

> On May 12th they took possession of the brigantine *John*, of Greenock, laden with
> pickled salmon and iron hoops, which was lying troy (or try, i.e. broadside to wind
> and waves) in the sea, without a soul on board, and which they sent to Liverpool.

Thereafter Gyles chased, fought and captured several ships and such exploits became
commonplace, though the activities of the Liverpool privateers, for all their vigour,
never matched the numerical successes of their French counter-parts who, with a
larger number of *armateurs* and a far larger enemy merchant fleet to plunder, exceeded
the British in this private war on trade.

More common among the run-of-the-mill merchantmen, was the experience of
the snow *Mary*, on passage from Liverpool to Jamaica. Taken by the French corsair
La Roche, she was recaptured nine days later by HMS *Torbay* whose captain impressed
all but two of the French prize-crew out of the *Mary* and put eight of his own men
aboard to assist the master of the *Mary* get the ship into port. Two nights later the two
Frenchmen broke into the master's cabin and murdered Captain Richmond while he
slept, then attacked the unarmed and unsuspecting crew on watch, confining them
below with those still in their hammocks. They then attempted to lay a course for

France, but were frustrated by one of the English prisoners who, having discovered a musket, found a loophole in a bulkhead and shot one of the bold French sailors dead. Sparing the other's life, they brought the *Mary* into Milford Haven. Other Liverpool ships were not so lucky: the *Landovery*, Captain Johnson, bound from her home port to Jamaica, fought-off a large French corsair for almost two hours before being taken, while on her way to Virginia the *John*, Captain Peter Gibson, was seized and scuttled by a French man-of-war.

Nevertheless, the ferocity of the privateers' war, conducted we must remember by officers and men who were mercantile in character, was far from insignificant. Off Tobago in October 1756, Captain Augustine Gwyn's *Catherine* 'had a very close and sharp engagement for eight hours with a large French snow, which struck to the Liverpool vessel'. Unfortunately soon afterwards the prize was retaken and run on shore 'through the gross negligence of the prize-master'. Gwyn was in the service of Messrs John Tarleton & Co., a firm engaged in the slave trade as well as fitting out a number of privateers, and was frequently in action. In the following year he was commanding the *Fame*, described as a 300-ton frigate of twenty guns and roughly the equivalent of a naval sloop-of-war. In her he took a small French corsair and engaged a squadron of three French privateers. Success in having prizes legally condemned – and thereby paying the wages and expenses of the capturing privateer – was almost as risky as their seizure. When Gwyn took 'a Dutch sloop, laden with French sugars' his prize-money was by no means certain, for:

> …the Dutch are artful traders, probably they may evade our laws and escape with impunity, which too many have done this war, notwithstanding their being notorious carriers of contraband goods to our natural enemy.

Back early into the fray was Captain Fortunatus Wright, still in Leghorn with his family, who now built a small privateer, the *St George*. The Tuscan government, though neutral, was not indifferent to the French and 'took measures to prevent the English ships in port from increasing their armament, either for defence as merchant ships, or for privateering purposes'. Wright cunningly acceded to these strictures and the *St George* commissioned with a paltry four small cannon and a complement of two dozen men. Wright left Leghorn with a certificate of compliance with the Tuscan regulations signed by the Governor on 25 July 1756, escorting a small convoy of four homeward bound British ships which had 'in vain waited for a ship of war'.

Wright's reputation and intentions had been called to the attention of the French and the King had issued an edict that the status of *chevalier* of St Louis a pension of 3,000 livres and command of a French warship would reward the man who brought Wright to France dead or alive. To this potent *douceur* the merchants of Marseilles had added a promised bonus of twice the value of the *St George*. Aware of the trap set for him, Wright had made arrangements that the homeward ships would load extra guns and, heaving-to beyond the limits of the port, eight guns were transferred to the *St George* while a further fifty-five seamen – 'Slavonians, Venetians, Italians, Swiss and a few English' – were engaged from the complements of the merchantmen.

At eight o'clock next morning, according to a letter written by an English merchant at Leghorn to a correspondent in Liverpool:

> ...a French privateer of 16 guns, with above 200 men on board, who had been cruising a month off our harbour [i.e. Leghorn], in order to intercept the English ships, bore down upon them. Capt. Wright made a signal for his convoy to run and save themselves, whilst he boldly lay by for the enemy; about twelve the engagement began in sight of above ten thousand of the well-wishers of the French, but in three-quarters-of-an-hour he silenced he xebeck, who had made off (ill-shattered) with her oars; had there been any wind, Capt. Wright would easily have taken her. Two other privateers appearing in sight and attempting to cut off his convoy, hindered his continuing the chase, he choosing rather to protect them than to run the risque of their being taken. Next morning he brought them safe back into this port. He lost his lieutenant and four men, and had 8 others wounded; but the xebeck suffered very much ... he maltreated her so much that it is generally believed they lost above 80 men, besides their captain and lieutenant.[16]

The English factory granted Wright a gratuity of £120, but the Tuscan authorities detained the *St George*, to which affront Wright waved his Letter-of-Marque-and-Reprisal, only to have two armed Tuscan snows move alongside and arrest him. The authorities claimed Wright had deceived them by arming his vessel beyond the regulations, he – quite rightly – claimed otherwise and a diplomatic wrangle ensued, not helped by the failure of the wretched Byng to relieve the garrison of Port Mahon and its consequent fall.

But Byng's failure – and his recall home to face an hostile and fatal court-martial – resulted in his replacement by Sir Edward Hawke. Two months later the new commander-in chief sent Captain Sir William Burnaby with 'the *Jersey* of sixty guns, and the *Isis* of 50 guns, to Leghorn to demand from the Magistrates Capt. Fortunatus Wright ... whom they have detained, and has only given them three days to consider of it'. Faced with this the authorities relented and two days after the men-of-war arrived, on 25 September Wright was released. Wright's *St George* left with a crew of '150 brave fellows', sailing in company with sixteen laden English merchantmen under the protection of the *Jersey* and *Isis*. As they passed the mole at Leghorn 'The fort fired by way of disapprobation at parting with him, three guns, but not with any design to do damage'.

Wright now began an active cruise against the enemy but, with the loss of Minorca, he was deprived of a base from which to operate in the central and eastern Mediterranean and was to find many hands turned against him. Having beaten off a French man-of-war in October 1756, he sent in to Malta two rich French prizes, the *Immaculate Conception* and *Esperance*, worth £15,000, but his own welcome in Valletta for stores was unfriendly. The knights had adopted an hostile attitude to British shipping, Captain Robert Miller, master of the *Lark* complaining that:

...our ships, persons and colours are treated with the utmost scandal, shame and indignity, even to the highest degree, and with such cruel severity that it is almost impossible for anybody to believe it that have not been eye-witnesses to it...

Into this atmosphere sailed the notorious Wright, Miller reporting that 'Capt. Fortunatus Wright, of the *St George* privateer, has been used here in a most barbarous manner...'

Wright had attempted to enlist and provide slops for British seamen landed from prizes taken by French corsairs but was ordered to land them, an order reinforced by the presence of a galley whose commander had orders to sink his ship having 'boar[ed] him and cut every soul to pieces' if he failed to comply. Wright was obliged to comply and put to sea on 22 October, being followed twenty-four hours later – as the neutrality laws provided – by a large French corsair of thirty-eight guns commanded by Capitaine Arnoux. This vessel was 'a prodigious dull sailer' and Wright manoeuvred round her 'just to aggravate' Arnoux, before making off. Within a few weeks Wright had sent in to Valletta and Leghorn two more French prizes, followed by a wheat-laden vessel valued at £9,000 sent in to Cagliari. Most of these ships belonged to Marseilles where:

...two ships of 20 guns and a settee of equal force, and all well-manned, are there fitting out purposely for him, with orders to give him no quarter, but burn him on board.[17]

The English writer, one of Wright's backers at Leghorn, added in *post scriptum*, 'the two [war]ships are fitting out by the King of France, and the Settee by the Chamber of Commerce of Marseilles; and that they have orders to set him on fire in any road where they may find him'.

With the defeat of Byng the French considered the Mediterranean their own, and with some justification for as the same writer explains 'the disgraceful situation we are all in, and the miserable state of our trade, the French Privateers in these seas being innumerable'. Writing at the time of Admiral Byng's execution, Horace Mann, the British envoy to Florence, the Tuscan capital, bemoaned the lack of British naval power in the Mediterranean.

Echoing Voltaire's famous epigram upon Byng's shooting, Mann told Horace Walpole:

Let us hope that the sentence may produce ... some reformation in the conduct of our sea-officers, which was so publickly criticised in the late war. I wish we could see a fleet in these parts now. Some thing must be done to recover our maritime reputation. The sea swarms with French Privateers, that daily take all the merchant ships that venture out. I have dissuaded the people [i.e. British traders] at Leghorn from sending many ships away that are laden for above a Million sterling, which, we know, the French have stationed several Privateers and Ships of war to wait for. They have advice boats continually going backwards and forwards, and others are at anchor at Porto (illegible), to be ready to follow Captain Wright and his prizes that had taken refuge at Port Ferrajo [Elba], from whence, if they can escape, we daily expect them at Leghorn. A plan has been agreed upon to indemnify the Captains of the Merchant Ships, who are ruined by laying, at a vast expense, in port by making a small average on the goods they have on board, otherwise they would have ventured out all hazards.

Indeed the valuable and mutual Anglo-Tuscan trade was so retarded that it caused lamentations in Florence where the economy was affected. Mann informed the Tuscan Government that this was a self-inflicted wound on their part, for the partiality of their policies, their treatment of British merchants and the insult offered to Captain Wright who was advised by the British consul at Leghorn to keep out of sight of the port, though 'he might send all the French prizes he had made to Leghorn … in deposit…'. Florence, meanwhile, agreed to enforce strict neutrality.

As Wright continued to send in prizes, a Liverpool newspaper of March 1757 noted that 'a large privateer is fitting out for Captain Fortunatus Wright, which is to be sent to him as soon as ready, and then he will be commodore of three ships'. One of these was the *King George*, into which Wright had transferred by the New Year when he encountered one of the French men-of-war fitted out to destroy him. This was the twenty-six-gun *Hirondelle* and Wright fought two inconclusive actions with her off Malta before both put into Valletta on 2 January 1757 to refit. Having been hulled, it was imperative that the *King George* was hove down, but Wright was denied permission to careen. Once again Captain Burnaby and HMS *Jersey* came to his rescue and both made for Leghorn from whence Burnaby convoyed four British ships blockaded in the port by two French men-of-war.

Whether or not Wright succeeded in careening the *King George* is uncertain, for his end is mysterious. Encouraged by Mann's promise to protect his prizes in Leghorn, he left Malta in March with one of them under his wing. On the 16th both vessels ran into heavy weather, the prize-master losing sight of his principal, and presuming Wright 'with 60 stout fellows' to have foundered. In the following months intelligence arrived that Wright had sent another prize into Messina while news from the masters of the British privateers *Anson*, Captain Gersham Speers, *Blakeney*, Captain Fowler, and the *King of Prussia*, Captain Mackaffee, passed on reports of sightings of Wright, but the truth was that no friendly face set eyes on him after he had left Malta. That the *King George* foundered through having been hulled – and perhaps inadequately repaired – in her action with the *Hirondelle* seems the most likely explanation. What is certain is that, despite the presence of other privateers, the successful Mackaffee included, Wright was sorely missed, for in July Mann again deplored 'The trade of Leghorn, upon which the whole wealth of this state chiefly depends, is reduced to its lowest ebb … Captain Wright … did great service … in the beginning of the war…'

Elsewhere commerce was badly affected by French corsairs. In 1757 all but two vessels sailing from Carolina with cargoes of indigo had been seized, 'Much to the honour of a nation possessed of above 200 men-of-war!' one newspaper exclaimed sarcastically. Calls for more properly organised convoys were raised and the Admiralty defensively declared that if:

> …any commanders of men-of-war had been defective in their duty of convoying or protecting their [i.e. the merchants to whom this letter was addressed] ships, or pursuing privateers … they should be dealt with according to their deserts.

Despite assurances of this nature, it was claimed that between August 1756 and February 1757 seventy British vessels were taken off Antigua alone. The masters of deeply laden merchantmen often had difficulty in keeping up with fast frigates sent to escort convoys and often lacked all protection, even in home waters where the French lurked. The commander of a corsair told the master of the *Dolly & Nancy* which he had just captured 'not a league off Beachy Head' that he did not fear British naval cruisers because 'they will not chase us if we don't hoist French colours'.

Often the resistance put up by armed merchant ships was impressive. Captain Marshall of the *Trafford*, returning to Liverpool from Virginia in December 1757, was attacked by a French corsair whom he fought for four and a half hours before being obliged to strike through lack of ammunition. Marshall was by no means unique, but hundreds of merchant seafarers, masters, mates and men, were imprisoned, although a few, like Captain Joseph Clarke of the *Windsor*, escaped. Captain Isaac Winn of the *Dolly & Nancy*, bemoaning the lack of naval protection and the failure of a man-of-war's captain to respond to his request to join a convoy, wrote eloquently of his plight to his owners:

> Thus, gentlemen, you have lost a good ship and a good freight, and we all that we had on board, and our liberty. I am in the common prison, without so much as a shirt to shift myself with, having nothing but what I had on when taken. They allow me four pence a day to live upon, out of which I pay for myself and mate, otherwise I must lie amongst straw and filth with the rest of my poor fellows. This is hard usage. Notwithstanding I can sooner forgive the authors of it than the villains who commanded the … two men-of-war, who, if they had suffered us to join them, might have prevented our being taken. Rage and vexation hinder me from adding any more…

Occasionally a well-armed merchantman might act in place of a warship as convoy escort, as did Captain Walter Barber of the *Resolution* of Liverpool. Returning to his home port to refit his ship as a privateer Barber undertook to convoy thirty-three merchantmen from The Downs to Spithead. On the passage 'We were for forty hours visited by three French privateers, till Captain Barber beat them off. He is the most honourable commander I ever was under' wrote one of the masters involved.[18] Unfortunately this situation was all too rare and losses of British vessels was serious.

Occasionally a corsair would not trouble to send in his prize but would ransom her at sea on some cognisance. Captaine Jean Maubeaule of the twenty-two-gun *Jupiter* of Bayonne allowed Captain Spears of the *Granville* to continue his voyage from North

Carolina to Liverpool with his cargo of tar and tobacco on a guarantee of £500 being paid him on arrival. Spears was obliged to surrender his chief mate, Alexander Scott, as surety against payment. Shortly afterwards Maubeaule took the *Knutsford*, Captain Sefton, Liverpool for St Kitts, and on a similar basis ransomed her for 1,500 guineas. The *Jupiter* also seized the *Aurora*, Captain Josiah Wilson, in June 1758, but Maubeaule was not willing to extend the arrangement to all his captures. Ransoming agents from the *armateurs* came over from France to negotiate the return of ships, the agent from Dunquerque reckoning that of the 136 British bottoms taken between 27 January 1756 and 5 March 1758, no less than seventy-eight had been ransomed. Generally, however, the balance sheet was about even:

> From the commencement of the war up to July 12th, 1757, the French had taken 637 British vessels; the ships taken from the French during the same period were 681 merchantmen and 91 privateers, making a total of 772. It was calculated that the English [sic] had profited by captures upwards of two millions.[19]

Notwithstanding such a general average, specific losses were immensely damaging to Great Britain which, unlike France, was no longer self-sufficient in her ability to feed her population and generate a war-chest. That a well-manned navy was necessary to protect trade was undisputed, but, as in previous wars, friction between the Royal Navy's impress service and the seamen belonging to merchant ships got out of hand. The navy stationed press tenders in various strategic places into which rounded-up seamen were held pending their shipment to a naval port, where they were entered into commissioning men-of-war. The best known of these tenders lay off the Tower of London and regularly took resentful men confined below padlocked gratings down to Chatham, not without the occasional affray resulting in broken heads and much unhappiness. There were other tenders, one of which lay off Hoylake near Liverpool. Early in the war, in October 1756, men confined in this impress tender, the *Bolton*, rose in a body, overwhelmed the sentries, beat-up the *Bolton's* mate and seized the vessel. The mate died of his severe wounds and about forty men escaped into the stews of Liverpool while the authorities mustered forces to retake the *Bolton* and apprehend the escaped seamen. Recovering the vessel was easy, since no one remained to defend her. Finding the 'mutinous deserters', which is what these wretches had become in law, was less so. One of these desperados was apprehended and Lieutenant John Siddal was attempting to carry his prisoner down to a boat when he and his press-gang were attacked by a mob intent on rescuing the arrested seaman. Later the mob liberated another recaptured mutineer from the Watch-house, breaking the ribs of the master-of-the-watch.

Another incident occurred as the Greenland whaler *Golden Lyon* entered the Mersey were H. M. Frigate *Vengeance* lay anchored in want of seamen. The *Vengeance* was commissioning as a man-of-war, having recently been captured from the French by the British frigate *Hussar*. Like the former corsair from St Malo, the *Golden Lyon* had also been French, a merchantman named *Le Lion d'Or*, taken by a Liverpool privateer at the very end of the War of the Austrian Succession. The privateer's owners, the firm of Goore and Bulkeley, finding little employment for their acquired ship with the onset of peace, determined to fit her for a new venture, intending to send her north, to the whaling grounds off Spitsbergen. To this end they had sought like-minded backers and they were joined by fellow share-holders who were almost all owners of slavers and privateers, men such as Manesty, Ogden, Cunliffe, Crosbie, and Tarleton. The *Golden Lyon* is recorded as having been placed in Liverpool's first commercial graving dock before leaving the port in 1752 as the first whaler to be owned on Merseyside. It was on her return from a subsequent whaling expedition in 1758 that she fell in with the *Vengeance*.[20]

The man-of-war's boats awaited new arrivals off the fairway buoys near the bar and then followed incoming vessels until they were within range of the *Vengeance*'s guns. This practice was adopted as the *Golden Lyon* ran in, the lieutenant in the boats hailing the whaler and announcing his intention of impressing all of her crew except the officers unless they entered the Royal Navy as volunteers. The response from Captain Thompson's crew was that 'as they belonged to the Greenland fishery they would not be impressed, and to enforce their words, brandished their long knives and harpoons'. As they were by now within pistol shot of the *Vengeance* the naval lieutenant had by now clambered aboard. As he did so the *Golden Lyon*'s crew bundled Thompson and his officers into the cabin and took over the ship, crowding on sail to pass out of range of the man-of-war's guns as rapidly as possible. The lieutenant was retained on board as a hostage while the naval sailors, faced with flensing irons, dropped back into their boats towing astern. The *Vengeance* opened fire, several shot damaging the *Golden Lyon* while others fell in Liverpool itself, although without inflicting much damage.

It being high water the *Golden Lyon*'s crew released Thompson and worked their way quickly into dock and next day:

> …proceeded to the Custom-house, to give bond, and to renew their protections [press-exemptions], according to Act of Parliament. Immediately after they had done, a large party of the press gang forced themselves into the Custom-house, fired several pistols, and committed other outrages, crowning the whole by impressing Captain Thompson and five of his crew. The rest escaped by various ways, some risking life and limb by jumping through the windows; others climbed on the house tops and over the walls. Whilst the press gang was taking the impressed men down to the water side, they were hooted by some women, one of whom 'was shot through the legs with a brace of balls'.

Thompson was later released while the magistrates, one of whom had been in the Custom House at the time and had been ill-used, determined to 'prosecute the ruffians for their insolence'. However, this threat did nothing to temper naval arrogance; within a short time the inward-bound slaver *Ingram* received the same treatment and her crew again secured her master and mates in an attempt to escape. Unfortunately the turn of the tide prevented this and all the *Ingram*'s crew were brought aboard the

Vengeance whereupon the *Ingram's* entire company, her master and chief mate alone excepted, were 'tied up, stripped, and whipped' by order of the *Vengeance's* captain whose name the reporting newspaper suppresses. 'This needs no comment,' the newspaper states, then goes on to say: 'for had the seamen committed any offence against the laws of this realm, they were entitled an Englishman's right'. Writing in 1897 Gomer Williams adds that:

> It is no exaggeration to say that in some respects, the British sailor at this time, and for long afterwards, was worse off than the negroes he assisted to oppress. His freedom was a sham.

As for reparation in law, the owner was in a better position than his employee, for the very person of the wretched sailor was itself the prize and, assuming the unlikely fact that he could afford it, he was physically unable to be able to bring a case to court. A few cases were brought by owners; one by a Mr Nickelson, shipowner of Poole, was heard in London before Chief Justice Wilkes and a special jury. Nickelson was awarded £1,000 against Captain John Fortescue of HMS *Prince Edward* for impressing the crew out of Nickelson's *Thomas and Elizabeth*. The ship had been on passage from Newfoundland towards Poole and the consequence of Fortescue's act was claimed to have been the loss of the ship.

Impressing men out of the merchants' service and into that of the nation, while under the imperative of a state of war, was not only often carried out illegally, but it seriously threatened the regularity of trade which, notwithstanding hostilities, must necessarily continue in order for the country to pay her way. Anxiety as to the impact of this enforced movement of labour – felt early in the war – provoked some ire in mercantile circles and on 25 June 1756 a number of affected gentlemen met in the King's Arms tavern in London's Change Alley to discuss the matter and propose a solution. Under the energetic leadership of a prolific pamphleteer and member of the Russia Company, Jonas Hanway,[21] they determined to form The Marine Society which undertook to remove from the streets of London a number of vagrant men and those impoverished urchins, many of whom were homeless orphans, whose mischiefs, thefts and general nuisance was commonly the prelude to lives of crime. These would be housed, clothed, fed and given a basic educational training – along with the inevitable bible, prayer-book and volume of edifying sermons – to become sailors, or at least go to sea with a view to becoming fully fledged seamen in due course. This application of vigorous 'Christian mercantilism', attacking as it did the presence of such obvious and shameful poverty on the streets of the capital, attracted donations from the great and the good of the day. Donors ranged from the actor David Garrick to the naval heroes Anson, Boscawen and Hawke – and later with a small gift, Nelson – but the organisation was mainly funded by such well-motivated trading institutions like Hanway's Russia Company. From this convergence of interests and, most notably the self-interest of the merchants, arose the notion that 'vanity hath built more hospitals than virtue' and certainly both merchant shipping and the Royal Navy itself benefited

The Marine Society Committee at work and using as premises
the Merchant Seamen's Office in the Royal Exchange. In the
right foreground the ragged street urchins are being brought in
and turned into the smart sailor boys on the left. The girls to the
ragged boys' rear are also being rescued from a life on the streets.
The Marine Society sent many thousands of boys to sea in both the
Royal Navy and the merchant service properly clothed, shod and
prepared for duties aboard ship. (© Courtesy of The Marine Society)

from a steady supply of man-power. Intending to wind itself up at the end of the war,
The Marine Society endures to this day, its first of many static training ships, the *Beatty*,
being moored off Deptford in September 1786 shortly after Hanway's death.

While the well-heeled London-based merchants generated a practical solution to
their dilemma by means of their own pockets, others were content to profit from
engaging the French in the *guerre de course* at which they were so proficient. In the
summer of 1758 a number of privateers from London and Liverpool, cruising in the
Bay of Biscay, fell in with a large French East Indiaman, *Le Prince de Conti*, on her way
to Pondicherry. The 800-ton vessel was well armed and commanded by Capitaine
de la Motte, who fought a gallant action and was holding off the attentions of the
London privateers *St George*, Captain Robinson, *Black Prince*, Captain Creighton, and
Boscawen, Captain Harden, when these were joined by the two Liverpool vessels *Isaac*,
Captain David Clatworthy, and *Shark*, Captain Abraham Harden, whose appearance

settled the issue. Although the outcome was soured by arguments as to who had clinched the surrender of De la Motte, *Le Prince de Conti* was valued at £100,000 and had on board an additional large undisclosed sum of money intended for trading 'for English goods' in India.[22]

Such were the profits in privateering that even the peace-espousing Quakers of Philadelphia were moved to take part and the *Sprye* was fitted out with twenty-two 9-pounders and 208 men for a cruise in the West Indies under command of an aptly named Quaker commander, Captain Obadiah Bold. Despite this and other colonial ventures, Liverpool remained the principal port from which British privateers emerged. Fortunatus Wright's partner and later Liverpool harbour-master, Captain William Hutchinson, went into partnership with one Henry Hardwar and others, to fit out the twenty-two-gun *Liverpool*. 'One of the finest privateers belonging to this period' she sailed on 10 June 1757, losing a man overboard before crossing the Mersey bar, but a few days later was in chase of an enemy. Hutchinson caught up with the *Grand Marquis de Tournay*, Capitaine François Dellmar, and in taking her after a sharp action released the master and crew of the brig *Sarah* of Bristol. The prize was laden with sugar, coffee, indigo, hides and logwood valued at £20,000, while the ship herself, also auctioned after condemnation as a lawful prize, was 'of 450-tons burthen, [a] prime sailer and pierced for 22 guns'. Hutchinson 'would not permit the least article to be taken from any of the French prisoners, and to the honour of the whole crew, each man behaved well'. On his next cruise Hutchinson retook the *Sampson*, captured while on her way to Bristol from Antigua with sugar rum and ginger, after which he engaged a French privateer and drove her on her home coast, seized a fishing vessel and then, having fallen in with the privateer *Fame* from Guernsey, decided to cruise in company and mount a ruse.

With the *Fame*, acting the part of a French corsair, and the *Liverpool* her submissive prize, both entered the Gironde. By this means they quickly seized the ship *Turbot* with a cargo of flour, pork, beef, brandy, laced hats and other apparel; the brig *La Muette* full of baled goods, small arms, wine and other stores; and the brig *Six Freres*, carrying a cargo of wine, flour, pork, soap, butter, candles, 'sweet and lamp oyl', Dutch cheeses, nails, twine, small arms, shoes, wood-hoops, canvas and 'one bale of shirts for negroes'. The *Fame* convoyed these prizes homewards but unfortunately *La Muette* was lost in St Bride's Bay on the Pembrokeshire coast 'where the natives plundered all that was saved of her cargo'.

On her own way home the *Liverpool* came to the assistance of a vessel presumed under attack from a large ship which Hutchinson mistakenly assumed to be a French privateer. With darkness coming on Hutchinson boldly ranged up to engage the 'Frenchman' and 'mistakenly' hailed him in French, whereupon the stranger opened fire and carried away some of the *Liverpool*'s top-hamper and gear. Hutchinson had caught a tartar; the 'Frenchman' turned out to be HM Frigate *Antelope* and the ship she had been engaging a smaller French corsair. The *Liverpool*'s crew sustained twenty-eight wounded from this unfortunate affair, after which six more died of their wounds and Hutchinson soon had 103 men disabled with wounds or fever. One of these was a young volunteer, a Mr James Holt, a member of a family to become well-known among Liverpool shipping families in the next century.

Hutchinson's next cruise took him into the Mediterranean, sending prizes into Leghorn, having assumed the mantle of his former partner. On his way home he took a French corsair, *Le Roi Gaspard*, and two Dutchmen on their way from St Eustatia with sugar, coffee and indigo. This was Hutchinson's last cruise in the *Liverpool*; he went ashore to pursue commercial interests. After a short hiatus the *Liverpool* was sold and took up a career as an ordinary merchantman. Hutchinson's venture seems not to have prospered, for by February 1759 he began his association with the port of Liverpool as principal water-bailiff, dock- and harbour-master, 'a position he held for about forty years'.

A curious incident followed soon after he took up his new post. Hutchinson was accosted by a former privateersman named Murphy who confronted him with a loaded pistol and accused him of being 'a damned villain'. Non-plussed, Hutchinson swiftly disarmed Murphy at the instant he fired the pistol and the assailant was tried at Lancaster Assizes and sentenced to serve in the Royal Navy for life. Hutchinson's later achievements at Liverpool outweigh those of his sea career, but he had risen by his own efforts and his own admission from his first appointment 'as cook of a small collier' to become one of the first thoroughly technical exponents of his profession. Born in Newcastle-on-Tyne his early years attest to the value of the English east-coast trade as a nursery for seamen.

> The best lessons for tacking and working to windward … are in the colliers bound to London, where many great ships are constantly employed, and where wages are paid by the voyage, so that interest makes them dexterous and industrious to manage their ships with few men in a complete manner in narrow channels, more so than, perhaps, in any other trade by sea in the world.[23]

He added that this mastery in the open sea belonged to 'those in the East India trade', a statement arising from his having made several voyages to India, the first to Madras in 1738 during which he had been prostrated for three months by scurvy. In his cure he had taken tea and, on a subsequent trip to Canton, grew enamoured of the brew. Hutchinson had served in the navy as mate of a bomb-tender before joining a merchantman engaged in the Mediterranean trade during the voyage of which he met Fortunatus Wright and afterwards commanded their jointly owned ship *Lowestoffe*, mentioned earlier.

In the later stages of his life in Liverpool, Hutchinson's alliance with two Liverpudlian mathematicians, Richard Holden and his son, produced a serious and valuable analysis of tides from which tide-tables were calculated. In his published works Hutchinson vigorously promoted a more technical and organised approach to the training of ship-masters and mates. He remarked:

...that there was no hidden or unknown principle concerned in the art of building, sailing, working and managing of ships, but the laws of motion, the pressure of fluids, and the properties of the lever which are all well known to British Philosophers.

It appalled him to consider that a great maritime nation relied upon mercantile officers who 'were left entirely to learn their duty by their own and other people's misfortunes'.

During his tenure of office as harbour-master, Hutchinson made assiduous observations of the weather, anticipating Admiral Beaufort with a 'table of winds', while his treatise, *Practical Seamanship*, was adopted as a standard work in several educational establishments such as Sir Thomas Frankland's Maritime School at Chelsea. Hutchinson was an acquaintance of the great civil engineer John Smeaton and a practical experimenter whose designs for two ships, the West Indiamen *Hall* and *Elizabeth*, made them 'greyhounds of the Atlantic'. Mindful of the fates of many seamen and their dependants, Hutchinson was instrumental in founding Liverpool's own Marine Society, subscribing to it and supporting it for the remainder of his life. From 1798 he also gave £20 per annum to a subscription designed to ease the tax-burden in paying for the war with France. He died in February 1801 after a life which was 'one unwearied scene of industrious usefulness', one of the most admirable of British seamen of whom almost nothing is today remembered.

The practice of ordinary merchantmen being furnished with a Letter-of-Marque in order to be armed, defend themselves and, if lucky, claim prize-money, often induced masters to take risks. In May 1759 Captain Birch of the *Upton*, off the Canaries on her way out to the Gambia, took a prize valued at £5,000. Some, such as Frierson of the *Prince Frederick*, Parke of the *Providence* and Quirk of the *Prussian Hero* – whom we met earlier when master of Peter Holme's snow *Betty* – all escaped after beating off an attack, in Quirk's case of five corsairs. On the other hand the previous February when outward-bound to the West Indies, Captain Seth Houghton of the *Catherine*, armed with twelve guns and a crew of thirty-five, was engaged by a French privateer of vastly superior force. In an action lasting from 07.00 to 16.00 the *Catherine's* crew inflicted casualties, but suffered in proportion and, in the débâcle of surrender, a boy was drowned. The French knew the value of concentrating at certain loci on a trade route and, in an action off Antigua in May, a group of five corsairs attacked four British merchantmen from Liverpool, Dumfries and Cork. These were the *Wheel of Fortune*, Captain Lethwayte, the *Eward*, Captain Kevish, the *Swan*, Captain Slazer, and the *Cork Packet*, Captain Champion, which beat off their attackers.

Among the most successful of the French corsairs was the Dunkirker François Thurot in the *Marshal Belleisle* who commanded a small squadron of corsairs active in the North Channel and Irish Sea, effectively placing Liverpool in a state of blockade early in 1760. There was irony in this for, after a disastrous start, the tide of war had turned in Britain's favour and 1759 had seen many remarkable victories for British arms in India, Canada and elsewhere. Known to history as the *Annus Mirabilis*, this was not readily appreciated in Liverpool where, early in the year, forty-five Liverpool merchants and shipowners requested the owner of the *Liverpool Advertiser* to cease publishing any intelligence of ship-movements, such was the threat posed by Thurot. Moreover, Thurot's mastery of the Irish Sea was thought to presage a major descent on Liverpool by the French in the absence of a Royal Naval squadron to defend it. Consequently the port-city was obliged to place itself in a state of defence. Bastions and outworks were thrown up, a militia battalion was raised and shipowners and slave-merchants took on military ranks at the head of their privately funded infantry companies.

In fact Thurot's expedition, a joint-stock enterprise by the *armateurs* of his native Dunquerque, had begun in October 1759 and was aimed at Ireland, that perennial and unattainable target of French ambition, and was indeed to have coincided with an invasion of England mounted by the French army and navy which the Royal Navy had actually thwarted by a brilliant action in which Admiral Sir Edward Hawke's fleet had chased De Conflans onto the rocks at Quiberon Bay on 20 November. Nevertheless, Thurot, having briefly withdrawn to recruit in Norwegian waters, occupied the Ulster port of Carrickfergus where he fell out with the regular French army officers commanding a detachment of troops intended to take Belfast. He then withdrew, landing 600 men on Islay and stealing cattle Soon afterwards, on 28 February 1760, three British naval frigates under Captain Elliott brought Thurot's force to battle off the Calf of Man, killed its leader, captured his three remaining vessels and ended the threat.[24] When the news reached Liverpool the volunteer troops were ordered to muster under the mayor – now 'Colonel' Spencer, supported by the shipowners Ingram and Tarleton, both of whom were 'captains' commanding companies. The volunteers paraded:

…all clothed in their new uniforms at their own private expense: the Colonel's company in blue, lapelled and faced with buff; Capt. Ingram's in scarlet coast and breeches, lapelled and faced with green; green waistcoats, gold laced hats and queue [pig-tailed] wigs; and Captain Tarleton's in blue, with gold vellum button holes; Captain Johnson's company of the tran of artillery wear the uniform of the navy, blue and buff with gold laced hats.

The battalion were joined by the Lincolnshire militia and passed in review order before the Earl of Scarborough.

For the common seamen faced with the twin dangers of an enemy at home – in the form of the navy's impress service – and at sea the prospect of a French prison, it was unsurprising that they occasionally resorted to desperate measures. The most common of these was desertion, usually after the pre-voyage payment of an advance or, in the case of privateers, a bounty. Even commanders of Hutchinson's reputation suffered from such an indignity and descriptions of deserters were rapidly circulated with notice of rewards offered for information about them.[25]

Like their British counterparts, despite the contrasting 'humanity' claimed by contemporary newspapers, French prisons were much feared.26 Personal robbery was the first experience of capture endured by merchant seamen taken at sea by corsairs or French naval vessels, but more especially the former. Captain James Settle of the *Annabella*, taken by the *Luce* of Brest in November 1756, reported his men were stripped almost naked. An anonymous master writing from confinement in Bayonne complained of the lack of distinction between officers and men, contrasting French officers allowed their liberty on parole in Petersfield with his own unhappy situation.

> No one is permitted to speak to us without the commandant's leave; our letters are all opened and read … and we are not allowed to purchase any necessaries from the town's people, but must take everything from the commandant's mistress who charges us at the rate of two shillings for what she buys in the town for sixpence…

Referring to the privateers fitting out at Bayonne, the same master pleaded for an exchange of prisoners by a cartel, otherwise:

> I am afraid that many of our common sailors, who are now about 200 prisoners on this castle, will be induced by threats or promises to take on in the enemy's service, where they are offered great encouragement.

Other privations endured by merchant commanders at Brest included being immured:

> …in a dungeon 40 feet under the ground, and not permitted fire or candle … they had straw to lie upon, but were obliged to pay dear for it. As to the provisions allowed them per day, it was three ounces of poor beef, such of brought to our markets would be burnt… They were indulged with three half pints of sour white wine per day, but debarred from water, which if sweet, was much better; but to do them some justice, they had sufficient bread. What was most singular is that they were debarred of laying out their own money, or drawing bills, no person being permitted to come near them; in short … they were treated worse than we treat dogs…

Some specific instances of mistreatment are also adduced by reports deposed by nine merchant masters – and we must remind ourselves that these men were not naval warriors – who had been repatriated to Plymouth after an exchange by cartel in January 1759.

> At their arrival at Vannes they were put among common felons, who were condemned to die, in the most nauseous gaol. The case of poor Capt. Gordon and his ship's company is a most deplorable one; the whole crew perished in the French ship they were taken in, she being lost on some rocks near the shore; the crew, who were all confined in irons, were by the French captain called English dogs, and

told they should perish as such, and would not suffer a man to let them out. Their behaviour to Capt. Turner was likewise very cruel, and to the English prisoners in general, forcing them to enter into their service. This can never go unnoticed by those in power.

Needless to say, it did.

Not all had such a hard time, and it was better to be captured in the West Indies where confinement was less painful and often shorter, prisoners consuming valuable viands on an island and being more readily exchanged. Captain Holme of the *Austin* was carried into Martinique from where the French then operated seventy-four corsairs. Holme was given a modest but adequate victualling allowance and after only eight days was 'sent up to Barbadoes [sic] in a cartel ship, and returned home passenger in the *Merrimack*'.

Despite the incursion of Monsieur Thurot and the alarum given to Liverpool, the achievements of the marvellous year of 1759 greatly reduced the risks to British trade which once again rapidly recovered. It would be February 1763 before the Treaty of Paris ended the Seven Years War, but the burden of self-defence was largely lifted from the shoulders of the ship-masters of the merchants' service long before and privateering consequently declined.

In addition to their own seizures, much good service had been achieved by privateers in recapturing prizes taken by the French, in restoring British bottoms and their ladings to their rightful owners after the privateers had made their profit. In March 1758 the *Spy*, Captain Robert Grimshaw, and *Resolution*, Captain McKee, having taken a Spanish ship, came up with the *Marlborough*, originally bound to London from Jamaica full of sugar, rum, pimento, hides and mahogany. On 31 August following, Gwyn's *Fame* fell in with the *Truelove* of Lancaster which had been taken by Thurot in the *Marshal Belleisle* and released her. Another restoration occurred to Captain Quirk's snow *Betty*, which had been taken by the corsair *Le Comte de St Florentine* when homeward bound from Jamaica. The prize was encountered by the New York privateer *Royal Hunter*, retaken and sent in to Rhode Island, while *Le Comte de St Florentine* was herself later captured. Equally lucky was the *Speedwell*, bound from Virginia to London with tobacco, indigo, pig iron and barrel staves. She was retaken after capture by the *Tyger*, Captain Burrowes, on his way from Liverpool to Jamaica.

Such recaptures, of which these are but a few examples, were economically important, for the seizure of a merchantman in terms of associated and potential monetary loss was often more than the face value of the vessel and her cargo. The number of ships belonging to Liverpool alone, taken during the Seven Years War by French corsairs, amounted to 143. As Gomer Williams points out:

> …probably one-third of the captured ships were slavers, a fact which added enormously to the losses, each slave ship representing three distinct sources of profit in a single round voyage.

However, in analysing the situation over a century later, the antiquary and architect Sir James Picton, is cogent:

> The pursuits of the Liverpool Merchants … will not bear very severe scrutiny in a moral point of view… The Practice of privateering could not but blunt the feelings of humanity of those engaged in it, combining as it did the greed of the gambler with the ferocity of the pirate. War is hateful in any form, but undertaken by a nation with the discipline and courtesies of a regular force, it assumes an amount of dignity which hides to some extent its harsher features; whilst marauding expeditions undertaken by private parties combine all the evils without any of the heroism of war; greed is the motive power, and robbery and murder the means of its gratification. Its influence on the community which encourages it cannot but be deleterious.

Picton, a gentleman of means occupying morality's tump, ignores the rawer facts of eighteenth century maritime life. Let Williams – who quotes Picton – have the last word upon this conflict as it was waged by the mercantile sea service:

> On the other hand, there were sentiments and qualities evoked and developed in connection with privateering, that tended to raise those who had fallen to the lowest depths. To be fired with enthusiasm, to cruise about the seas … to face death manfully 'for the honour of Liverpool,' and even for pelf, if not for King and Country, must have done good to many a bankrupt soul and pocket and could scarcely deteriorate the men who embarked upon such work.

Perhaps; it was a brutal age and ports like Liverpool were scarcely places to find the best in mankind for the growing conurbations drew to them the desperate and the dispossessed, men and women moved out of their natural environment by Enclosure Acts and all the upheaval that was converting the rural cottager into the industrial wage-slave. From Ireland as well as rural England these masses gravitated towards the new industrial cities, particularly Liverpool, Manchester and Glasgow, becoming the causes of epidemics, but also prompting the first stirrings of public health and – on the part of the manipulating capitalists who profited from shipowning, slavery and sugar – extraordinary philanthropy.

Most of the indigent men then flooding into Liverpool simply went to sea.

NOTES

1. As a 'ship' the *Planter* possessed three masts, fore, main and mizzen, each crossed by yards setting so-called square sails. Triangular jibs were set on the foremast stays leading to the bowsprit and between the masts staysails were deployed. The mizzen also carried a fore-and aft sail, sometimes at this period called – confusingly – a mizzen course, but later referred to as a spanker or driver. This three-masted, square rig specifically defines the full-rigged ship.

2. Hutchinson's buoyage system, adopted in many ports other than Liverpool was eclipsed in British waters around 1939 but had long since migrated across the Atlantic to be retained by the Americans. In 1977, in modified form, it became the International Association of Lighthouse Authorities' (IALA) Region B and pertains today throughout the Americas, North and South, Korea, Japan and the Philippines.

3. The lighthouses on the Isle of Man remain under the Northern Lighthouse Board today, though buoyage around the island is the responsibility of Trinity House. The disfavour of the Liverpool merchants marked a period during which the Elder Brethren were ambiguous about the development of lighthouses and predated their assumption of greater responsibilities, expertise and an explosion of enterprise in the later nineteenth century.

4. Parry and Sherlock, *A Short History of the West Indies*, p129 *et seq.*

5. The circumnavigating privateer commander Woodes Rogers' first term as governor of the Bahamas ended in 1721. He was appointed a second time in 1729 and died in post in 1732 as mentioned in an earlier chapter.

6. The daughter of an attorney, Anne Bonny sailed with and secretly married the pirate 'Calico Jack' Rackham. Mary Read had taken to soldiering in the War of the Spanish Succession but joined Rackham's crew. When Rackham – who proved cowardly – was captured in 1720, both women were reprieved from the death sentences passed on them on account of their being pregnant, but Read died in prison of typhus; Bonny's end is uncertain.

7. Teach had 'married' several times, the last time to a sixteen year old. This final wedding was said to have been officiated at by Eden. During one of his drunken dinners, Teach fired his pistols to test his officers' reactions. One shot, fired under the table, wounded his gunner, Israel Hands, in the knee. Hands subsequently left Teach's employ and became a well-known beggar on London's streets and was immortalised by Robert Louis Stevenson in *Treasure Island*.

8. The opinionated, influential and obnoxious Mather was involved in the Salem, New England, witchcraft trials, evidence perhaps that twelve is too young for university entrance.

9. Pares, *War and Trade in the West Indies*, p41 and p61. As was mentioned elsewhere Jenkins was reputed to have carried his ear with him, even unto the grave.

10. An account of the bungled attempt on Cartagena may be found in the pages of Tobias Smollett's novel *Roderick Random*. Smollett was present as a naval surgeon's mate.

11. One of Anson's lost ships was the *Wager*, which was embayed on the south-west coast of Patagonia and went to pieces. As a result of the disintegration of her crew, following that of their ship, the Admiralty afterwards maintained that a crew owed a duty of obedience to the commanding officer notwithstanding the loss of their ship. This meant that from 1748 a naval ship's company remained on pay until the commission of their ship was finally terminated by the court-martial which sat to determine the cause of her loss. Such a measure was taken to avoid mutinous, or disobedient, behaviour predicated on the fact that no duty of obedience was owed since up to that date a naval seaman's pay stopped when his ship was lost, as was claimed by the Wager's so-called 'mutineers'. This rectification in the Royal Navy, had no equivalence in the merchant service and it was not until 1943, in the middle of the Second World War, that it was applied to many merchant seamen.

    The celebrated action between HMS *Centurion* – the single ship to which Anson's misadventure had been reduced – and the armed merchantman *Nuestra Señora de Covadonga* fought in the Pacific on 20 June 1743 made a success of Anson's circumnavigation. The prize's cargo realised £500,000 and required thirty-two wagons to carry it in triumph to London, making Anson both a peer and a rich man.

12. This first capture of Louisbourg was accomplished by the Royal Navy and what were called 'Provincial' troops raised in the Thirteen Colonies. The exchange for Madras irritated the American colonists who thought the action high-handed and dismissive of their own martial valour. This stoked anti-Governmental sentiments which would find fruitful ground once the French had been defeated in Canada by 1763.

13. Middleton was one of a small band of men who, having made significant contributions to exploration, suffered from the Admiralty's casual manner of exploiting them for their talents. Not all were suitable as career naval officers: Dampier has been noted elsewhere, as has Halley. Dalrymple was, of course, repudiated largely on the Admiralty's experience of mavericks from outside its own ambit. Only the candidate preferred over Dalrymple, James Cook, seems to have impressed the navy, though not without resistance, but he had abandoned his mercantile career as a mate and given up an offered command to go to sea in the Royal Navy as an able seaman. He was therefore 'home-grown', though his abilities had first been acquired in Walker's Whitby colliers.

14. Boscawen's modest victory was offset by the disastrous ambush laid by the French and their native allies on the banks of the Monongahela for General Braddock's column which was to have crossed the mountains and rolled the French back to the Great Lakes. It was a prefiguring of the war with the rebellious American colonists.

15. And a tiny foothold in Canada, the French retaining the twin islands of St Pierre and Miquelon – which remain French territory – in the Gulf of St Lawrence on the grounds that a base for their cod-fishery on the Grand Banks was indispensable.

16. Quoted by Gomer Williams, p51 *et seq.*

17. The anglicised version of *saettia*, a lightly built, versatile galley common throughout the Mediterranean and commonly used as a naval vessel, corsair or trader was settee.

18. Among the *Resolution's* crew was a 'seaman' who was discovered to be a young woman. She would not reveal 'her name or quality; only that she had left home on account of a breach of promise of her lover'.

19. Gomer Williams, p115.

20. A Captain Metcalfe preceded and followed Thompson in command of the *Golden Lyon* and he was in command of her when she was later lost in the ice in 1765. Thompson seems to have been in command of her replacement, the new *Golden Lion*.

21. Jonas Hanway, the son of a naval victualling agent and brother of a naval officer, was one of London's eccentrics and said to be the first man in the city to use an umbrella. Born in 1712, as a young man he served in trading houses in Lisbon and St Petersburg, from where he made his journey into Persia, surviving privation and warfare, and encountering the redoubtable Captain Woodroofe – mentioned earlier. Hanway's travels, especially his seasick passages across the North and Baltic Seas, induced in him 'melancholy impressions of the danger of sea life'.

22. Clatworthy made several successful captures in *Isaac* which was an exceptionally able little sixteen-gun sloop. Later sold to colonial interests in America, she reappeared in British waters under rebel colours as the American *General Mifflin* during the War of American Independence and wrought a great deal of havoc against British shipping. Part of the 'Continental Navy' the *General Mifflin's* builder is said by Howard Chappelle, in his *History of the American Sailing Navy*, to be unknown, but Gomer Williams is specific on the vessel's origins.

23. Hutchinson goes on to say that a 'travelling French gentleman of rank' on seeing this sight had held up his hands and exclaimed 'that it was there that France was conquered'.

24. These were the *Marshal Belleisle* of fifty-four guns, the *Blanque* of thirty-six guns and the *Thurot* of twenty guns. One vessel had parted company with Thurot and while in the island one of Hutchinson's smacks, there loading with kelp for Liverpool, was plundered of flour. An eyewitness reported 'a number of English and Irish in the crews'.

25. These are of passing interest. John Coulston, a deserter from Hutchinson's *Liverpool* was 'a middle-aged man, about 5 foot 7 inches high, wears his own hair, brown complexion, and very much marked with the small pox. Had on, when he went away, a cheque shirt and 2 waistcoats, one made of white flannel, trimmed round with black tape and black buttons, and the other a blue frize; wore a brown pair of fustian breeches, dark blue stockings and round pewter buckles. Any person who will secure him … shall receive a handsome reward.' John Smith 'had on a blue rug great coat, a brown frize coat under it, a curled light coloured wig, and a slouched hat'. He was 'much addicted to gambling' as was Robert Maxwell who was also 'very much pitted with small pox…'

26. The original prison for Frenchmen in Liverpool was the old castle built by the Stanleys but such were the problems incarcerating men there that in December 1756 the Admiralty rented assembly rooms in Water Street for their confinement, equipping them man-of-war fashion with issues of hammocks and slops accordingly. 'It's to be hoped [that this] will be a means of procuring our countrymen, who have fallen into their hands, better usage than hitherto'.

PART THREE

'The Grandest Society of Merchants in the Universe'

British Shipping in the Indian and Pacific Oceans
1707–1793

For you, ye midgets of a bygone day,
That floating on a breeze of ceaseless strife,
With greedy rivalry of passions rife,
Felt naught of hidden workings in the fray,
That pushed you hither thither on the way
Of greater doings in a larger life,
And hurt and slew you with the callous knife
Of fate, do I this history essay.

Sir Richard Temple (1850–1931)
To the victims aboard the Worcester

SIX

'THEIR BLACK AND BLOODY FLAGS'

The Contest for the Indian Ocean, 1708–1763

Around 1700, during the period of uncertainty prior to the formation of the 'United' East India Companies, trade to India was relatively free of restriction. In 1699 the English parliament had passed an act allowing ships, known officially as 'Special Stock Ships' but more generally as 'Free Traders', to engage in oriental trade hitherto denied them by monopoly. However, the boards of both the 'Old' and the 'New' Companies sought to restrict what they still regarded as interloping, forbidding their officials in India to treat with the supercargoes of these trespassers. Faced with this threat to profitability the 'Old' Company in particular stepped up its traditional war on the excesses of private trade amongst its own employees. Like the Customs House, the Company employed 'tide-waiters' who intercepted incoming ships, boarded them and rummaged for more goods than Company employees were permitted, or for proscribed articles upon which they imposed a duty. Homeward bound in 1684 Edward Barlow described how the *Kent*:

> …met a ketch, which had our East India Company's waiters, which are sent by them on board of all ships coming from India to oversee and look whether they can see or find any person that brings any mulctable goods home with them, and if they hear of any, to inform the Company of it, although a man may have but a piece or two for his own use or for his wife and family.

Barlow deeply resented this intrusion into his personal affairs, ending sarcastically:

> I having two pieces of calico which cost in India both together five shillings and ninepence, they put to me four shillings [duty] … before I could have them in my

own possessions, the Company showing such kindness to poor seamen, their waiters being then as welcome to us as water in a ship which is ready to sink.

Barlow's admission is the more telling in that he was submitted to this nuisance when first mate of the *Kent*. Nor was he much luckier in the *Wentworth*, for while the power of the Old Company waned under competitive strain, that of the government waxed as it seized any prospect of revenue. In 1701 Barlow, investing in silks, lacquer-ware and tea, found that in the *Wentworth's* absence, Government import duty had been raised to 15 per cent and this was only payable after the goods had been auctioned and their value determined by market forces. This obliged Barlow and his colleagues to pay warehousing fees and to be filched of 'wateragge, wharfrige, portrige and cartrige'. Although claiming he lost on the tea and lacquer-ware, of the £908 his silk raised at auction, Barlow received £454. This was undoubtedly profitable and whilst receiving less than he had hoped, the persistent nature of the traffic leaves little doubt that, despite impositions, it paid.[1]

The severity with which the Court of the Old Company sought to cling onto its privileges was to precipitate an international constitutional crisis, a profound miscarriage of justice, and an event the echoes of which linger to this day. It all centred upon two merchant ships.

Circumstances having made the turn of the century suddenly bright with opportunity for interloping in India, many shipowners sought to barge in. One man to do so was Captain Thomas Bowrey who had himself sailed in Indiamen before taking to the Country-trade. From 1669 until 1688 'he wandered incessantly about the Bay of Bengal, and … the Malay Archipelago' as master of a Country-ship. Returning to Wapping with a small fortune he settled to become a well-respected figure in the shipping world and a Younger Brother of Trinity House. Possessed of an 'insatiable curiosity' Bowrey took an interest in anything maritime, building a small yacht, the *Duck*, in which he made coastal trips in the southern North Sea, consequently publishing sailing directions for the English coast. Constantly seeking opportunities and information Bowrey instructed his ship-masters to enquire into prospects for whaling and to collect vocabularies of local languages. He wrote an account of his experiences in Indian and Malay waters and a *Dictionary of English and Malay* which appeared in 1701, the first commercial lexicon aimed at assisting trade. Bowrey was the part-owner of seven vessels, to several of which he was ship's husband, and he acted as a broker, bringing together investors to charter other ships to take advantage of the commercial lacuna in India.

This period unfortunately coincided with the War of the Spanish Succession during which French privateers were active in the English Channel and it became common practice for ships to avoid them by passing round the north of Scotland. This did not guarantee safety, for one of Bowrey's vessels, the *Mary Galley* on her way home from India in 1707, was taken by French corsairs off Jutland. Another of his ships was the 150-ton *Worcester* and she was to have a profound effect upon history.

At his accession to the English throne in 1603 James VI of Scotland had united the two kingdoms as 'Great Britain', but they remained separate entities, with their own privy councils, parliaments and established churches. James I, as he now became, was keen to make Great Britain one political state, beginning a Unionist movement which became a goal for the farsighted. Acts were passed that facilitated greater co-operation, ending ancient border conflict and, after the case of the *Postnati* of 1608, establishing that everyone 'born in England or Scotland after the union of the two crowns, were entitled to all the privileges of the citizens of either country'. There was one important exception to this, and it was to play a crucial part in what occurred a century later. As for Union, resistance and mutual antipathy confounded James's cherished scheme and the easily diverted king gave it up. Arguments in favour of Union simmered on but were eclipsed by the troubles of James's successor, Charles I, and the English Civil War. Although Scotland supported Charles Stuart after his father's execution, this only led to the invasion of Scotland by Parliamentary forces and further national humiliations. More were added at the Restoration.

In 1663 Charles II assented to the second Navigation Act which protected English shipping excluding Scottish vessels from importing goods into England. Although salt, corn and fish coming from Scotland and seal-oil from Russia were exempted, all of which could come into England in Scots bottoms, the general curtailment of opportunity in favour of English shipping infuriated the Scots. Compared with England, Scotland was a poor and backward country, split between the remote and archaic Highlands and the aspiring but struggling Lowlands. Nevertheless: 'The Scots were an energetic commercial nation whenever the political condition ... admitted general attention to commerce...' They had a small merchant fleet engaged in trade with the Baltic states, in particular in timber and flax; and a considerable fishing fleet which worked the Iceland and Newfoundland banks. Attempts to establish Scottish colonies had failed, particularly in Nova Scotia, but an agitation remained to establish a 'colony of refuge' in North America.

But it was envy of the riches of London, excited chiefly by the wealth of the East India Companies that sharpened mercantile appetite in Scotland. Despite this ruthless application of Mun's mercantilist arguments in which England determined that Scotland should 'neither participate in her trading nor be permitted to create a like system for herself', the Scots defiantly struck back, determined to form a joint-stock company of their own. On 14 June 1695 an act was passed in Edinburgh for the 'encouragement of foreign trade' and a fortnight later 'A Company Tradeing to Affrica and the Indies' was incorporated. It was deliberately modelled upon the two English East India Companies and it intended raising capital of £600,000 equally from both Kingdoms. In London its chief advocate was the Scots-born but English-bred merchant William Paterson who was, at this time, also a keen instigator of the establishment of the Bank of England.[2] Paterson was among the English backers who, in only nine days, raised the requisite £300,000 for what – to the torment in particular of the Old East India Company – Paterson's friends called 'The Scottish East India Company'. As for the Old Company, the value of its stock fell sharply in the face of apparent new competition, initiating the beginning of the Old Company's troubles. Any members of its own board discovered putting money into the rival Scottish outfit were kicked out, beginning a 'series of rash insults to Scotland, which, rendering the Union necessary, were at the same time a sad impediment to its progress'. So aroused were the Directors of the Old Company that they laid the matter before Parliament, the up-shot of which was the ruling-out of English investment in the new joint-stock enterprise. In December 1695 the Scots were left to go it alone. This they perceived as a contemptuous act.

To float The Africa Company, as it was now misleadingly called, the Scots had to reduce the required capital to £400,000, but investment from a relatively poor nation was slow. What could be raised in a few days in London, took six months in Scotland. However, seen as a measure of national honour, small investors promised much. People in all walks of Scots life stumped-up, but even so the company was under-subscribed. Paterson, meanwhile, had resigned from the Bank of England's board to mature a scheme for a Scottish colony at Dairen, on the Isthmus of Panama.[3] Whilst freighting ships for India as intended, The Africa Company's board – under Paterson's influence – now turned its attention to this new project which caused a further popularly accepted change of name to 'The Dairen Company'. The first self-inflicted disaster occurred with the shift of policy. The building of a fleet of East Indiamen at Glasgow collapsed, and with it the first phase of the Company's sad existence. However, this was obscured by enthusiasm for the new proposal. Almost the whole of Scottish industry supported the colonial enterprise and on 26 July 1696, 'amid bright sunshine and the plaudits of a vast assemblage', three ships left Leith Road bound for the Caribbean.

On 4 November the colonists landed on the Isthmus where, bereft of any expertise and in the face of active Spanish hostility, the emigrants attempted a settlement. It was an abject failure, utterly unsupported from Scotland for eighteen crucial months after which, in June 1699, the 'miserable remnant' gave up and sailed for home. By this time belated help was on its way; between May and September a number of ships left Scotland bound for Dairen, all of which arrived far too late and only one of which, the *Caledonia*, Captain Robert Drummond, returned. Despite the mismanagement of the Company's directors which caused 'the loss of 2,000 lives and £200,000,' it was 'almost universally believed in Scotland that England was responsible for the fiasco'. The ruin of so many investors caused the whole of Scotland to seethe with indignation, coinciding as it did with the poor harvests of 'the seven ill years' of 1693–1700. The effect upon the Scottish economy was catastrophic. 'Investments had been made beyond the quantity of capital available,' Defoe remarked: 'The stock was a dead weight upon a great many families'. Widespread debt, despair and depopulation ensued, nurturing a deep-seated sense of grievance. King William III's Government doggedly pursued the mooted Union but took no action to ameliorate the ruination north of the border. The Scottish nation's wrath fell upon what it conceived to be the author of its great misfortune: the Old East India Company in London and 'Mutual enmity was at its highest.' Amid rejection by the Scottish parliament of all William III's overtures to bring about Union, King William's horse stumbled on a molehill, mortally injuring him and leaving to Queen Anne two kingdoms on the brink of war.[4]

To this simmering hatred, the Old East India Company now made its own inimitable contribution. While perceptive English statesmen saw that Scotland must either 'be subdued and held [by force of arms], or must participate in the English trading privileges', the Directors of the Old Company insisted on forcing the very exclusivity of those privileges. In an attempt at self-rescue, the rump of the Dairen Company had chartered a single ship, the *Annandale*.[5] In February 1705 she lay at anchor in The Downs, attempting to embark some English seamen prior to taking up a charter to sail for India and recoup in part The Dairen Company's losses. To her owners she was a legal, free-trading, 'Extra Stock' vessel. To the Old Company's directors in London she was an unwanted interloper, but they could do nothing to stop her sailing. Until, that is, she recruited English sailors.

In the eyes of the Old Company's directors in London, the *Annandale* was a 'foreign ship' and – while Scotsmen could serve on English ships, under James I's reforms – the provisions of the Old Company's charter proscribed reciprocity, so in the act of recruiting Englishmen the *Annandale* breached their charter. The Old Company went to law and the law supported it: the *Annandale* was sailing no-where. The news of the ship's arrest reached Roderick Mackenzie, 'the energetic secretary of the Dairen Company in Edinburgh' who nursed an animus against all things English.

Then, on 31 July 1704, Thomas Bowrey's equally free-trading ship *Worcester* put into Leith Roads on her north-about homeward voyage from India to London. Captain Green was under instructions to seek the escort of a man-of-war to the Thames. In the *Worcester* Mackenzie saw a fortuitous means of making good the loss of the *Annandale*, but in seeking a justification for action he descended to vengeance. Ignoring the germane fact that the *Worcester* was neither beneficially owned nor chartered to the Old East India Company, Mackenzie seized his opportunity. He laid charges against the master and ship's company of the *Worcester*, initially as a reprisal for the seizure of the *Annandale* but, as the rumoured – and exaggerated – value of the ship excited a gross cupidity, he went a step too far. Green and his men were, he alleged, pirates. The ship:

> …was seized by a stratagem, and her officers and crew eventually tried for piracy, presumably of a Scottish ship, the *Speedy Return*, commanded by that Robert Drummond who had brought home the *Caledonia*, the one ship of the Dairen Company which returned to Scotland from the short-lived colony… [T]he accused were all convicted and her unfortunate captain, Thomas Green, and two others [the mate, one John Madder who was, ironically, a Scotsman, and James Simpson, the gunner] were hanged at Leith on 11 April 1705.[6]

No one in Edinburgh knew at the time what had happened to the *Speedy Return* or her crew, but Mackenzie had gone to tortuous lengths to achieve his objective. Counting upon the prevailing anti-English feeling abroad, and after careful enquiry, he cunningly suborned his 'witnesses', carefully selecting members of the crew with grievances, and getting them to swear affidavits in favour of his stratagem. Those who co-operated, of course, avoided the ultimate penalty for piracy, thus when it came to the trial the case was based upon fabricated and unsubstantiated evidence, sufficiently convincing to produce a verdict pleasing to Mackenzie.

The consequences of this appalling act of reprisal and consequent travesty of justice are soon told. Complex and slow to gather momentum, the fate of Green and his officers served to break the stalemate in the protracted negotiations that still pursued Union.[7] On 15 July 1706 the English Commissioners insisted the Dairen Company was finally wound up.

> Indeed, after the case of the *Worcester*, its mere existence was a danger to English commerce, but, by an act of extraordinary grace for the period, they recommended that its shares should be purchased at the value of the nominally paid-up capital, roughly £220,000, together with 5 per cent. interest to 11 May, 1707, thereon. Thus was a total of about £223,000 reached, which sum was duly distributed after much calculation to the shareholders ruined, not by any act of the English who paid this compensation, but by the maladministration of the Company's Scottish Directors.[8]

Despite opposition in both London and Edinburgh, the treaty agreed between the two countries was converted into an act applicable to 'the law of all Great Britain… On 6 March, 1707, Queen Anne came to the House of Lords and solemnly gave the Royal Assent to one of the greatest acts of statesmanship performed in the British Isles'. Thus, the fates of two obscure merchantmen played a pathetic part in a great event, an event which was, *inter alia*, of material consequence to the history of the British mercantile marine in which the Scots were to play so dynamic a part. But even as the United Kingdom of Great Britain rose, the Old East India Company was expiring.

Coincident in 1707 with the unification of the crown's two kingdoms was the creation of the British 'United' East India Company, mentioned in the conclusion of Chapter One. This mercantile enterprise, newly forged from the merger of the two rivals was to grow into a commercial and political entity of extraordinary power and influence, and the event is as noteworthy to British history as the Act of Union itself. Although other countries possessed East India Companies, it was to be the contribution of the British Company to establish an empire. This began with the death of Aurangzeb – that other momentous event of 1707 – but only manifested itself properly in 1717 when the Mughal authorities, in disarray after the passing of the emperor, granted the Company minor territorial rights; these would prove a useful springboard later. In the short-term the anarchy into which India slowly descended encouraged the new and now 'Honourable' East India Company to increase its sepoy forces in defence of its own interests as they came under threat. This military capacity ashore soon far exceeded the corresponding naval might of the Bombay Marine – which was escorting Mughal vessels bound to Jeddah on the annual *haj* – and would in turn serve the Company's aggrandisement very well, but for the time being trade-protection in Indian waters meant rather more than the guarding of privileges and the prosecuting of legal suits in England.[9]

For many years commerce in the Indian Ocean had suffered from piracy. As has been mentioned, English policies created a piratical migration from the West Indies into the Indian Ocean where it combined with local enmities arising from the disintegration of the Mughal Empire. Simultaneously local chieftains took to the sea, happily raiding any ships owned by the European nations, with little or no fear of reprisals. One Arab fleet ousted the Portuguese from Mombasa and settled at Muscat. They also threatened Gombroon (Bandar Abbas), compelling the despatch of the Indiaman *Nassau* to act as a guard-ship for the town. But in the last years of Aurangzeb's reign these indigenous sea-rovers were joined by the newcomers at Madagascar where the rogues displaced from the Antilles had settled. Others made indiscriminate raids upon trade mounted from the Mascarene Islands, chiefly Mauritius, which until 1710 when it was taken over by the French East India Company and renamed Île de France, was held by the Dutch.[10] The Dutch, though again close to England with the accession of William III, nevertheless cynically manipulated the troubles of the Old Company in the closing years of the seventeenth century by suggesting to the Mughal emperor that the English specialised in piracy. Alas, the malicious assertion was not entirely untrue, not least because it arose in part from within the Company itself.

In 1690 the crew of the Country-ship *Unity*, led by a man named John Gilliam, rose and seized their own ship, cruising piratically for some time. Then in 1696 in Bombay the crews of the Company ketch *Josiah* and the Indiamen *Mocha* plotted mutiny. One weakness from which the Company suffered at this time was in the quality of its seamen. A lack of man-power caused indiscriminate recruitment, and often a preference for Europeans rather than lascars, meant inviting vipers into a ship. This had been the case in these two vessels. Having stolen the *Josiah*, her new masters' cruise was short. With most of them ashore in the Nicobar Islands, the two-man anchor-watch discovered neither of them was eager to turn pirate and, cutting the cable, they made sail, bringing the ship into Aceh road from where she was soon afterwards returned to Bombay.

Equally unwisely, but probably unwittingly, Captain Leonard Edgecumbe of the *Mocha* had signed-on some former pirates. When the ship was off Aceh the mutineers rose, seized the arms-chest and killed Edgecumbe. Twenty-seven officers and loyal hands were cast adrift in a boat and left to their fate. The *Mocha* now began a three-year cruise, taking numerous vessels in eastern waters under the self-styled 'Captain' Culliford. In 1697 the *Satisfaction*, Captain Willocks, was captured by the *Mocha* and her tender, a captured vessel called the *Charming Mary*. After being rifled, the *Satisfaction* was released, but Willocks was obliged to remain as a pilot to the pirates. He was eventually released when his services were dispensed with. Later that year the *Mocha,* now renamed *Resolution*, attacked the Company's ship *Dorrill* in the Malacca Strait but was driven off after a fierce engagement lasting three hours. That year pirates also seized a Portuguese vessel on her way to Macao and plundered and sank an English-owned Country-ship named *Diamond*. Elsewhere, to rub salt into an open wound, the Company lost the *Dorothea* and the *Bedford*, both of which were captured by a French man-of-war. The latter was afterwards redeemed by her owner,

Richard Dorrill, and sold on to Sir Henry Gore (who recommissioned her into the Company's service only to lose her off Mauritius in 1703 in a cyclone). Unfortunately, the Peace of Ryswick that ended hostilities with the French in September 1697 did not stop piracy: it was now rampant.

The pirates' base at Madagascar sat athwart the route out from London, command-ing the Mozambique Channel where, in the adjacent Comoro Islands, India-bound vessels stopped to take on board 'wood and water'. It was upon these shores that groups of outlaws settled in some style, bringing with them from the Caribbean a rough, fraternal democracy enshrined in Libertalia on the island's northern tip. This, however, was only limited to themselves: 'These pirates, unexpectedly elevated to the dignity of petty princes, and being destitute of honourable principle, used their power with the most wanton barbarity.' The indigenous population of Madagascar were:

> ...divided into small nations ... who carry on a continual war with each other. The prisoners taken in war are either rendered slaves to the conquerors, sold, or slain according to pleasure. When the pirates first settled among them, their alliance was much courted ... and those whom they joined were always successful in their wars, the natives being ignorant of the use if firearms... By these means they in a little time became very formidable, and the prisoners whom they took in war they employed in cultivating the ground, and the most beautiful of the women they married ... as many as they could conveniently maintain. The natural result was, they separated, each choosing a convenient place for himself, where he lived ... surrounded by his wives, slaves, and dependants. Nor was it long before jarring interests excited them also to draw the sword against each other... Thus like scoundrels they lived...

It was a lifestyle not without its attractions to desperate men deracinated by civil war, the excesses of judicial suppression in the wake of Monmouth's rebellion, as well as religious conflict in Europe. Woodes Rogers had given them a scare when he arrived in the *Delicia* of forty guns on a slaving expedition earlier in the century but many remained and remained active, acquiring a taste for the easy pickings of passing India-bound vessels with forays further north, along the Malabar coast and into the Arabian seas where they also engaged in trade as the mood suited them. They had little to fear from anyone and grew emboldened.

Ranging up into the Red Sea, the freebooters intercepted Mughal vessels and proved such a curse that the Emperor Aurangzeb suspended trade with the English until he had arranged for their armed protection of his ships, mentioned previously. This did not put an end to the matter, as we have seen. In 1695 John Avery, in company with two other vessels, fell upon Aurangzeb's own *Ganj-i-Salwai* as she bore pilgrims to Jeddah for the overland trek to Mecca. Avery took a booty which was estimated to have realised £325,000. He then 'freed the ship ... without torturing the people; but carried a young Mogul lady with him, and some of her servants, who had been at Mecca,' causing a major affront to the imperial dignity. The Company's president at Surat, Mr Annersley, was beside himself as he and forty other Englishmen were thrown into prison to protect them from an angry mob. The Governor of Bombay, Sir John Gayer, attempted to temporise, only to be told that: 'The English, Dutch and French should put to sea in search of the thieves.'

To support his raiding Avery intending transferring his base to Perim, in the Strait of Bab-el-Mandeb at the entrance to the Red Sea, but after digging through rock and finding no water the project was abandoned and Avery withdrew to Madagascar. Others soon afterwards arrived in the area, one vicious party attacking a Bombay-owned Country-ship laden with Arab steeds bound for Surat. She was commanded by an Englishman named Sawbridge who so irritated the pirates with his protests against their actions that they sewed up his mouth. Having plundered the ship the pirates set her on fire, horses and all, and landed Sawbridge and his crew near Aden where, soon afterwards, Sawbridge died.

Further outrages followed by boldly 'flying English colours' Avery placed a large price upon his head, laid there by both the Lord Chief Justice of England and the Court of Directors. But at this point Avery – 'a man with more cunning than courage' – had vanished and the commitment of three of the Company's armed cruisers to the escort of Mughal ships from Jeddah to Surat in March 1698 eased the animosity between the Company and Aurangzeb.[11] It also deterred Captain William Kidd, who had now arrived in the Red Sea, from attacking a convoy.

William Kidd had originally been furnished with a Letter-of-Marque, along with a privateering commission to root-out pirates in Madagascar plus powers of Reprisal to attack the French. He commanded the *Adventure Galley*, a fast vessel of thirty guns and about seventy men. On his passage he spoke with Commodore Warren, then in the South Atlantic with a squadron of four men-of-war protecting the trade north of St Helena. Kidd arrived at Madagascar in February 1697 and began searching for his quarry without success and with diminishing stores. The *Adventure* was foul and in need of repair and he borrowed money to acquire stores from some Frenchmen in the Comoros. He also seems to have increased his gang to about 'two hundred men', probably by recruiting disaffected pirates resident among the islands, which may explain his sudden change of heart. Kidd encountered several Indiamen in the offing but did not molest them, sailing north for the Red Sea, to land at Perim.

Here, in January 1698, Kidd seems to have undergone a diabolical conversion, suborning his men who seemed nothing loathe to consent 'to go on account', a euphemism meaning to turn pirate. Despatching a boat across the strait towards the Yemeni coast he gained intelligence of 'fourteen or fifteen ships, ready to sail, some with English, some with Dutch, and some with Moorish colours' all lying at Mocha. As the convoy came south through the Strait of Bab-el-Mandeb, Kidd attacked. The *Adventure* had a brief encounter with the Indiaman *Sceptre*, of which Edward Barlow was first mate, but a Dutch man-of-war escorting the convoy bore down to engage and Kidd escaped. Kidd now withdrew to cruise on the Malabar coast where he took an Arab vessel from Aden, torturing her English master, Captain Parker, and his Portuguese comprador. Kidd now embarked on raids on coastal shipping in the course of which he murdered his own gunner, Moore, in a fit of temper. Later, taking water, his cooper was killed by the local inhabitants; Kidd landed, burnt their houses and executed one prisoner.

His next interception was the *Quedah Merchant*, a 400-ton Mughal ship from Surat in which a Mughal *vizier* had an interest and which an Englishman named Wright commanded. Robbing her Armenian supercargoes and passengers, trading her cargo and dumping her crew ashore, Kidd now took her over and manned both his ships 'principally by crews of Europeans'. Taking both vessels back to Madagascar he fell in with Culliford in the *Resolution*, the former *Mocha*. The two men conceived an alliance of sorts and Kidd abandoned the worn-out *Adventurer* in favour of the staunchly teak-built *Quedah Merchant*. Then, though weakened by desertions, Kidd sailed east towards Amboina, concocting a complicated plan by which means, by virtue of stolen documents, his original commission and the influence he flattered himself he commanded at court, he thought to escape the consequences of his actions. To this end he returned in due course to New York where he thought his fortune would purchase him further friends. In his imagination 'all would be hushed, and that justice would but wink at him'.

In Kidd's absence, faced with innumerable horrid predations in what Sir John Gayer thought of as the Company's preserves, the Governor of Bombay had not been idle. Desperately Gayer wrote home for help, pleading the assistance of the Royal Navy, while on 1 January 1699, Aurangzeb, who 'attributed the piracies to the English,' placed guards on the English, French and Dutch factories at Surat. Gayer, meanwhile, had ordered the Company's ships in Bombay prepared for a service and a few days later the Company's yacht *Benjamin* arrived with despatches.[12] Comforted by their contents, Gayer accordingly embarked himself, sailing north to Surat in the *Benjamin*, with the HCSs *Mary* and *Thomas*, and the ketch *Josiah* – now restored to her rightful owners. On arrival at Swally on 11 January he informed Aurangzeb that he could not guarantee to defeat the pirates, but that the Company's squadron would protect a convoy to Mocha and that His Majesty's Government were despatching a squadron of warships from England. After some negotiations Gayer secured the freeing of the beleaguered factories and, in concert with the French and Dutch representatives, signed a bond of security against any future losses caused by the pirates. Gayer then sent both Company cruisers and Indiamen along the Malabar coast on an offensive sweep.

Gayer's intervention was made in the nick of time, for an impatient and affronted Aurangzeb had just issued an order 'for putting a final embargo on the trade of all Europeans in his dominions'. This he now reversed. Nor had the other trading nations been idle and all three put up large bonds while men-of-war from each were assigned a station. A Dutch squadron of three vessels was to cover the Mocha trade, the French would stand guarantee for the Persian Gulf and the English were entrusted with 'what were termed the Southern Indian Seas'.

In response to Gayer's intelligence the English Government had in the meanwhile passed an act against piracy. The English squadron charged with sweeping Indian seas clear of pirates was that of Commodore Warren's, which consisted of four men-of-war,

HMSs *Anglesea* and *Harwich*, each of forty-eight guns, the *Hastings* of thirty-four and the twenty-gun *Lizard*. In an attempt to end the business at a stroke the Government had offered a free pardon to all pirates who turned themselves in by the end of April 1699, who had perpetrated their crimes east of the Cape of Good Hope, and south of a line between Socotra and Cape Comorin. Warren bore authority to accept submission but two names were expressly excepted from this amnesty: those of John Avery and William Kidd.

Warren was only partially successful: for piracy was never long absent from these waters. Nevertheless Culliford's *Mocha* surrendered to him off Madagascar, though their initial insurrection told against them and fourteen of her crew were clapped in irons. Brought home they were afterwards tried in London and hanged beside the Thames in 1701. Kidd too was repatriated from New York where, far from friends, he had found only enemies. Many of his former crew, mostly those who ran from him in Madagascar, turned King's evidence in exchange for pardons. Kidd, among several others, was arraigned at an Admiralty Sessions held at the Old Bailey in 1701 on charges of piracy and the murder of the gunner, Moore: he was condemned to death.

> Wherefore, about a week after, Capt. Kidd, Nicholas Churchill, James How, Gabriel Loff, Hugh Parrot, Abel Owen, and Darby Mullins, were executed at the Execution Dock, and afterwards hung up in chains, at some distance from each other, down the river, where their bodies hung exposed for a long period.

Although the desiccating corpses of Kidd and his ilk hung in their riverside gibbets long after the passing of the old century, they were far distant from the Indian Ocean and within a few months hostilities had again broken out. While the War of the Spanish Succession drenched the fields of Europe in blood, it disrupted trade very little in these distant seas, but the preoccupation of naval forces with grand strategy in the Mediterranean and the Caribbean withdrew what small forces had been deployed in the east. Warren had died and been succeeded by Commodore Littleton who became embroiled in 'unseemly disputes' with the Company's officials. The *Harwich* had been wrecked off the Chinese coast and Littleton was now summoned home. Disdaining the traders, Littleton's ships:

> …had done nothing to suppress the pirates, and had returned home with cargoes of private goods … the Indian seas, therefore, had been left with no other defence than what the guns of the Company's ships could afford…[13]

The war, of course, destroyed the co-operation that had briefly pertained among trading competitors on the Indian littoral who now found themselves enemies. All this created conditions on the high seas in which piracy again flourished, for there yet remained the pirate colonies on the Malagasy coast.

Among the vessels passing Madagascar were those newly admitted to the trade, the privately owned Separate-Stock vessels which enjoyed no protection. Moreover, one of the reasons these ships were so resented by the East India Companies, Old and New, and by the new United Company after amalgamation, was because their presence and conduct in Travancore, Peshwa, Gaikwar and Scind proved troublesome. Their presence acted as a lure for pirates while their conduct in trading – not always with the requisite rectitude – upset the delicate stability between the Company's factors, native traders, local chiefs and the shipping of all parties: the European East India Companies, the Persians, Mughals and Arabs.

The vulnerability of these vessels and the effect of their capture were remarked upon in March 1703 by the Old Company's Council at Surat.

> [W]hile such ships are permitted to come out … the pirates [will not] want fresh ships while they can so easily be supplied with theirs… They have long since taken the *Speaker* and *Prosperous*…

A Captain Leckie had just arrived in the '*Constant Friend*, a private subscription [i.e. a Separate-Stock ship] of about 250 tons…' Leckie had a cargo worth £4,000 to trade and had already called at Aceh. After Surat the *Constant Friend* was going to Gombroon and Basra but Leckie reported a narrow escape from pirates off the Madagascan coast. The two private ships *Speaker* and *Prosperous* had, as the Council noted, become pirate ships. The *Speaker* had been taken some years earlier by a gang under 'Captain' John Bowen. In 1700 she was on the Malabar coast.

> The pirates here met with no manner of inconveniences in carrying on their designs, for it was made so much a trade, that the merchants of one town never scrupled the buying commodities taken from another, though but ten miles distant, in a public sale: furnishing the robbers … with all the necessaries, even of vessels…

Among Bowen's prizes was another free-trader, the Separate-Stock ship *Borneo*, Captain Conoway, which he had taken off Caliquilon, Travancore, on her way from Bengal. Bowen quickly disposed of her cargo and sailed south. Heading for Madagascar, the *Speaker* ran into heavy weather which drove her to leeward and, 'being negligent in their steering,' she ran aground on St Thomas's reef off Mauritius and was lost. Bowen and most of his men made it ashore.

> They met here [Mauritius] with all the civility and good treatment imaginable. Bowen was complimented in a particular manner by the [Dutch] governor, and splendidly entertained in his house; the sick men were put, with great care, into the fort, and cured by their doctor, and no supplies of any sort, wanting for the rest. They spent here three months, but yet resolving to set down at Madagascar, they bought a sloop, which they converted into a brigantine, and about the middle of March 1701, departed, having first taken formal leave of the governor, by making a present of two thousand five hundred pieces of eight; leaving him with the wreck of their ship, with the guns, stores, and everything else that was saved. The governor, on his part,

supplied them with necessaries for their voyage ... and gave them a kind invitation to make that island a place of refreshment in the course of their future adventures, promising that nothing should be wanting to them that his government afforded.

Finding 'a fruitful plain' on the side of a river on the east side of the Malagasy coast Bowen's crew laid up their brigantine and took the remainder of the year to establish a fort and settlement at Maritan. After a while, however, they 'became dissatisfied with their new situation, having a hankering mind after their old employment'. They had begun refitting their little vessel when providence offered them a better. Into the bay in the New Year, in quest of wood and water, sailed the *Speedy Return* and the *Content*. Both of these vessels were Scottish, owned by the Dairen Company and commanded by Captains Robert Drummond and Alexander Stewart respectively. Drummond had been slaving and was deceived by the appearance of Maritan, coming ashore with Andrew Wilky, his surgeon. Bowen, meanwhile, put off in a boat on the pretence of purchasing some goods from the *Speedy Return*, boarded her with his boat's crew and, accosting the mate, produced small arms and seized the ship.

> The surprise was sudden ... Bowen ... burnt the Dutch brigantine ... cleaned and fitted the [*Speedy Return*] ... took water, provisions, and what necessaries were wanting, and made ready for new adventures.

Having cruised unsuccessfully off the Mascarene Islands, Bowen returned to Madagascar where he encountered a Captain Howard with whom he made an alliance.

Howard had meanwhile made himself master of the *Prosperous*, which was part-owned by Thomas Bowrey, owner of the ill-fated *Worcester*. She had fallen foul of 'Captain' Thomas Howard off the Comoro Islands. Howard was a lighterman's son and merchant sailor who had gone to the bad in the West Indies, deserting his ship and with twenty confederates stealing a turtling schooner. Gradually increasing the size of their vessel by turning over from one capture to another and recruiting their number as they went, the gang was soon raiding the coast of Virginia under a rogue named James. When a man-of-war appeared on the coast they made for Guinea 'where they took a great number of ships of many nations, all of which they rifled...' In due course they attacked and captured a Portuguese man-of-war of thirty-eight guns, 'carried her in shore, and ripped off her upper deck, made her deep-waisted, by cutting down some of her gunnel. This prize they named the *Alexander*.' Forcing into their company 'carpenters, caulkers and surgeons' their hellish progress continued round the Cape of Good Hope until they ran aground in the Comoros where Howard and a few others deserted, heading for Madagascar itself. Hereabouts for some months Howard and others engaged in acts of savagery and deception until:

> ...the *Prosperous*, a ship of thirty-six guns, commanded by Capt. Hilliard, came in, which Howard and some other pirates (with the assistance of the Boatswain and some of the crew belonging to the ship) seized. In taking this ship the captain and

his chief mate were killed, and several others wounded. Howard was by the company declared captain. Several of the ship's crew took on with them…

Having doubled the island, 'they found some of the *Speaker's* company [men left at Maritan], whom they took on board, and made up their complement, about seventy men.' Howard then embroiled his crew in a war with a settled Dutch pirate after which he declined to fight a powerful Dutch East Indiaman and finally fell in with Bowen himself 'about Christmas 1702' off Mayotta.

The conjoined gangs now took the free-trader *Pembroke* as she came into the anchorage for water on 10 March 1703. Swarming aboard, the pirates took the ship, killing the mate and plundering her. Having removed Captain Woolley (also referred to as Whaley) to use as a pilot they let the *Pembroke* go under her second mate, the two crews falling out over which ship Woolley should be confined aboard. With their dispute settled, the two ships separated to reprovision, careen and prepare for a joint venture, meeting in due course off Surat. Here they harried local trade, Bowen in the *Speedy Return* going in chase of a:

> Moorish ship of seven hundred tons, bound from the Gulf of Mocha to Surat. The pirates brought the prize into Rajapora [sic] … where they plundered her; the merchandise they sold to the natives; but a small sum of current gold … amounting to £22,000 they put into their pockets.

Their capture had been owned by Abdul Ghafur who had been trading in Arab horses. Off Surat Howard seized a second prize from which they took 'the best of her cargo, the most valuable of which was 84,000 sequins, a piece of about ten shillings each, and then they let her drift…' Having decided to transfer into one of the captured vessels, the *Prosperous* and *Speedy Return* were burnt. At Rajapur they mustered:

> …one hundred and sixty four fighting men; forty three only were English, the greater number French, the rest Danes, Swedes, and Dutch. They took on board seventy Indians to do the drudgery of the ship, and mounted fifty six guns, calling her the *Defiance*, and sailed from Rajapora the latter end of October, in the year 1703, to cruise on the coast of Malabar.

Proceeding to reprovision at Cochin they were informed by a Dutch merchant to whom they had previously sold plundered goods that a local-ship named the *Rhimae* lay not far away in Mud Bay. Here, meanwhile, 'people from the [Dutch] factory flocked aboard every hour, and dealt with them as in open market, for all sorts of merchandise, refreshments, jewels, and plate, returning with coffers of money…' The pirates decided against attacking the *Rhimae* on account of the uncertain depth in Mud Bay and the failing health of Woolley, whom they here released. Soon afterwards they sailed, again falling in with the *Pembroke*, which having been loaded with a cargo of sugar at Madras was on passage to Surat. They plundered her afresh before Bowen made for Mauritius and, presumably, a warm welcome from the dissembling Dutch governor. Howard appears to have remained on the coast of Travancore, where he 'retired among the natives … married a woman of the country and being a morose, ill-natured fellow, and using her ill, was murdered by her relations'. In Mauritius Bowen died in retirement and was 'buried in the highway, for the priest would not allow him holy ground…'

Bowen and Howard were not the only pirates active in the Arabian Sea. Better known are the names of Avery and Kidd, but this yarn has been related at length for its wider significance in connection with the capture of the *Speedy Return*, its distant impact on the crew of the *Worcester*, and of events at Surat. Learning of the outrages on 31 August 1703, along with the collaboration of local factors, Colt, the new governor at Surat, was so enraged that he had several of them thrown into prison. Such was the inconvenience caused to several free English and Dutch vessels trading cargo at Swally Hole that their masters turned their guns on the port. Colt was compelled to climb down, another humiliation of the East India Company by free-traders.[14]

For those in Surat responsible for protecting trade the nightmare went on. Gayer had been placed under confinement by the Mughals until piracy was extirpated. Two ships, the *Severn* and *Scarborough*, were fitted out as men-of-war with 'Captain Richards, formerly in the Company's service, being appointed Commodore with instructions to cruise between Madagascar and Mocha, and to convoy the Mocha fleet thence to Surat…' Indeed Company resources were stretched thin as the Marathas, Beluchis and Mekranis poured into the vacuum left after the death of Aurangzeb. Bombay was threatened and the Company's seamen were drafted out of its Maritime Service and into its Marine. Elsewhere even the free-traders like Alexander Hamilton, with consignments of cargo worth £10,000, were obliged to mount operations ashore to deliver trade-goods to their destinations. In secret alliance with the Marathas, the Portuguese began to reassert their power and Surat was effectively invested. Plundering of vessels continued with Arab pirates building their ships in Pegu and thereafter infesting the Bay of Bengal, notwithstanding the arrival of a small naval squadron, which proved ineffectual.[15]

There were now four factions competing for mastery of the waters surrounding the Indian subcontinent: the Europeans, led by the British; the Marathas, the Mughals and the Arabs. In the case of the last three, all could muster fleets of some size and in 1715 a powerful Arab squadron 'kept all the sea coast in awe from Cape Comorin to the Red Sea'. The most dangerous, however, was the Maratha squadron under Kanhoji Angrey who by dint of ability had risen from seaman to *Surhail*, or grand admiral of the Maratha fleet. He was to dominate the Konkan coast – of which he was named viceroy – which stretched south from Bombay beyond Goa to Karwar and Mangalore. It consisted of rocky promontories and indented bays, with the estuaries of rivers descending from the Western Ghats providing anchorage and careenage, often protected by offshore islands. It was in marked contrast with the palm-lined sands of the Malabari coast further south, providing numerous rocky promontories upon no few of which impregnable fortresses, such as that at Gheriah, had been raised. Gheriah, massively reinforced by Kanhoji Angrey, together with the off-lying island of Malwan, lay 200 miles south of Bombay, centrally commanding the Konkan coast and its coastwise shipping.

It is, as John Keay points out, 'a peculiarly English conceit' to regard as pirates legitimate local sovereign rulers on India's west coast 'who maintained a squadron of fighting ships' to secure their coasts and trade.[16] Although the Mughals had engaged the East India Company to protect Mughal shipping, this had led the Company's servants to arrogate to themselves an assumption that John Company was *the* local naval power. As the Mughal writ waned, the smaller feudatories took charge of their own affairs. Such was the Maratha fleet under Kanhohi Angrey. 'One man's pirate is another man's patriot; in Maratha eyes the worst offenders were undoubtedly those ships which flew the Company's flag' not just because the English – and they were still largely English – vessels disdained to seek or pay for Angrey's *dastak*, or passports, but because men like Kidd and his successors – not to mention interlopers – had flown something approximating it and, as the Dutch were constantly saying, piracy was endemic amongst the English.[17]

Angrey's career was to be long and he had begun it in 1710 by possessing the island of Khanderi, not far from Bombay, but protected by extensive shallows. That year his *grabs* had engaged the *Godolphin* for two days, during which time Captain John Ap-Rice had driven them off, though his ship was so badly damaged that she was condemned when she arrived at Bombay.[18] Angrey struck again in November 1712, the ketch *Anne*, on her way in a small convoy from Karwar to Bombay, was taken by four *grabs*.[19] Among the prisoners was Katherine Chown, a young, pregnant woman widowed for the second time during the action.[20]

Off Goa in December 1712 two Angrian *grabs* manoeuvred against the outbound Indiamen *Somers*, Captain Eustace Peacocke, and *Grantham*, Captain Jonathan Collett. The two ships were becalmed, so hoisted out their boats and sent them to counter-attack the *grabs*. After an exchange of fire the *grabs* made off, making Angrey wary of engaging the Company's ships in future.

In the face of this perceived effrontery, an attempt to raise an Anglo-Portuguese expedition to attack Angrey at Colaba failed because the Portuguese were luke-warm, preferring to respect Maratha rights, and because the gravid Widow Chown lay there in Angrey's clutches, if not his arms. Instead a Company officer was sent to open negotiations. Discovering Mrs Chown possessed of her virtue but in a state of near naked disarray 'the Scots lieutenant well named Mackintosh' wrapped her up.[21] Following Katherine Chown's ransom a truce was arranged between Angrey and the Company, the latter undertaking to ensure that only British ships would wear the Company's ensign.

This, of course, was impossible to enforce, not least because the Company's striped, 'grid-iron' ensign was easily confused with the plain red ensign and either – or both – were a great convenience and a handy disguise. With Indian, Company and Anglo-Indian free-traders all notionally 'English', only chaos could ensue, which it did, though the pettifogging Company officials smoothed the difficulties – at least in their own legalistic imaginations – by asserting that the flag covered the cargo. Thus any vessel carrying a cargo consigned in any way under the Company's auspices was inviolate, and certificates were issued to any ship sailing from Bombay possessing any connection with the Company's trade. When they were intercepted by Angrey's forces and their Maratha *dastaks* were demanded, the Company's passports were airily waved, the Maratha duties were refused and British 'rights' claimed. Though much was made of Maratha infamy at the time, the Company method could scarcely be called an 'honourable' practice.

Nevertheless, Charles Boone, the new governor of Bombay, was now confronted with a serious decline in the Company's position and the parlous state of its affairs. With the random piracies of Arabs, Gujaratis and the home-grown renegades from Madagascar, threats to the Company's factories the length of the coast combining with an increasingly hostile Maratha force at sea under Kanhoji Angrey, Boone determined to put Bombay in a state of defence, building a circumvallation. Pleading for recruits from as far away as England he also decided to strengthen the Company's sea-power, laying down two armed vessels in Surat. These, the *Britannia*, eighteen guns, and the *Fame*, sixteen guns, were built in six months and commissioned with joint complements of 260 men, a company of marines each, and placed under the command of Captains Weeks and Passwater respectively. While these were building in the north, in Konkan waters, Angrey took four Indian vessels laded by the Company, and attacked the British Country-ship *President*. The Maratha *grabs* were beaten off with heavy losses to them, leaving eleven dead and thirty wounded among the *President*'s people. The subsequent flurry of indignation and recrimination between all the injured and aggrieved parties rumbled on for some time.

Once commissioned, the *Britannia* and *Fame* carried out a sweep along the coast, intermittently skirmishing with a few of Angrey's *grabs* and arriving at Bombay amid the thunder of saluting guns between the ships and the castle. Here, meanwhile, Boone had ordered more tonnage: twenty *grabs* and *gallivats*. He had also had built the armed sloop *Defiance*, Captain Matthews, and the 'escort and guard ship' *Victory* of twenty-four guns. Boone's actions placed the Bombay Marine on a proper footing, providing for its finances – in excess of £51,000 *per annum* – but he had yet to appoint a senior officer. Hitherto the Bombay Marine had consisted of only one thirty-two-gun armed ship, four heavy 'grab-ships, mounting between 20 and 28-guns, and twenty *grabs* and *gallivats* armed with between 5 and 12-guns'. None of the officers at Boone's disposal were suitable to serve as commodore.

In selecting a senior officer for this new force Boone chose Captain Alexander Hamilton. No longer a young man, Hamilton had spent thirty years in eastern waters, rising by dint of cheek and intelligence to a position of influence, commanding and owning Country-ships, a free-trader who was among the first to have enjoyed the pleasures of Thailand, roistered at Whampoa and knew all that there was to know about trading among the Mergui islands or with the Bugis of the Sulu Sea. 'How,' Keay asks, 'a private trader, renowned for his outspoken criticism of the Company and cordially detested by its factors from Gombroon to Canton, came by the command of its Bombay fleet is something of a mystery,' but perhaps the answer lay in recent events.

In the previous year, 1716, the Gujerati Sangarians based at Beyt, in the Gulf of Kutch, learned of the British Country-ship *Morning Star* passing between Gombroon and Surat with a valuable cargo on the Company's account. Accordingly the *Morning Star* was ambushed by a large force of eight vessels and 'about two thousand men' intending to overwhelm the *Morning Star*'s British officers and their lascar crew. The intermittent fight lasted two days, but the *Morning Star* escaped, though leaving twenty-four Indian merchants in the hands of the Sangarians from whom they had to be ransomed for £600. The ship's master and owner was Alexander Hamilton.

> Belying his years, the Captain had shown great courage and resourcefulness in dis-
> engaging from them and it was presumably news of this action which commended
> him to the Bombay Council as a doughty commander. He was promptly engaged at
> eighty rupees a month...[22]

By now the state of the besieged factories was critical. These had proliferated as trade had increased and stretched from Cambay in the north to Anjengo in the south. As the political anarchy grew and military raids increased along the coast, many had been attacked or surrounded and, at Anjengo, most of the English had been barba-rously killed.[23] Angrey, with a fleet of ten *grabs* of up to 400 tons and thirty guns, and fifty *gallivats* some of 120 tons and mounting four to ten guns, now effectively com-manded the Konkan coast. He had little trouble recruiting. 'Animated by a lust for plunder, there now flocked to his standard numerous adventurers, including renegade Christians, mostly Dutch and Portuguese, Arabs, Mussulmen and Negroes, a most daring and desperate band'.[24]

Deciding that Karwar must first be relieved owing to the situation of the factory some distance from the sea which rendered it 'nothing but a genteel prison', Boone ordered Hamilton and the new squadron of the Marine to relieve it. As soon as the monsoon moderated in the autumn, Hamilton's force arrived offshore where:

> The seas run so high ... that there was great difficulty in landing in the teeth of
> an enemy, who had ten times our numbers, so that the first attempt at landing was
> unsuccessful by our men's neglect and disobedience to the orders ... and about four
> score of our bravest fellows were cut off, and some taken prisoners; but, about six
> weeks after, we had some revenge on the enemy in an engagement on the side of a
> hill... We were in daily expectation of more forces ... but we harassed the enemy at
> night in burning villages ... and at sea we took some vessels laden with salt going to
> the enemy, and three ships ... coming from Arabia with horses... However, when
> our reinforcements came, we could muster in our fleet, of seamen and soldiers, two
> thousand two hundred and fifty men. The enemy raised on the strand some batter-
> ies to hinder our landing, and we took two of the prizes ... and laid them ashore
> at high water to batter their batteries, and keep the enemy at a distance with their

great shot, till our men were landed and drawn up. Each of our floating batteries
were covered with [the armed ships]. When all was ready, we landed [all our men]
… without the least hindrance … for they were preparing to flee to the woods;
but our … land-officers were so long in drawing up of their men in a confounded
hollow square, that the enemy took courage, and, with horse and foot, came running
towards our men, firing and wounding some as they marched in their ranks, which
our Commandant seeing pulled off his red coat and vanished. Some other as valiant
soldiers followed, and threw down their arms. We lost in this skirmish about two
hundred and fifty, but our floating batteries would not permit the enemy to pursue
far, nor durst they stay to gather up our scattered arms, so about eighty sailors went
on the field of battle, and brought on board the Commodore [Hamilton's *Victory*]
about two hundred stand of arms, most of them loaded. However, the enemy had
some loss too, for we found eleven dead horses, and saw many fires along the foot of
the hills to burn their dead…[25]

It was almost a disaster; only the seamen from the Bombay Marine had prevented
a complete débâcle. The two sides drew apart and, using an intermediary, a Seid
friendly to both, ten days later 'peace was proclaimed on best terms for both parties'.
But Hamilton had had enough. On top of the Company's military officers, who had
behaved cravenly, he disliked the self-serving and arrogant conduct of the Company's
local factors which, he considered, did little for relations with the Indians with whom
he – and most of the locally based and established interlopers – necessarily enjoyed
good relations. After the expedition to Karwar he resigned to resume the more con-
genial life of a free-trader. He had held his commission scarcely six months.

In the last months of 1717 Angrey's vessels seized the richly laden *Success*. Built
for the East India Company's own account, the *Success* had made two voyages from
England under Captain Thomas Clapham. By now, however, she was engaged
in the cross-trade between Bombay, Mocha and Surat, owned or chartered to the
Company's Indian agent at Surat. Angrey also waylaid and plundered at gun-point
another Company ship, though he desisted from carrying her off, thus demonstrating that he paid a good deal more attention to his agreements than his opponents.
However, when the reports of Angrey's latest 'piracies' reached Bombay it inflamed
Governor Boone and his Council.

An alarmed Boone sent the usual written protest: 'Let the bottom [i.e. ship] be
whose it will, the money lent on it is worth more than the ship and the goods [in her]
are English, [as] you well know'. That might be the case Kanhoji Angrey responded,
'but tomorrow Your Excellency will say that you intend to freight fifty or an hundred
ships of Surat merchants. If so, what occasion do they have to take the *dastak* that they
formerly took off me'. Angrey raided Bombay harbour where he seized an innocent
grab to make his point that: 'From this day forward, what God gives, I shall take'. But
time was passing and Boone was impatient. The new season approached, and with it
the arrival of 'the fleet' from England. God forbid that it should fall into the hands of
Angrey! As Hamilton's force returned from Karwar, new plans were laid. The soldiers

available to Boone were a mixed bunch, composed of steady sepoy infantry under regular Company officers, with additional 'sentinels' raised from the commercial population of European merchants, their partners, Company 'writers' and counting house clerks. Mostly bachelors, these volunteered in some numbers under the persuasion of alcohol, bonuses and the attractions of the mess life. Depending upon social status some of these gentlemen were given Company commissions and assumed the ranks of field-officers for which they had not the slightest aptitude, a fact that went some way to explain Hamilton's failure and his own contempt for them. As for the seaborne assets, the battered *Success* was turned into an armed ship, the other vessels were assembled and a man was sought to carry Boone's designs into effect.

In April 1718, just before the onset of the strong south-west monsoon in May but after Angrey had withdrawn most of his vessels into his refuge at Gheriah for the Indian equivalent of 'winter-quarters', Boone decided to attack. Given the concentration of the Maratha fleet in the river estuary under the rampart of the fortress and behind a boom protected in turn by the out-work of Malwan Island, Boone's offensive looked promising. But it was hurried and ill-organised. In the face of the natural obstacles and the quality of the troops it scarcely needed the hostility of an enemy to confound it. The Bombay squadron, led by a certain Commodore Berlew, proceeded in considerable force, and on 11 April began operations against the fortifications. An attack by fire-ships and explosion vessels, one of which was called the *Terrible Bomb*, could not break the boom, while a landing party sent ashore to seize the landward end, struggled through a swamp where it was 'raked by fire' from the fortress. For a week Berlew's pressed Indiamen bombarded the place, but their broadsides lacked the weight of metal of men-of-war and the shoal water prevented them coming in close enough to have any effect at all. In the face of this the new commodore declared 'the place was impregnable'. After furious exertions and 'great loss' Berlew withdrew.

Another attack on Angrey's men at Khanderi made in October 1718 also failed, again through incompetence. Only ten miles from Bombay, the appearance of Angrey himself cut the Company's force off from seaward, whereupon it retreated ignominiously under the batteries of Bombay castle. A third attempt in 1719 was frustrated by a small Portuguese squadron that, instead of blockading the island, let boats pass while the landing party put ashore was driven off with bloody loss. It was all very half-hearted and humiliating, and it would have deterred a lesser man than Boone. In desperation and in consideration of the shallows, he ordered the construction of 'a great and mighty floating machine' named *The Phram* which was, 'by the nicest composition cannon-proof'. This monster mounted a dozen 48-pounder siege guns and, it followed that: 'It must of course prove of great service to us against any of those castles, which we could approach near enough to cannonade'.

In April 1720 Angrey, continuing to harry the coastal trade, captured the British Country-ship *Charlotte* after a defence in which the *Charlotte's* people emptied their powder magazine. The ship was carried under the guns of Gheriah and plundered. Boone, meanwhile, amid a multitude of troubles, was also playing host to a Captain Macrae who had arrived in July in a battered hulk with a tale of the loss of his

Indiaman to Malagasy pirates – as will be presently explained. In the meantime a separate raid was made on Angrey's stronghold by a force led by a Mr Walter Brown and consisting of the armed Country-ships *London* and *Candois*, with two other vessels, some *grabs* and *gallivats*, which succeeded in burning sixteen small vessels in the anchorage before being repulsed.

On their return they came in sight of two strange vessels, the pirate ships of which Macrae had given notice. Boone was now informed that these, which included the pirated Indiaman, were in the Arabian Sea. Incensed that Brown had done nothing against these, Boone commissioned Macrae to scour the coast for them, a circumstance that deprived the governor of proceeding against Gheriah until the following spring, by which time *The Phram* was ready. She disappointed all expectations, throwing her balls short and proving vulnerable to returned fire from the elevation of the embrasures of Gheriah. Maratha *grabs* threatened an attack on her and *The Phram* was withdrawn under the sluggish tow of a ship. Finally, when the *grabs* pressed forward the monster was set on fire, cut adrift and abandoned. Two of Angrey's *grabs* were likewise burned and with this as their only success the British force returned to Bombay its tail once again between its legs.

With Angrey's cruisers active, pirates in the offing, Bombay's trade compromised and the Company's factories everywhere in trouble – that at Gombroon being attacked by four thousand Beluchi horsemen – Boone was at his wit's end. Macrae's sweep had proved unsuccessful, as we shall see, though Boone received numerous reports of several vessels to the southward of Goa having been taken, along with protests of 'English' ships pillaging Portuguese and Dutch cargoes. Boone daily expected reinforcements from home, whither he had written a stream of increasingly desperate pleas. At last, while the Bombay Marine was retreating in humiliation from Gheriah, Commodore Thomas Mathews was on his way with a squadron of men-of-war. Hopes ran high in expectation: all would be well with a professional naval officer on hand to enforce matters. But although Mathews had discretionary orders to protect the trade of western India, his primary objective was the destruction of the buccaneers of the Malagasy coast. He had no idea, as he doubled the Cape of Good Hope, that the most vicious of these were eluding all attempts to catch them far to the north, in Indian waters.

The lawless settlers of Madagascar had continued to thrive on piracy and the East India Company had continued to suffer. On 20 July 1720, when on her maiden outward voyage the HCS *Cassandra*, commanded by Captain James Macrae, put into the anchorage off Joanna (Anjouan), a watering place in the Comoro Islands off the north-east coast of Madagascar. Here they joined an Ostend-flagged free-trader and another Indiaman, the HCS *Greenwich*, Captain Richard Kirby.

Shortly after Macrae anchored, the two Indiamen were approached by some canoes arriving from the adjacent island of Mayotta. The men in them claimed their ship, the *Indian Queen*, had run ashore when on passage from the Guinea cost towards the East Indies, and she was now undergoing repairs. The two commanders quickly realised the men were pirates sailing under Olivier de la Bouche. 'Captain Kirby and I,' Macrae reported later:

> ...concluding that it might be of great service to the East India Company to destroy such a nest of rogues, were ready to sail for that purpose on the 17th August, about eight o'clock in the morning, when we discovered two pirates standing into the bay... I immediately went on board the *Greenwich*, where they seemed very diligent in preparation for an engagement, and I left Captain Kirby with mutual promises of standing by each other.

Kirby and Macrae had also solicited the aid of the Ostender, 'of twenty-two guns' whose 'captain had promised heartily to engage with us'.

The two pirate ships were the *Victory* and *Fancy*, both of over thirty guns and carrying the gangs of the pirates England and Taylor.[26] Unfortunately for Macrae the wind was light, and in the pirates' favour, for having 'unmoored' Macrae made sail, finding it necessary to bring two of his boats 'a-head to tow me close to the *Greenwich*...' Kirby's ship, however, 'being open to a valley and a breeze, made the best of his way from me,' followed by the Ostend ship.

> About half-an-hour after twelve, I called several times to the *Greenwich* to bear down to our assistance, and fired a shot at him, but to no purpose, for though we did not doubt but he would join us because, when he got about a league from us he brought his ship to and looked on, yet both he and the Ostender basely deserted us, and left us engaged with barbarous and inhuman enemies, with their black and bloody flags hanging over us, without the least appearance of ever escaping, but to be cut to pieces... [N]ot withstanding their superiority, we engaged them both about three hours; during which time the biggest of them received some shot betwixt wind and water, which made her keep off a little to stop her leaks. The other endeavoured all she could to board us, by rowing with her oars, being within a ship's length of us above an hour; but ... we shot all her oars to pieces ... and by consequence saved out lives.
>
>   About four o'clock most of the officers and men posted on the quarterdeck-being killed and wounded, the largest ship [the *Fancy* under Taylor] making up to us with diligence, being still within a cable's length of us, often giving us a broadside, there being now no hopes of Captain Kirby coming to our assistance, we endeavoured to run ashore; and, though we drew four feet more of water than the pirate...he stuck on a higher ground ... so was disappointed a second time from boarding us. Here we had a more violent engagement than before: all my officers and most of my men behaved with unexpected courage; and, as we had a considerable advantage by having a broadside to his bow, we did him great damage; so, that had Captain Kirby come in then, I believe we should have taken both the vessels, for we had one of them sure; but the other pirate [England's *Victory*] (who was still firing at us,) seeing the *Greenwich* did not offer to assist us, supplied his consort with three boats full of

fresh men. About five in the evening the *Greenwich* stood clear away to sea, leaving us struggling hard for life, in the very jaws of death…

By this time, many of my men being killed, and no hopes left us of escaping being all murdered by enraged barbarous conquerors, I ordered all that could to get into the long-boat, under the cover of the smoke of our guns; so that, with what some did in boats, and others by swimming, most of us that were able got ashore by seven o'clock. When the pirates came aboard, they cut three of our wounded men to pieces. I with some of my people made what haste I could to King's town, twenty-five miles from us, where I arrived next day, almost dead with the fatigue and loss of blood, having been sorely wounded in the head by a musket ball.

Macrae was lucky to survive, for the hoisting of the piratical 'black flag' to indicate no allegiance was owed to a nation-state had been accompanied by the 'bloody flag' a red banner announcing that no quarter would be given and the attacked would have to fight or die. Clearly a man of resource, Macrae now had another stroke of luck. 'King's town' was the name given to the village on Joanna wherein the local chieftain dwelt. Here Macrae learned that Captains England and Taylor had offered a reward for his capture and, had not the local 'king and all his chief people' hated the pirates and been in Macrae's favour, this might well have delivered up the redoubtable commander into their hands. Instead Macrae caused a report that he had died of his wounds to be circulated, 'which much abated their fury'. He also learned the identity of the gangs' leader, Edward England, quondam mate of a West Indiaman. What followed is curious; an indication of the intimacy of the maritime community at the time, but also of the ease with which the harshness of a seaman's existence and the lasciviousness of life as an hedonistic outlaw so easily seduced men into piracy. Ten days later, largely recovered, hoping the pirates' malice was easing and having had some contact with them, Macrae:

…began to consider the dismal condition we were reduced to; being in a place where we had no hopes of getting a passage home, all of us in a manner naked, not having had time to bring with us either a shirt or a pair of shoes, except what we had on. Having obtained leave to go on board the pirates with a promise of safety, several of the chief of them knew me, and some of them had sailed with me, which I found to be of great advantage; because, notwithstanding their promise, some of them would have cut me to pieces, and all that would not enter with them [those of Macrae's men who would not join the pirates], had it not been for their chief captain, Edward England, and some others whom I knew. They talked of burning one of their ships, which we had so entirely disabled as to be no father useful to them, and to fit the *Cassandra* in her room. But in the end … they made me a present of the said shattered ship, which was Dutch-built, and called the *Fancy*; her burden was about three hundred tons. I procured also a hundred and twenty-nine bales of the Company's cloth, though they would not give me a rag of my own clothes.

Having rescued himself and most of his people - though he was obliged to leave 'some officers and men' as hostages with the pirates – Macrae now set about refitting the damaged *Fancy*. He reported the departure of England and Taylor in the *Victory* and *Cassandra* on 3 September, while, with incredible resource and labour, Macrae:

> ...with the jury masts, and such old sails as they left me, made a shift to do the like on the 8th together with forty-three of my ship's crew, including two passengers and twelve soldiers; having no more than five tuns of water aboard. After a passage of forty-eight days, I arrived here [at Bombay] on the 26th October, almost naked and starved, having been reduced to a pint of water a day, and almost in despair of ever seeing land, by reason of the calms we met with between the coast of Arabia and Malabar.
>
> We had in all thirteen men killed and twenty-four wounded; and we were told that we destroyed about ninety or a hundred of the pirates. When they left us, there were about three hundred whites and eighty blacks in both ships.

In his report to the Court of Directors, written at Bombay on 16 November 1720, Macrae did not mince words in explaining the loss of his ship, nor of his dutiful assiduity in looking after his employers' best interests:

> I am persuaded had our consort of the *Greenwich* done his duty, we had destroyed both of them, and got two hundred thousand pounds for our owners and selves; whereas the loss of the *Cassandra* may justly be imputed to his deserting us. I have delivered all the bales that were given to me into the company's warehouse, for which the governor and council have ordered me a reward.

Macrae's conduct had been of the highest order, both in respect of the Company and his crew. He had fought his ship with boldness and courage and sustained a head-wound. Despite the approbation of, and material reward by, Boone and the Council; and notwithstanding the apparent grandeur of his station as an East India commander, even now his circumstances were far from happy and his future uncertain. (How much more so the fates of those two score of men who survived with him.)

> Our governor, Mr Boon [sic], who is extremely kind and civil to me, had ordered me home with the packet; but Captain Harvey who had a prior promise, being come in with the fleet, goes in my room. The governor had promised me a country voyage to help to make up my losses, and would have me stay and accompany him to England next year.

The preference afforded to Harvey – who had probably come out in the *St George* which arrived at Bombay to be stationed there as a guard ship for the Company's Marine – could probably not be avoided by Boone. The Governor's solicitude for the unfortunate but resourceful Macrae is obvious and the impression made on the equally remarkable Boone was to have consequences, but whether or not Macrae made any money from a voyage or two 'on speculation' in a Country-ship, seems unlikely as his name reappears later in this extraordinary period and he may well have taken some part in the operations under Hamilton and Berwell. Notwithstanding his conduct, Macrae's loss of the HCS *Cassandra* was the East India Company's worse case of losses to piracy. Perhaps it was as well, given this and Macrae's damning condemnation, that Richard Kirby did not survive the voyage of the *Greenwich*. He died – perhaps by his own hand – in August 1721 while his ship lay at Bandar Abbas in the Strait of Hormuz. Yet this is nowhere near the end of the tale, the strands of which are tortuous.

During the negotiations for a ship with the pirates, Edward England revealed to Macrae that his own influence among the outlaws was waning in favour of his confederate, Taylor, 'chiefly because the latter was more savage and brutal'. Realising England's situation offered a distasteful but necessary collaboration Macrae, meeting Taylor on the *Fancy*'s quarterdeck, kept Taylor in good humour making 'the punch to flow in great abundance' and employing 'every artifice to soothe the mind of that ferocious villain'. Macrae's stock also rose on account of the sudden appearance of a man with whom he had formerly sailed.[27]

> It happened that a pirate, with a prodigious pair of whiskers, a wooden leg, and stuck round with pistols, came blustering and swearing upon the quarter-deck, enquiring "where was Captain Mackra [sic]." He [Macrae] naturally supposed that this barbarous-looking fellow would be his executioner, but, as he approached, he took the captain by the hand, swearing "that he was an honest fellow, and that he had formerly sailed with him, and would stand by him; and let him see the man who would touch him." This terminated the dispute [over Macrae's future], and Captain Taylor's disposition was so much ameliorated with punch, that he consented that the old pirate ship, and so many bales of cloth, should be given to Mackra, and then sank into the arms of intoxication. England now pressed Mackra to hasten away, lest the ruffian, upon his becoming sober, should not only retract his word, but give liberty to the crew to cut him and his men to pieces.[28]

Giving Macrae his liberty was seen by the band of thugs as 'inconsistent with piratical policy'. They feared that England's 'gentle temper' and 'generosity' toward Macrae had compromised them and that the Company's retribution would swiftly follow. By his kindness to Macrae, England had sealed his own fate. When Taylor in *Cassandra* and with the *Victory* in company left Joanna on 3 September, he headed for the Mascarene Islands. Here, on Réunion, near Mauritius, Edward England and three men loyal to him were marooned. The four men 'exerted their industry and ingenuity', built a boat and made for Madagascar, where they landed to join their fellows, many of whom were integrated into the local population. Here England fades a little from this history. Not so Taylor.

He, with his hostages, now headed north, into the Arabian Sea and fell in with two Arab vessels with cargoes of horses from Muscat. Capturing them and treating their passengers and crew barbarously, Taylor was obliged to set them on fire, horses and all, on being approached by what looked like hostile ships. Taylor now found himself not in a sea which he could dominate by rapine and terror, but one in which the contending parties were several and the complexities of which he barely understood. Although he captured several small craft, the crews of which he tortured for information and to satisfy his sadistic appetites; and although he made bold but ineffective demonstrations, usually under the British red ensign, he achieved little in the way of prizes to satisfy his men. The *Victory* was not in good condition and was increasingly fouled by weed, and on one occasion Taylor came within sight of the Company's force falling back from an attack on Angrey's stronghold, as previously related.

Taylor now struck south of Goa, stretching down the coast to Karwar and raiding coastal shipping, but with little material success. The pirates were now short of water and they withdrew to the Laccadive Islands (Lakshadweep). Here they took water and terrorised the inhabitants. With most of their men away fishing, the pirates 'used the defenceless women in a brutal manner, destroyed many of their fruit trees, and set some of their houses on fire'. However, the anchorage was exposed, they lost several anchors and some of their number in boats upturned in the surf. Their sexual appetites satiated they now considered the other, and determined to reprovision by a raid on the Dutch factory at Cochin. Reaching the coast far to the north near Tellichery, they seized a small coastal vessel whose crew told them of Macrae having been on the coast in an armed ship of the Bombay Marine. This incensed Taylor, who conceived Macrae as a base ingrate. Off Calicut Taylor sent his boats in to cut out an anchored Country-ship, but the guns from the fort drove them off. However, they withdrew with a prisoner, a Company officer taking passage in the little ship, who they converted into an hostage.

Arriving off Cochin, they saluted the fort with eleven guns, to be responded to in like manner. Having sent a letter ashore, bum-boats came out and they began to buy food. Taylor also received a message that he could purchase chandlery and any necessary 'naval stores' a few miles down the coast where there were those willing to trade with them illegally. Taylor readily assented to this and in due course came to an anchor, whereupon canoes ran alongside and supplied them in abundance. Among these was their contact, a man known as John Trumpet. He generously brought a boat load:

> …of arrack, and sixty bales of sugar, as a present from the governor … receiving, in return, a table clock and … a gold watch, the spoil of captain Mackra's vessel. When the provisions were all on board, Trumpet was rewarded with about six or seven thousand pounds, was saluted with three cheers, and eleven guns; and several handsful of silver were thrown into the boat, for the men to gather at pleasure.[29]

Trumpet surprised them further, for he sent out more stores on board the next morning and also apprised of the expected forthcoming passage of a laden ship belonging to the brother of Governor Boone. This was more to the liking of Taylor and his gang and they cruised along the coast in anticipation, eventually sighting a promising looking vessel. Now the wind fell light and the *Victory* and *Cassandra* drifted apart but, as night fell, Taylor and his confederates decided to seize their victim next morning. At dawn, however, they were 'almost ensnared in the trap laid for them', for five ships were seen. 'The pirates were in the greatest dread lest it should be Captain Mackra [sic], of whose activity and courage they had formerly sufficient proof'. But Macrae was too far off; as the wind came up a chase ensued and only one of his *grabs* gained on Taylor who escaped to the southward.

After a Christmas debauch, the *Victory* and *Cassandra* made for Mauritius, taking on the way a large Portuguese vessel aboard which was the Viceroy of Goa and his suite. The ship had been disabled in bad weather and, despite being well armed, was deceived by Taylor's two ships wearing the British ensign. Plundering the vessel which yielded: 'Besides other valuable articles and specie, they found in her diamonds to the amount of four million dollars' they also extorted ransom for Conde de Ericeira and his people before landing them. Taking another ship with a large number of slaves – allegedly two thousand – they made for Madagascar with their prize, but this appears to have been retaken and instead headed for Mozambique. Meanwhile Taylor and his fellow malefactors, after months of frustration, enjoyed all the riches that ruthless crime invariably gains.[30] At Madagascar the pirates had shared their spoil, each man supposedly having forty-two diamonds at a time when the only source of the precious stones was India. They then assembled a parliament and decided upon their future. Many resolved to settle and join the other superannuated villains now squatting in settlements along the coast. Taylor, however, had other plans. Condemning the *Victory* to be burnt, the *Cassandra* was put in hand and thoroughly refitted.

While Taylor's ships had been about their villainy, Commodore Mathews had been on his way to the Indian Ocean. At the Cape he had received intelligence from the French governor of Pondicherry and the Company's governor at Madras that the 'English and American' pirates in the Indian seas commanded eleven vessels and fifteen hundred men, of which Taylor's two ships were only a small part. Mathews was also advised that these men were elusive, some seasonally migrating to the coasts of Brazil and Guinea, others remaining in Madagascar and the Comoro Islands. Mathews made for Madagascar, discovering Edward England on the off-lying island known as St Mary's. Quite what Mathews got up to is difficult to determine, for he appears to have negotiated with England – 'the Commodore had some discourse with them' – but to little or no effect. Clearly dislodging the pirates from their lair was beyond him and, since his conduct in India seems on a par, we may assume Mathews achieved nothing. Hamilton remarks that on St Mary's the pirates had 'left behind them some marks of their robberies, for in some places they found pepper a foot thick, lying on the ground…' As for attacking the pirates by sending the men-of-war's boats up the rivers along whose shores the felons had retired, Mathews demurred, excusing himself on the grounds that it 'would be impractical, since they [the pirates] could have easily distressed the boat's [sic] crews out of the woods'. England would not treat with him, but was not detained, and now fades entirely from our ken.

Matthews [sic] sailed for Bombay where he acted in a high-handed manner, claiming precedence by virtue of his [naval] commission and was soon planning a series
of voyages designed to ensure for himself a handsome share of the Company's profits. He seemed bent on discrediting the Company and, worse still, he completely
repudiated the Company's contention that any ship carrying a consignment was
entitled to fly English colours, thus in effect supporting Kanhoji's case.[31]

Mathews's motives for this are less to do with animosity towards the Company, which
he undoubtedly harboured, but out of disgust that Indian Country-ships should
have the effrontery to fly the British red ensign. Although this is today the ensign
of all private British craft, in 1722 it was the senior of the three squadronal ensigns
of the Royal Navy, aggrandised in recent memory with the additional saltire of
St Andrew by the Union. With a laxity for which it was to become famous, ships
in the British merchants' service – whether beneficially owned by Britons, Parsees
or Anglo-Indians, aware of the equally strict regulations governing the wearing of
the Company's striped colours – invariably adopted the red ensign of Great Britain.
Given this state of affairs, it was possible for almost anyone remotely involved with
flying ensigns to either take offence or offer an insult on several points of precedence
or convention. Possessed of a royal commission and being the man he seems to have
been, Mathews clearly availed himself of all of them. Fortunately he is soon disposed
of. Boone ate humble pie, cobbled together an alliance with the Portuguese and
assembled an adequate force of several men-of-war, transports, an artillery train and
6,500 men. These he sent against Kanhoji Angrey at Colaba.

Anglo-Portuguese relations were bad. Irregular fighting had broken out between
them but they agreed to supply soldiers. Unfortunately, owing to a secret accommodation with Angrey which preserved their shipping from interception, the
Portuguese did not press their attack. Mathews's 'contributed nothing except 200
marines … [whose] bravery had been conspicuous' and it was yet another blunder-
ing disaster, Boone's fourth. The Dutch were no more successful in an assault on
Viziadroog where, despite having seven heavily armed ships and a bomb-ketch, 'they
were repulsed with great loss'.

Boone's time was now up; he sailed for home a disappointed man who had
done his utmost. Mathews went upon a trading progress to Surat and then round
Cape Comorin to Bengal. In the Hughli he was importuned by a distressed widow,
Katherine Gyfford, who pleaded that the Company were holding her against her
will, having an unjust claim of £9,000 against one or other of her several husbands'
estates. Suitably inflamed at the effrontery of a bunch of merchants to distress so
obvious a lady, Mathews promptly offered her strength of his arms and the consolation of his bed. While her legal wranglings rumbled on almost until her burial in
Madras in 1745, his career ended in 1748 in dismissal. It was remarked of him that:
''Tis wonderful how void Admiral Mathews is of commonsense, good manners, or
knowledge of the world.'

The villainous Taylor had in the meantime refitted the *Cassandra* and, having sworn-in a crew, sailed for Africa. While roistering along the coast of Mozambique he heard of the hue-and-cry and decamped from before Maputo. Leaving Delagoa Bay in December 1722, Taylor sailed for the Caribbean where, at Portobello, he turned *Cassandra* over to the Spanish, on condition that he was granted a commission in their navy. The ship was taken into the royal navy of Spain as a 5th Rate while Taylor, no doubt as good a naval officer as Mathews, retired to a life of ease and luxurious obscurity.

It only remains to recount the fate of the redoubtable Captain Macrae who, after his fruitless exertions in pursuit of Taylor, returned to Bombay. Here, he was selected to undertake a confidential mission to Benkulen where he dealt 'so successfully with the commercial abuses rampant there' that his conduct recommended him for higher-office. After a period as deputy governor at Fort St David, Benkulen, in January 1725 he was made Governor of Fort St George and Madras, an office he held until his resignation on 14 May 1730. Although 'stern and arbitrary', his conduct was highly acceptable to the Company for he was 'emphatically' commercial, undertaking fiscal and administrative reforms, establishing a mint, stabilising the rate of exchange between a plethora of currencies and the export of silver. He returned home with a fortune estimated at £100,000 in specie and diamonds 'as his best investment', to buy an estate in his native Ayrshire. Here this remarkable man adopted the five grandchildren of his benefactor.

This period was the nadir of British fortunes in Western India. The hesitant Portuguese made legitimate what had long been in part accomplished: a peace with Kanhoji Angrey. Thereafter their power irreversibly declined. The Dutch and French fared little better, as the Maratha fleet dominated the coast and no trade could pass except in convoy. Secure in his fastness at Colaba, Angrey was untouchable, the best that could be achieved being a series of retaliations on both sides. In 1723 a Company *grab* was sunk, for which reprisal a Maratha vessel was seized; but following an exchange of letters and of prisoners both parties lapsed into a brief cold war. Then in 1727 'a richly-laden ship belonging to the Company, which, together with other prizes, was taken into his fortified harbours' warmed things up. The following year Kanhoji sent emissaries to Bombay to propose a peace, but then his ships took a small Company vessel, the *King William*, and carried off Captain McNeale. An attempt by McNeale to escape ended in his being confined in irons and beaten, a captivity that ended any pretence at peace and lasted, for McNeale, some time. An alliance was made with Angrey's enemies but amounted to nothing and the Company failed to capitalise from schisms in the Angrey family arising from Kanhoji's death in 1729. After a bloody power-struggle in which eyes were put out, lives lost and Colaba was carried by assault, Kanhoji's estate was divided, one half making overtures towards Bombay. The other, where the old man's mantle fell upon one of his many bastards, took on a more dangerous aspect.

The bastard in question, Manhoji Angrey, moved swiftly. At war with his neighbours, he gained territory that brought him within a stone's throw of Bombay, commanding the approaches to Salsette Island. Thereafter followed a period of sea and land warfare in which the Company's ships, having been left alone for some time, now began to suffer. In January 1732 the *Ockham*, Captain William Jobson, was attacked off Dabhul as she approached Bombay from London. The eight galleys were unable to place themselves ahead and astern of the Indiaman which was unmolested on account of the light breeze that allowed Jobson to retain command of his ship; backing and filling his sails, he inflicted a defeat upon the Angrian vessels and was left to proceed upon his voyage. So far so good, but Jobson had had a hard fight of it and, *pour encourage les autres*, Jobson's men, who had plied their guns to such effect, were paid a bonus of two months' extra pay. However, on 26 December 1735 the *Derby*, was attacked off Suvarnadrug by an Angrian force sent out by Sambhaji Angrey from Gheriah. She came off less well. Captain Abraham Anselme did not have the benefit of much wind and the nine galleys, five *grabs* and fifteen *gallivats*, manned by about eight hundred men, were able to take advantageous stations on his near immobile ship. Ahead and astern, clear of the Indiaman's broadside, the Maratha squadron hammered the *Derby*. Raked from both ends and with the ship dismasted, Anselme's men began to lose heart. The first mate fell, five seamen were killed and six were seriously wounded. Anselme perceived his position was hopeless and struck his colours. It was a dire moment, for the *Derby* carried in her holds a vast quantity of naval stores (to refit the Indiamen in the dockyard at Bombay), ammunition and the annual imprest in silver dollars: the Company's trading capital for the year. [32]

The *Derby* was boarded and carried into Suvarnadrug where her crew were imprisoned. Although eventually ransomed by the Governor of Bombay eleven months later, Anselme was to die on the homeward voyage, a broken man. The two half-brothers, Manhoji and Sambhaji Angrey, maintained a modest civil strife between themselves and a robust war on two fronts: on land against their hereditary enemies, and at sea against the Company. At Bombay, the governor's council, eager to hit back, promoted reprisals in which the Bombay Marine participated without, however, covering itself in glory. The best it achieved was an attack on 22 December 1738 under Commodore Bagwell on a fleet of *grabs* in the estuary near Rajapur during which the Maratha admiral was slain. This was offset the same day by the loss of the *Anne*, a Company *grab*, along with some other laden coastal craft.

Elsewhere other Indian rovers were abroad. In 1734 Captain Radford Nunn of the Bombay Marine was despatched in the sloop *London* with a bomb ketch and five *gallivats* to make a punitive raid on the Gujarati coast. 'After a sharp fight' with the loss of four men Nunn and his party carried off their booty, valued at 3,650 rupees, which the Bombay Council awarded them, 'but the Court of Directors meanly reversed this order, and claimed a moiety for themselves'. The tit-for-tat quality of this coastal warfare is illustrated by the swift revenge which, six months later occasioned the loss of the *Antelope*, a Marine *gallivat* escorting 'some richly freighted vessels' to Cambay. By preconcerted arrangement the *Antelope*'s pilot ran her aground and, jumping overboard, swam ashore.

The *Antelope* was speedily assailed by a strong force of pirates, and, although gallantly defended for a time, further resistance was rendered hopeless by the explosion of her magazine. Ten Europeans, two Lascars, and two Sepoys perished; and the officer in command and one seaman were the only Europeans that survived.

Nunn was back in action on Christmas Day 1738 at the southern end of the coastline notionally 'under' the Bombay Presidency in an action ashore near Tellicherry, a fight described by Low as 'the first war in which the English of Western India showed any military skill, or contended with field artillery and what was called a regular army...' Notwithstanding this, it altered little: trade along the coast remained under constant threat.

So serious were the injuries inflicted by these pirates, and so heavy the expense of fitting out ships to protect trade, that the Company were prevented from making their usual investments, and, in their alarm, even began to anticipate the extinction of their commerce in Western India.[33]

Matters were now imperceptibly coming to a head. In 1738 the Parsee shipbuilder Lowji Wadia had been tempted south from Surat to Bombay. Here he established a ship-yard constructing vessels out of the durable Malabar teak that grew in profusion on the Western Ghats. Wadia established a dynasty that was to build ships for both the East India Company's Marine and its Maritime branches, as well as Anglo-Indian Country-owners and, when the timber crisis reached a peak in the Napoleonic War, for the Royal Navy.[34] Of equal moment and great strategic importance was the digging out of a graving-dock as part of the Wadia yard. This was, for many years, the only dry-dock available to British ships – the Royal Navy included – in eastern seas. Next came indications that Sambhaji was seeking a quieter life, for in January 1739 he made a proposal to Bombay, offering unmolested passage along the Konkan coast in return for all ships taking up the *dastak*. Since this came with a demand for an annual pension of two million rupees it was rejected by Bombay, not least because Sambhaji had already possessed himself of most of the Company's liquid assets with the *Derby*.

As Sambhaji fumed, his half-brother Manhoji stirred. Despite protestations of amity, warfare flared all along the coast until 'misfortune changed his disposition' and the new governor, Stephen Law, agreed to treat with him. As a consequence Law sent the Bombay Marine's vessels to pursue Sambhaji who retired towards Suvanadrug and, after a humbling 'by the English squadron and a co-operating Mahratta force, under the Peshwa's son ... Nana Sahib ... hastily patched up a truce'. Sambhaji had, nevertheless, thereby preserved the Angrian fortress at Colaba.

By now the Maratha power was immense and 'mustered regular armies, with well equipped artillery trains'. It had disposed of most of the remoter Portuguese posts – one reason for the weakness of the Anglo-Portuguese alliance – though the Bombay Marine had convoyed remnant Portuguese garrisons to safety. With an officer of the Marine named Inchbird acting as intermediary, a peace was concluded between the

Maratha Peshwa and the Portuguese on 14 October 1740. Among the terms was the withdrawal of Maratha forces from Salsette, greatly improving the position of Bombay.

While these events were in train, they had little effect upon the Angrias who were steadily detaching themselves from the Maratha Peshwa. On 9 November 1739, the Konkan coast:

> Was devastated by a frightful storm, in which three of the finest *grabs* of the Bombay Marine, completely armed and equipped, and commanded by three experienced captains, Rigby, Sandilands, and Nunn, foundered, leaving not a fragment to tell of their fate.

A revivified Sambhaji immediately raided Bombay harbour, 'carrying away fourteen fishing boats, with eighty-four men'. His ambitions now stretched further. In late December 1739 the HCS *Harrington* anchored off Tellicherry a little distance off three other ships. The road was the assembly anchorage for coastal convoys and the *Harrington* joined another Indiaman, the *Halifax*, and two Country-ships, the *Ceres* and *Pulteney*. Captain John Blake of the *Halifax* had begun the voyage as his ship's second mate but six months out Captain Manley had died of fever and the mate, Mr John Aston, had been promoted commander. The *Halifax* was for some months employed in the cross trades and on 30 September 1737 had been caught in a tremendous cyclone and driven ashore. Although not badly damaged, at first the ship was considered a constructive loss and she was abandoned; but when Aston also died of fever, Blake decided otherwise. Plaguing the council at Madras until they agreed to him making an attempt to haul the ship off, Blake accomplished this feat and was rewarded with her command. In March the *Halifax* left the Hughli and, on her way to England, made for Bombay to complete her cargo. If the *Halifax*'s commander was a notable character, the *Harrington*'s was an international celebrity.

Captain Robert Jenkins had famously lost his left ear – or a part of it, the matter was discussed earlier – when off Havana in 1731. During the agitation that followed his mutilation by Spanish coast-guard officers, his much later appearance before the bar of the House of Commons and the consequent outcry that eventually provoked 'The War of Jenkins' Ear', a new hereditary bottom had been laid down to the order of Jonathan Collett for the East India Company at Perry's Blackwall yard. The new ship was to be named *Reward* in compliment to Jenkins, though her name was changed on her launching in late 1732 to *Harrington*. Jenkins was by now – 1739 – on his fourth eastern voyage in her, still accompanied by his pickled ear.

A week into the New Year and the four ships were still waiting for their escort, but instead of an armed ship of the Bombay Marine, on the evening of 9 January 1740, fifteen Angrian vessels, six of them heavily armed 'frigate-sized' *grabs*, stood in towards Tellicherry Road in line abreast. Singling out the *Harrington* as being slightly separated from the others, they bore down upon the Indiaman, firing their bow guns. Jenkins weighed, cleared for action and began to move towards the other ships, greeting his attackers with his stern chasers. After a few minutes, with the sea-breeze filling in,

Jenkins decided to tack and, standing our towards the Angrian line, swung and fired three broadsides before the engagement became general. A desultory action rumbled on for five hours, before the Angrian squadron withdrew a little; both sides licked their wounds and repaired battle-damage. Jenkins remained under easy sail and when, at about five o'clock next morning, the Angrians returned to the attack, Jenkins made sail to meet them. There seemed now a reluctance on the part of the Angrians to come to close quarters, but Jenkins was on the offensive and closed with the large *grabs*. Now all six clustered about him, but Jenkins's gunners so handled their weapons that none got close enough to run their bowsprits over the *Harrington* and gain access to her decks – their preferred tactic. The Indiaman dismasted the Angrian admiral's *grab* and the *gallivats* came in under oars to tow her out of trouble. This they achieved by doing so directly to windward, thus preventing Jenkins from giving chase. Jenkins, however, had not only exhausted his men, he had spent all his powder so, 'knowing that it was his best policy to look his enemy in the face, he lay to for three hours, but they did not venture to renew the engagement.'

Jenkins seems not to have been supported by Blake in *Halifax*, but he was rewarded at Bombay, where the council awarded him 300 guineas and appointed him as Commodore of the Bombay Marine. However, he did not survive long, succumbing to fever and 'a flux' on 17 December 1742, and was buried with his severed ear. While the *Harrington* and her consorts had survived, other ships did not. The Bombay ship-owners – Britons, Parsees and others – suffered a string of losses while the Company's Marine did its limited best. Then, in the face of the treaty with the Maratha Peshwa, the Court of Directors ordered a reduction in the establishment of the Bombay Marine, a decision they were almost immediately to rue for 'the mercantile marine, now larger than ever, suffered serious losses from pirates'.

Besides a host of lesser losses, the Country-ship *Princess Augusta* was captured when coming from Benkulen in 1742, and that year a *gallivat* named the *Tiger*, having been disabled by a waterspout, was seized by pirates. Raids were made on vessels off Surat and the situation the length of the coast became confused. Whilst professing alliance with the British in Bombay, Manoji Angrey continued to plunder the coastal trade until, upon Sambhaji seizing an English ketch off Colaba, Manoji inexplicably rescued it. When themselves making coastal passages, the large, armed Indiamen were ordered to escort and protect the small indigenous craft, themselves confined to convoy. One such, escorted by the HCSs *Montague*, Captain Fielder Freeman, and *Warwick*, Captain Richard Shuter, was harried for a day and a night by seven *grabs* and eight *gallivats* belonging to Sambhaji Angrey; the Angrians succeeded in triumphantly carrying off 'five vessels and a Portuguese ketch'. So bad were the raids that the bankers of Bombay refused all trade-advances and coastal commerce almost ground to a halt.

Upon this desperate situation were now heaped further coals. The war with Spain hitherto named after Captain Jenkins' ear had now metamorphosed into a trial of strength in Europe, swiftly resolving the problem of Austrian Succession but rumbling interminably on. On 31 March 1744 hostilities had opened between Great Britain and France, a fact that marks a watershed upon the other side of which, eclipsing the mari-

time wars along the western coast of the subcontinent, the Company emerged in India
as a politico-military power in deadly conflict with the French. The struggle with
the French whose victories included the capture of Madras, supersedes the history of
trade; yet that trade went on to have its subtle, unrecognised effect upon the outcome.
Part of this, almost incidentally, was the final destruction of the Angrian pirates.

In view of the general European war and the probable appearance of French cruisers
in the Indian Ocean, all East India commanders were issued with Letters-of-Marque-
and-Reprisal. The Court of Directors further ordered the construction of a frigate
for the Bombay Marine from an English shipyard. As the French attacked Madras in
October 1746, the HCS *Princess Mary*, Captain George Martin, on her way to Calcutta
but stopping off Madras, was scuttled before she fell into enemy hands. Later, after the
French took the city, the ship was refloated, repaired and commissioned into the
French royal navy as a 5th Rate. She did not long remain thus, for she was wrecked at
Goa in the following July but the rest of the French squadron that had doubled Cape
Comorin to seek pickings on the west coast had more luck. In September 1747 the
two French frigates *Apollo* and *Anglesea* (a British capture), arrived off Bombay where
they daringly cut out the Indiaman *Anson*, Captain Charles Foulis.

Some accommodation was reached after a parley by which the Anson's crew were
released. These men, as much an embarrassment to the government of Bombay as to
their captors, were – as a matter of expedience – turned over into the Marine, most
being sent to the *grab Bombay*. To men expecting to return to England at some future
date, the prospect of indefinite service in eastern waters was unacceptable. As far as
they were concerned this high-handed action amounted to impressment and was
not to be tolerated for long. The *Bombay*, being sent upon a cruise to cover the trade,
lay off Rajapur at anchor on the evening of the 1 March 1748. Commander Samuel
Hough was at dinner with his two mates and the surgeon when the men broke into
the cabin in a body demanding their immediate release. There was a scuffle in which
shots were exchanged, without causing any fatalities but, upon the mutineers crying
out that resistance was useless, Hough:

> ...flung his sword away, and, standing unarmed before the whole body of seamen,
> asked them, in God's name, why they behaved thus. They told him in reply that they
> had no complaints to make of their officers; but having been trepanned into the
> Company's service, they were resolved to have their liberty or die.

Hough was now separated from his officers and, after seven hours of negotiations in
which 'it was remarkable that ... not a man touched a drop of liquor', Hough finally
secured an agreement that the men would return to duty on a promise that they
would be repatriated to England. Unable to punish an entire vessel's company, the
Council adopted the dishonourable scheme of entering the men in men-of-war then
arriving at Bombay on their way home after service in the Bay of Bengal.[35] To this
mutiny was now added another humiliation, the loss of the *Restoration*, a twenty-gun
grab manned by eighty Europeans and fifty-one lascars. Built in the Bombay Dockyard

she was the Marine's flagship, usually flying the Commodore's broad pendant, and her capture by Tulaji Angrey was the very nadir of the Bombay Marine's fortunes. Tulaji had succeeded Sambhaji and repudiated any allegiance to the Maratha Peshwa with whom he was soon at war. Secure in his fortresses Tulaji's writ ran the length of the coast, a prince rather than a pirate. He attacked indiscriminately, his *grabs* picking at the flanks of the convoys, even those as large as thirty-six vessels and, in 1749, taking a large forty-gun French Indiaman belonging to *La Compagnie des Indes*. Again Bombay sought help from the Royal Navy, a squadron of whose ships was in the Bay of Bengal where a transformation in the Company's affairs was underway under the emerging military capacity of one of its own officers, Robert Clive. On the western side of the Deccan too, a change of wind was occurring, with the appointment of William James as commodore of the Bombay Marine.

James had been born in Pembrokeshire in 1721, beginning his life behind the plough, but at twelve he went to sea. Following an apprenticeship he served as a servant in the navy under Hawke, but soon returned to merchant ships, obtaining a post as master 'in the Virginia trade'. During the War of Jenkins' Ear his ship was captured by a Spanish man-of-war and James, with his crew, were imprisoned in the Morro Castle at Havana. In due course they were all liberated and put aboard a brig sailing for South Carolina, but the brig was old and leaked badly; when they ran into a gale the ancient hull was so wracked that she began to founder. James called for volunteers and escaped in the longboat shortly before the brig disappeared. Such was the hurry in which they abandoned ship that they only had a small keg of water and a bag of biscuit on which to subsist. For twenty days the survivors drifted aimlessly until they sighted land and struggled ashore ten miles from Havana. 'Only one of the party … died from the effects of the severe sufferings they had endured; the others indeed lost the use of their limbs for a considerable time, but, ultimately, they all recovered'.

After a few months they were put aboard a British vessel and returned home, James to marry the landlady of the Red Cow, a public-house in Wapping. What effect this had on his joining the Bombay Marine is uncertain, but he arrived there in 1747 and proved himself so zealous that in two years he had risen to commander. Appointed to the twenty-eight-gun frigate *Guardian*, the following year he was ordered to take the ketch *Drake* and the frigate *Bombay* under his orders and proceed south, towards Tellicherry, with a convoy of seventy coastal vessels. North of Goa they were attacked by sixteen *grabs* and *gallivats*, 'mounting from four to twenty-two guns each, and crowded with men'. These belonged to Tulaji Angrey and they expected easy pickings. James, however, threw out the signal for the convoy to head south in a body, and drew his three armed vessels off towards the approaching Angrian squadron in line. After a lively engagement of over two hours during which one large *gallivat* was sunk and several others damaged, the Angrians withdrew towards Gheriah with James in pursuit, harrying them and inflicting casualties at small loss to his own men. Meanwhile the entire convoy had escaped to arrive safely at Tellicherry.

James, on returning to Bombay, received the thanks of the new governor, Richard Bourchier, and found himself appointed commodore of the Marine in 1751, to hoist

Severndroog Castle, the grand folly raised on Shooter's Hill near Greenwich, London, by his widow as a memorial to her husband, Sir William James. This drawing by Donald Maxwell was executed about 1927. (From a private collection)

his broad pendant in the forty-four-gun *Protector*, the especially English-built frigate that now acted as the Marine's flagship. The dynamism of Commodore James in securing the safety of commerce was soon apparent. A small squadron of the Marine was dispatched to Surat and, with another sent to patrol the Gulf of Cambay and the Kaythiawar peninsula, several pirate craft were destroyed, stabilising the trade north of Bombay. James himself, 'with a strong squadron' cruised continuously throughout the seasonal winter months to protect shipping along the Konkan and Kanara coasts. This virtually blockaded the Angrians 'who did not dare again to attack the ships of the Marine', creating a stalemate which persisted until 1755 during which Bombay prospered mightily. The city had become 'the grand storehouse of all the Arabian and Persian commerce', described by Surgeon Edward Ives in 1754 as 'perhaps the most flourishing of any this day in the universe'. This was an extraordinary change of circumstances which could only improve: Under Robert Clive the Company's army was victorious across the Deccan, and Madras was recovered from the French in 1748 as a consequence of the treaty ending the War of the Austrian Succession.

Moreover, in the New Year of 1755 it was anticipated that the naval squadron under Admiral Watson would arrive with sufficient force to dislodge and destroy the

Angrians from all their strongholds. Through diplomacy Bourchier had concluded an alliance with the Peshwa to eject the insolent Tanhoji from Suvarnadrug and Viziadrug, but Watson lingered at distant Trincomalee, sheltering from the oncoming south-west monsoon in May. The situation could not wait upon events and Bourchier determined to act before the coming of the rains: James was ordered to mount an expedition. At the heart of the force were the *Protector*, the twenty-eight-gun *Bombay*, the *Swallow* of sixteen guns and the two bomb-vessels, *Triumph* and *Viper*. On 25 March 1755 these units of the Bombay Marine were joined by the Peshwa's fleet of seven *grabs* and six *gallivats*. Ashore there were ten thousand Maratha warriors.

On their approaching Suvarnadrug – known then as 'Severndroog' – on the 29th Angria's fleet cut and ran; although pursued by the *Protector* they were able to escape from James who anchored off Suvarnadrug on 2 April, eager to force the fortress to capitulate before the onset of the onshore winds of the monsoon. Ashore the Maratha army invested the place from the landward side but their batteries were too distant from the outworks to have any effect, a fact that irritated James. The commodore accordingly sent boats in to sound the estuary that ran under the ramparts of the fort and constituted the Angrian harbour. Finding sufficient water, he took in the two bombs and the *Protector*, opening a cannonade and bombardment which, in the first day threw eight hundred shot and shell at the walls. During the night a deserter informed James that although the shell bursts were effective, the bombardment of the walls was ineffectual since they were of solid rock and eighteen feet thick. He suggested that there was deep water on the eastern side of the island.

Early on the 3rd, the *Protector* was warped in again, followed by the *Viper* and *Triumph*. Under a heavy fire from batteries mounting sixty-six guns, James anchored with only a foot of water beneath the frigate's keel. Clapping a spring on his cable, the *Protector* was swung to bring her broadside to bear and returned fire but she was so close that, even when the quoins were all knocked out, the *Protector's* guns could not be sufficiently elevated to hit the high ramparts. However, being within musket-shot, the men in the tops were able to sweep the parapet and drove the Angrian gunners from their pieces. Although the Maratha fleet kept their distance, the *Swallow* and *Bombay* moved in and added their broadsides, while the bombs threw their shells over the walls. After four hours, the north-east bastion began to crumble while a bursting shell set a store-room on fire. By directing the musketry to concentrate on the burning store, James kept the fire-fighting parties away and allowed the fire to gain a hold and before long the fort was ablaze. At eleven o'clock that night the flames reached the grand magazine. The explosion drove the battered garrison into the out-lying fortifications. Emboldened by this success, the Maratha land-forces exerted themselves and attacked. However, at daylight as the fire died away, the Angrians attempted to get back into the main fortress to hold-out until reinforcements arrived. Seeing the Marathas were unable or unwilling to pursue the Angrians into the fort, and anxious that he did not lose the initiative, James ordered the *Protector* to renew the bombardment and, under its cover, landed a party of seamen 'who, with great intrepidity, ran up [to] the gate, and cutting down the sally-port with their axes, forced their way into it; upon this the garrison surrendered' and the British union flag floated above the ruined fortress.

In the fort were found a great part of the *Derby's* cargo while the anchorage contained three Dutch prizes. These recovered, the squadron proceeded along the coast and, on 8 April, without further loss of life, accepted the surrender of the fort at Bankot, ten miles away. On 11th, under the terms of the agreement with the Peshwa, the Union flag was lowered from the ramparts of Suvarnadrug and the place was handed over to the Maratha forces. With the onset of the monsoon imminent, Bourchier over-ruled James's desire to press an immediate attack on Dabaul and the squadron returned to Bombay.

That November, a month after the end of the strong south-west monsoon, Admiral Charles Watson arrived with Rear Admiral George Pocock, a squadron of four ships-of-the-line and two sloops-of-war, British regular artillery and a battalion of the Company's sepoys, the latter under Lieutenant Colonel Clive. The presence of Clive was circumstantial, peace having been patched up with the French. Watson was joined by the ten vessels of the Bombay Marine and the opening of a campaign against Geriah was characterised by a wrangle over the division of the spoils. Considering actually seizing them a prerequisite, James offered to lead a reconnaissance of this most feared fastness of Tulaji Angrey, an offer that was readily accepted. James was back in Bombay by 22 December when he laid the report of his survey before the council-of-war constituted for the purpose of reducing Gheriah.

James's exploit is now quite forgotten, but was remarkable for its audacity. He arrived off Gheriah on 14 December in the *Protector*, with the twenty-eight-gun frigates *Revenge* and *Guardian*. Here he:

> ...saw the enemy's fleet, consisting of three three-mast[ed] *grabs*, eight ketches, and twelve or fourteen *galivats* [sic] in the harbour, rigged and their sails bent, with one three-mast *grab* having only her lower masts rigged. I stood into seven fathoms water, when I think I was within point-blank shot of the fort, but they did not fire at us. I was exceedingly surprised at finding the place so widely different from what I had heard it represented. I assure you, Sir, it is not to be called high, nor, in my opinion strong...[36]

And so it proved. Watson, Pocock and Clive left Bombay on 7 February 1756 with HMSs *Kent* of seventy guns and flying Watson's flag; *Cumberland*, sixty-six guns; flying that of Pocock; *Tiger*, sixty guns, *Salisbury*, fifty guns; the sloops-of-war *Bridgewater*, twenty, and *Kingfisher*, sixteen. Commodore James flying his broad pendant in *Protector*, forty-four, commanded the Company's squadron which consisted of the twenty-eight-gun frigates *Revenge*, *Guardian* and *Bombay*, the sloop *Swallow*, sixteen guns, and the bomb-vessels *Drake*, *Warren*, *Triumph*, *Viper* and *Despatch*. Four large Maratha *grabs* and forty *gallivats* reinforced the fleet. All the Angrian forts along the coast had been systematically reduced and Maratha land-forces were co-operating. On 12 February Watson's four ships-of-the-line and the *Protector* stood in to bombard the forts, the smaller vessels worked inshore to attack the shipping and dockyard. At close range the engagement was heavy, both from the fort and the Angrian *grabs*, but a shell from one of the bomb-vessels fell on board the Bombay Marine's former flag-ship *Restoration*, lying a prize of Tulaji Angrey. The vessel caught fire and this quickly spread among the crowded vessels, packed together in the harbour and 'the whole of the piratical fleet was speedily involved in the conflagration'.

Clive now landed his infantry and invested the landward side to cut Tulaji off from communication with the Marathas, of which he was suspected. That evening, having beat a parley, Watson sent in a flag of truce with a summons to surrender. This was rejected and the following morning the bombardment recommenced. Finally, about five o'clock next evening the white flag appeared and the business was accomplished. Only nineteen in killed and wounded were lost to the British in this affair which yielded an immense treasure to the captors, besides liberating a number of prisoners, two hundred cannon, six mortars and a vast quantity of powder, shot and shell. Most agreeable were 'one hundred thousand pounds sterling in silver rupees'.

Tulaji's fleet had, before the fire, comprised one seventy-four-gun ship, two of sixty-six guns on the stocks, eight *grabs* of varying size and sixty *gallivats*. Tulaji, who had sent the Peshwa's emissaries away with obscenities ringing in their ears, was ironed and flung into the Peshwa's prison where he subsequently died. Watson retired to Madras and, after some delay, Gheriah was handed over to the Peshwa. The Maratha fleet remained in being, based upon Gheriah, from whence it issued from time to time, and there were further bloody encounters with the Bombay Marine. Even as late as 1775:

> The Dutch, French and Portuguese cannot sail by or near their [the Maratha] coast in safety, without being strongly convoyed. A very few months since, five or six merchant ships sailed from Goa, bound for Surat and the isle of Diu [a Portuguese island in the Gulf of Cambay], under the convoy of a man-of-war of sixty-four guns, which they attacked with their frigates, and after putting it to flight made prizes of his whole convoy (which were Portuguese), and carried them safely into Gheriah.

So, although Gheriah had been given over to the Peshwa in accordance with the agreement with him, and although from time-to-time it acted against the Company, in Maratha hands it tended to erode the competition of others and, in general, respected all vessels trading under, or protected by, the British flag. This was clear evidence of the Company's growing power.

William James was in action again, shortly after the fall of Gheriah, when, in the *Revenge*, he fell in with a thirty-four-gun French frigate, *L'Indienne*, newly arrived on the coast from Mauritius and meditating mischief. Having been attacked, James and his men offered fierce resistance and prevailed in the action so that James carried his prize into Bombay and with her the news of renewed war. But this was not the end of his accomplishments. Bourchier was now desperate to pass on the news of war as quickly as possible, but the conventional wisdom was that the onset of the rain-bearing south-west monsoon effectively cut off Bombay from the other Presidencies between May and October. This caused great anxiety, so James offered a solution, having long pondered the problem. Seeking the cause of the dramatic seasonal change of the wind, James argued that it had something to do with the salient nature of the Indian subcontinent, and that

> ...by sailing out of the influence of the south-west monsoon, it was possible for a vessel to reach a latitude where variable gales prevailed, and that by such a means a communication might be kept up between the different parts of the Company's set-tlements on both sides of the Indian Peninsula. He, accordingly, sailed from Bombay in the middle of the monsoon, got into favourable weather to the southward, and arrived on the Coromandel coast, to the surprise of the whole settlement, after a voyage nearly as short, in point of fact, as was ordinarily made during the fine weather of the north-east monsoon.

James's passage in the *Revenge* – 'at that time a feat unexampled in the navigation of those seas' – not only bore the news of the renewal of hostilities with France but five hundred soldiers to reinforce Fort William. James's arrival enabled Watson and Clive to seize the initiative and to force the Hughli: in the following months they recaptured Calcutta after five months in the hands of Siraj-ud-Dowla and then took the French post at Chandanagar, thereby opening a campaign which, by the end of the Seven Years War in 1763, would leave the French with only a toehold in India at Pondicherry.[37] James played little part in this, beyond briefly blockading Pondicherry in the *Revenge* with HM Frigate *Triton*, for in 1759 – that year of victories – he quietly returned home.[38]

As a result of his booty from Gheriah, James was a relatively wealthy man.[38] He was also a widower, for now he married a Miss Goddard and settled south-east of London at Park Farm, near Eltham. As a reward for his services the Court of Directors presented James with a gold-hilted sword and election to their company. He rose to become chairman and in July 1769 he was sworn-in as an Elder Brother of Trinity House, to be elected Deputy-Master in 1775. In July 1779 he was made a baronet and he sat in the Commons as MP for Looe, and for Joshua Reynolds for posterity. When the French declared war in support of the American rebels, James produced a plan for the capture of Pondicherry, for which he received 'a handsome service of plate'. He died on the day of his daughter's wedding, 16 December 1783, it is said of an apoplexy brought on by reading the draft of the proposed India Bill which was intended to curb the power of the East India Company.

In the following year a revised India Bill was passed. This imposed a superintending Board of Control to remove from the Company's hands all matters in the Company's territories relating to administration, revenue, diplomacy and war. Commodore Sir William James would have been horrified, but he is not quite forgotten for his widow perpetuated his memory with the erection of 'Sevendroog Castle' upon the summit of Shooter's Hill. The folly – 'after a design by Mr Jupp' – commemorates James's part in the capture of the Angrian stronghold of Suvarnadrug, the securing of British commercial hegemony over the coasts of Malabar, Kankara and Konkan and by extension the supreme status of the city of Calcutta.

On the eve of the Seven Years War an observer in the River Thames could scarcely have guessed that the British had not been granted everything that a bountiful providence could bestow. The country had not only triumphed over enemies abroad, it had survived the last gasp of the second and younger Stuart Pretender, leaving it internally secure. Britain's naval achievements were implanted in the national psyche, its difficulties having earlier inspired James Thomson to write, and Thomas Arne to set to music, *Rule Britannia*. After the Treaty of Paris at the war's end in 1763, British power in the east exceeded that of all other European countries. Had a Londoner sought the fundamental reason for this, it lay under his nose, in the Thames as Henry Fielding had observed as early as 1754 :

> Besides the ships in the docks, we saw many on the water; the yatchts [sic] are sights of great parade, and the king's body yatcht is, I believe, unequalled in any country for convenience as well as magnificence... We saw likewise several Indiamen just returned from their voyage. These are, I believe, the largest and finest vessels which are anywhere employed in commercial affairs. The colliers, likewise, which are very numerous, and even assemble in fleets, are ships of great bulk; and if we descend to those used in the American, African, and European trades, and pass through those which visit our own coasts, to the small craft that lie between Chatham and the Tower, the whole forms a most pleasing object to the eye, as well as warming to the heart...[39]

It was now that 'the Grandest Company of Merchants in the Universe' came fully into their own.

NOTES

1. Barlow's few pounds profit was as nothing compared with the private fortunes made by those Company servants ashore who had multiple opportunities for dabbling and better chances of escaping any duties. In 1699 Elihu Yale returned from India with a fortune of £175,000. He had 'gone out' as 'a writer', or book-keeper, at an annual emolument of £10 in 1672. Able and astute, by 1687 he had risen to be Governor of Madras and traded privately in everything from diamonds to timber, surviving accusations of malfeasance and abuse of power. His fortune, equivalent to half the Company's working capital for that same year, was in part used to establish the American university that today bears his name.
2. See Chapter Three, Note 12.
3. A member of the Merchant Taylor's Company, Paterson accompanied the expedition but had little influence on events which were put in the hands of a council whose members quarrelled. He returned to take part in the formulation of the treaty leading to the Act of Union and in negotiations which culminated in the 'Sinking Fund' and the scheme of 1717 for the consolidation of the national debt. He died in 1719.

4. When, at the end of 1702 Queen Anne's last child died and the English Parliament settled the succession on the House of Hanover, the Scottish Parliament demurred, an agitation which awoke the ambitions of the Stuart Pretender slumbering in retirement at Saint Germain.

5. An added irony to this sorry tale is that while the *Annandale* was named after one of the representatives of the *Scottish* Crown, she had been chartered to The Dairen Company by the *Welsh* part-shipowner Captain John Ap-Rice. He also appears to have been in command of the *Annandale* at the time of her arrest and one suspects collusion between him and the Old Company. Ap-Rice's conduct throughout is suspicious. He knew Bowrey and was in the employ of the *English* East India Company. See Note 18 below.

6. Temple, *The Tragedy of the* Worcester, p65. The 'stratagem' involved besides Mackenzie and a dozen accomplices, the presence of a lieutenant of a Scots man-of-war lying at anchor in the road. Sir Richard Temple goes into the entire matter in great forensic detail. Drummond, the commander of the *Speedy Return*, remained to live out his life in Madagascar. He was not murdered by Green.

7. In his *History of the Union of Great Britain* of 1709, Daniel Defoe says of the 'affairs in both Kingdoms introductory to a Treaty of Union', that the 'clashings of interest' over the Dairen Company, the affairs at Glencoe, the disagreements over the Succession and 'the seizing the ship *Worcester* and execution of Captain Green and several others' were crucial.

8. Temple, p66. The money formed part of an 'Equivalent Fund' that was agreed to settle 'disputable fiscal matters between the two countries, in favour of Scotland'.

9. With its Bengal equivalent, the fore-runner of the Indian Navy, the Bombay Marine was in almost continuous action in these years. The Marine Service of the Honourable Company – as distinct from the mercantile Maritime Service – was habitually disparaged by the officers of the Royal Navy in the same way that 'Sepoy Generals' like Arthur Wellesley were by army officers. The colloquial naval slang was the 'Bombay Buccaneers'. See C.R. Low, *The History of the Indian Navy, 1613–1863*, Vol.1.

10. The islands had been first discovered by the Portuguese navigator Dom Pedro Mascarenhas in 1505, hence its collective name. Mauritius itself was named by the Dutch after Prince Maurice of Orange, a name to which it reverted after being taken by the British in 1810.

11. Eventually Avery tricked his accomplices of their ill-gotten gains and made his way to the West Indies. Here he sold his ship and escaped, though five of his men were caught and hanged. In England his attempts to launder his money failed, he was deceived in turn by a group of Bristol merchants with whom he conspired and he died in Bideford.

12. The *Benjamin* had just been completed for Sir Josiah Child.

13. On his way home Littleton called at Madagascar and, according to Captain Alexander Hamilton of the Bombay Marine in his *A New Account of the East Indies*, of 1727, had some of the pirates aboard HMS *Anglesea* where, by another account, a number were given pardons. Hamilton also states that Littleton supplied the pirates with some heavy tackle to enable them to careen their ships, making plain the hint that the commodore laid himself open to charges of venality. Whether or not Littleton was seduced by an ample compensation from the pirates' booty is uncertain, but he may well have covered himself by the issue of pardons, relying on the protection of others back at Bombay whose private goods his ships were carrying home.

14. Gayer had superseded Annersley at Surat, displeased with his conduct.

15. Among other demonstrations, the Portuguese had taken a British Country-ship from pirates and claimed her as a prize, refusing to restore her to her owners.

16. Keay, *The Honourable Company*, p255.

17. The question of ensigns was a moot one and complex beyond the dreams of vexillologists, but false colours were often flown as a legitimate *ruse de guerre* to close

an enemy, a tactic well understood by the English pirates. Also, a distinction has to be made between the Country free-traders some of whom, like Alexander Hamilton, were ensconced among and a part of local commerce – and who therefore sought to maintain the *status quo* – and the interlopers from Europe who, like the pirates when minded to trade their booty, often wore English colours but behaved badly and cheated when and where they could. Truly, as John Keay calls it, this was 'The Dark Age' in Britain's relationship with India.

18. It is almost certain that this Captain John Ap-Rice is the same man who part-owned and possibly commanded the free-trader *Annandale*. Sources indicate that he had been involved in some of the murky doings at Benkulen mentioned in Chapter One, there is a suspicious gap in his HEIC service around the period in which the *Annandale* was freighted for the Dairen Company and he may well have in some way colluded to have the *Annandale* arrested. His appointment to the *Godolphin* was possibly a reward for services rendered to the HEIC, but his service ends unusually as he appears to have been 'replaced' in 1710.

19. The etymology of '*grab*' is complex, as is the spelling, while the actual definition is imprecise because the word, which appears in Arabic as well as Indian dialects, meant slightly different things in different places and at different times. In Indian waters in the eighteenth century the *ghurab* (but also *al-ghurâb*, *ghoráb*, *ghourab*, *gharab* and *qarib*) was essentially smaller than a western vessel but was usually, at least in part, square-rigged, some had bipod or tripod masts and a long bowsprit, which proved useful for boarding.

20. Katherine was ransomed, only to be widowed a third time when Gyfford was mutilated at Anjengo (see Note 22 below). She became something of a white icon, beloved by the hagiographers of imperialism.

21. John Keay's wry joke is irresistible. *The Honourable Company*, p259.

22. Keay, p252 *et seq*.

23. Gyfford, the governor, 'had his tongue cut out, the tongue was then nailed to his chest, and he then nailed to a log and sent floating down the river. The rest … were simply dismembered; just twenty horribly mangled survivors made it back to the fort'. Katherine, née Cooke, formerly Harvey and Chown was thus widowed a third time. Keay, *The Honourable Company*, p253.

24. Low, C.R., *History of the Indian Navy, 1613–1863*, p97 *et seq*, Vol.1. Low is partial, casting Kanhoji Angrey as nothing better than a pirate comparable with Avery, Kidd, Bowen, Taylor and the like. Keay sets the matter right.

25. Low, p95, *et seq*, quotes Hamilton at length. Hamilton's disgust remains almost palpable, for he omits his own name from his account of the affair.

26. England's ship the *Victory* was formerly the *Peterborough* of Bristol, a slaver taken in the Atlantic.

27. James Macrae, probably because he was a Scot and could not have joined the Company's service much before, had come into it directly as commander. This argues he had both a good reputation and considerable experience. His encounter with his former shipmates suggests this was mixed and was probably acquired in slavers and the Africa/West India trade. Macrae was born in poverty in Ayrshire, losing his father in infancy. His mother was a washerwoman but the bright James attracted the attention of a 'violer' named Hew M'Quayre. The musician gave him some education and around 1692 Macrae went to sea, only much later joining the Company's service.

28. A curious footnote to this event is that Macrae's reprehensible old shipmate with the whiskers and wooden leg is supposed to have inspired Robert Louis Stevenson with the character and appearance of Long John Silver in *Treasure Island*.

29. The account leaves many unanswered questions, not least the identity of Trumpet, but one assumes that at some stage the anonymous Company officer was ransomed. The alternative was that, in the sequel, he was killed.

30. The taking of a seventy-gun Portuguese ship in identical circumstances is also claimed for Captain Condin, or Condent. Condin is also associated with the capture of the *Cassandra*, Captain Macraigh (sic), though less certainly. He seems to have been active at this time and was included in the warning given to Mathews at the Cape. The likelihood is that his ship, the *Dragon*, was probably in the offing on both occasions.

31. Keay, p262 *et seq.*

32. While Low predictably says the men fought 'gallantly', Keay writes of the resistance being 'feeble'; Cotton expatiates: 'they fought with little spirit' attributing this to discontent 'at the captain not offering them the usual encouragement to fight by hoisting two treasure chests on deck'. If so, it was a consequential defalcation. Cotton then adds that Anselme surrendered overruling 'those who were willing to continue', quoting Biddulph as his source but stating that Downing 'says that *Derby*'s crew stood most gallantly by the ship and captain, and held out till they were quite overpowered.' The losses indicated by Hackman are not severe but the surrender is indisputable and was most likely caused by the predicament of the ship and the inevitability of defeat. It was a quite acceptable practice in naval – never mind mercantile – warfare, to surrender to a superior force do avoid 'an excessive effusion of blood' – provided always that one had defended the honour of the flag.

33. Low, Vol. 1, p106.

34. As an example of the Wadia shipyard's output the frigate *Trincomalee*, built in 1816, remains afloat at Hartlepool today.

35. There were some other seditious incidents in the Bombay Marine at this time. A surgeon named William Willis was punished for 'exciting discontent' and four seamen were flogged for the same offence. Generally the white seamen in the Company's marine were there by choice, having settled in India, whereas the men in the Indiamen were under articles for a single voyage and the transferring of them was both stupid and arrogant.

36. The contribution made by Commodore James in reconnoitring and surveying Gheriah is rarely acknowledged and affords one example of the eclipse of the service rendered by mercantile officers. Rodger, *The Command of the Ocean*, p274-5, referring to the attack on Gheriah, states that: 'This operational chart-making was to be one of the keys to British success in amphibious operations all over the world, and it was the more noteworthy in that the Royal Navy had as yet no reputation for hydrography in general.' The inference is plain, William James's part is not admitted; the taking of Gheriah was a triumph for the Royal Navy, notwithstanding the crucial part played by a merchant sea-officer.

37. Watson died soon afterwards, handing over to Rear Admiral George Pocock. Meanwhile in the autumn of 1757 Commodore Stevens of the Royal Navy reinforced Bombay; he then met Pocock at Madras in early 1758. Pocock's fleet fought the French Indian squadron under d'Aché off Cuddalore on 29 April 1758, again off Negapatam on 3 August, and finally off Pondicherry on 10 September 1759.

38. Not as wealthy as Watson, who had £10,000 prize-money from Gheriah, or Clive and Pocock, who each had £5,000. James probably obtained about £4,000 to which other accruals made up his fortune.

39. Fielding, H., *A Voyage to Lisbon*, John Long, London, 1907.

SEVEN

'APPOINTMENTS OF GREAT EMOLUMENT'

The Vicissitudes of Eastern Trade, 1708–1793

It was the fate of the East India Company to excite jealousy throughout its history. This was largely on account of the tales of personal wealth that came home, evidenced by the conspicuous riches of the new, *arriviste* nabobs. It was bruited abroad that riches were easily come by and, if not in the Company's service, then on its fringes. In *The Trade and Navigation of Great Britain* of 1733 Joshua Gee had admitted that:

> The Licences given by the Company to private Merchants, to carry on a coasting trade in India, has been of great Advantage to this Nation, and several Merchants that transported themselves thither, have by that Means been abled not only to pay Debts here, but also to put themselves into a Way of raising Fortunes for themselves and Families.

In addition to those profiting from the Country-trade were others closer to the Company who were, in effect, parasitic upon it. Among these who preyed upon John Company, the closest to home were those shipowners who sought high rates for the charter of their vessels. In India, there was a second layer of naked self-interest: unscrupulous Company servants, from writers upwards by way of factors to the coun-cillors and governors, all of whom were intent on feathering their own nests. Back in London, grudging parliamentarians, mindful of the country's dependence upon revenues raised from import duties on the one hand, and their personal exclusion from the Court of Directors on the other, constantly sought to regulate the Company. Outside London the jealous merchants of Bristol which by the second half of the century was in decline and to whose complaints have to be added those from an up-

and-coming Liverpool where the slave-trade – and in wartime privateering – were attracting investment. Lastly, but among the home-grown parasites, was the Royal Navy. In a century of maritime warfare an increasingly competent and powerful navy invoked its powers in defence of the realm to help itself to merchant seamen.

Men-of-war often pressed seamen out of merchantmen to the point of ruining the profitability of their voyages as we shall have occasion to observe. Although a merchant ship's master, mates and apprentices were exempt from seizure, little or no consideration was spared for the fate of a ship, the state's wants over-riding those of any private citizen. Moreover, as a matter of case-law it was established that the deprivation of a seaman's liberty was acceptable if preserving the greater liberties of the majority of Englishmen ashore. This offensive arrogance might be pleaded against, but the process was lengthy and usually futile. Naval high-handedness – which was to be one of the primary causes of war with the United States in 1812 – became endemic in the hours of the Royal Navy's greatest need of man-power. With a large and vigorous merchant marine to plunder, the navy had no need to consider manning its ships a matter for its own planners. Left to individual commanding officers, the problem was solved by draconian measures.

For their part, ship-masters could not avoid some contact with the Royal Navy, for they had to square the advantages of convoy against the risk of the impressment of their crews. It is a subject that will be aired repeatedly, but for the East India Company, with its close association with the state making it particularly vulnerable, impressment was a grave issue. As early as 1710 the Company's secretary, Thomas Woolley, remonstrated with the Admiralty that officers and men of the Impress Service, having heard a number of sailors were being paid at East India House actually invaded the Company's headquarters in Leadenhall Street 'on a pretence of searching for seamen'. Such behaviour occasionally passed the bounds of any propriety, as when during the same War of the Spanish Succession, a Lieutenant Hutchinson, cruising for seamen in the Channel in a smack, followed the HCS *Cardonell* into The Downs and the moment she was anchored, boarded her. Captain William Mawson protested he must be left sufficient hands to bring the ship safely into the Thames, but Hutchinson took out of her all her able seamen and, in defiance of Mawson's fury and the officer's press exemption, her second mate.

Such state abduction against its own law-abiding citizens was commonly enforced by small arms. Occasionally a man-of-war's 'great guns' were employed, even in peace time. In August 1734 the *Duke of Lorraine's* commander, Captain Christopher Wilson, made a complaint to the Court of Directors who ordered the Secretary inform Their Lordships at the Admiralty that:

> …the men of war at the Nore treated him more like an enemy than a Merchant Ship coming into Port in such weather as he had, it being very bad, they firing near Twenty Shott at his Ship, some of which came among the Rigging, might have been of dangerous consequence to the Ship, and to the Company who had a Cargo on board to the Value of Two hundred thousand Pounds, This action being what the

Company did not expect from any of the Men of War, as the Captain of the *Duke of Lorraine* has assured the Court that he lowered his sails, and did what was safe to be done, they have commanded me to signify the same to you...

True that in this case the purpose of the aggression is obscure, but it is far less so in a later instance, perpetrated in 1781 by a zealous young post-captain named Horatio Nelson. In the West Indies in 1779 Nelson was in command of the sloop-of-war *Badger*. When the master of the homeward bound merchantman *Amity Hall* protested at Nelson's impressments of his men, Nelson lost his temper. Nelson was acting, it was alleged, in defiance of a convention that left unmolested a laden and homeward-bound vessel faced with an ocean passage. Nelson vindictively assumed the master 'insubordinate' and poached his men. He proved even more unpleasant in 1781, towards the end of the dreary war that had begun against the American colonists and ended against half of Europe. In October 1781 Nelson, at Sheerness and now in command of the frigate *Albemarle*, received orders to proceed in company with two other men-of-war to Helsingborg in Denmark, to escort home the last of the year's Baltic trade. Before leaving, however, he was given another task.

With his ships short of men Admiral Roddam, the port-admiral at the Nore, ordered Captain Nelson to intercept a number of in-bound Indiamen which had been reported passing The Downs on their returning from China. They would reach the Nore after nightfall and Nelson was to press men out of them without the use of undue force. Zealous as ever Nelson queried Roddam's orders as to the amount of permissible force. Then, at ten o'clock in the evening with the Indiamen almost upon him in the darkness, Nelson cut and buoyed his cable. Making sail he came up with the leading Indiaman and hailed her, ordering her to bring-to. The commander of the Indiaman refused, whereupon:

> We compelled them to anchor, firing 26 nine p[ounder]s shotted at their masts and rigging. We likewise bro' to 3 others & anchored ourselves alongside the Headmost of them. At 12 sent the boat on board the *Haswell*... They threatened resistance & til Daylight was given them to consider on it. At 5 a.m. Weighed and run alongside the *Haswell* upon which her men entered for H.M.Service...[1]

The Indiaman was actually the ill-fated *Halsewell* commanded by Captain Richard Peirce. The men taken out of the *Halsewell* were not only returning home after an absence of two years, seven and a half months – having begun their voyage on 7 March 1779 – but were being carted off for an indefinite period. It was this sort of action that inflamed merchant seamen against the authorities and undermined discipline in these ships after the end of the war. It was also the converse to the glories of 'England expects...' and at variance with the naval cant of protecting a vessel proceeding upon her lawful occasions.[2]

The British Government's relationship with the East India Company was complex. Since neither could do without the other, the whip-hand passed between them according to circumstances. In general, however the Company was subjected to increasing regulation in the eighteenth century. To some extent this assisted the Company. In 1708 parliament had passed the Convoys and Cruisers Act, raising an expectation that commerce would have the full support of naval might. Although there were to be catastrophic exceptions, insofar as the Company was concerned, the extreme value of its cargoes had a degree of naval protection. Another advantage derived from state involvement occurred in 1715 when the government extended the Company's monopoly as sole traders between China and Great Britain. Ultimately this would prove a drain on its Indian resources of silver and required a high level of bribery – as much as £2 millions annually – it nevertheless extended the Company's life. From about 1729 commodities from China were paid for by exports of Indian cotton goods, but the shortfall in the balance of payments began to be paid for by small quantities of Malwa opium. Although this was largely grown under the Company's auspices, it was not allowed in Company ships with consequences we shall later observe. However, by 1753, despite its importation being illegal, the Chinese authorities at Whampoa put a duty on the import of opium, a practice known as 'squeeze'.

Other factors detracted from the advantages of such dubious goings-on. The self-serving practice of private-building by Directors in yards owned by their associates was terminated by an Act of 1710. Under the new act Directors were forbidden to own and hire ships to the Company; instead a ship was chartered for a number of voyages at so much per ton of cargo, the Company guaranteeing a certain tonnage. Ships were to be taken up by ballot and no tenders were acceptable unless made by open tender by a master and two owners. Although the market was thus theoretically opened for shipbuilders, many of whom sought to fleece John Company, such was the size, cost and specialisation of an Indiaman that their construction remained in the hands of a clique. These men, collectively known as 'the Marine Interest', not only built Indiamen, they owned them.

Like other ships of the time, each Indiamen was owned by a small syndicate of whom one was the majority share-holder. East India masters, or commanders as the ships' captains were increasingly styled, were often included and many aspired to become the principal share-holders. In the hands of these general managing owners, or ship's husbands, lay the patronage attached to the appointment of commanders, for the Act of 1710 also forbade the unqualified selling of master's posts, an evil that had often placed incompetent place-seekers in command, as was the case experienced by Edward Barlow when chief mate in the *Fleet*. Notwithstanding such transactions might cost as much as £10,000 'there was no service equal to it, or more difficult to get into, requiring great interest'.

As was to be expected of an organisation run largely by practical seafaring men, the Company was in the vanguard of technical innovation. By 1761 copper sheathing had been introduced to combat *teredo navalis*, more than doubling the life of an East Indiaman. Even so, the ships were 'generally run for about four voyages, when they were held to be worn out'. Even given the appetite of the ship-worm and the vicissitudes of the service, it was an extravagant system that required 'about thirty ships every year', but it ensured a steady stream of orders for the ship-yards and a high quality of new-built ships for the task. When sold out of service or, if genuinely worm-eaten and rotten, broken-up, each Indiaman's slot was taken up by a new vessel which was hired to replace her after having been 'built upon the bottom' of the old vessel. A 'right' of continuity was asserted by the owner of the first ship – invariably a member of the Marine Interest – and so a succession of 'hereditary bottoms' were built until 1796, when a reforming spirit pervaded certain members of the Court of Directors and the system was abolished. Nevertheless a tradition of retaining the same name for a succession of ships remained to confuse a later age.

Another by-law of 1773 ensured that a ship's freight-rate had to be re-negotiated after four voyages and led, in 1780, to arguments over the calculation of the formula – consisting of fitting-out and running costs – which had arisen during the war with the American rebels. By this time the war involved Great Britain in hostilities with most of the maritime nations of Europe, most significantly in this case, the Dutch. Insurance premiums had increased alarmingly and the haggling, though it ended in compromise, was confusing, since most of the Directors were also managing-owners and suffered a severe conflict of interest in respect of their own pockets and the Company's coffers. Another argument arose over the freight rate which had risen alarmingly. The independent Directors wished to pay no more than £32; the owners would accept no less than £35. In 1783, as the war ended and after internal lobbying, the votes of the Court favoured a policy of advertising for tenders outside the Marine Interest. Twenty-eight vessels were offered but the Company's surveyors could find none of British-build fit for the arduous duty of an eastern voyage, foreign bottoms being excluded. These findings are suspicious, but the Court accepted them and perhaps was glad to do so as much as the hard-line owners, for chartering outside the familiar ring threatened the precious monopoly, and that in turn threatened them all. With the Company requiring a gross tonnage of 10,000, the matter was settled at £33 per ton.

Typical of the inner circle of the Marine Interest who ran the Honourable East India Company at this time was Robert Wigram, the orphaned son of a ship-master who had been lost at sea. Wigram left his native Wexford for London where he was taken under the wing of a family friend, Dr Allen. Allen told him that he had come to a city 'where, if you tumble down, no one will pick you up', but Wigram possessed a modest capital of £200 which he was keen to invest and Allen helped him to secure an appointment as surgeon in the *Admiral Watson*. The HCS *Admiral Watson* was a small Indiaman of only 430 tons which, under the command of John Blewitt, sailed from Spithead on 20 February 1764 bound for Benkulen. During the voyage Wigram made friends with Second Officer William Money who advised him in the matter of private trade. Wigram made a second voyage to Benkulen in the *Duke of Richmond*, Captain Benjamin Godfrey, and his last as surgeon in the *British King*, Captain Richard Williamson. In her he met and befriended her chief officer, Joseph Cotton, afterwards an influential Deputy Master of Trinity House. This time the ship went on from Sumatra to China where the twenty-eight-year-old Wigram contracted

Sir Robert Wigram,
1744–1830. The son of a
merchant and privateer
commander, Wigram
began his career as an
East India Company
surgeon, then as a trader
in pharmaceuticals before
becoming a ship-owner,
ship-builder and one
of the first shipping
magnates at the heart of
the East India Company.
He became a Unitarian
through the influence
of his wife and was a
colleague of Huddart.
(Author's Collection.
Original source
unknown)

opthalmia. With his chosen career in ruins but possessing a knowledge of medicines, trade and the orient, Wigram turned now to becoming a drug-merchant in London. His private enterprise had increased his personal capital to £3,000 and after ten years he had made enough money to move to Walthamstow House where he enjoyed country pursuits and rode into town every day with his son Money Wigram, named in honour of his old friend.[3]

In 1790 Wigram decided to invest in shipping while continuing as a drug-merchant. It was a good time to diversify: the independence of the United States had actually increased the volume of trade between the former mother-country and her quondam colony while opportunities in Canada and India were opening up. Wigram bought an 800-ton vessel, the *General Goddard* which had been built to the usual specifications of the Honourable East India Company and had just completed her fourth chartered voyage. Her previous owner was none other than William Money, by now a ship's husband, East India Director and an Elder Brother of Trinity House. Wigram sent her east under the command of Thomas Wakefield and later that year had the 1,200-ton *True Briton* built by John and William Wells at Deptford for the service of the East India Company. Upon the outbreak of war in 1793, mindful of the need for transports, Wigram bought four more vessels and appointed William Taylor Money, son of his associate and friend, to the command of the *General Goddard*. Homeward bound off St Helena on the night

Part of a large group portrait of the Merchant Elder Brethren of Trinity House in uniform. Many of the assembled ship-masters were connected with the East India Company. Jospeh Huddart is seated on the extreme right, with Anthony Calvert fourth from the right. From a painting by Gainsborough Dupont dated 1794. (© Courtesy of Trinity House)

of the 2 May 1794 the *General Goddard* encountered a number of Dutch merchantmen also homeward from Java. Unwilling allies of the French, the Dutch nervously fired at the British Indiaman who kept company with them until daybreak, holding her fire until the British frigate *Sceptre* arrived on the scene. In the ensuing action seven Dutch Indiamen were captured and brought into St Helen's Road, an action which earned Captain Money £60,000 in prize-money.[4]

Wigram's shipowning prospered and at one time he owned twenty-three East Indiamen, the same as the number of children he produced from two marriages. He extended his business associations with other East India Company commanders and directors, many of whom were Younger or Elder Brethren of Trinity House.[5] Despite his association with the Company, Wigram never joined the Court of Directors but in December 1802 he was elected MP for Fowey and supported Pitt, who later honoured him with a baronetcy. After Pitt's early death, Wigram sat briefly for Wexford.

In 1805 he bought part of Perry and Wells's ship-yard at Blackwall (Wells had been a Company commander) and backed Joseph Huddart's patent hemp cable-making process. In 1810 Wigram became chairman of the East India Dock Company, whose enormous and secure wet-dock opened that year. He also became a partner in a brewing company and in 1812 acquired the whole of the Blackwall ship-yard, establishing the shipbuilding company of Wigram, Wells and Green that was – with some changes of name – to become famous as the producers of the East Indiamen's successors, the Blackwall 'frigates' of the post-Napoleonic War period. Wigram retired at sixty-seven, selling the shipyard to George Green and two of his own sons, Henry Loftus Wigram and Money Wigram, both of whom had been sent to live at the ship-yard as teenagers to learn the craft and business.

Wigram was typical of the Marine Interest which operated so close an inner circle that, once an East Indiaman ship was built:

> There was never any written engagement on the part of either the owners or the Company as to the continuance of these charters, but the custom of contract was so well established that both parties mutually relied upon it, and considered themselves bound by ties of honour to observe their implied customary engagements. When, therefore, a ship's turn arrived to be employed [by ballot], the owner, as a matter of form, submitted a tender in writing to be engaged, and proposed a particular person to be captain, and this tender and proposal were always accepted. Thus the owners of these East Indiamen had everything in their own hands, and the favour of one of them was a fine thing to obtain, leading to appointments of great emolument.

Chief of these was, of course, that of a ship's master and commander. These men and their fortunes were bound together and each must trust the other. In respect of their joint interests and those of the Company, these were in turn made congruent by a binding oath of loyalty. A Company commander and the senior four mates swore to be 'true and faithful' to the Company for whose benefit their ship was employed. Once arrangements for a voyage were under way a commander's allegiance shifted; he became the agent of the Court of Directors, taking aboard a cash imprest for necessary disbursements during the months and years ahead and sometimes a great deal more, as we saw in the case of Captain Anselme and the *Derby*. Once secured, the position of an East India commander was not merely enviable; it was heritable and, of itself, conferred patronage in respect of others eager to serve the Company in order to serve themselves. The ties that bound these men extended beyond mere business and were often dynastic, involving marriage-settlements and nepotism, all regular and deeply ensconced features of eighteenth century Georgian Britain. Yet, as it did in the Royal Navy, the system worked remarkably well, for it was circumscribed by certain controls: opportunities were open only to those sea-officers who had passed their examinations – often oral and not particularly taxing – but who must have served sufficient sea-time. Promotion required an officer – or mate in the merchant's service, a mate in the Royal Navy being a junior warrant officer only slightly superior to a midshipman – to have served first as a midshipman. After a voyage as fifth or sixth mate, then another as third or fourth, and a further one as first (chief) or second mate, promotion to master and commander rested upon the social interest an officer could then command. However, it also depended upon his purse, because purchase of command was permitted until its abolition, along with 'hereditary bottoms', in the reforms of 1796. With the right connections it was therefore possible to rise to command after three voyages, or in about four and a half years, but the sea-time and qualifications were obligatory and incompetence was not tolerated – too much rested upon the reliability and quality of the Company's officers.

There was, though, the matter of religion. As for officers in the army and navy, it was necessary for a Company officer to be a member of the Established Church, such was the fear in the eighteenth century of Popery and insurrection under the Stuart Pretenders to the throne. However, given the pragmatism of the age, it does not surprise to find a sole exception to prove the rule. Captain Edward Arlond was a Roman Catholic but was appointed by William Gostlin, a principal managing-owner, to command the new *Duke of Buccleugh* in 1713. Arlond, moreover, appears not to have had held any previous rank in the Company's service, an irregularity which perhaps attracted the attention of the Directors, but such was his outstanding reputation as a seaman and ship-master that both his lack of experience in the Company's service and his faith were overlooked. Indeed, having commanded the *Duke of Buccleugh* for a three-year voyage to Bombay and the Indian coast, the ship was turned over to a new commander and in July 1721 purchased by Arlond himself. Arlond thereafter remained proprietor until his ship was sold out of the Company's service at Lloyd's Coffee House.

Remuneration among the lower officers was poor and 'it required a private capital of at least five hundred pounds to enable a man to arrive at the position of second mate, which was the lowest station wherein the pay and allowances afforded a maintenance'. Nevertheless, competition for berths was fierce and often an aspiring youth could be helped by a captain's favour, hence the attraction of beginning a career as a 'captain's servant', which carried with it no menial tasks beyond a polite subservience. Abuses occurred but probably less-so than in the contemporary Royal Navy since, beneath it all, commerce and profit was the only business of the Company's servants, ashore and afloat. Incompetence and profitable seafaring did not go hand-in-hand for long.

Nor did the social status of an East India commander fall far below the cachet that attached to a post-captain in the Royal Navy, hence the resentment at the insolence of junior naval officers in charge of press-gangs. In the eyes of many the riches implied by command of an East Indiaman far exceeded those attaching to naval service. Once east of St Helena, where the Company's grid-iron ensign replaced the red ensign of a standard British merchantman, the commander of a Company ship enjoyed immense privilege, especially as the political and administrative power of the Company's writ extended ever deeper into the Indian hinterland. Going ashore to call upon the Governor in Fort St George at Madras in a gig whose crew were as smartly turned out as that of any crack frigate, a Commander ranked with members of the local President's Council. He was saluted by thirteen guns and the turning out of the Company's guard. Moreover, although a naval captain might augment his meagre pay by the single percentage allowed him if he carried chests of specie or bullion, plus his prize money, the 'great emoluments' accruing to a Company commander were somewhat more regular, though by no means guaranteed.

The captain of an East Indiaman, in addition to his pay and allowances, had the right of free outwards freight to the extent of fifty tons, being only debarred from exporting certain articles, such as woollens, metals, and warlike stores. On the homeward voyage he was allotted twenty [space] tons of free freight, each of thirty-two [cubic] feet; but this tonnage was bound to consist of certain scheduled goods, and duties were payable thereon to the Company. As the rate of freight in those days was about £25 a ton, this privilege was a valuable one. Of course much depended upon the skill and good management of the individual commander, the risk of the market, his knowledge of its requirements, and his own connections and interest to procure him a good profit. In addition to free tonnage, he further enjoyed certain advantages in the carrying of passengers, for although the allowance of passage [table] money outward and homeward was arbitrarily fixed by the Company, there being a certain number of passengers [usually the Company's own employees, factors, writers, clerk, and in due course officers of the Bombay and Bengal armies and the wives and families of senior civil servants and military figures] assigned to each vessel, and their fares duly determined, ranging from £95 for a subaltern and assistant surgeon to £235 for a general officer, with from one and a half to three and a half tons of free baggage, exclusive of bedding and furniture for their cabins, yet it was possible for captains, by giving up their own apartments and accommodation to make very considerable sums for themselves. In short, the gains to a prudent commander averaged from £4,000 to £5,000 a voyage, sometimes perhaps falling as low as £2,000, but at others rising to £10,000 and £20,000. The time occupied from the period of a ship commencing receipt of her outward cargo to her being finally cleared of her homeward one was generally from fourteen to eighteen months, and three or four voyages assured any man a very handsome fortune.

Thus wrote Robert Eastwick – who served as an officer in two Indiamen before commanding a Country-ship – of the very end of the eighteenth century, though the practices and procedures stood from its beginning. While a captain might give up his own apartments to a senior Company official and his family, it meant imposing on his chief mate and displacing him, with a consequent knock-on effect down the chain of command, the sixth mate ending up back among the midshipmen whose company he had so lately left. No matter; consolation lay in the wider allowances for private trade which was increasingly permitted to all the officers, the petty officers and many of the seamen in proportion to rank and rating. Matters changed after Barlow's day and this 'official' scale was augmented by a sideline, accompanied by nods-and-winks, which upon occasion – and especially when word of a fashionable demand for some such frippery as egrets' feathers got abroad – resulted in the decks of an Indiaman being stuffed with private trade-goods.

Merchant seamen of all classes and in all manner of ships indulged in private trade. It was one reason why men went to sea, though normally opportunities were not large and profits modest. A man might accumulate sufficient to buy an inn, especially a cook or purser able to work on the quantities of stores where some

Robert Eastwick, 1772–1865. Originally an East India Company officer, Eastwick took advantage of opportunities in India and rapidly rose to command of a country-ship. (Author's Collection)

creative accounting could be done, or where a little light-fingered embezzlement or quiet selling of ship's stores were possible. The opportunities available to East India officers and men was of a different order and to this end they would often combine into syndicates, even to the extent of acquiring investors outside the ship, and agents to do the buying and selling in their absence. Such an increase in available capital on the one hand, and deduction of commission on the other, made a berth aboard an East Indiaman attractive, and the occupier thereof a man of parts. This was facilitated by the commanders and officers in the Company's fleet enjoying the privilege of financing this private trade by being allowed 'certificates on the Court' in London.

Despite the heavy duty laid upon private imports in 1701 and so anathematised by Barlow, increased allowances mitigated its effect until in 1803 when such goods were held not to be merchandise, but only intended for private use, which the importer had to certify. The degree to which individuals thereby perjured themselves may be guessed at.

One steward took out to India 'some prime articles of saddlery, likewise the best London-made shoes and boots' which 'always yielded a hundred per cent in Bengal'. As the century progressed and with time the British territories expanded, so too did the ex-patriate population, ladies and their maids included, to create a constantly enlarging market for 'Europe goods'. Almost all of life's embellishing artefacts and commodities were supplied not by the Company's exports, but by the private trade of its marine employees. In June 1786 Mrs Creighton and Miss Tranter:

> ...beg[ged] leave to acquaint the ladies of the settlement that they have purchased the whole of the millinery and haberdashery contained in the investment of Mr Thomas Denton, chief officer of the *Phoenix* (Captain James Rattray) which ... reached her moorings in the River Hooghly [sic] on 30 May.

Mrs Eliza Fay, having also set up an emporium in Calcutta, that same October and consequent upon the arrival of the HCS *Ravensworth*, announced that 'Captain Roddam and Mr Burdekin's investments of Haberdashery are exposed for sale'. Both emporia stocked the millinery of Madame Beauvois and included besides 'caps, hats and turbans', 'superb ... dresses of the latest fashion'. Occasionally officers pushed their luck, overstepping the bounds set by the Company. In 1742 Captain Charles Birkhead was removed from the command of the *Queen Caroline* for illicit trading, contrary to the Company's rules.

Some able commanders established quite complex business empires whose tentacles extended deep into society at home as well as in the orient. It is hard to find a more comprehensive list than that of Captain Robert Taylor of the *Earl Talbot*. He arrived in the Hughli in May 1786, though the observations are those of the diarist William Hickey, then not long arrived in Bengal as an attorney attached to the Supreme Court at Calcutta. Taylor advertised:

> ...claret, red port, Madeira, old hock, porter, cider, ale, pale beer, rum and gin, pineapple cheese, pickles confectionery, hardware, hats, jewellery, plate, perfumery, haberdashery, cutlery, fishing tackle, and prints of droll and political characters.

Another, Captain Charles Chisholme of the *Glatton*, brought out in 1778 a quantity of Madeira, only to find the market flooded and the price depreciated. Fortunately he had also acquired a large pack of hounds 'then in great demand by the Bengal sportsmen'. With 150 pipes of madeira on his hands he instructed his purser to offer two pair of hounds at the market price with every purchase of four pipes of Madeira at 300 rupees per pipe; he cleaned up.

Clearly the sportsmen of Bengal were a fruitful market, particularly in the matter of English hounds. A son of the Earl of Balcarres, Robert Lindsay, on his way to Calcutta aboard the *Prince of Wales* to take up a vacancy for a writer, reported that when Captain Jonathan Court put the passengers on a short allowance of water, the hounds were not. 'We then determined to lodge a complaint against him upon our landing ... [but] on approaching the shore [Court] thought it prudent to make an ample apology and all was forgiven'.

Calcutta had become a great city, full of vices and spices, which, for all its perceived excesses still struck new-comers with wonder. In 1789 Abdul Lateef Shushtari, arriving from Hyderabad, remarked that:

The city now contains around five thousand imposing ... houses of stone or brick
and stucco... Seven hundred pairs of oxen and carts are appointed by the Company
to take rubbish daily from streets and markets out of the city... Grain and rice are
plentiful and cheap ... big ships come from Europe and China ... filled with precious goods and fine cloths, so that velvets and satins, porcelains and glassware have
become commonplace. In the harbour at Calcutta there are over 1,000 large and
small ships at anchor, and constantly the captains [of the large vessels] fire cannons
to signal arrival and departure...

The practice of firing salutes was but part of a ritual that came with the status of command of an Indiaman, the quasi-naval end to a spectrum that rested its other firmly
upon private trade. Success in such 'adventures' often enabled a commander to buy
into the Marine Interest and thereby become a ship's husband and managing owner.
Much, therefore, rode upon an individual commander's acumen and his knowledge
of the market, both in India for manufactured goods and luxuries, and back in Great
Britain for the exotica of the orient. Often the trade was a high-risk business and a
captain might lose his investment – even his shirt – in these risky 'private ventures',
for the length of a passage might destroy a market or the near simultaneous arrival of
a number of East Indiamen with like-minded commanders, flood it. This happened
in 1769. Private losses were immense, especially in glassware which had been much
requested the previous year and with which every officer had stocked up. Since the
Company levied a duty upon these imports, when another glut in 1789 threatened
the imminent ruin of numerous commanders and officers, it provoked a petition
for a remission of all duties. This was acceded to, not so much out of compassion for
the distressed importers, as for the maintenance of the suppliers who kept the growing British community supplied with their wants and luxuries. Thus, despite these
vicissitudes, the trade was on balance beneficial to all parties. Even at the height of
the Napoleonic War in 1806 and 1807, when the French were waging a particular
effective *guerre de course* in the Indian Ocean, private trade was about 8 per cent of the
overall value of the Company's traffic.

Not all made their fortunes quickly, some not at all. Envy bred rivalry and the
occasional feud. Given that an East Indiaman lasted for about the same time in
which a captain could amass enough wealth to be a made-man, length of service
as commander is often an index of commercial acuity. It was not a position to be
relinquished for no good reason, but some served only a single voyage. Success bred
success, their patronage was sought for Company aspirants, even their hand in marriage. Others were less favoured; some were utterly luckless. One of these last was
John Wordsworth, the poet's brother, who complained that he had failed to make
his fortune, a fact which clearly embittered him. It was therefore doubly unfortunate
that his life ended tragically. Wordsworth had gone to sea in 1771 and, having served
in two Indiamen, first as captain's servant and then as midshipman, he spent a year as
a master's mate in HMS *Ruby* in the West Indies. In 1778, however, he was 'taken up'
by William Dent, a Director and owner, and signed on as third mate of the 804-ton

Earl of Sandwich. In his mid-twenties Wordsworth made a voyage to Bombay during which the sickness of others caused him to rise rapidly and he was promoted to commander for the ship's next voyage to Madras and China. The *Earl of Sandwich* sailed on 11 March 1783, returning home on 4 April 1785 to be broken-up after a survey considered her unfit for further service.

After a spell ashore, Wordsworth was appointed by Dent to the new 1,183-ton *Earl of Abergavenny*, launched at Harwich in August 1789. He made two China voyages in her before Dent sold her to the Royal Navy in September 1794.[6] Dent, however, ordered a replacement which was built at Northfleet on the Thames. The second *Earl of Abergavenny* was one of the largest class of Indiamen at 1,460-tons and she sailed on her maiden voyage for Bombay and China on 18 March 1797. Following this, between 1799 and 1804, Wordsworth made three voyages to 'China direct', and left on 1 February 1805 for Bombay and onwards to China again. Having by this time commanded no less than seven voyages in three ships, by all the rules of the game, Wordsworth ought to have made his pile, becoming, if not a land-owning gentleman, then a ship's husband as his cousin was to do. Instead his luck ran out. Thrashing his way down Channel at on a wintry evening he had the misfortune to run the *Earl of Abergavenny* on the Shambles Bank off Portland Bill. In an area of strong tides the ship was holed and, although she had floated off on the flood tide by 8 pm, she sank before Wordsworth could run her onto a flat, sandy beach near Weymouth. Next morning when a rescue was mounted, only her masts and yards remained above water. Although exonerated at the subsequent enquiry, which attributed the blame to another's faulty conning, Wordsworth had perished with many others at his post of duty.

The fate of the *Earl of Abergavenny* – a grounding followed by total loss – occurred all too often. A similar fate had overtaken the HCS *Earl of Dartmouth* which sailed for home from Madras on 8 June 1782 commanded by David Thomson. She encountered bad weather, lost spars and was driven disabled hundreds of miles to leeward in heavy south-westerly monsoon weather, right across the Bay of Bengal, to ground on Car Nicobar Island. Thirty-one lives were lost in the wreck and the survivors were rescued by the HCS *Chapman*. Such dreadful casualties arose from a variety of causes besides a pilot's error or bad weather. As we shall have reason to note in the following volumes of this history, losses of Indiamen, like those of ordinary merchantmen, were all too frequent. Misadventure – whether from Acts of God or human failings, such as storms or fire – were, and remain, impossible to protect against. Faulty navigation owing to the inadequacy of contemporary methods, particularly the uncertainty of longitude was part of the risks attendent upon a voyage and depended entirely upon individual professional competence, training, proper equipment and opportunities to observe or calculate a position, but even when all these things were in place, there remained the problem of poorly surveyed waters and a lack of accurate charts. For years both the Royal Navy and the merchant's service had suffered from lack of investment by both the state and commerce in proper measures being taken to produce comprehensive charts or reliable instruments.

By the end of the century chronometers derived from John Harrison's No 4 were neither widely available nor yet commonly carried and navigation in the open ocean remained imperfect. But it was in the coastal waters, particularly those of the eastern seas, that real danger lurked and strenuous efforts were made by the Company to remedy the deficiency. Indeed, the very business of garnering hydrographic information was itself full of danger. In 1783, the Company's despatch vessel, the fourteen-gun *Antelope*, having delivered letters for the Select Committee at Canton, sailed for Calcutta on the 20 July. Captain Henry Wilson was intending to carry out some surveying among the Pelew Islands (Palau Islands, part of the Carolines) on the return passage but on the 9 August, on approaching the archipelago, the *Antelope* struck a reef and shivered to pieces. Salvaging what they could of the wreck and subsisting on a small, neighbouring and uninhabited island, the crew – with considerable local help – constructed a small schooner which they named the *Oroolong* and in which they left the islands on 12 November, bound for Macao. With them they took the king's son, Lee Boo, and on 30 November they arrived back at Macao where the Tsongtoc and Hoppo, 'expressing great Concern for their Misfortune,' allowed Wilson and his men to proceed upstream to Whampoa and join an Indiaman for the passage home.[7]

However, Wilson's orders were part of a wider attempt by the Company to reduce the risks to its ships in eastern waters, formalising the work begun many years earlier by its pioneering ship-masters. To this end surveyors like Alexander Dalrymple and James Horsburgh were officially appointed and tasked, while much valuable supplementary hydrographic work was accomplished by many East India commanders in the normal course of their voyages. The surveying skills of Sir William James have already been remarked in connection with the attack on Gheriah, but the majority of this work was entirely driven by commerce.

Alexander Dalrymple had gone out to Madras as a fifteen-year-old writer in 1753. '[H]eadstrong in youth as he would become cantankerous in age' he became interested in the voyage records of successive Indiamen, attracted to waters east of India and the possibility of establishing a permanent Company base from which to derive better benefit from the rapidly growing commerce with China, a trade upon which the Company was becoming increasingly financially dependent. Imperial opposition to the Company establishing trading posts in China, as had been achieved in India, led to the focus of all trade at Whampoa, a roadstead in the Pearl River some distance below Canton, with the Portuguese post at Macao providing the best depot to be hoped for by the Europeans in the face of what was felt by them to be an unreasonable intransigence on the part of the Chinese emperor. Macao was also useful as a retreat for the young gentlemen 'writers' and the supercargoes who handled the seasonal trade during the worst of the summer heat. These men were permitted to man the counting-houses of the Company's factory in Canton itself only while the Indiamen lay discharging and loading downstream at Whampoa.

In September 1758 the HCS *Pitt* arrived at Madras, bound ultimately for China. The *Pitt* had been built two years previously as the *Pondicherry* for the French *Compagnie des Indes* but after the outbreak of the Seven Years War had been captured by HMS

Alexander Dalrymple,
1737–1808, Hydrographic
Surveyor and Hydrographer
to the Honourable East India
Company, and later the British
Admiralty. (© Courtesy of the
National Portrait Gallery)

Dover in January 1757. That October she was purchased by the Honourable East India
Company and refitted at Blackwall. Commanded by Captain William Wilson the *Pitt*
proceeded to Plymouth to embark Colonel William Draper and the 64th Regiment
of Foot, troops sent out in support of the Company's regiments and the 39th Foot
then in Madras.[8] Although a fast ship, the *Pitt* arrived too late in the season to carry
favourable winds through the South China Sea to Whampoa, for by the autumn the
north-east monsoon had set in. Knowing that news of the outbreak of the war had
been brought by a circuitous route through the Sunda Strait and by way of the Straits
of Malacca, Wilson pondered his chances of making a similar loop which would give
him a slant by which to approach the Pearl River from the south-east, rather than the
south. Consulting Dalrymple he discovered the young man had abstracted the log of
Captain John Saris of the *Clove* who, as previously noted, had years earlier ventured to
Japan from Bantam. Dalrymple was convinced a suitable passage existed through the
Indonesian archipelago between the Moluccas and New Guinea and, having obtained
the blessing of President Pigot, leader of the Madras Council, Wilson set off. With the
Pitt went the ketch *Success* of the Bombay Marine, to act as a surveying tender.

Wilson was successful and reached Whampoa early in 1759, naming the new route
after his ship. Although the intention had been to utilise the channel to avoid head-
winds rather than for any strategic purpose, 'Pitt's Passage' became extremely useful
in either direction. The long detour through the Moluccas and east of the Philippines

not only gave access to Canton irrespective of the prevailing monsoon in the South China Sea, it also dodged any enemy forces in the Sunda Strait. Moreover, it conferred upon British-flagged shipping a claim on free navigation through the Dutch East Indies. All these factors were of growing importance for, with the export of Malwa opium to China steadily increasing – about 1,000 chests a year by 1760 – a new and subsequently important component to Britain's oriental trade was emerging. East Indiamen were expressly forbidden to carry opium, despite the fact that the Company held a monopoly of its production in Bengal, so the carriage of the drug was undertaken by Country-ships which, by the end of the eighteenth century, made up a large proportion of the so-called 'China Fleet' and as such they were as vulnerable in war as Company ships, hence the benefits of what would come to be called the Eastern, as well as Pitt's Passage.

In pursuance of all this licit and illicit traffic Dalrymple himself was selected by Governor Pigot of the Madras Presidency to carry out a 'Secret Service': an extensive survey in the presidency vessel *Cuddalore*. He left Madras in the HCS *Winchelsea*, commanded by Thomas Howe, and transferred to the *Cuddalore* under Captain Baker in the Strait of Malacca, whereupon they set off for Macao, Taiwan and the Philippines, Dalrymple taking over the direction of the schooner.

Meanwhile the *Success* had been sent north under James Flint. The increasing value of the China trade, and especially in its importation of tea, was creating problems for the Company. Duty on exported tea was extracted by the Chinese authorities who manipulated the rivalries of the competing European East India companies at one end of the world, while equal extortion in the way of import duty was practised by the British at the other. While the Chinese exactions were less than those of the home government – which by this time had risen above the cost price of the tea in question – the Company's Directors and Court in Leadenhall Street had little choice but to bow before the latter, even boasting of their patriotic contribution to the Exchequer. They were less content to submit to the levies at Canton, not least because these were exacted with Celestial disdain on the one hand and were considered – with a reciprocal and xenophobic contempt on the other – to amount to subsidising a foreign power. At Macao the Select Committee of supercargoes, the governing trading body of the Company *in situ*, determined on advancing an initiative and for this they chose James Flint, sending him, accompanied by one of their number, to Ningpo to open commerce through that port.

Flint had been sent out to Macao in 1736 as an orphaned child by some enterprising soul who hit upon the notion that while it proved almost impossible for a mature Briton to learn Chinese, an untutored child might accomplish the task with a facility only enjoyed by the very young. These successful endeavours to make him 'acquainted with the Mandareen' were interrupted by a passage to Madras three years later after which he was returned to Macao and apprenticed to Chinese merchants. Dressing and living as a 'Celestial' – as the Chinese were frequently known – Flint travelled extensively in southern China and learned not only Mandarin, but the difficult dialect of Fukien. Utterly loyal to the Company, 'who occasionally relieved his penury', Flint was in Canton as interpreter to the supercargoes in 1746 at a rate of 90 *taels* for every Indiaman he assisted.

Flint and his companion were received 'very graciously' at Ningpo and trading was carried out with the cargo they had brought in the *Success*. Flint and his colleague returned to Macao and the following year two vessels loaded at Ningpo to which place Flint now expected to be appointed on a permanent basis. But one lot of monopolists had encountered another: the Co-Hong of Chinese merchants at Canton had protested to the Emperor at this circumvention of their privileges and the breaking of the imperial edict forbidding foreigners to trade anywhere other than through Canton. There followed a consequential imperial decree proscribing any trade through Ningpo.

In early 1759 Wilson arrived in the *Pitt* with the *Success* in company, and the latter was taken over for a renewal of an attempt to open trade in defiance of the Emperor's decree. Thus when Wilson sailed in the *Pitt* and made his way through the Eastern Passage, Flint went north. His was a remarkable 'embassy', 'a solitary, pig-tailed Englishman,' in John Keay's phrase, 'with no official credentials and the most presumptuous of communications … would be lucky to get away with his life'.

The *Success* was refused entry at Ningpo where the officials, having incurred imperial wrath once, went in fear of their own lives and would not even permit the purchase of necessary stores. Flint left a copy of his petition there and then continued north, shadowed by imperial war-junks. The *Success* arrived at the Taku Bar where, by an extraordinary coincidence, Flint ran into the local mandarin who had formerly been at Canton. As the official's 'guest' Flint was allowed to proceed upstream to Tientsin (Tianjin) where the mandarin suggested taking refuge in the claim that Flint had been the victim of 'stress of weather'. The latter, however, maintained that this would not answer his purpose and the two men now decided that if Flint distributed copies of his petition among all the local officials they would 'for fear of each other will not think to keep it from the Emperor'. His friend required that Flint paid him well for this service, *cumshaw* that was well invested, for an Imperial edict recalled the Hoppo and ordered Flint, in the company of two mandarins from the court in the Forbidden City, to return overland to Canton and enquire into the grievances of the British. The two imperial commissioners dealt out the Emperor's displeasure to the disgraced Hoppo's staff and the Co-Hong merchants, but enquired into the identity of the East India Company's Chinese collaborators and simply reverted to allowing trade only through Canton.

After their departure Flint was summoned before the Imperial Viceroy. In expectation of trouble, the Company's Selectmen accompanied him, to be deprived of their swords and forced to their knees when they refused to *kowtow* in the Viceroy's presence. The loyal Flint was sentenced to three months detention at Macao, after which he was banished from China. His Chinese accomplice, who had assisted him in drafting the petition, was strangled and all the objections enumerated in the petition were reinforced by revised imperial decree. Despite the Company sending Captain Nicholas Skottowe of the HCS *Royal George* to protest to the Viceroy and secure Flint's release, Flint served his sentence and was eventually deported. Matters remained exactly as before, the only concession being permission for Company officials to reside within the Pale of their factories in Canton throughout the year.

Meanwhile Dalrymple had not been idle. He too nursed ideas of establishing a trading base free of the Viceroy, the Hoppo and the Co-Hong and in 1759 had taken the *Cuddalore* along the north coast of Luzon. He was at Macao when Flint was sentenced and then sailed down the coast of Indo-China, carrying out a running survey of Hainan and Annam, anchoring off Da Nang. Of this voyage he afterwards wrote that:

> My journal of the coast of Hainan is perhaps the most imperfect of any in my whole voyage, it was on my first setting out in command of the *Cuddalore*, the Chief Mate was not an artist and had all the prejudice which constantly attends ignorance. He was besides very careless at keeping the log.

Dalrymple's standards were high and he did not suffer fools.

Dalrymple next returned to Macao, where he was to render a more immediate service to his employers. Despite the British and John Company's gains on the Indian subcontinent under Robert Clive, the French were successful elsewhere in the Indian Ocean and in 1760 a French naval squadron drove the Company's people out of their pepper-plantations along the south-west coast of Sumatra by seizing Benkulen which was 'shamelessly' surrendered. The French then lay in the Sunda Strait in ambush for the expected 'China Fleet'. Word reached Whampoa where six laden Indiamen were ready to sail and to outwit this stratagem Dalrymple and the *Cuddalorre* joined the commodore to pilot the fleet through the Sulu Sea. Despite the *Cuddalore*'s leadsmen being constantly in the chains sounding, the passage through the reef-strewn waters of the Sulu archipelago south-west of Zamboanga in January 1761, resulted in one of the Indiamen running aground to become a total loss. The remaining five pressed on, anchoring off the large island of Jolo, home of the Sultan of Sulu, with whom Dalrymple concluded a trading contract. Having carried out a hasty survey of Jolo, the *Cuddalore* accompanied the Indiamen through the Macassar Strait and into the Indian Ocean by way of the Sape Strait between Sumbawa and Komodo. This route was, he wrote later in his *Memoir Concerning the Passages to and from China*, 'the most eligible Passage to China for Ships getting into the Latitude of five degrees South to the eastward of Java before the beginning of November, or perhaps later.' Off Sumbawa Dalrymple took leave of the Indiamen which proceeded to Madras, the *Cuddalore* continuing her surveying, particularly of the new passage. During the rest of the year Dalrymple continued charting the beautiful Sulu archipelago, finding safe passages through the string of islands. On completion of this he sailed north, to Luzon, and made a survey of Manila Bay, returning to Madras in early 1762.

Dalrymple now pleaded the utility of a permanent post in the Sulu area, clear of Dutch and Spanish claims and interference, and received permission to explore on behalf of the Company. Given command of the smaller snow *London* and with one James Rennel, later Surveyor-General of Bengal, Dalrymple explored the coast of Borneo (Sabah) and selected the island of Balambangan in the Balabac Strait as a new base for a Company station. This was part of the territory of the Sultan of Sulu and negotiations were opened to obtain a grant of the island which was officially ceded in September 1762. Dalrymple wanted Balambangan colonised by Chinese and established as a free port but, despite the endorsement of both the Court of Directors and – for it was deemed to be necessary – the approval of the British Government, the project ultimately failed.

One reason was attributable to Dalrymple himself: he set the price of his services too high, wanting almost vice-regal powers in Balambangan, believing that he could establish 'a great and permanent extension of the Company's commerce'. Amid rumours of his having raised troops and recruited 2,000 Chinese coolies in Manila for his private purposes, his demands were rejected out of hand. None of this was true, but Dalrymple's manner only added to the furore, and his obstinate refusal to compromise undermined the project. Although a minor post was established in Balambangan in 1772 it never amounted to much and was a drain on resources. Dalrymple's project, along with his influence, was eclipsed at least for a while.

On his return to London in 1765, Dalrymple was elected to the Royal Society and it was intended by that body that he should lead the expedition to the Pacific in 1768 to observe the transit of Venus from Otaheite. In 1767 he published a pamphlet that claimed the existence of a 'Southern Continent' which lay between its 'eastern part discovered by Juan Fernandez' and 'the western coast seen by Tasman'. Such a landmass, Dalrymple asseverated, had a probable population of 'more than fifty millions... There is at present no trade from Europe thither, though the scraps from this table would be sufficient to maintain the Power, Dominion and Sovereignty of Britain, by employing all its manufacturing and ships'. This display of finely worded expertise buttered no parsnips at the Admiralty. Their Lordships insisted that the proposed expedition should be led by a naval officer and Dalrymple's name gave way to that of James Cook.

Disappointed, Dalrymple employed his embittered time in producing a number of charts of the East Indies and a handbook on nautical surveying, taking part in the Royal Society's then current debate on the existence of *Terra Australis Incognita*, whence Cook was later directed. After a brief return to Madras as a member of the Council there in 1776, Dalrymple was formally appointed as the first Hydrographer to the Honourable East India Company in 1779, producing beautifully engraved folios of charts for East India Company commanders, along with sailing directions to accompany them.

His running surveys were attended by the difficulties of determining longitude, though he did his best with lunar observations, but he nevertheless established the Company's hydrographic credentials long before the Admiralty troubled itself to do so properly on behalf of His Majesty's ships. Dalrymple's work proved of enormous use, opening up the navigation of the East Indies and increasing the professional expertise of the Company's officer corps. In 1764, for example, a small convoy of Indiamen escorted by HMS *Falmouth* were directed to proceed from Manila by way of Sulu 'and thence between Borneo and Celebes' (Sulawesi) towards Madras, the route that Dalrymple had pioneered.

Eclipsed by Cook in the nation's hagiography, Dalrymple was an advanced thinker. In 1769, even before the American colonies had rebelled, Dalrymple perceived in the stirrings of discontent, a world in which colonies played only a part in the aggrandisement of Great Britain, a world in which sea-power through trade was the prime dynamic. 'It must be obvious,' he wrote in *A Historical Collection of the Several Voyages and Discoveries in the South Pacific Ocean*:

> That if colonies are aiming at independence, and endeavouring to break off all connection with the Mother Country, the only means of preventing these intentions, and of securing the power and prosperity of the Mother Country, must be by extending its commerce to distant nations who can have no connection with those discontented colonies.

Trade, Dalrymple presciently asserts from his experience in the Orient, is the true goal and this lay beyond mere imperialist colonialism. He was a century ahead of his time, though his thesis found resonant echoes in Adam Smith's *Inquiry into the Nature and Causes of the Wealth of Nations*, published in 1776 and the year of the Declaration of Independence of the United States of America.

If they did not share Dalrymple's foresightedness, it was in their own self-interest for commanders of Indiamen to undertake hydrographic surveying as, where and when opportunity offered, for it was well understood that much was to be expected from the trade with China, both on the Company's behalf and in respect of private trade. Most understood the need for a safe haven between India and China, for the eastern archipelago was increasingly infested with pirates. However, establishing such a post was an uncertain business and Balambangan 'proved a short-lived and abject fiasco,' led, as it was, by one of Benkulen's 'ever venal factors, [who] plumbed new depths of embezzlement and was soon driven back to sea by the outraged Suluans'. This wretch received the severe disapprobation of the Court of Directors who considered that he 'exhibited a scene of irregularity, duplicity and presumption not to be equalled upon the records of the Company'. Balambangan was to enjoy a brief revival under Robert Farquar, but Farquar's transfer to Penang in 1805 ended the flirtation.

Nevertheless Dalrymple's flickering torch for a British post in the Far East was picked up and carried by others. Captain Thomas Forrest was a Country commander who shared Dalrymple's ambitions to extend British trade beyond the confines of the Company's immediate and conservative interest, and moreover, beyond the reach of the Dutch or Spanish. He had gone to Balambangan and from there sought fresh sources of spices in a purchased and converted Suluan prau he named *Tartar*. In this small craft he had skirted the coast of Irian Jaya and discovered new nutmeg forests. Passing through the Gilolo Strait west of New Guinea he sailed north to Mindanao obtaining trading concessions from local chiefs before returning to Balambangan only to find its new 'colonists' had moved to Borneo on the failure of their offshore enterprise. Undeterred, Forrest sailed west, through the Singapore Strait and up the Strait of Malacca until his crew refused to go any further. By this time he had reached the Sultanate of Kedah, near Pulo Penang, and here the tiny *Tartar* was sold for less than £10. In due course, Forrest continued north, scouting the Mergui archipelago where once, long ago, Samuel 'Siamese' White had held his venal sway.

Dalrymple, meanwhile, busied himself correlating and incorporating much of the work of men like Forrest, even if they were not Company servants. Others included Walter Alves who succeeded Dalrymple in command of the snow *London*. He too ventured along the coast of Mindanao and in 1765 sailed 'among the islands on the Coast of China' in what, Keay records, was a voyage of some significance.

> On 12 February, in what seems to have been one of the earliest mentions of the place, he hauled to the north of the island he called 'Heong Kong'. 'The tide being done [I] anchored in six fathoms, mud, distant from Heong Kong about a mile, Lantao Peak bearing west, eight degrees south'.[9]

Alves was killed off the coast of Borneo when the *London* was boarded by *orang laut*, the amphibian 'sea-people' who traditionally preyed on the neighbouring islands but now enjoyed the novelty of passing European shipping. Another among the forgotten pantheon of mercantile surveyors was John McCluer who, having joined the Bombay Marine as a volunteer, had by 1784 been appointed lieutenant. Soon afterwards, in the *Scorpion*, he embarked on his career as an hydrographer, surveying the harbours of Muscat and Matruh which was extended in 1787 along the coast of the Persian Gulf from Basra to the Strait of Hormuz, work later published by Dalrymple. At the end of 1787 McCluer made the first full survey of Bombay harbour and then spent over two years working along the Indian coast, including the Lashadweep – or Laccadive – Islands, from Diu Head to Cape Comorin. McCluer operated from the small *Experiment* ably seconded by Lieutenant John Proctor in a *pattamar* as tender, often in defiance of the Angrian corsairs still infesting the coast. Later McCluer had assistance from Lieutenants Ringrove, Skinner and Wedgeborough, and surveyed Mocha Road in the Red Sea. Such was the quality of the work of McCluer and his colleagues that it was used by Dalrymple and his successors, particularly James Horsburgh, in working up sailing instructions for the Company's vessels.

Such was McCluer's achievement that in late August 1790 he was promoted to commander and appointed to the *Panther*. On the 23rd the *Panther*, with the *Endeavour* commanded by First Lieutenant William Drummond in company, was despatched on another surveying voyage. This was intended to undertake the work Wilson had been sent to oversee in the *Antelope* seven years earlier when the ship had been wrecked and among his officers were Proctor, Wedgeborough and Robert White, the two latter of whom had been midshipmen in the *Antelope*. McCluer's two ships carried out running surveys while working along the coast of Java towards the isolated Pelew Islands, lying in Latitude 7° 00' North, Longitude 134° 30' East where they arrived on 22 January 1791. McCluer was greeted by the local king, who recognised Wedgeborough and White, and embraced as a friend even though he brought the melancholy news of the death of the king's son Lee Boo. McCluer also brought gifts, cattle and seeds, which the king greeted with enthusiasm allowing McCluer to occupy the island of Amallikala and establish Fort Abercrombie as British territory.

McCluer now left Proctor, who had succeeded to the command of the *Endeavour* upon the death of Drummond, to continue the survey while he took the *Panther* to Macao for supplies and to send his despatches to India. Proctor was also to 'instruct the Natives in the use of the tools of husbandry, and in the cultivation of rice grounds and gardens, for which seeds had been brought in abundance'. Proctor also assisted the king in a war with his neighbours, the musketry of the Company's seamen proving fatally effective.

In due course McCluer rejoined Proctor, and both *Panther* and *Endeavour* sailed for the western extremity of New Guinea to resume surveying, discovering McCluer Inlet (Teluk Berau) and calling at Amboina and Seram, before heading east along the southern coast of New Guinea. On the 26 November they were attacked by natives who killed Nicholson, the *Panther*'s surgeon, and wounded four seamen by arrows. Despite this set-back, which McCluer wisely refused to punish punitively, they reached Tanjong Vals on 21 December. McCluer now headed south, across the Torres Strait with his leadsman sounding continuously until within sight of New Holland, whereupon he turned westwards towards Timor. After replenishing his stores and enjoying a cordial reception from Van Schilling, the Dutch governor, McCluer made for Benkulen to forward his findings to London, one of which was the presence of the nutmeg on islands of the coast of New Guinea. That done, he then turned back towards Amalikalla. Reaching the Pelews by way of Sulu, where he picked up more grain, seeds and cattle, on 20 January 1793 McCluer directed Proctor to proceed to Macao independently in *Endeavour* and thence homewards in one of the Company's ships to report to the Court of Directors in London. At Macao Proctor found HMS *Lion* and the HCS *Hindostan* attending Lord Macartney's embassy to Peking, a description of which is left to the following volume, *Britannia's Realm*.

McCluer had delegated this important duty to Proctor for personal reasons, though these were in part disguised, for on 2 February 1793 McCluer, 'considering that he had fulfilled the objects of his mission' took the unusual step of resigning his command in favour of his first lieutenant. Wedgeborough took the *Panther* first to Macao and then Bombay, arriving on 17 August 1793. Meanwhile, retaining the *Panther*'s launch, McCluer remained in the Pelew Islands to 'enlighten … the minds of the noble islanders' and on 27 June, his resignation notwithstanding, he was promoted to captain in the Bombay Marine. McCluer's desire to 'civilise' and 'ameliorate' the condition of the native population is said to have been only part of his motive for remaining behind. It seems that at the age of thirty-one he had been captivated by the beauty of the local women, one of whom he made his mistress, although back in India he had a Malabari lover who bore him a daughter named Margaret. He resided among his new friends for fifteen months, at the end of which he set off in the launch for Ternate, but found the weather against him and resolved, with no instruments or charts, to put about for Macao, 1,600 miles away, arriving sick but alive after surviving on coconuts. After recovering from his ordeal, McCluer purchased a small vessel, the *Venus*, with a bill of exchange against the Bombay Marine, but before he sailed for the Pelew Islands to embark his native women and friends he was persuaded by a fellow officer of the Marine, John Hayes, to relieve the small settlement Hayes had established at Dorey, in Geelvink Bay on the north coast of New Guinea. Having attended to this, McCluer proceeded to the Pelew islands and, having embarked 'several Natives of both sexes', he began his passage to India. At Benkulen he met the HCS *Europa*, Captain Augustus Applegarth, and the Bombay Marine's frigate *Bombay*, aboard which he transferred some of the women before he set off across the Bay of Bengal. Neither McCluer nor the *Venus* was ever heard of again.

After subsisting on the charity of Lieutenant Snook, one of McCluer's officers, his women and friends sent to India in the *Bombay* were in 1797 eventually repatriated at the Company's expense to their homeland. This was engineered on the instigation of Wedgeborough, by this time commander of the HCS *Princess Royal*, and Captain Henry Wilson whose loss of the *Antelope* fourteen years earlier had begun this extraordinary story.

Only one further visit was made to the Pelew Islands by a vessel of the Bombay Marine, a new *Antelope*, a fourteen-gun brig built in 1793 which, under the command of Captain Nathaniel Tucker, called there in March 1802 when bound to India from Macao with despatches. A further footnote might be added concerning Lieutenant John Hayes, who had persuaded McCluer to call at Geelvink Bay when both men met in Macao. Hayes was then in command of the *Duke of Clarence* and *Duchess* and himself on a surveying voyage that would take his two vessels south to what was still then called Van Diemen's land, those parts of New Guinea and Java untouched by McCluer and Proctor, and a host of islands stretching westwards. Unhappily the whole of these protracted endeavours were lost when the ship conveying Hayes's charts and journals was captured by a French cruiser.

Hayes himself was absent so long that, nothing having been heard from him, it was assumed that his expedition had been lost. His pay, and that of his men, was stopped, reducing their dependants 'to great distress', ended only when 'the gallant Hayes sailed into Bombay one day'. Hayes went on to enjoy an active and distinguished career and we shall meet him again, though his surveying days were over.

When, at last in 1795 the British Admiralty finally decided to establish an Hydrographic Department it was to Alexander Dalrymple that Their Lordships were compelled to turn in some desperation. In this Dalrymple reversed his fate in 1768, for it would have been Cook who occupied that office had he not been murdered in Kealakekua Bay. The cantankerous and ageing Dalrymple therefore concurrently held the office of hydrographer to both the Royal Navy and the Honourable East India Company until his enforced retirement. He died three weeks later on 19 June 1808 at the age of seventy. In the cause of his death is reflected something of the turbulence of his life, for it is variously attributed to gangrene or 'of chagrin caused by his dismissal' from his post Hydrographer of the Navy. Dalrymple's relationship with Their Lordships was never easy; he was reluctant to publish unverified charts and had first to work through a mass of material of variable quality and disparate method, for which he was only allowed a tiny staff and modest budget. Notwithstanding these difficulties, which were undertaken in old age, he established a state department whose contribution to navigation, geography and the natural sciences was huge and upon which, of course, the British mercantile marine came to rely.[10]

Dalrymple was to have one more impact upon eastern commerce, and one for which his influence has been entirely forgotten. For long the booming trade with China had brought with it concerns about its vulnerability and its financing. It was vulnerable to interloping, of which more later, to interdiction in wartime and to exactions in the way of levies by both the exporting Chinese and the British government eager to benefit from importing its highly desirable commodities, most notably tea. But of more immediate concern to the Directors and the factors was the actual financing of the China trade. English exports were no more wanted in China than in India, but that mattered less than their refusal in China. Flint's attempts to open trade with the colder climes of north China had been made in the hope that a market would be found for English woollens, still a major English export in the Company's ships. All these hopes foundered and the burgeoning trade was instead paid for by silver specie. As John Keay succinctly puts it: 'At the very moment Clive was reporting that the revenues in Bengal should obviate the need to export treasure for the India trade, treasure for the China trade was draining its resources as never before'.[11]

It was impossible to finance the China deficit by using the Bengal surplus because, apart from a limited market in Indian cottons and Patna saltpetre, no Indian exports found favour in Canton. Or at least none that could be legally shipped, for the one commodity that found a ready outlet – and which was both produced by the Company and taken thither in limited quantities by the Country-trade – was opium. Dalrymple's analysis of China's import trade identified other needs: gold-dust, tin, furs, leather, pepper, spices and the bird's nests and shark's fins that complemented native rice. All travelled either overland from south-east Asia, or arrived in Chinese junks from the East Indies. Indian cottons and opium found a ready market in the East Indies and Dalrymple suggested a three-way trade, cotton and opium to the islands of the East Indies, and their produce in British bottoms to China. To some extent this trade was already under-way, carried out in the British or Indian-owned, Indian-based Country-ships which, as they had the Muslim *baggalas* in the Indian seas, now drove the Chinese junks out of their traditional trade.

Increasingly this Country-trade was a factor within the Company's trading empire – in it, but not strictly speaking of it – and its success was actually at the Company's expense, for Company servants engaged in it, not merely dabbling, but often to the extent of prejudicing the Company's legitimate claim on their time. What had begun as a free-entrepreneurial offshoot to the Persian Gulf and Arabia Felix, now flourished in the other direction. Indeed the Company's insistence – by the Court of Directors in distant London – upon its monopoly of the carrying trade to and from Britain, had blinded it to the opportunities in what was parochially thought of as mere 'local trading'. Its servants had not been so blinkered. The corrupt and relatively isolated factors operating from a re-occupied Benkulen began trading collectively on their own account: one reason for their factory's poor performance insofar as the Company's auditors were concerned. Elsewhere other syndicates were forming, trading with Kedah and other Malayan places; Aceh on Sumatra's north coast; with the Burmese of the Mergui archipelago and the Bugis merchants of the East Indies. These 'associations', shipowners of substantial vessels, were also the precursors of later shipping agencies and they failed in only one respect.

Taken as the sum of its separate parts, this was a highly successful business, suffering only from difficulties arising from equivalence of currencies. Trade was usually valued in gold pagodas (standardised in 1818 as worth 3.5 rupees), but 'gold cobangs' derived from as far afield as Japan, Mexican dollars and the ubiquitous silver rupee were among the multitude of 'cash' in circulation, making calculation complex and rake-off a ready means of nest-lining. Country-ships were owned by a number of racial groups, ex-patriate Persians and Armenians, as well at Britons, along with native Mughals, Golconda Muslims, Hindu Tamils and Zoroastrian Parsees based principally in Bombay and Calcutta but in many other places too. Nor was ownership confined to the mercantile classes; the Nawab of Arcot owned at least two 400-ton ships, the *Success Galley* and the *Nawab of Arcot*, both commanded by English masters. Others were commanded by Indian *nacodas*, who often acted as their own compradors, or supercargoes, while on most ships commanded by Britons – and here we should note a significant influx of Scotsmen – there went a *dubash* or interpreter. In time many Europeans learnt one or more of the native dialects and all added to the indiscriminate, practical and grammar-defying argot known as 'pidgin'. Alongside the ships, literally, existed an army of labourers and officials, from the humble and untouchable coolie, upwards through foremen and tally-clerks by way of harbour-officials, tax-farmers and revenue collectors to the merchants and shipowners.[12]

Often far larger than many British-built merchantmen and constructed of durable teak many Country-ships rivalled or exceeded the grandest Indiamen. They were usually built on conventional European lines and sufficient to impress one English observer who remarked: 'Behold the finest fleet of merchant shipping in the world'. It was no idle boast as, despite Dutch domination of Java, this trade was conducted eastwards from the Indian coast to Aceh, Kedah, Perak, Pegu, Mergui, Rangoon, 'Junk Ceylon' (Phuket), Malacca and beyond into the China Seas. In 1788 the Court of Directors signed a trading agreement with the Spanish Royal Philippine Company, which had been formed three years earlier, initiating a further cross-trade. Exports from India consisted of textiles,[13] salt and saltpetre, and tobacco from Jaffna; with imports of pepper, betelnuts, timber, rattans, gum dammar (rosin), benjamin (benzoin or incense), sticklac (a resin produced from an insect and laid down on sticks), horses, sugar, arrack, tung oil, ivory, cumin seed and Sumatran gold-dust. One interesting product exported from India alongside cotton piece-goods were ready-made garments: trousers, under-pants, shirts, skirts and blouses, much of which went to Batavia in exchange for copper, arrack and sugar. Westwards, passing Gombroon (Bandar Abbas) and Qeshm, to Bussourah (Bushehr) and Basra in the Persian Gulf, and in

the Red Sea beyond Mocha, ships reached Jeddah, Kosseir, Tor and Suez, importing horses, dates, weapons and coffee. This was a trade not without its dangers, the
extensive reefs in both the Persian Gulf and, more especially, the Red Sea, proved hazardous. In November 1809, the Country-ships *Diamond, Futty Allebhoy* and *Bussora
Packet* were returning to Bombay from Basra when the *Diamond* and *Futty Allebhoy*
both struck on shoals north-west of Nabiyu Farur. The weather was hazy with a
strong wind and the ships beat on the reefs until they were bilged. Almost all of the
passengers and crews got ashore but, on the sea abating, Captain Benson led a party
back aboard the *Diamond* to find his cargo of Arab horses in a terrible state and their
handlers responsible for the rifling of the ship. Fortunately Captain Clement of the
Bussora Packet, finding his ship alone, put back and rescued the others the following
day. Many other County-ships engaged in this trade were lost, the *Arran* in 1809.

As always coastal shipping reacted to politico-military events. During the intermittent Mysore Wars food shortages in the Carnatic led to imports of food-grains from
which shipping benefited. On the other hand the near contemporaneous Burmese
Mon rebellion caused the abandonment of shipbuilding on the Irrawaddy where
it had long been established. With this trade went a diaspora of merchants' representatives, similarly reflecting a wide racial mix but all indissolubly linked with the
great trading-web that thrived under the Company's grand umbrella and focussed on
Calcutta. As to its political hold, John Company, while assiduous in its tax-farming,
was content to leave daily administration to the local *nawabs* and *rajas*, but was quick
to intervene when its commercial interests were at stake.

Almost everywhere trade throve, even the French enjoyed a period of great
prosperity with their own Country-vessels and traders based on Pondicherry and
Chandarnagar on the Hughli, but all attempts to establish factories outside the subcontinent foundered. The Sultan of Aceh would have none of it when approached
by Forrest on another of his voyages; the Dutch headed-off all attempts to gain a
foothold in the Rhio Islands, south of modern Singapore. It was not for want of
trying on the part of the Company's servants. Beyond the repossessed Benkulen's Fort
St David, attempts were made to establish trading posts elsewhere in the East Indies,
on Java and Borneo, even modern Vietnam at Tourane. But matters at Benkulen were
not satisfactory, its official trading deficit troubling the Court of Directors in London
and the President and Council at Madras. A shabby attempt was made to trade Malwa
opium for spices smuggled out from under the noses of the Dutch, and this encouraged both Company and private 'Country' enterprise. Such machinations could not
be kept from Batavia and, while Benkulen factors squealed about the British right
of navigation through Dutch waters, the Dutch countered that such a right did not
include trading within their colonies. They might have added nor on private account.
The only solution seemed to be relocation, a solution which was to wait a generation
and a genius.

The need for another factory was driven by the increasing need for a mid-way
base or depot between India and China. The situation became more acute during the
American War of Independence when a French squadron under the incomparable

De Suffren almost dominated the Bay of Bengal. Although never fully satisfactory in answering the purpose, success of a kind was gained in 1786 when Captain Francis Light, a former naval officer who had become a Country commander working for the Madras Association – a private firm – persuaded the Sultan of Kedah to cede Pulo Penang, which Light renamed Prince of Wales Island.[14] One of the young men sent there on the Company's behalf was one Stamford Raffles who, for the time being, stood in the shadow of others but was among the youngest of the rising generation.

Dalrymple's successor as the Company's hydrographer was James Horsburgh. From the age of twenty-two in 1784 Horsburgh was at sea in the Company's ships, surviving ship-wreck on Diego Garcia in the Indian Ocean in 1786. A born surveyor and observer of natural phenomena, the Royal Society published his findings on the diurnal variation of barometric pressure which he had studied between 1802–1804, and elected him a Fellow in 1806. His charts had appeared under Dalrymple's aegis and, after assuming Dalrymple's mantle, in 1808 he produced the *East India Directory* for which he received 100 guineas from the Court of Directors. Horsburgh assisted the Royal Navy's Hydrographer in resolving the confusion of longitudes and preparing a list of places whose exact meridian was to be established during a proposed naval expedition. James Horsburgh was a founder member of the Royal Geographical Society in 1830 and continued in the East India Office as hydrographer until his death six years later, leaving his name to a reef and lighthouse at the eastern end of the Singapore Strait.

Although the exploits of the Bombay Marine lie largely outside the scope of this narrative, it is meet to remark that the Marine furnished a number of surveying officers whose work contributed to the safe expansion of British trade by adding to the folios of Dalrymple and Horsburgh. Mindful of the ordeal of the survivors of the HCSs *Winterton*, *Grosvenor* and other vessels, after the loss of the HCS *Earl Talbot* in the South China Sea in 1800 mentioned earlier, the Bombay Marine's two surveying vessels the *Intrepid* and *Comet* were sent to search for survivors. Both were in turn lost without trace and Lieutenant McCluer, who had made his name under Dalrymple with extensive surveys of the Persian Gulf and west coast of India, was dispatched on a search for a port of refuge for vessels threatened by a typhoon. Between 1806 and 1820 Captain Daniel Ross surveyed the Kwantung coast east and west of Macao, the coast of Cochin China, Hainan, Taiwan and the Straits of Malacca, being appointed Marine Surveyor-General in 1809 to facilitate the operational co-ordination of surveying throughout the region.[15]

Increasingly detailed work was carried out. Under Captain Maxfield, working in the Bay of Bengal, a new anchorage was found inside the Armagon shoal suitable as a refuge in the north east monsoon which rendered Madras Road such a hazard. The constant depredations of pirates attacking shipping passing up to Basra in the Persian Gulf drew the Bombay Marine into naval operations and to facilitate this Captain Maugham was despatched with a number of officers to carry out a full survey of the gulf. As time passed and the steamer route was established between Suez and Bombay, further work was carried out in the Arabian and Red Seas The latter was under-

Joseph Huddart, 1741–1816, East India Company Commander and Elder Brother of Trinity House. Huddart carried out extensive surveys in the Far East and on the home coast. Later he became a wealthy manufacturer of cable-laid rope and chain anchor cable. A colleague of Sir Robert Wigram. (Author's Collection)

taken in 1829 in the *Hugh Lindsay*, the first steamer built in India, under Commander Robert Moresby who took his ship beyond the Straits of Bab-el-Mandeb, the 'Gate of Tears'. Moresby followed up this preliminary work in the sloop *Palinurus*, and Captain Elwon in the brig *Benares* carried out more detailed work which was 'as perfect as labour and skill can make it'. This occupied a period of four and a half years which took its toll of the surveying officers, after which, under Captain Haynes, the *Palinurus* charted the coast of the Hadramaut and the island of Socotra off the Horn of Africa. One reason for such surveys was the increasing need of coaling stations for both merchant and naval steamers and these were afterwards established at Perim Island, in the Strait of Bab-el-Mandeb, and at Aden on the Yemen coast to the eastwards.

So much for the Bengal Marine; among the commanders of the Company's commercial Maritime Service Joseph Huddart was one of many whose contribution to hydrography has been less regarded than that of Dalrymple or Horsburgh, but whose cumulative data amounted to a mass of information.[16] Born in 1740 Huddart belonged to the old school, going to sea and soon commanding a brig in the coasting trade. In 1768, after building another brig to his own design at Maryport, Cumbria, he traded to North America. In 1771, on a visit to London, he met Sir Richard Hotham who 'husbanded two ships in the Honourable East India Company's service… Sir Richard was so much pleased with the judicious remarks Mr Huddart made on this occasion,

as to express a strong desire that he should … enter into the Company's service…'
Discovering that he would have to serve first as fourth officer the ambitious Huddart
declined, but in 1773 Hotham persuaded him to sail in that capacity in the HCS *York*
bound for Benkulen and, without putting up a bond, Huddart was promised command of the ship when Captain Hayter resigned. Employing a master in his own ship,
Huddart agreed and during the *York's* voyage he produced a survey of the west coast
of Sumatra and the anchorage at Benkulen. Hayter, however, was disobliging.

Huddart was another victim of the inflated expectations attached to private
trade which, from time-to-time, slumped. He lost £120 on his investment on one
voyage, which persuaded him to quit the service, but with rebellion in prospect
in America matters were little better in his former employment, so he resumed
coastal trading in the *Patience* until in October 1776, when on Hotham's behalf,
he 'under took to superintend the curing of provisions at Cork for [Hotham's]
ships in the Company's service'. These were then shipped to London in Huddart's
own vessel. Huddart, meanwhile, having sold his Sumatran survey to Mr Sayer,
'an eminent chart-seller in Fleet-street', became engaged by Sayer to survey the
Irish Sea. Huddart sent his own brig off to trade in the Baltic and chartered a small
vessel to undertake the survey, which was very well done. 'The emolument derived
from this undertaking was inconsiderable, the celebrity acquired by it was great'
and led to the Company again soliciting Huddart's services as first mate of a new
Indiaman, the *Royal Admiral*. The Company's nominated commander dying before
the commencement of the voyage, Huddart was accordingly appointed, in defiance of the regulations – for he had only made one voyage not two and that in an
inferior rank – and at the disadvantage of having to exploit his dead predecessor's
investments. This he did to the satisfaction of the executors of the late commander
during the voyage to Bombay which lasted from April 1778 to January 1780 and
upon which he took his son William as a midshipman. On the outward voyage, one
of the convoy in which the Indiamen sailed struck a rock in the approaches to Table
Bay and Huddart and his son went off in one of the *Royal Admiral's* boats to locate
the position of the rock. The boat was upset by a heavy breaker and all survived,
though Huddart lost his surveying instruments.

On Huddart's second voyage to Bombay the *Royal Admiral* was put under the
orders of Admiral Sir Edward Hughes and took part in supporting operations against
the Dutch at Jagginaultporam and Negapatam and it was August 1783 by the time
the *Royal Admiral* returned to Britain. Thereafter Huddart rose in the Company's
service, making a success of his third voyage both in pecuniary terms and in charting the Basses Reef, off Sri Lanka, carrying out a running survey of the Gaspar
Strait – which afterwards astonished commentators on the accuracy of its longitudes
– and charting Simon's Bay, Table Bay and False Bay, all in South Africa. Huddart's
fourth and last voyage in the *Royal Admiral* was to Bombay and thence onwards to
Canton. Huddart's was a remarkable record; he had continually employed himself
in surveying and collecting information, using his talent for navigation and nautical
astronomy so that:

…he was enabled, by the eclipse of Jupiter's satellites, to ascertain the longitude of Bombay with greater precision than had been done by any former geographer. He [also] observed an annular and central eclipse of the sun when in China; he went some distance to accomplish this object, and thus determined with greater accuracy the longitude. Together with several other Surveys, he completed one of the whole Peninsula from Bombay to Coringa [near Cape Godavari], also one of the River … from Canton to the island of Sankeet…

Huddart retired from the sea to establish a private observatory and workshop in which he became a skilled horologist. Being a Younger Brother of Trinity House he was called upon in 1790 to carry out a survey of the Haisbro Gat off the Norfolk coast and it was following this that he was elected an Elder Brother, assisting with the Corporation's work as the lighthouse authority for England and Wales throughout the years of the Revolutionary and Napoleonic Wars during which the Corporation raised a military force to defend the Thames against invasion. He was instrumental in the completion of the Longships lighthouse off Land's End, and in establishing beacons on the Runnelstone and Wolf Rock. Indeed his work at Trinity House increased his knowledge of seamarks, and also of dredging and spoil management; but that was not all. He conducted surveys of the Scottish coast and offshore islands, and suggested improvements to several ports throughout Britain and Ireland, including several of the Royal Dockyards. Huddart also became a member of the Royal Society and a director of several enterprises to provide adequate wet-dock facilities in London, in particular the East India Dock, opened in 1806. In 1800 he had commissioned a factory for spinning a new and improved rope intended to give greater strength for ship's anchor cables, a patent method from which he made a fortune. At the same time he carried out experiments in hull form with his East India colleague and shipbuilder Sir Robert Wigram at Blackwall. Sadly, it was admitted by his familial biographer, that 'owing to the application by Captain Huddart of his high mathematical knowledge and language in noting the experiments, little can be made of them' which meant that after their author's death they appear to have been lost to posterity.

Many of Huddart's surveys had been published by the chart-maker Laurie and he was instrumental as an influential member of the Court of the Trinity House in encouraging the pursuit of a more aggressive policy of providing proper seamarks in the form of new and improved lighthouses and lightvessels which, until his time had been largely left in private hands.[17] Even approaching death Huddart's observational method did not fail him, for he kept a record of his declining state almost until his demise in August 1816.

Despite a growing trade and the enrichments of its servants, the Company's affairs were again heading for trouble in the early 1770s. In theory the East India Company was to remit annually to the Treasury the sum of £400,000 but in 1772, with fifty-five laden Indiamen at sea, it was obliged to seek a loan of £1,000,000. As a consequence a Parliamentary Committee was appointed to look into its affairs which, under close scrutiny, proved none too savoury. Despite that fact that freight rates were far too high – a more competitive commercial rate being two thirds of that charged – it emerged that the Company's structure made the milking of it too easy and that its most trusted and elevated officials were not noted for their probity or rectitude. Sucked into the vacuum left by the corruption and failure of the Mughal Empire at the turn of the century, the growing military power of the Company on land, where it had destroyed the French and their Indian allies and suppressed revolt by Tippoo Sahib, led its officials to overweening acts among which extortion and personal gain supplanted the considerations of commercial enhancement. In short, its servants had lost sight of the fact that trade was, after all, the Company's *raison d'être* and that they were merely its commercial servants.

As a consequence of this corruption, the government passed two acts through parliament, the first authorising the desired loan, the second exacting its price. The India, or Regulating, Act of 1773 – that which was alleged to have caused the apoplectic death of Sir William James – removed the Company's control over its territorial gains, appointing a supreme Governor-General at Calcutta at a handsome salary of £25,000 per annum. The first such lucky man was an insider, Warren Hastings, who had previously served as Export Warehouse-keeper at Madras before rising by stages to become Governor of Bengal.[18] Supporting him was to be a Supreme Court and judicature – to which William Hickey was appointed – with a salaried Council as advisors. All Company Presidencies were henceforth subordinate to this gubernatorial regime. Thus, whilst retaining operational control of its day-to-day affairs, the actual government of what was now effectively British India, was under the British crown. At the same time the Company's charter was renewed and, in order to ensure its continued viability this included a monopoly on the trade in tea from China.

The consequences of these acts along with the Company's woes were not inconsiderable. Tea drinking had grown exponentially since its first appearance on the market a few years earlier. Tea was widely believed to be a panacea for all ills and although expensive, had rapidly become extremely popular as a beverage, not least in the American Colonies. In 1773 three chartered ships were sent to Boston in order to take advantage of the market there. They were not, as is often claimed, Indiamen, not least because the Company was excluded from trade with the Americas by an act of 1698, but Extra-Ships carrying a cargo whose sale would be beneficial to the Company.[19] Unfortunately, the addition of a small duty by Lord North's government in following the hated Stamp Act and other Coercive Acts in previous years led to an explosion of wrath among the susceptible and agitated population. Although North's duty was but a 'peppercorn of principle', its presumption in taxing citizens bereft of representation in the imperial parliament led to a wild demonstration of protestors dressed as Mohawk Indians who, boarding the ships in the night, tossed 342 chests of tea into the harbour. The Boston Tea Party convinced the ladies of Massachusetts that coffee was a more suitable and appropriate beverage and the event, though it led to impositions until the loss was made good, contributed to the Declaration of Independence made in Philadelphia three years later.

At the time, however, the incident was of little moment in Leadenhall Street. The loss of the American tea market scarcely mattered, for a remarkable upsurge in tea consumption at home more than made up for it. Following a parliamentary enquiry into smuggling, the government of the elder Pitt had decided to reduce the duties on several imports from India. The effect of this upon the duty on tea increased its consumption still further so that it was no longer a luxury but widely available even among the labouring classes. This increased demand threefold and proved timely, rapidly repairing the Company's finances and in the late 1770s it was decided to build a larger class of Indiaman. Aimed at making economies of scale, the former 800-ton class were now to be increasingly superseded by ships which within fifteen years would reach 1,200 to 1,400 tons burthen.

Prior to the introduction of the new ships, around 1789, a thorough overhaul of the Company's Maritime Service was undertaken, one effect of which was to improve the professional services of the ship's officers, another to increase the life of a vessel in the Company's service from four to six voyages. So, as the larger ships came into service, a regulation allowed the commanders and officers to take up any capacity unused by the Company's outward lading for the purposes of private trade, and any on the homeward passage to be utilised by 'the Company's servants and merchants residing under the Company's protection in India … at a reasonable freight'. This was on top of the existing allowances and by this means an increasing volume of private trade made up the lading and the value of an Indiaman's freight.

Whatever stuck to the fingers of the Company's servants in India, it was to China that the Court of Directors now looked to for commercial profit and the China trade that prolonged the life of a Company that was – at least in India – now far from a mere commercial entity.

NOTES

1. The *Albemarle*'s first lieutenant, Martin Hinton, quoted by Roger Knight, *Nelson, The Pursuit of Victory*, p65. Knight states that none of the East India commanders complained, which hints that only a few men were taken, but it does not rule out the possibility that a protest was lodged but ignored.

2. Relationships between the two services often became heated, particularly when officers of the Royal Navy and the Bombay Marine came into conflict. Keble Chatterton mentions in *The Old East Indiamen* (p146 *et seq*) one such case of friction arising from attempts to press men out of Company vessels. It is not out of place to emphasise this incident, adding as it does to the reasons for animosity arising between the mercantile marine and the Royal Navy, for it was to permeate and often poison the relationship between the two. In 1804 Captain Lord George Stuart of HMS *Arrogant*, then lying at Bombay as a hulked receiving ship, summoned the commander of the HEIC's cruiser *Ternate*, a sixteen-gun brig, to answer a charge of having in a previous vessel – the Company's brig-of-war *Fly* – harboured a deserter from the *Arrogant*. The officer commanding the *Ternate*, Thomas Dade Beaty, refused, challenging Stuart's authority to issue commands to officers of the Company's Marine. Knowing Beaty to have gone ashore next evening, Stuart boarded the *Ternate*, mustered her crew, took out of her six

prime seamen – though whether he recovered his deserter is unclear – and demanded Beaty attend him on board *Arrogant* next morning. A voluminous correspondence ensued. The 'Superintendent of the Hon'ble Company's Marine', Beaty's immediate superior, judged Stuart's action 'very harsh and indecent', writing to the Governor at Bombay that: 'If the crews are to be impressed…I humbly presume I cannot expect to retain one seaman in the Service'. This wretched affair is not mentioned in C.R. Low's *History of the Indian Navy, 1616–1863*, although Beaty appears in a list of First Lieutenants of the Bombay Marine. He was in the *Viper* in 1802, the ill-fated *Fly* in 1803 and the *Ternate* in 1804.

3. He is said to have ridden into the city daily at the head of a small cavalcade of seven of his sons, all of whom had interests in what had become a family business empire. Among his other sons the seventh, Sir James Wigram, became an eminent judge and his tenth, Joseph Cotton Wigram, became Bishop of Rochester. Wigram's habit of honouring his friends by giving their names to his sons was continued in the sixteenth, William Pitt Wigram, but the dynastic affectation went risibly awry when his eldest son, Sir Robert, coined the surname FitzWygram, an affectation dropped by the sixth baronet, Sir Edgar, grandson of Money Wigram, in 1920. Wigram's second son William was a member of the HEIC's Court for forty-one years.

4. Captain William Taylor Money subsequently became Superintendent of the Bombay Marine and held the post until 1813 when he retired and was superseded by Captain Henry Meriton. He also was later an Elder Brother of Trinity House.

5. Among other senior members of the fraternity at this time who were either owners or HEIC commanders – all having been ship-masters as a prerequisite to being Elder Brethren – were Captains Anthony Calvert, John Woolmore, John Cotton, Joseph Cotton, Henry Pelly, William Money, George Probyn, Philip Bromfield, Robert Preston, John Defell, John Sealy, George Curtis, Richard Lewin, George Ballantyne, Robert Burrowes and Isaac Robinson.

6. With the outbreak of the French Revolutionary War the year before, the Royal Navy bought a number of stoutly built East Indiamen particularly for convoy duties and foreign stations. Dent's ship was renamed HMS *Abergavenny* as a fifty-four-gun, 4th Rate, served until 1807 when she was sold for breaking up.

7. Not be confused with Tucker's brig-sloop *Antelope* built in Bombay in 1793 for the Bombay Marine. Prince Lee Boo died of small-pox in December 1784 and lies buried in Rotherhithe churchyard where the HEIC erected a monument to him.

8. Madras was under threat from the French under De Lally and Draper's arrival was timely for the forces defending it were led by Colonel Aldercron of the 39th Foot who had arrived in 1756 on the outbreak of war. The 39th were the first regular royal line regiment to serve in India. As an officer bearing the king's commission Aldercron was automatically senior to the officers of the Company's armies but proved incompetent and had no knowledge of Indian conditions, so that for three years the Madras council tried to get 'the use of Aldercron's troops without Aldercron'. This they succeeded in doing upon the eve of the regiment's recall, whereupon half its strength signed up for service in the Company's armed service. Amid this activity it is easy to overlook the Seven Years War by which British hegemony increased so tremendously across India, leaving the French with only Pondicherry and the Portuguese the imperial vestige of Goa. (By the Methuen Treaty of 1703 Britain and Portugal were bound in alliance, thus facilitating co-operation at both Goa and, more important to this history, Macao.)

   As related, in October 1758 Colonel Draper had arrived with his regiment at Fort George in the HCS *Pitt*, Captain William Wilson. Afterwards he played a key role a largely forgotten British military triumph of the Seven Years War, the capture of Manila. Having thrown back De Lally from the ramparts of Fort George, Colonel Draper sailed aboard an Indiaman in *mufti* to the Pearl River to discuss with the supercargoes of the Select Committee resident there the state of Spanish power in the Philippines. The focus of Draper's enquiries was Manila and the state of repair of the *Intramuros*, the city's defensive citadel, along with the defences at Cavite, the neighbouring shipbuilding arsenal. Draper then returned to London, where the First Lord of the Admiralty was Lord Anson. Anson had personal knowledge of the Spanish in the Pacific and had made his fortune from the capture of the *Nuestra Señora de Corbadonga*, mentioned earlier. Having secured confidential governmental approval for an expedition against the Spanish at Manila, Draper returned to Madras aboard the frigate *Argo*. Arriving in June 1762 he transmitted the Ministry's orders to the flag-officer there, Rear Admiral Samuel Cornish. (Cornish's origins are obscure but seem rooted in merchant shipping. He is said by some authorities to have, like James Cook, come up the hard way and had begun his career as a merchant seaman in colliers working between London and the Tyne. Others, Rodger included, suggest he was the son of a ship-master in the West India trade. Either way he knew his business and his operation, conducted thousands of miles from a proper base, was a credit to him and his fleet.) The objective of destroying Spanish power in the Pacific had collateral benefits, for Cornish's squadron was worn out. Clive's victories had not come cheap and the admiral was anxious for his ships in Madras's open roadstead with the cyclone season imminent. Manila Bay was a tempting refuge, while the facilities at Cavite offered cheap refitting.

Draper mustered his own infantry battalion, the 79th Foot, and an artillery battery, he had perforce to supplement this with 'a composition of the deserters of all nations whom I take with me more to ease the fears and apprehensions of the people of Madras than any service I can expect from them…' (Draper to Lord Egremont, 27 July 1762.) These were embarked with stores, ammunition and guns in Cornish's flagship, HMS *Norfolk* and the squadron of four other ships-of-the-line and two frigates besides the *Argo*. A detachment of the Company's sepoys was also embarked and the former forty-four-gun *Southsea Castle* was reduced to assist as an armed transport.

The British squadron entered Manila Bay at sunset on 23 September and, a fortnight later Draper's 'banditti' stormed the ramparts, aided by Filipino 'patriots' who wished for the overthrow of their Spanish masters. The operation was nearly upset by the onset of wild weather whilst the landing was being effected. Several men were drowned in landing, the ships' boats being upset in the heavy surf and the *Southsea Castle* parted her cable and drove ashore. However, though a wreck, her grounding on hard sand facilitated the discharge of the artillery which was dragged up the beach on coconut matting. A siege battery was established and began to bombard the adjacent San Diego bastion, enabling the assault to be made on 6 October. The negotiations with the Archbishop were tortuous and conducted in Latin, but in due course Cornish's weary warships were repaired and refitted at Cavite and the city yielded a good deal of plunder. But all attempts to establish a British foothold foundered in Manila as surely as they had at Balambangan. News of peace ended the British intervention and, notwithstanding a long wrangle between London and Madrid, the balance of half of the agreed ransom of four million dollars never materialised. Finally – despite the daring of the raid – the city was returned to Spain at the peace negotiations in Paris which were concluded on 10 February 1763, eight days before the agreement between Cornish and Draper, and the Archbishop of Manila – hence the Spanish refusal to honour the bill of exchange. Florida and Minorca were esteemed more valuable than distant Manila to the British Ministry and the Company's expectations were disappointed.

9. Keay, J., *The Honourable Company*, p357.
10. Dalrymple's candidacy for commanding the voyage to observe the transit of Venus from Tahiti was dismissed by the Admiralty because of his insistence on being given a post-

captain's commission in the Royal Navy. The Admiralty refused point-blank, having regretted such promotions as Dampier's and, more recently, Edmund Halley's. Dalrymple's high-opinion of himself, though in many ways justified, did not work in his favour and he would have proved an irascible commander.

11. Keay, p359.

12. The names of many such posts were assimilated into the waterfront slang familiar to generations of seafarers, as were many of the duties and establishments associated with cargo-storage and handling. It also provided a diversity of near synonyms. The name bank-shall for a warehouse, derives from *baksaal*, a word common in the Carnatic, while a synonym for a storage facility is go-down, deriving from a Tamil or Telugu root. Such words, courtesy of the seamen who used them, spread widely, so one finds bank-shalls on the shores of the Pearl River and go-downs in the Malay peninsula. For a wonderful vocabularic wallow, see Hobson-Jobson, *The Anglo-Indian Dictionary*.

13. The list of textiles is complex and redolent of many localities and traditional processes: *muri*, or *more*, was cotton cloth, *bethiles* were muslins and there was long-cloth blue and long-cloth white, *salempores*, *allegeas*, *succatoons*, chintzes and *palempores*.

14. The Madras Association was owned by Jourdain, Sulivan and de Souza and was based at Fort George. Its ships traded in Indian cottons, selling them to Malay and Bugis merchants in Malaya and Indonesia and buying trade-goods for China, thus cutting out the traditional Chinese junks. The Association had agencies in Aceh and Kedah and effectively operated a local monopoly. In 1770 the Directors in London ordered Madras to take over this trade on behalf of the HEIC, but the Sultan refused. See Keay, p360. Raffles in due course solved the problem of an intermediate British settlement by founding Singapore (See Vol. 3, *Masters Under God*).

15. Following Cook's three voyages, his young protégés founded the core of what, in the following century, would prove to be a remarkable achievement by the Royal Navy, the charting of almost all the world's oceans. In 1791 George Vancouver was surveying in north-west Pacific and in 1795 Flinders and Bass were exploring the Australian coasts. Surveying was increasingly perceived as a government, that is to say, a naval task and this remarkable generation of naval surveyors has eclipsed the earlier mercantile practitioners.

16. The principal of merchant masters – and any other mariners – contributing to the common pool of knowledge is still maintained by way of 'hydrographic notes' in which any relevant observations are communicated to the Hydrographic Office.

17. See Woodman, R. and Wilson, J., *The Lighthouses of Trinity House* and Woodman R., *Keepers of the Sea*. During this period Lowestoft Lighthouse had long been in the Corporation's keeping and in 1806 the Eddystone lighthouse passed out of private hands and was taken under Trinity House management. New lights were also provided at Haisbrough, the Longships, Flamborough Head and South Stack with light-vessels being established off the Newarp, Owers and the Sunk shoals. Full control of all English, Welsh and Channel Island lighthouses did not pass directly under Trinity House's national management until 1836. Lighthouses in Scotland and the Isle of Man had been under the management of the Commissioners for Northern Lights in Edinburgh, and those of the island of Ireland under the Commissioners for Irish Lights at Dublin, since 1786. England and Wales were, therefore, under an archaic system for some fifty years after other parts of the United Kingdom.

18. Hastings reformed the revenues, improved the judicial system and waged war against the Marathas, who remained a threat to the Company's hegemony, but in rooting out corruption he made enemies and resigned in 1784. Reaching home he faced impeachment for alleged extortion and aggression. The subsequent trial lasted from 1788 to 1795, at the end of which Hastings was acquitted. He was, however, financially ruined. He died in 1818.

19. Sir Evan Cotton is quite clear on the point of these ships not being regular Indiamen. See *East Indiamen*, p105.

POST SCRIPTUM

By following events such as the fate of Captain John Wordsworth and the HCS *Earl of Abergavenny* we have run ahead. Indeed the vicissitudes of eastern trade have carried us beyond that great British historical mile-stone, the Treaty of Paris ending the Seven Years War in 1763, and we have ignored the subsequent national humiliation that followed defeat on land and sea in 1781 which rendered the thirteen British colonies in North America independent, and over-run the next major event, the outbreak of the French Revolutionary War in 1793. For reasons already explained, this cannot be helped, but the interested reader is invited to return to the main narrative in Volume Two, *Britannia's Realm*, which covers events in the Atlantic and Arctic Oceans from 1763 until the outbreak of the Great War with France in 1793, before following the adventures of British merchant seafarers through the War of the French Revolution, the brief Peace of Amiens and the long years of the Napoleonic War. The part played by British merchant shipping in the defeat of French ambition, has been largely ignored by conventional naval historians. Its ability to carry wealth-generating commodities in support of the home economy and to provide the means with which to subsidise European alliances against the French was critical to the successful outcome of the war, while the supply of British military operations was another important contribution. Furthermore the ability of merchant shipping to defend itself against the corsairs unleashed by France's vigorous *guerre de course* – again much under-estimated in effect and extent by main-stream history – was an additional burden. Such a struggle was often heroic, running alongside the ceaseless fight against the elements and the consequential tragedies and disasters that added to the appalling toll of lives and *matériel* that under-wrote *Britannia's Realm*.

Even before the end of the Great War with France the first primitive steam-vessels had made their appearance on rivers and estuaries, and by 1816 the first coastal passages were being undertaken by paddle steamers. The progress of British steam navigation and the extraordinary events that marked the mid-part of the nineteenth century follow in the third volume, *Masters Under God*.

The story continues in *More Days, More Dollars*, and is concluded in *Fiddler's Green*.

BIBLIOGRAPHY

PUBLISHED MATERIAL

All published in London unless otherwise stated

Arasaratnam, S., *Maritime Commerce and English Power, Southeast India, 1750–1800*, Variorum, Aldershot, 1996

Armstrong, R., *The Merchantmen* (Vol.3 of *A History of Seafaring*), Ernest Benn, 1969

Barrett, C.R.B. (Editor), *The Trinity House*, Lawrence and Bullen, 1893

Barrow, T., *The Whaling Trade of North-East England, 1750–1850*, University of Sunderland Press, Sunderland, 2001

Baumber, M., *General-at-Sea, Robert Blake and the Seventeenth Century Revolution in Naval Warfare*, John Murray, 1989

Beaglehole, J.C., *The Life of Captain James Cook*, Stanford University Press, Stanford, California, 1974

Biddulph, J., *The Pirates of Malabar*, South, Elder & Co., 1907

Blackmore, E., *The British Mercantile Marine: A Short Historical Review*, Charles Griffin, 1897

Bowditch, N., *American Practical Navigator*, Defense Mapping Agency Hydrographic/Topographic Center, Washington, 1984

Brooks, L., and Ducé, R.H. (editors), *Seafarers, Ships and Cargoes*, University of London Press, 1951

Brown, C.H., *Nicholls's Seamanship and Nautical Knowledge*, Brown, Son & Ferguson, Glasgow, 1958

Brown, R.D., *The Port of London*, Terence Dalton, Lavenham, 1978

Bulley, A., *The Bombay Country Ships, 1790–1833*, Curzon, Richmond, 2000

    Free Mariner, John Adolphus Pope in the East Indies, 1786–1821, British Association for Cemeteries in South East Asia, Putney, 1992

Cameron, A. and Farndon, R., *Scenes from Sea and City, Lloyd's List, 1734–1984*, Lloyd's List, London 1984

Carse, R., *The Age of Piracy*, Robert Hale, 1959

Charton, B. and Tietjen, J., *Seas and Oceans*, Collins, 1989

Chatterton, E.K., *Valiant Sailormen*, Hurst and Blackett, 1936

    The Mercantile Marine, Heinemann, 1923

    Windjammers and Shellbacks, Fisher Unwin, 1926

    Ventures and Voyages, Rich and Cowan, 1935

    The Old East Indiamen, Conway Maritime, 1971

    Seamen All, Philip Allan & Co. Ltd, 1928

Childers, S. (Editor), *A Mariner of England, An Account of the Career Of William Richardson… as told by himself*, Conway Maritime, 1970

Clowes, W.L., *The Royal Navy, A History*, AMC Press (reprint), New York, 1966

Coates, W.H., *The Good Old Days of Shipping*, The 'Times of India' Press, Bombay (Mumbai), 1900

    The Old 'Country Trade' of the East Indies, Imray, Laurie, Norie & Wilson, 1911

Coggeshall, G., *A History of American Privateers and Letters-of-Marque*, C.T. Evans, New York, 1856

Cole, S., *Our Home Ports*, Effingham Wilson, 1923

Collis, M., *Siamese White*, Faber and Faber, 1936

    British Merchant Adventurers, Collins, 1942

Compton, H. (editor), *A Master Mariner, Being the Life and Adventures of Captain Robert Willian Eastwick*, T. Fisher Unwin, 1891

Cordingly, D., *Life Among the Pirates*, Little, Brown, 1995

Cornewall-Jones, R.J., *The British Merchant Service*, Sampson Low, Marston, 1898

Cotton, Sir E., *East Indiamen*, The Batchworth Press, 1949

Cotton, J., *Memoir on the Origin and Incorporation of the Trinity House of Deptford Strond*, Darling, 1818

Cowen, R.C., *Frontiers of the Sea*, Gollancz, 1960

Dalrymple, W., *A Historical Collection of the Several Voyages and Discoveries in the South Pacific Ocean*, two volumes, 1769

Damer-Powell, J.W., *Bristol Privateers and Ships of War*, J.W.Arrowsmith, Bristol, 1930

Dann, J.C. (editor), *The Nagle Journal*, Weidenfeld and Nicolson, New York, 1988

Davis, R., *The Rise of the English Shipping Industry in the 17th and 18th Centuries*, David & Charles, 1962

Dearden, S., *A Nest of Corsairs, The Fighting Karamanlis of Tripoli*, John Murray, 1976

Defoe, D., *History of the Union of Great Britain*, Edinburgh, 1709

Dow, G.F., *Slave Ships and Slaving*, Marine Research Society, Salem, Mass, 1927

Earle, P., Sailors, *English Merchant Seamen, 1650–1775*, Methuen, 1998

Ellacott, S.E., *The Seaman*, two volumes, Abelard-Schuman, 1970

Ellis, H., *A Voyage to Hudson's Bay by the* Dobbs Galley *and* California, Dublin, 1749

Esquemeling, J., *The Buccaneers of America*, George Allen, 1911

Equiano, O., *The Interesting Narrative and Other Writings*, Penguin, 2003

Falconer, W., *Marine Dictionary (1780)*, David & Charles Reprints, Newton Abbot, 1970

Farrington, A., *A Biographical Index of East India Company Maritime Service Officers, 1600–1834*, The British Library, 1999

Fielding, H., *The Journal of a Voyage to Lisbon*, John Long, 1907

Foreman, S., *Shoes and Ships and Sealing Wax, An Illustrated History of the Board of Trade, 1786–1986*, HMSO, 1986

Garstin, C., (editor), *Samuel Kelly: An Eighteenth Century Seaman whose days have been few and evil, to which is added remarks etc. on places he visited during his pilgrimage in this wilderness*, Jonathan Cape, 1925

Gibson, J.F. *Brocklebanks, 1770–1950*, two volumes, Henry Young, Liverpool, 1953

Gill, C., *Merchants and Mariners of the 18th Century*, Edward Arnold, 1961

Gibb, D.E.W., *Lloyd's of London, A Study in Individualism*, Lloyd's, 1972

Grey, C., *Pirates of the Eastern Seas (1618–1723)*, Sampson Low, Marston, 1933

Gurney, A., *Compass, A Story of Exploration and Innovation*, W.W.Norton, New York, 2004

Hackman, R., *Ships of the East India Company*, World Ship Society, Gravesend, 2001

Haring, C.H., *The Buccaneers in the West Indies in the XVII Centuries*, Methuen & Co., 1910

Harris, G.G. *Trinity House of Deptford Transactions, 1609–35*, London Record Society, 1983

Haws, D. and Hurst, A.A, *The Maritime History of the World*, two volumes, Teredo Books, Brighton, 1985

Hayter, A., *The Wreck of the* Abergavenny*: The Wordsworths and Catastrophe*, Pan Books, 2003

HMSO, *The Mariner's Handbook*, Sixth Edition, 1989
    Ocean Passages for the World, Third Edition, 1973
    Seafarers and Their Ships, 1955

Hood, J., *Marked for Misfortune*, Conway, 2003

Hope, R., *A New History of British Shipping*, John Murray, 1990
    Poor Jack, Chatham, 2001
    The Merchant Navy, Stanford Maritime, 1980

Huddart, J., *A Memoir of the Late Captain Joseph Huddart*, W. Phillips, 1821

Huddart, W., *Unpathed Waters, The Life and Times of Joseph Huddart FRS, 1741–1816*, Quiller Press, 1989

Hunter, H.C., *How England got its Merchant Marine, 1066–1776*, National Council of American Shipbuilders, New York, 1935

Hutchinson, W., *A Treatise on Practical Seamanship*, Scolar Maritime Library Reprint, 1979

Johnson, H., *A General History of the Pyrates*, London, 1746

Keay, J., *The Honourable Company, A History of the English East India Company*, Harper Collins, 1991

Kemp, P. (editor) *The Oxford Companion to Ships and the Sea*, OUP, Oxford, 1988

Kendall, C.W., *Private Men-of-War*, Philip Allan, 1931

Knight, R., *The Pursuit of Victory, The Life and Achievement of Horatio Nelson*, Allen Lane, 2005

Lane-Poole, S., *The Barbary Corsairs*, Fisher Unwin, 1890

Linebaugh, P., and Rediker, M., *The Many-Headed Hydra*, Beacon Press, Boston, 2000

Lubbock, B., (editor), *Barlow's Journal, 1677–1703*, Hurst & Blackett, 1934

MacGregor, D., *Merchant Sailing Ships, 1775–1815*, Argus Books, Watford, 1980
    Fast Sailing Ships, Their Design and Construction, 1775–1875, Conway, 1988
    Schooners in Four Centuries, Argus Books, Hemel Hempstead, 1982

Macintyre, D., *The Privateers*, Paul Elek, 1975

Mackenzie-Grieve, A., *The Last Years of the English Slave Trade, Liverpool 1750–1807*, Putnam, London, 1941

Maclay, E.S., *A History of American Privateers*, Sampson Low, Marston & Co., 1900

Mannix, D.P. and Cowley, M., *Black Cargoes, A History of the Atlantic Slave Trade, 1518–1865*, Penguin, 2002

Marshall, P.J., *East Indian Fortunes, The British in Bengal in the Eighteenth Century*, Oxford University Press, 1976

Mathias, P. and Pearsall, A.W.H., *Shipping: A Survey of Historical Records*, David & Charles, Newton Abbot, 1971

Milton, G., *White Gold*, Hodder and Stoughton, 2004

Morse, H.B., *The East India Company Trading to China, 1635–1834*, five volumes, Oxford University Press, undated (*c.*1860)

Moyse-Bartlett, H., *A History of the Merchant Navy*, Harrap, 1937

Naish, G., *The Interwoven Lives of George Vancouver, Archibald Menzies, Joseph Whidbey and Peter Puget, Exploring the Pacific Northwest Coast, Canadian Studies*, Vol.17, The Edward Mellen Press, Lewiston, New York, 1996

Norie, J.W., *A Complete Epitome of Navigation*, Charles Wilson, 1864

Norman, C.B. *The Corsairs of France*, Sampson Low, Marston, Searle & Rivington, 1887

Owen, N., *Journal of a Slave-Dealer*, George Routledge, 1930

Pares, R., *War and Trade in the West Indies*, Frank Cass, 1963

Parry, J.H. and Sherlock, P.M., *A Short History of the West Indies*, Macmillan, 1971

Rediker, M., *Between the Devil and the Deep Blue Sea*, Cambridge University Press, Cambridge, 1987

Read, A., *The Coastwise Trade of the United Kingdom*, George Thompson, 1925

Rinman, T. and Brodefors, R., *The Commercial History of Shipping*, Rinman & Lindén AB, Gothenburg, 1983

Ritchie, G.S., *The Admiralty Chart, British Naval Hydrography in the Nineteenth Century*, The Pentland Press, 1995

Rodger, N.A.M., *The Safeguard of the Sea*, Harper Collins, 1997
    Command of the Ocean, Penguin/Allen Lane, 2004

Rosser, W.H., *The Law of Storms Considered Practically*, Charles Wilson, 1876

Rutter, O., *Red Ensign, A History of Convoy*, Robert Hale, 1942

Samhaber, E., *Merchants Make History*, Harrap, 1963

Schwarz, S., *Slave Captain*, Bridge Books, Wrexham, 1995

Senior, C., *A Nation of Pirates, English Piracy in its Heyday*, David & Charles, Newton Abbot, 1976

Smith, K., Wattes, C.T. and Watts, M.J., *Records of Merchant Shipping and Seamen*, Public Records Office Guide No 20, PRO Publications, 1998

Stamp, D., *The World, A General Geography*, Longmans, 1966

Statham, E.P., *Privateers and Privateering*, Hutchinson, 1910

Sutton, J., *Lords of the East, the East India Company and its Ships*, Conway, 1981

Sugden, J., *Nelson, A Dream of Glory*, Jonathan Cape, 2004

Temple, R.C. *The Tragedy of the 'Worcester', 1704–1705*, Ernest Benn, 1930

Thomas, H., *The Slave Trade, The History of the Atlantic Slave Trade 1440–1870*, Simon & Schuster, New York, 1997

Thomas, R.E., *Stowage: The Properties and Stowage of Cargoes*, Revised Edition, Brown, Son and Ferguson Ltd, Glasgow, 1963

Thomson, G.M. *Sir Francis Drake*, Secker and Warburg, 1972

Tracy, N., *Attack on Maritime Trade*, University of Toronto Press, Toponto, 1991

Trinder, I. *The Harwich Packets, 1635–1834*, Trinder, Colchester, 1998

Unknown, *Lives of Pirates, &c*, Milner and Sowerby, Halifax, 1865

Villiers, A., *Vanished Fleets*, Geoffrey Bles, 1931
    Monsoon Seas, The Story of the Indian Ocean, McGraw-Hill, New York, 1952
    Voyaging with the Wind, HMSO, 1975

Watson, L., *Heaven's Breath, A Natural History of the Wind*, Coronet, 1985

Wild, A., *The East India Company, Trade and Conquest from 1600*, HarperCollins, 2000

Williams, G., *Voyages of Delusion*, HarperCollins, 2003

Williamson, J.A., *The Ocean in English History*, Clarendon, Oxford, 1941

Wilson, C., *Seamanship; Both in Theory and Practice*, Norie and Wilson, 1841

Whormby, J., *An Account of the Corporation of Trinity House of Deptford Strond and of Sea Marks in General*, Smith and Ebbs, 1746

Woodman, R.M., *The History of the Ship*, Conway, 1997
    ... *of Daring Temper*, The Marine Society, 2006
    Keepers of the Sea, Revised Edition, Chaffcutter, Ware, 2005
    with Wilson, J., *The Lighthouses of Trinity House*, Thomas Reed, Bradford on Avon, 2002

OTHER SOURCES

Reference has been made to the *Oxford Dictionary of National Biography* and other information has also been culled over a period of many years from a variety of sources, including the *Mariner's Mirror*, *Naval Chronicle* and contemporary organs.

INDEX

If you are interested in purchasing other books published by The History Press,
or in case you have difficulty finding any History Press books in your local bookshop,
you can also place orders directly through our website
www.thehistorypress.co.uk